Accolades for *Rocky M* ~~~~~~

"An essential reference for any traveling fly fisher. Current, accurate and precise information with great maps and GPS references. If you fish the West, you're a fool not to have this book!"

— Jack Dennis, fly-fishing author, videographer and merchant,
  Jackson Hole, Wyoming

"Finally, a book that covers the 'best of the West.' Steve Cook's new book, *Rocky Mountain Fly Fishing,* is a must-have resource for readers who wish to fly fish the great rivers of the West. Steve's writing style (in the tradition of his first book, *Utah Fishing Guide*) shines in his attention to detail. He answers our questions of what, when, where and how before we ever ask them! From river to river, *Rocky Mountain Fly Fishing* will become your greatest travel companion by putting the best information available for each destination directly into your hands."

— Dennis Breer, owner, Trout Creek Flies, Dutch John, Utah

"Steve Cook's *Rocky Mountain Fly Fishing* is a valuable compilation of information, maps, and hatch and fly pattern recommendations that will benefit any fly fisher hoping to gain insight into the West's great Blue Ribbon waters."

— Steve Schmidt, owner, Western Rivers Flyfisher, Salt Lake City, Utah

"A dream book filled with precisely the type of detailed information — hatch schedules, public access points, terrific maps with GPS coordinates, lists of local fly shops and much more — an angler needs to expertly sample the famous trout waters of the Rocky Mountain West. As far as fly-fishing guidebooks go, this is definitely one of the most complete and useful."

— Bill Schneider, publisher, Falcon Publishing, Helena, Montana

"Steve Cook has done it again. His guide to the best trout streams in the Rocky Mountain region is great. He not only tells you what flies to use and when, but also specific tactics on how to fish them. This will be a great guide to the fly fisher traveling throughout the West and looking for the best places to wet a line."

— Wes Johnson, Chairman, Utah Council of Trout Unlimited

Publisher:
Bryan Brandenburg
AmazingOutdoors.com
6322 South 3000 East, Suite G-50
Salt Lake City, Utah 84121
Phone number/s: (801) 858-3450,
toll-free (800) 366-8824
www.AmazingOutdoors.com

Editors:
Stephen A. Jackson
Marcia C. Dibble
Dave Webb

Contributing writers:
Michael Ferguson
Andy Fitzburgh
Kory Kapaloski
Berris "Bear" Samples
Larry Tullis
Guy Turck

Art Director and cover design:
Cory Maylett

Artists:
Greg Pearson
Mike Stidham

Uncredited photos:
Steve Cook

Cover photo:
Tom Montgomery/Tony Stone

Back cover photos *(clockwise from left)*:
Mark Williams,
Steve Schmidt (three photos)

Contributing photographers:
Char Alexander
Stu Asahina
Buzz Basini
Jeff Beck
Dennis Breer
Brad Cutler
Tom Ferris
Willie Holdman/Sundance Resort
Bob Johnson
Leonard Kleiman
Mikey Langford
Sherri Mann
John McColgan
Richard Munoz
Peter Rigstad
Steve Schmidt
Darren Sutherland
Larry Tullis
Mark Williams
Richard Winkler

Maps:
Peter Strohmeyer and
Paula Rudd/MindMeld *works*

Printer:
Bertelsmann Services Inc.
Valencia, California

Library of Congress Catalog Card Number: 00-109180
ISBN: 0-9671738-6-8

fly rocky mountain fishing

Blue Ribbon Rivers of the American West

By Steve Cook

In memory of my father —
the best times we spent were on the water

Acknowledgments

lthough a single name appears on the cover, this book represents the contributions of many people who share a passion for the mountains and rivers of our American West. I would like to begin by thanking the many fly fishers who spent a moment with me over this last year as I traveled the Rockies on a quest for information. You shared your stories, flies and food with me as well as your insights on fly fishing, and many of my best memories of this past season are of our brief interactions on riverbanks across the West. Special thanks to Richard Munoz, whom I met on the Gunnison.

Several good friends shared my travels and brought friendship and camaraderie to my work on the road. Thanks go out to Jeff Beck, Ken Davis, Hank Kiley, Dave Lattimore, Bud Murray, Bill Shan, Bill Young and Brad Cutler. Brad made several trips with me this season, becoming a rather accomplished fly fisher in the process.

The anglers who know a river best are the ones who guide others or spend their days in fly shops freely dispensing their knowledge as well as their love of the sport. Many of these ardent professionals have donated their time and knowledge for inclusion in this book. We are grateful to: Del DeSpain of Bighorn Fly and Tackle in Billings, MT; Blaine Heaps of Bud Lilly's Trout Shop in West Yellowstone, MT; Bob Burk of Cimarron Creek in Montrose, CO; Woody Canon and Chuck Schell of Driftwood Dories in Salt Lake City, UT; Barry Kirkpatrick of Cutthroat Anglers in Silverthorne, CO; Rich Speer of Flies and Lies in Deckers, CO; Mitch Hurt of Fine & Far Guide Service in Livingston, MT; Mark Forslund of Four Seasons Fly Fishers in Murray, UT; Art Rowell of Fryingpan Anglers in Basalt, CO; Tony Reinhardt and Cole Hobbs of The Grizzly Hackle in Missoula, MT; Mark Silver of iGage in Salt Lake City, UT; Morrison Simms of Jack Dennis Fishing in Jackson, WY; John Rainey and Alain Pinto of Los Rios Anglers in Taos, NM; Jerry Lappier of Missouri River Trout Shop and Lodge in Craig, MT; Shaun Lawson of South Fork Lodge in Swan Valley, ID; Buzz Basini of Spring Creek Specialists in Livingston, MT; Jim Santa of Sturtevants in Hailey, ID; Dennis Breer of Trout Creek Flies in Dutch John, UT; Nicholas St. George and Steve Bielenberg of the Watershed in Dillon, MT.

Trout Bum 2 is the fly shop just down the street from my home in Park City, Utah, and Rick Hansen, Jason Holloway and Jon "Harley" Jackson were all very helpful with their insights into both Utah rivers and other streams throughout the region. Bruce "Goose" Juhl of Trout Bum 2 and Destination Sports not only helped with several destinations but also took the time to read the full manuscript.

Our friends at Western Rivers Flyfisher in Salt Lake City gave the project a lot of support over and above the contributions of individuals, but most importantly they were the guys I went to hang out with to get recharged.

Much of what I have learned about the Green River in Utah was passed down to me by Emmett Heath of Green River Outfitters. His example of comportment and passion for fishing sets the ideal standard I strive to reach.

There are not thanks enough for Mikey Langford of Henry's Fork Anglers and Zac White, formerly of Madison River Outfitters. Between these two young men there is nearly 20 years of guiding experience in the West Yellowstone area. Even though Mikey is finishing his last year of law school and Zac is committed to a new career that has kept him off the river most of this year, they both donated their time and knowledge to make our coverage of the greater Yellowstone region as complete as possible.

Tom Pettengill of the Utah Division of Wildlife Resources, Rob Keith of the Wyoming Game and Fish Department, and Dick Oswald of Montana Fish, Wildlife & Parks all took time out of their busy schedules to help me with research. Thanks also to Dr. Daniel L. Gustafson of Montana State University for his assistance on questions regarding entomology.

We are again privileged to exhibit the artwork of Greg Pearson, whose artistic talents are as great as his fishing abilities. The trout renderings in our appendix are the fine work of Mike Stidham. Many photographers also contributed images for the book. They are: Char Alexander, Stu Asahina, John McColgan, Tom Ferris, Bob Johnson, Leonard Kleiman, Sherri Mann, Peter Rigstad, Darren Sutherland and Richard Winkler. Mark Williams is a talented photographer who provided many rich and warm pictures for these pages. His contribution is matched only by that of Steve Schmidt of Western Rivers Flyfisher. We are again grateful for the opportunity to display the fruits of Steve's years of fishing photography. Our cover photo is the work of the gifted Tom Montgomery.

This volume also benefits from the generous efforts of several fine writers. Michael Ferguson contributed "Using GPS" while "To Net or Not to Net" comes from Guy Turck of High Country Flies. Berris "Bear" Samples took time out from his busy writing and fishing schedule to write our piece on "Fly Casting Western Waters." Look for his new book entitled *30 Days to Better Flycasting* for more of his great instruction. Larry Tullis is the talented and widely published writer who prepared "Fly-fishing Techniques" and "Kickboats for Fishing." Kory Kapaloski of Trout Bum 2 wrote the section on "Drift Boats and Rafts" and Andy Fitzhugh of Western Rivers Flyfisher contributed the article on "Wading Safety."

We are most flattered by the foreword that was written for us by Cathy Beck. We have long admired her photography and writing and feel honored to receive such a fine recommendation.

Thanks to Peter Strohmeyer and Paula Rudd of MindMeld *works* for their great work on the maps and their patience in the final days. Stephen A. Jackson has again added polish to my words, and his deft competence with the English language is apparent throughout the text.

The team at AmazingOutdoors.com has been wonderful to work with on this book. We would like to thank Marcia Dibble for her careful and concise editing, Sam Webb for his advice and direction on fishing issues, Cory Maylett for his open-minded approach and our great cover design, and Dave Webb for shepherding this work to completion. A very heartfelt "thank you" goes to Bryan Brandenburg for his vision of what is possible and the support to bring the goal to fruition.

My final thanks are to Lisa Cook, my wife, part-time fishing companion and best friend. No words can convey my gratitude for your efforts on this book.

Table of Contents

Foreword

By Cathy Beck

When Steve asked me to write the foreword to this book, I asked myself if we needed yet another "where to go" book on the Rocky Mountains or anywhere else for that matter. But after getting to know him and seeing the book proofs, I soon realized that this book is different from the rest. He's done his homework and has put in an incredible amount of time and research making sure every destination is as complete and accurate as possible.

The book contains many of my favorite streams and rivers, places Barry and I fish every year. Yet as I read this book, I learned something new about every one of these old favorites. There's just enough history on each destination to make it interesting. And, when I read about the places where I have not yet fished, I wanted to go, right now. This book will do that to you.

The section on GPS was an education for me, and maybe it will be for you too. For new anglers, there is help on casting and tips on netting, whirling disease, boats and rafts that will help us all and keep us informed. The information on whirling disease alone should be a wake-up call to all of us — a reminder of how fragile our streams are and what we can do to help prevent this disease from spreading. The section on wading safety is very important to every angler who steps into the water. Inexperienced anglers can easily get into trouble wading, and this information just might save a life sometime. It's important stuff.

For the angler who is planning a trip to one of these destinations, there is information on what time of year is best to go, what hatches to expect and even recommended fly patterns. There is information on tactics, accessibility, accommodations, fly shops and even area attractions for the nonfisherman. There are maps, GPS coordinates and even web sites for checking water flows!

I would suggest getting comfortable, because I don't think you'll put this book down after reading about one or two rivers. You'll have to look ahead, go around the bend, to see what else is there.

Cathy Beck *is the author of* Cathy Beck's Fly-Fishing Handbook *and co-author of* Fly-Fishing the Flats *with her husband, Barry. Together they own Raven Creek Photography in Benton, Pennsylania, and host guided fly-fishing tours around the world.*

INTRODUCTION

The Rocky Mountain West

The Rocky Mountain chain forms the strong, rugged backbone of the North American continent. Made up of nearly 100 separate ranges, the Rockies stretch for 3,000 miles, from northern Canada down into New Mexico. This broad mountain system spreads out over 300 miles in places, and its highest summits are found in the state of Colorado, with more than 50 peaks that reach above 14,000 feet. Mount Elbert is the highest of these at 14,433 feet.

These mountains are the product of violent volcanic activity and the implacable advances of massive tectonic plates in collision. Portions of the southern Rockies were formed between 400 million to 600 million years ago, while younger ranges uplifted in the late Cretaceous period, about 60 million to 140 million years ago. Burgeoning mountains like the Tetons are the result of rapid upthrust that has occurred in the last 9 million years, and the Yellowstone region continues to rise up slightly each year as the underlying magma chamber slowly fills and causes the earth's surface to bulge in this gradually evolving province.

The erosive forces of ice and snow have carved many of the valleys that hold our rivers of today. The high peaks of Colorado were glaciated as recently as 8,000 years ago, and these flowing ice fields still exist in the Wind River Range and other high points of the northern Rockies, even though global warming is causing the rapid retreat of glaciers throughout North America. The "little ice age" saw glaciers advancing for several centuries and only ended around 1860.

Flowing water continues to cut and shape our mountains as run-off and snowmelt seek to escape the high mountains. Rivers on the east side of the Continental Divide make their way to the Mississippi and the Gulf of Mexico. Most of the water west of the divide in the northern Rockies makes its way to the Columbia River and the Pacific Ocean, while farther south the Great Basin traps water in the stagnant Great Salt Lake, whose only outlet is the sky above. Waters west of the divide in the southern Rockies have carved our most impressive river courses, such as the Grand Canyon and Black Canyon of the Gunnison. The Colorado River drains this region, but unfortunately, man's ever-growing thirst prevents the river's flow from ever reaching its goal in the Gulf of California.

The climate of the Rocky Mountains is heavily influenced by altitude. At moderate elevations, weather is fairly temperate, with cold winters and fairly cool summers, although higher elevations and low humidity combine to make the summer sun quite intense at times. The highest portions of the Rockies enjoy an alpine climate with severe winters and short, cool summers. The relatively high elevations of this region can make for very changeable weather. Annual precipitation is highest in the Northern Rockies, which receive nearly three times the moisture that falls on the mountains to the south.

The Rockies are home to a variety of wildlife that have successfully adapted to the challenging mountain environment. Grizzly bears, black bears, mountain lions

PHOTO: STEVE SCHMIDT

Another recent immigrant to the West — the rainbow.

and wolves make up the top tier of the food chain and feed upon ungulates such as elk, moose, mule deer and whitetail deer. Mountain goats and bighorn sheep occupy the highest elevations, along with smaller mammals such as pikas and marmots. Bison still thrive in Yellowstone National Park, and the ubiquitous coyote can be found throughout the region. Bald eagle populations have rebounded in the West, and golden eagles are also a common sight. Peregrine falcons, great horned owls and osprey still search for prey in the rugged mountains, and waterfowl make their annual migrations through the area. The native cutthroat trout subspecies have been joined by rainbow trout from the West Coast, brook trout from the East and brown trout from Europe. Grayling still persist in the Big Hole River in Montana, while kokanee salmon and lake trout can occasionally be found in some Rocky Mountain Rivers.

The first humans appeared in the Rockies sometime between 8,000 and 10,000 B.C. These wanderers developed different customs and habits to help them cope with the harsh lands they inhabited. At the time of the early exploration by Europeans, Nez Percé were found in Idaho, Flatheads occupied lands in what is now Montana, and Shoshone Indians were in Wyoming and Idaho. Utes were spread throughout Utah and Colorado, while southwestern tribes like the Navajo, Hopi and Pueblo were located along the southern edge of the Rockies. Although the Blackfoot, Cheyenne and Crow lived primarliy on the Great Plains, they did make their way into the mountains as well.

Brown trout were imported to the U.S. from Europe and eventually made their way to the Rocky Mountains.

Spanish explorers entered the southern Rocky Mountains in the sixteenth century, and members of the Dominguez-Escalante expedition were the first Europeans to see much of this country as they traveled in search of a route to California in 1776. Lewis and Clark's Voyage of Discovery, begun in 1803, was the first expedition into the area by the fledgling United States. Their findings, combined with the Louisiana Purchase, opened the door for the fur trade to move into the Rockies. The fur trade flourished during the 1820s and 1830s, when the rugged and independent mountain men trapped in the winters and gathered together for rendezvous in the summers.

By the mid-1800s the dream of land ownership was drawing settlers west in increasing numbers. Settlements small and large began to spring up in the Rocky Mountain region as the United Sates fulfilled what many believed to be her "manifest destiny": becoming a transcontinental nation stretching from the Atlantic Ocean to the Pacific.

The stability of the United States was quickly drawn into question with the advent of the Civil War. While the focus of the war was east of the Mississippi, it still had a large effect on many towns and settlements in the Rockies, such as Virginia City. The gold that was discovered here was vital to both the Union and Confederate governments to support their war efforts. Located in what was then Idaho territory, the predominantly Confederate population of Virginia City constantly disrupted the North's attempts to rule the town. To solidify Union control, the Montana Territory was founded, including Virginia City within its boundaries. Abraham Lincoln's friend Sidney Edgerton was appointed as governor and the Vigilantes were formed to curb escalating violence.

As the Civil War ended, the period most of us associate with the Wild West commenced, and a series of Indian Wars began that culminated in Custer's defeat at the Little Bighorn in 1876. While Native Americans were being rounded up and forced onto reservations, some of the West's most famous outlaws were beginning their careers in crime.

Born Robert Leroy Parker in Beaver, Utah, in 1866, Butch Cassidy stole his first horse as a young man. He soon teamed up another horse thief, Harry Longabaugh, aka the Sundance Kid (who took the name after jailtime in Sundance, Wyoming). They began robbing banks and trains with their gang, which became known as the Wild Bunch. As their fame grew, so did the reward for their capture, until the pair finally fled to South America in 1901.

As law and order became firmly established in the region, the chief impediment to further settlement in the West was the shortage of water for agriculture. This issue was addressed with the establishment of the U. S. Reclamation Service (predecessor to the Bureau of Reclamation) in 1902. Several water projects were begun, including Pathfinder Dam on the North Platte in Wyoming and the Gunnison Tunnel in Colorado. Dam building has continued into recent times, with the completion of Jordanelle Reservoir on the Provo River in 1996. Throughout the twentieth century, water projects have helped to form the communities and lifestyles of today's Rocky Mountains, as well as creating some of our best trout fisheries.

While agriculture has historically formed the economic base of much of the region, tourism is becoming increasingly important to local businesses and is now a major industry in the Rocky Mountains. More than a dozen national parks combine with national monuments, the Wild and Scenic Rivers system, BLM lands and state parks and wildlife management areas to give visitors great opportunities to experience the wide and expansive landscapes of the Rocky Mountain West. Many mountain towns cater to tourists, and the growing number of ski resorts increases the options for lodgings in these areas.

The increasing popularity of fly fishing means that anglers can find full-service fly shops and outfitters near most of the great rivers of the region. Experienced guides will be available for most rivers, and travelers new to the sport can often take a casting lesson or rent the necessary equipment for their first experience on the river. Many fans of the sport believe that this Rocky Mountain Region holds some of the finest trout rivers of North America. Whether you live among the Rocky Mountains, or visit them to cast a line, we hope that you will enjoy the rich heritage of the land as well as the brightly colored trout that swim its rivers.

How to Use This Guide

ur purpose is to provide readers with a tool that will enhance their enjoyment of fishing on the great trout rivers of the Rocky Mountains. We hope to stimulate your desire to experience new waters and provide you with the practical information that will ease trip planning and allow you to make the best use of your time. Remember that our information is only a starting point. A few printed pages are not enough to capture the many nuances of dynamic, living river systems. It is not so much what is known about a fishery that captures our imagination, but that which lies waiting to be discovered.

Issues of time and space have forced us to limit the number of rivers covered in this volume. We recognize that there are many other rivers that are worthy of inclusion, but, when time or logistics prevented us from giving them the attention they deserved, they were omitted with the hope of including them in future volumes. For information on **Other Rocky Mountain Rivers**, refer to the **Appendix** on page 410 or check for articles on the web at *www.AmazingOutdoors.com.*

Although anglers are drawn to rivers by the fish that reside there, it is interests and experiences beyond fishing that make for a full and satisfying journey. For this reason, we have included information about history, geology or biology with the intent of transmitting a sense of place that encompasses each river and its surrounding area.

General Season Dates and Bag & Possession Limits are listed for each state, as well as any **Special Regulations and Fees** that apply to specific rivers. The information is from the game laws in effect in 2000 and is included solely for the convenience of our readers, primarily to aid in planning a trip. Anglers should always obtain a current copy of the fishing regulations for the state they intend to fish and understand them thoroughly before heading to the river.

We believe that good fly fishers will discover a way to catch fish on whatever water they find themselves. With the **Tactics** section of the text, we hope you will be able to shortcut the process. The suggestions in this section merely represent techniques that have been successful for others.

Our **Hatch Charts** concentrate on the rivers' main hatches, which are the ones we believe to be most important to fly fishers. **Suggested Fly Patterns** include imitations that are widely known and can be found in most any fly shop. We also include some local patterns that may only be available in the immediate area.

The **How to Get There** section will be helpful to anglers booking flights as well as those who drive to the rivers covered in this book. As anglers, we find information on **Accessibility** to be of the greatest importance, and when this information is combined with the **Maps** and **GPS Coordinates**, it should be relatively easy for anglers to find their way to the stretch of river that has captured their interest. If you are planning to float a section of river, always check with local sources as river conditions can change from year to year. Log jams or new construction can create new hazards to avoid.

When to Go contains information on the fishing conditions that are normally found during different seasons of the year. This section is intended to help readers plan trips that coincide with a river's best fishing, but don't forget the old adage: "The best time to go fishing is whenever you can."

In the **Resources**, you will find listings for campgrounds, lodging and outfitters to help you make reservations for your trips.

When planning your trips to the blue ribbon rivers of the Rocky Mountains, we recommend two sources of additional maps to help you find your way. DeLorme produces an *Atlas and Gazetteer* for each of the states covered in this guide. These useful books offer 1/250,000 scale topographic maps of the entire state and can greatly aid navigation. In performing the research for this book, we had the privilege of using *All Topo Maps* by iGage. These four to six compact disk sets hold digital copies of all of the USGS 1:24,000 scale topographic maps for each state, including several well-designed and useful software options. If you are headed into the backcountry, this software is invaluable, allowing you to customize and print your own highly detailed topographic maps, and create and load waypoint files into your GPS unit. Measurement features give you realistic distances for hiking trail and river sections.

Whether you use this book to visit every river listed or just to fuel your imagination during cold winter months, we hope it will contribute to your enjoyment of our shared sport and that perhaps we might meet on a quiet stretch of river and share a story about our days on the water.

Using GPS

By Michael Ferguson

apidly increasing numbers of outdoor enthusiasts are purchasing Global Positioning System (GPS) receivers. These units now sell for as little as $100 and have become much more user-friendly. There is still a learning curve for users, but the time spent is well-invested as GPS offers huge benefits to anyone who spends time in the outdoors. GPS is just a tool, but a powerful one. It will give you the opportunity to go farther with greater comfort and allow you to focus more of your attention on why you are outdoors in the first place.

HOW GPS WORKS

Your GPS receiver depends on a constellation of 24 satellites. Each satellite constantly transmits a stream of radio messages. Your receiver uses those messages to calculate its (your) position. It does this by determining its distance from several satellites (3 or more) in known positions. Your receiver can only calculate a position in 2-D mode with three satellites. It then has to depend on the last known elevation to generate a solution. In mountainous terrain this can induce error exceeding one mile. Make sure you can determine if your receiver is in 2-D mode and don't rely on it at such times. Satellite coverage has greatly improved in recent years and you can usually acquire the necessary four satellites for 3-D operation. Getting out in the open will help, or simply wait for better coverage as satellites move overhead.

SELECTIVE AVAILABILITY

GPS receivers became more accurate on May 1, 2000, when President Clinton ordered the U.S. military to stop Selective Availability (the scrambling of satellite signals used by civilians).

Artificial errors were intentionally introduced into the satellite signals for years for national security reasons, giving the military a far more accurate system than civilians.

The military will still be able to scramble the signals on a regional basis should it need to do so for national security reasons. But GPS users worldwide will not be affected by such GPS degradations, and businesses reliant on GPS will be able to continue to operate at peak efficiency.

LAND NAVIGATION WITH GPS

The Global Positioning System is the most significant development in land navigation since the invention of the compass. GPS fundamentally changes the way you use a map. The coordinate system on the map was essentially irrelevant to the land navigator. Now, with GPS, coordinates are everything. Coordinates you read on the display of your receiver can be used to pinpoint your position on the map, and coordinates you obtain from the map or some other source (such as this guide) can be entered into your receiver so it can guide you to that location. It's safe to say that the key to unlocking the full potential of your GPS receiver is knowing how to work with coordinate systems. Make sure your GPS receiver is set to the same datum/format as the coordinates you are entering.

If coordinates are the key to GPS, distance and direction are the treasure. Once you have coordinates stored in your receiver's memory you're ready to navigate. Distance and direction are the foundation of GPS-based navigation.

A GPS receiver is in navigation mode when it has been told to "GoTo" a stored waypoint. There are many items of information associated with navigation mode, but distance and direction are easily the most important of these. Quite simply, they give you the exact distance and direction as the crow flies to the destination you selected. If there is a river between you and your destination you may not be able to literally follow the directions provided by your receiver. However, if you know the location of a bridge you can use it as an intermediate "GoTo" destination, then switch the "GoTo" to your final destination upon reaching the bridge. Obviously, this requires that you have two waypoints stored in your receiver: one for the final destination, and one for the bridge.

A more advanced way to deal with this scenario is to link the two waypoints into a route. A route is just several waypoints that have been linked into legs. Routes can be used to order waypoints so that a complicated path of travel is easier to follow. Also, most receivers automatically switch their "GoTo" to the next waypoint as you pass the current waypoint. A convenient touch.

USING A COMPASS WITH GPS

There are two distinct reasons compasses are important to GPS users. One reason is that although GPS receivers are very good at telling you the exact direction to your destination, they are very lousy at telling you what that direction is on the ground. Your GPS receiver will tell you it's 1.23 miles and a bearing of 312 degrees to the bridge, but it's your compass that will show you the real-world direction that is 312 degrees. When using a compass to follow the directions provided by your GPS receiver you need to make sure your GPS receiver and your compass are set for the same "type" of north.

A compass needle naturally aligns with the direction known as magnetic north, which is different than true (geographic) north. The difference between true north and magnetic north is known as magnetic declination. Some compasses can be adjusted for magnetic declination to display true north-based directions. Almost all GPS receivers have the option of providing direction readouts as either true directions or magnetic directions. The important thing is that you make sure both your receiver and your compass are set to give the same type of reading.

Very often when you perform a "GoTo" with your receiver you will not be able to actually see the destination you are "going to." A handy trick in this situation is to use your compass to find some visible distant landmark that is on the path to your destination. Now you can put both your compass and GPS receiver away until you reach that intermediate destination. Once you're there, haul out your receiver and compass and repeat this process.

The second reason compasses are an important accessory for a GPS user is more traditional. You guessed it, a compass also serves as a backup in case you lose the use of your GPS receiver. Whether it's due to a malfunction, drained batteries, your horse stepped on it, or whatever, when your GPS receiver stops working you need to know how to use just a map and compass to find your way. There's a saying among old mariners: "Never rely on a single navigation method." That's how they became old mariners. Hopefully, when the time comes to rely on those traditional navigation skills they will serve you well. It will take more effort (after all, saving effort is what GPS is all about), but those traditional skills can and should bail you out. In fact, quite a few GPS users have commented that using GPS has allowed them to improve their map and compass skills. That's because GPS provides instant feedback and verification, thereby allowing rapid gains in their confidence levels.

Michael Ferguson *is the author of* GPS Land Navigation and GPS Waypoints.

CONSERVATION

PHOTO: STEVE SCHMIDT

To Net or Not to Net

By Guy Turck

A common question at High Country Flies is whether it is better to net a trout or not. The short answer is... it depends. The long answer is that you shouldn't net a trout unless you have to. Having said that, there are times when it is appropriate to use a net.

The basic rule of thumb regarding the handling of trout is don't. Of course, this is not always practical, and we are sometimes forced to net or touch our catch. However, to the extent that it is possible, you want to avoid handling trout whether it be with your hands or a net.

One thing you should never do is net a small trout. It's simply not necessary and is potentially harmful to the trout. While no trout, large or small, should be manhandled, small trout are particularly susceptible to such mistreatment. They are very delicate little creatures. Mishandling small trout can dramatically increase their post-release mortality rates. They may swim away, apparently healthy, but the damage has been done.

Nets have a tendency to scrape off the protective mucous on a trout's skin. The mucous allows trout to easily slide through the water, reducing the effort required to get around in its environment. The mucous is also a barrier to bacteria and

PHOTO: STEVE SCHMIDT

Be sure the fish can hold itself upright on its own and has a bit of spunk in it before the final release.

fungi. To a certain extent, any net will remove some of this mucous, leaving the trout susceptible to disease.

The actual fabric of a net is an important factor in minimizing damage to trout. Rubber nets are the best at reducing the negative impacts of netting a trout but are really only practical when boat fishing. Soft-knotted cotton nets are acceptable but not as good as rubber. They are, of course, much more practical for wade fishermen, but hard to find. Woven synthetic nets, similar to nylon but softer, are in vogue with leading net manufacturers and are a pretty good compromise. Hard-knotted nylon nets, like you'd find in the Kmart fishing department, are the worst and should not be used, period.

So when is it a good idea to net a trout? When a good-sized trout is going ballistic and refuses to give up, that's when! Hard fightin', hard chargin' brutes with no quit in them are prime candidates for the net. The idea is to reduce the length of the fight, thereby reducing the overall amount of stress inflicted. In such cases the use of a net may be justified because you don't want to play the fish to exhaustion, which can increase post-release mortality rates. Use the net to keep the fight as short as possible.

Proper use of the net can also help minimize its impact. Net the fish, but keep it in the water. Let it catch its breath before lifting for a quick photo. Then, if necessary, return it to the net until it is fully revived. By keeping the netted trout in the water you are also helping reduce the friction between the trout's skin and the net fabric. Lifting the trout from the water while in the net will cause the net fabric to scrape the skin and remove mucous.

Once netted, a clean release is equally important to the trout's survival. Do not manhandle or, in any way, squeeze the fish. Do not stick your fingers in its gills. Keep the fish in the water as much as possible and fish barbless to ease hook removal. Be sure the fish can hold itself upright on its own and has a bit of spunk in it before the final release. And be sure to thank the fishing gods for your good fortune.

Bottom line: Never net a small trout and only net large trout to reduce the length of the fight.

Guy Turck *lives in Jackson, Wyoming, and is a fishing guide for High Country Flies. Turck is the designer of Turck's tarantula, which took first-place honors in the 2000 Jackson Hole One-Fly Event.*

Whirling Disease

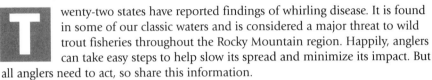 wenty-two states have reported findings of whirling disease. It is found in some of our classic waters and is considered a major threat to wild trout fisheries throughout the Rocky Mountain region. Happily, anglers can take easy steps to help slow its spread and minimize its impact. But all anglers need to act, so share this information.

The microscopic fish parasite responsible for whirling disease was accidentally introduced to the United States from Europe in 1958. Its initial impact was primarily felt at fish hatcheries, but it has now spread to major river systems where it has caused significant damage. The dramatic population collapse of rainbow trout in Montana's Madison River above Ennis Lake (from 3,300 rainbows per mile to 300 per mile) demonstrates the devastating effect whirling disease can have. However, studies show the rainbow population there is coming back, and scientists report considerable progress in the quest to identify natural processes that influence the spread of the disease and the severity of outbreaks.

Still, the disease continues to spread and wreak havoc on fish populations. Whirling disease is now present in 13 of Colorado's 15 major river systems, and rainbow populations in highly infected areas have crashed.

Young cutthroat trout have also proven to be susceptible to whirling disease. Recent research indicates that all species of cutthroat trout may be threatened or endangered in the next century unless human impact (including the spread of whirling disease) on their habitats is reduced.

Humans are not affected by whirling disease.

WHAT IS WHIRLING DISEASE?

Whirling disease is a condition that affects trout and salmon. It is caused by a microscopic parasite known as *Myxobolus cerebralis*. The parasite attacks the cartilage tissue of a fish's head and spine. Young fish may develop symptoms such as whirling behavior or a black tail; they may even die. If they survive, fish may develop head deformities or twisted spines.

Fish biologists believe there are other harmful effects, such as making fish more susceptible to predation and environmental disturbances, as well as impairing their ability to feed and reproduce.

The parasite exhibits a complex life cycle. In one stage it is hosted by small aquatic worms that are common in most waters. Host worms release the more fragile parasitic stage that must infect a trout within a few days or die. Infected trout carry very persistent spores that can survive in moist places for years. When an infected fish dies, these spores are released into the environment. The spores can be transferred to other waters on muddy boots or other fishing equipment.

Rainbow trout are the most susceptible game fish, followed by kokanee salmon, golden, cutthroat, brook and brown trout, and splake. Whitefish and grayling can be infected as well. Lake trout may be immune; other game fish species such as bass, bluegill, perch or walleye do not get whirling disease.

There is currently no known treatment or cure for fish infected with the parasite.

WHAT IS BEING DONE?

Whirling disease has been effectively eliminated in some hatcheries that can tap an uncontaminated water source. Attempts to eliminate the disease in the wild have been unsuccessful. Most work now centers on containment and control of the disease. Barriers have been installed in many areas to prevent infected fish from moving to unaffected areas. Programs have been developed to educate anglers about the problem, so they don't unwittingly spread the disease.

In addition, stocking policies have been changed. Fish from infected hatcheries are stocked only where the disease already exists. Some states now concentrate on stocking the more-resistant brown trout or hybrids into contaminated streams.

The Whirling Disease Foundation coordinates a national effort to combat whirling disease. Each year, the Foundation, Trout Unlimited, the U.S. Fish and Wildlife Service, and other sponsors host a Whirling Disease Symposium, bringing scientists and mangers together to discuss the latest whirling disease research and plan future research priorities. Over 200 university, state agency and federal scientists are now conducting research on the problem.

The Whirling Disease Foundation reports these promising developments:

❐ A water-filtering device has been developed that uses ultraviolet light to kill the whirling disease parasite in hatchery water sources.
❐ Studies indicate that disease hot spots exist in rivers, and that some hot spots may be no bigger than a banquet table or two. Knowing this, it may be possible to manage around or even clean up some of these hot spots, and increase the survival rate for nearby spawning trout.
❐ A Montana study successfully imprinted wild trout eggs with a coldwater spawning temperature. That may help the fry emerge earlier, thus avoiding the period of heavy infection.
❐ In Colorado, a test study is under way to filter the parasite from a heavily infected tributary, which may lower the mainstem infection.

WHAT CAN YOU DO?

Find out which waters are infected in the areas you plan to fish. That information can be obtained from the agency that manages fisheries in that state. Some agencies list infected waters on their Internet sites.

Follow the procedures outlined below every time you go fishing, and be particularly diligent when you know you've been fishing an infected water. (The disease is spreading rapidly, and a water may harbor the parasite for some time before it is detected, so make proper cleanup a normal part of your routine.)

❐ Thoroughly clean mud from all equipment before moving to another water, or to another section of the same water. Waders, boots, anchors, boats and boat trailers should all be carefully cleaned. Thoroughly dry equipment in the sun, if possible, before reuse. If you are traveling directly to other waters, clean your equipment with a 10% solution of chlorine bleach or use another set of equipment.

❏ Do not clean fish in any body of water other than the one in which the fish were caught. Adult fish can carry whirling disease without showing any deformities. In particular, the heads of infected fish contain the resistant spores. Do not dispose of fish parts in other waters.

❏ Never transport live fish. Upstream spread of whirling disease can be blocked by dams and diversions. Moving fish above these barriers can allow this disease to spread.

❏ Call the agency that manages the fishery if you observe the symptoms of whirling disease in fish or observe illegal stocking.

❏ Help to educate other anglers that you know or meet in the field. We all have to work together if whirling disease is to be controlled.

RESOURCES

The Whirling Disease Foundation web site offers detailed information about the disease; go online to *www.whirling-disease.org*.

Two other organizations involved in trout conservation efforts are Trout Unlimited (*www.tu.org*) and the Federation of Fly Fishers (*www.fedflyfishers.org*).

FISHING BASICS

Fly Casting Western Waters

By Bear Samples

recurring theme runs through any western fly fisher's experience — big waters, big wind and big fish. While anglers around the globe want to discuss these storied waters and their healthy, robust trout, these fish are rarely just easy "gimmies." Time after time in the West, a fly fisher must make a tricky presentation, a bull's-eye cast, or a casting distance that exceeds that of the smaller streams found closer to home. The West, perhaps more than any other trout region in the world, requires solid fly-casting skills to earn the reward of a leaping fish.

It is difficult to believe that fly fishers will travel hundreds and even thousands of miles to fish the classic waters of Montana or Idaho — yet not bring the necessary casting tricks to match the expensive graphite contained in their rod cases. Preparing for a trip should include a study of casting books and videos, any necessary lessons, and plenty of yard or park practice. When you sacrifice time, money and energy for a major adventure, the bother of some extra casting practice should be pretty low on the pain scale. The major reason that people will not work on their fly casting is that they possess the

Do not let the rod butt hinge more than 30 degrees from the wrist.

average ability required to deliver the fly and catch fish in average situations. But a raging wind will reduce a typical fly fisher to neophyte status. Difficult currents on the Provo River will give a guide just as much gray hair as the eager client — yet all too often it's no fish, no tip. Good casting produces good results, which means both more and better trout.

HINGING THE WRIST

The number one casting problem that keeps anglers from getting to fish is hinging, flexing or bending the wrist. The inability to flex the rod correctly causes the rod to fall low to the front and rear. Casting energy is dissipated to the outside

Bear's Casting Aid (right) helps prevent the floppy wrist syndrome shown above.

of a large casting loop, which often merely piles the line to the front of the angler. To cure this problem, I developed Bear's Casting Aid, a wrist-stiffening device that prevents the floppy-wrist syndrome (contact AmazingOutdoors.com for ordering information). With a tight wrist and a speed-up-and-stop casting stroke, anglers will become more adept at advanced casting techniques. In contrast to an under-powered loop, a tight loop produces maximum energy to cheat big winds and add distance. For a checkup, go to a local fly shop and have them evaluate your casting stroke and loop formation.

PICK-UP AND LAY-DOWN CAST

I agree with Gary Borger's philosophy of keeping your fly in the water and using as few false casts as possible. Accordingly, I use a pick-up and lay-down cast much of the time. If you begin with your line straight and rod tip low, along with a distinct stop to your power stroke, your line will always be on your rod tip with the rod properly loaded. It is not difficult to make this cast up to 50 feet. This is one of the primary casts when you are pounding the bank with a woolly bugger or grasshopper from a drift boat — tactics often used on the Green or other floatable rivers. Before you know it, you'll be making twice as many casts as your partner and covering a lot more water.

ROLL CASTING

When wading streamsides with willows and cottonwoods close to your back, a roll cast is indispensable. The Beaverhead and the Fryingpan both require regular roll casts. There are three key factors in grooving this cast:

1) lift your casting hand to about the height of your face;
2) stop the rod completely to allow the water tension to anchor the line; and

3) drive the cast forward in a straight line without hinging your wrist and making a large loop.

Another situation where this technique is essential is fishing dry flies upstream. Try to spot your target fish first, then lay your long leader and fly at least three or four feet above it. Strip your slack line in as the fly drifts toward you. With 10 or 15 feet of line remaining, roll cast your fly back into the feeding lane. On the Provo River, we drive fish crazy by "casting a hatch" until the browns are fooled by the artificial fly.

FALSE CASTING

I recommend spending extra time working on false casting. The false cast is the fore- and backcast sequence that keeps the fly in the air while serving other useful purposes, such as drying out a dry fly, lengthening your cast, hovering for accuracy, and changing direction of your cast. You can also false cast while you are changing positions on the stream. I've walked as far as 50 or 100 feet to the next rising fish by false casting the entire distance. If a fish shows itself in a rise form, you are instantly ready to put the fly on the water.

Many people incorrectly try to use false casting to distance their cast by putting lots of extra rod energy into their final presentation cast. It is more efficient to go through your false casting, then open up your line hand slightly on your forecast, which allows the line to shoot slightly from your loaded rod. This will easily get you an extra 10 or 15 feet on your cast.

Timing is the key factor in good false casting. Your casting loop should form a candy cane or "J" lying on its side as your line straightens to the rear and front. Do not allow your line to come totally straight. This causes the line to be pulled downward by gravity and the rod to unload. A good way to practice false casting is to turn sideways so you can watch your line unfurl to the rear. Remember to use the same casting energy to the rear and the front. One of the most common problems fly casters face is to underpower the backcast and hammer the forecast. This usually leads to a tailing loop because of the misapplication of power.

To change the direction of your cast, go through your regular false casting sequence, then when making your final presentation, drive your hand and rod tip toward your new target. It is not difficult to change your direction by 45 degrees. A typical scenario for this technique might be on the Henry's Fork. You are covering the stream with a dry fly that you cast quartering upstream. After putting a quick upstream mend into the drift, you allow the fly to pass in front of you and drift below you. You could then pick up the cast and fire it straight back upstream. But a better option is to reposition your cast by false casting and aiming your first forecast to the middle of your drift: Return the next false cast to the rear middle, then deliver your last front cast to the target area upstream.

LOB CASTING

One of my favorite techniques on places like the Green River below Fontenelle Dam is to fish with a large dry-fly attractor, like a foam beetle or Chernobyl ant, with a nymph dropper. Sometimes I bet the farm and extend a woolly bugger on the drop. I have had some nice results with this system. But using most casts, casting this dry/dropper rig is next to impossible unless you want to fight the frustration of constant tangles. Try a lob cast to avoid this knotty problem.

When the stream is flowing from right to left, the correct hand position for the lob cast is this across-the-body, backhand stance.

Practicing the lob cast is best done on stream with a full setup. This is one of the only instances when you might as well learn the cast while fishing. Begin with your line in the water to your front and extended about 25 or 30 feet. Roll the flies upstream in a quartering direction. Work your regular mends to allow for a drag-free float. On the hang down when the flies are directly below you, move the rod from side to side or lift the rod tip and drop it back. Swimming the flies can drive fish insane, so prepare for a vicious strike.

To begin a new lob cast, lift your rod and line until almost all of the line has pulled free of the water. You should have about five feet of line in contact with the water. Roll your rod 180 degrees in your hand, so that the rod guides are pointed skyward and the back of your hand (with the stream flowing from your right to left) is in front of your face. Make a backhand cast upstream and cast an open or medium-sized loop. This is accomplished by dropping your casting hand slightly at the end of the casting stroke.

Employing the lob cast instead of false casting will reduce line tangles. Also use the lob cast when doing regular strike indicator fishing. It is a big help if you use split shot or double nymphs.

CHEATING WESTERN WINDS

Fly fishing the West dictates that you will have to cast under windy conditions. I can recall numerous occasions where drifting a river was close to impossible in a wind — much less trying to cast. Make for better days by learning to cast during a blow.

The first step to good casting in the wind is to determine the wind direction. Your strongest cast is when the wind is blowing into your line-hand side. The wind blows the line and fly away from your body, and you make a normal cast. With the wind coming from your backside, apply more energy to your backcast while dropping low to the rear. By aiming high to the front on delivery, your cast will sail for more distance.

Sometimes the location of trout forces us to cast into the wind. When the wind attacks from your rod-hand side, make a full, low sidearm cast. In most cases, this will keep the fly away from your body. Another approach is to backcast with a three-quarters or full sidearm, then at the rear, tilt your hand and rod into the backhand position. Make your forecast with this backhand stroke that carries the fly and line away from your body on the line-hand side. If you were to follow the path of your rod tip, it would be scribing a wide oval path.

Casting into the wind is one of the most difficult parts of fly fishing. Many anglers leave good water to find another spot, or just throw in the towel, rather than trying techniques that help to shoot line, like the double haul, to get distance against the wind. One trick is to fish with one line size heavier than the rod manufacturer recommends. For example, for a 5-weight rod, use a 6-weight line. Anglers who have battled the wide Missouri or the Clarks Fork often use a 7-weight rod for dry flies in windy conditions.

Shooting line lets you release extra line to the front or rear on your false cast. With a loaded rod, release line from your line hand as the loop has begun to form off your rod tip on your forward cast. Make your loops as tight as possible so they can drive into the wind with high energy. Try to leave at least 30 feet of line out as you pick up line for a new cast. If you work your fly in too closely, say within 10 feet of the fly line out, you do not have enough line to bend the rod and load it properly.

Anglers rarely learn the technique of double hauling simply by reading a book or magazine article. Casting videos and live instruction aid people in positioning and timing for the double haul. A haul is a yank or downward pull by the line hand on the fly line that is performed in conjunction with the power stroke. It

PHOTO: AMAZINGOUTDOORS.COM

In hauling, the line hand follows the rod hand before the downward pull. No line slack is allowed to form between the line hand and stripping guide.

speeds up the line and places a bend in the rod tip. Double hauling provides the most energy possible to perform the work of cheating a headwind.

Another tactic is to throw your backcast high to the rear and have the wind "stand it up." This helps in loading your rod, which is driven low to the front and underneath the strength of the wind.

Practice is the key for all good fly casting. You can even practice with pantomime and imitate your casting strokes while you are sitting in your car, in the office or at the dinner table. Believe it or not, your casting will improve. Also, take a lesson from a certified instructor or guide — not just someone who catches fish. Unskilled teachers may only teach you their bad habits without recognizing your problem areas and how to correct them.

PRESENTATION CASTS

You must learn to keep your fly on target. When you think about rivers like the Madison, with pocket water formed by exposed rocks, it takes an exact cast to be in the fish zone. During a heavy insect hatch, trout will often hold in one position with the insects being washed toward the fish in a feeding lane. With close observation, you'll find that the fish will rarely move more than six inches to either side to eat. On the Provo River during a blue-winged olive blanket hatch, some browns won't even turn their heads!

Practice does make perfect, and accuracy practice can be a fun game. Begin with hula hoops as targets and eventually replace them with dinner plates. Place them on the lawn at selected distances and let the games begin. As you practice, try to hit the targets with backhand and sidearm casts, too. If it has just rained, you can practice roll casting on a parking lot (that's what that old line is good for!). It only takes a small amount of water to provide the correct surface tension to grab the line.

For your best accuracy, you need to move your casting hand from beside your body to in front of your body in line with your eyes. This is much like shooting a rifle or sighting a bow. Your casting stroke is limited, but if you need to cast longer distances, let the rod hand pass beside your head and over your shoulder. Work at accuracy until you can hit targets at 50 feet.

Presentation casts refer to the type of cast that is needed to present your fly in the most natural or drag-free manner. If you are planning a trip to a famous spring creek, like Armstrong's/DuPuy or Silver Creek where big trout often hold in the hardest to reach water, good presentation skills are essential. An easy cast to learn is the "S" cast. As the line comes off the rod tip upon delivery, shake your rod back and forth. These bends of line in the water are straightened by the current as your fly at the end floats naturally. Combined with a long leader, this cast will pay big dividends.

You will find many fishing situations where you want to cast over the main current to fish the calmer or slower-moving water on the opposite side. A reach cast is made by firing a regular overhead cast toward the target area. As the line has almost completely straightened, reach your rod in the direction of the upstream current by pushing your casting hand directly away from your body to the right or left. Let the line fall to the water and pull your rod back to the front position. This cast places a large amount of line on the current to present your fly drag-free.

With a long leader, a puddle cast is very effective. In your final casting sequence, drop your backcast slightly to the rear and aim your forecast higher than normal to the front. As the line straightens, lower your rod quickly and collapse your cast. The line ends up in a puddle or pile in the current. The result is an effective float for your fly.

Curve casts are used when you have to reach a fish behind an obstacle like a rock or sticks. For right-handers, if you cast slightly sidearm and stop the rod quickly as the rod tip is passing to the left, the line will follow the tip and kick sharply to the left. A curve to the right is created by underpowering your forecast as you move your rod slightly from right to left. This causes your line to fall with a moderate curve to the right.

Determination and practice will produce the necessary casting skills to prepare you for a western water adventure.

Berris "Bear" Samples *is a Federation of Fly Fishers certified master fly-casting instructor and teaches at Sage fly-fishing schools. He is the author of* 30 Days to Better Flycasting *and was voted the 1999 Western Rocky Mountain Fly Fisher of the Year by the FFF.*

Fly-fishing Techniques

By Larry Tullis

he three most important fly-fishing techniques focus on presenting dry flies, nymphs and streamers. Each technique has many permutations but still requires a knowledge of the basics. Time spent learning and practicing basic techniques will pay big dividends on the stream.

DRY-FLY TECHNIQUES

Dry flies imitate the adult stage of aquatic insects, but also include terrestrial insects such as grasshoppers, beetles, ants and cicadas. Dry-fly fishing is arguably the most enjoyable fly-fishing technique, because you can see the trout take the fly on the surface of the water, and the almost weightless fly is generally very easy to cast. Since you cast the weight of the line, not the weight of the lure, the lighter dry fly makes things easier for beginners. Hence, most anglers start with dry-fly fishing — even though other techniques often produce better results. Skilled anglers will also use dry flies when more advanced presentations are needed.

Most dry-fly fishing is done by casting up and across toward the midcurrent, or down and across toward a bank. You must identify your primary target — usually a rising trout or a good-looking trout feeding lie — and present the fly to a secondary target immediately upstream, several feet from the primary target. Remember that the rise form of a surface feeding trout drifts downstream, so you must cast well above where the rise form started. Trout often have a very limited strike zone, so casts and drifts must be accurate — unless you're just prospecting the water.

When imitating a specific floating insect, you are generally casting to individual trout; attractor flies are often best when you systematically try to cover the water searching for takers.

Once your cast is made, you must achieve a natural drift. If the fly lands on a tight line, the currents will immediately drag the fly in an unnatural manner. Experienced anglers often do much better because they know how to present the fly on a slack line, and get a long, natural-looking drift by using mending and other line-control techniques.

You'll see a belly develop in the fly line as the current pulls it downstream past your position. Use the rod tip to roll the floating line upstream and over, so it produces a mirror image of the previously dragging belly. This gives you additional slack line before the current "bellies" the line again. More than one mend is often needed, but don't overdo it. Mending often moves the fly and may put the fish off as much as current-caused drag will. Add some slack line immediately following the mend to allow the mend to work longer. A common mistake is to strip in the slack after mending, which defeats the purpose of the mend in the first place. Keep as many small "S"-curves in the line as possible as the dry fly drifts toward the primary target.

PHOTO: STEVE SCHMIDT

Trout often have a very limited strike zone, so casts and drifts must be accurate.

When a trout takes the fly from the surface, set the hook with a swift and firm sweep of the rod at a downstream angle. Strip in more line if the rod is not bent tight to the fish, but be prepared for the trout to take off. Allow the fish to pull slightly taut line through your fingers. Keep a smooth bend in the rod as you wear the fish down. If a large fish jumps, give it a little slack so a tail slap won't part the leader.

NYMPHING STRATEGIES

Nymphing is almost always the most productive way to fly fish because 90 percent or more of a trout's diet is made up of subsurface foods. A nymph is a generic term referring to a sunken imitation of aquatic insects, crustaceans, worms, leeches or fish eggs. Nymphing is the presentation technique you use to present a subsurface imitation in a natural manner.

The most common and easiest to learn nymphing strategy is to use a strike indicator and floating fly line. This floating yarn, foam, cork or dry-fly indicator gives you a reference point to watch (like a bobber used with natural baits) while the fly drifts naturally in the current. The strike indicator lets you track the sunken fly, helps ensure you are getting a natural drift, and lets you know when a trout hits the fly.

Place the indicator on a seven- to 12-foot tapered leader about one to two times the water depth from the fly (if the water to be fished is three feet deep, put the indicator three to six from the fly). Use a shorter distance for heavily weighted flies and a longer distance for lightly weighted flies. Weight the leader if the fly is

PHOTO: LARRY TULLIS

Use mending and line control to get a long, natural-looking drift.

not sufficiently weighted. Some nymphs are weighted with wire, lead or bead-heads so they will sink; others are tied without weight, and so the leader will need to be weighted instead.

Trout feed mostly in the lower third of the water column near the stream bottom but will sometimes suspend themselves near the surface to capture ascending insects. Using appropriate weight to get down — but not drag and snag the bottom — is essential. Weight should be adjusted regularly to match changing depth and water speed.

Just as in dry-fly fishing, the typical nymphing cast is up and across stream with appropriate slack introduced during the cast or subsequent mends to allow for a natural drift. Cast far enough above your primary target so the nymphs have time to sink down into the lower third of the depth before reaching the fish on a slack line.

Since this technique is more visual you will not feel the hit, so set the hook anytime the indicator dips under, shoots upstream, or looks in any way like it is straying from its natural drift pattern. Set the hook on any "hit" until you can distinguish between the current and a take. Never assume it is just the stream bottom or you'll miss lots of trout.

A dry fly as a strike indicator works very well on trout feeding in shallow water. Just hang some tippet material tied from the bend of the dry fly down to a nymph on six to 24 inches of leader. Two flies are usually better than one because you cover twice the water and give the fish a choice. The same is true when you use two nymphs instead of just one.

STREAMER PRESENTATIONS

A streamer is a generic term for many small fish (minnows, fry, smolt, etc.) imitations and may also include leech or crayfish imitations, since techniques and fly patterns are often interchangeable.

Unlike with nymph and dry-fly fishing, most streamer fishing is done on a tight line with an active retrieve of the line. Since a streamer simulates a frightened or injured baitfish, it must swim or dart in a lifelike manner. Cast to a likely place where a trout may be waiting and then strip in the line in short fast pulses or with longer, steady pulls. In deep water, you might want to use a heavily weighted fly or fast-sinking sink-tip fly line. Generally, let the line sink before starting the retrieve, but when casting near a bank or in shallow water, start the retrieve immediately.

As soon as the fly hits the water, bring the line over to the rod hand so you can strip the line in from behind one or two fingers of the rod hand. Never completely let go of the fly line. The retrieve should be done with the rod tip pointed directly at the fly, so there is always a tight line and hits are easily felt right through your fingers.

When a fish takes, it is usually obvious. Some hits, however, are soft and just feel funny. The line may go completely slack, or act like a rubber band starting to stretch. The hook should be set by simultaneously lifting the rod and stripping in some line, rather than pulling the rod tip sharply up and back. Game fish often try to stun their prey before devouring it, so you don't want to pull the fly out of the strike zone if the fish just nipped at the fly. Continue the retrieve until the take is solid.

Larry Tullis *lives in Salt Lake City and is a writer, photographer and fishing guide.*

ON THE RIVER

Kickboats for Fishing

By Larry Tullis

kickboat is a small watercraft designed to be used from a sitting position with fins on your feet for hands-free direction or drift control. Imagine a pontoon on each side of you with a comfortable seat in the middle. Many can be rigged with oars or motors, but the whole idea behind these boats is to be able to use fin power for better control and placement while fishing. They can also be used for a variety of nonfishing adventures, including hunting, wildlife watching, photography and scuba diving. Various sizes and designs are available, so choose one that suits your size and the type of water you will use it on.

Kickboats are generally bigger than float tubes but smaller than whitewater catarafts. Kickboats give you better portability, ease of use, and more launch options than a large cataraft, and they perform much better in most conditions than a float tube. They are also faster than float tubes, seat you higher, and have more options such as oars, motors and river-running capabilities.

CHOOSING A KICKBOAT

There is no ideal kickboat for everything. A great boat for swift rivers will be too heavy for backpacking; a high lakes watercraft will be far too small to run

PHOTO: LARRY TULLIS

Fins can be used for propulsion and also to control a kickboat's direction, leaving the fisher's hands free for serious business. Most kickboats also accommodate oars.

rivers. Decide whether you want a stillwater craft, a river machine, a lightweight portable, a heavy-duty design that needs a trailer, or one of the many midsize kick-boats that offer fair portability with good versatility for rivers and lakes.

For rivers, the watercraft should be at least eight feet long and have a some-what rockered (banana-shaped) hull for ease of maneuvering with fins in fast water. Flat pontoon shapes have better tracking features for stillwater but don't turn easily for use in rivers or windy lakes. Nine- to 11-foot long boats give you the capacity to do multi-day floats (with your camping gear), while shorter boats are great for day trips. If you want to use an electric motor, make sure a motor mount is available. Smaller kickboats often have no rowing option. Anglers on larger rivers will want to row rather than rely on fins to cover distances quickly or to negotiate tricky whitewater with more control. Experienced kickboaters often use fins through Class II and III rapids and rarely use the oars for anything but quick shut-tles from point A to B; however, oars are still nice to have. Some users prefer to forgo fins and just row to good wading spots.

HISTORY OF KICKBOATING

Although small pontoon-type boats have been used for hundreds, perhaps thousands, of years, fin power for these crafts has only been used since the '80s. Float tubes have been around since the '40s, but the genesis of kickboats came from float tubers who wanted a better fishing platform that had similar fin control. Brooks Bouldins' "Kikk Boat," and Daryl Osborne's "Water Otter" (and its prede-cessor the "Water Wagon") got things started commercially. New designs were seen every year as features were improved, and new companies like Buck's Bags, Outcast, Hobie, J.W Outfitters, Kingfisher, Watermaster, Tote-N-Float and Dave Scadden's Pontoon Craft came out with their versions of the ultimate kickboat. Many smaller companies build their own designs as well, and some large recreational equipment companies have produced imitations of competitors' models. Consult your local shop and get some expert advice before buying any model.

MANEUVERING A KICKBOAT

Begin learning kickboat control in a sheltered piece of stillwater. Whether you are using fins or oars, there are five basic maneuvers you need to learn.

First, kick or row in a straight line. This may be more difficult than you first anticipate, since most kickboats are designed to turn better than to track in a straight line. Just kick or row with equal power to both fins or oars. You will be traveling backward, so make sure you are not getting yourself into a dangerous spot. If your course varies, kick or row with one fin or oar a little harder or softer to compensate.

Second, spin on an axis. This means that from a dead stop you need to be able to spin clockwise and counter-clockwise. To do this, rotate one or both fins in a cir-cle right under your seat. You should be able to spin in both directions. This spin is necessary in order to aim your boat in a particular direction to cast, or preliminary to kicking in a new direction. Many small corrections are necessary due to wind or stream currents. You should be able to spin with the oars, too. Plant one oar in the water and row with the other. Stop and switch directions. Once you are comfortable doing this, try powering both oars in opposing directions. This will spin the boat even quicker.

The third maneuver is the power turn. Start by kicking backward in a straight line. Now angle both fins to the right or left of center slightly, while maintaining a steady cadence with both fins. If you kick to the right, your craft will take you backward to the right, and vice versa for the left. If using oars, row in a straight line and

The Deschutes is a specialty kickboat that can be used to fish rivers with rapids up to Class IV and V. Here designer Dave Scadden uses the boat to navigate the Henry's Fork near Surprise Falls.

begin rowing slightly harder or softer with one oar than the other. This will cause you to turn while maintaining power and speed. Unlike with fins, you can do this maneuver forward or backward with oars.

The fourth maneuver is designed to maintain control in moving water or wind. Should you stop kicking your fins, you will be buffeted by wind and currents and lose directional control — so your feet should constantly be maneuvering. In lakes, wind will blow you all over unless you learn to keep your back to the wind and a steady cadence with the fins to hold position. This is one of the real advantages of kickboats. You can hold position easily in the wind without an anchor and then instantly change position without having to raise anchor, fishing all the while.

In rivers, the current is constantly pushing you downstream while swirling currents try to spin your craft. Rotate the craft so your back is up-current and keep a slow kick going. This slows your drift down the river and makes it easy to keep you facing downstream to see obstacles and the next fishing spot. Don't fight the current and wear yourself out, just maintain control. Dragging one or both fins near the bottom where the water is slower can also help control your drift with less kicking, depending on water depth.

The fifth maneuver is the river ferry. A ferry is used to get you from one side of the river to the other, with the least amount of downward travel, or to maneuver through an obstacle-filled channel. You'll need to spin your watercraft so your back is aimed the direction you want to go and begin kicking in a straight line. If you aim too far downstream you'll pass lots of river before getting across. Likewise, if you try to fight the current while you cross, you'll just be wearing yourself out as the river pushes you farther downstream. Ideally, you can find the

PHOTO: LARRY TULLIS

By using a kickboat, anglers can work virtually every part of a river. This angler is floating through small rapids in scenic Bear Gulch, on Henry's Fork.

perfect angle that will take you across with the least effort and the least amount of downward momentum. Once you find the right angle, it seems that just a little effort pulls you right across. Oars obviously will get you across quicker, but fins do just fine with a little practice.

You will use many of these maneuvers in combination, especially in rivers. Say you're coming up to a rapid section with some logs and boulders. You decide the best spot to enter the rapids (usually the V-shaped slick water just before the first waves), ferry to that spot, and then straighten up so you're facing downstream. If there is a rock dead center, you'll need to rotate to one side and kick or row to avoid it, then rotate so you face downstream again before you need to spin the other direction to avoid a log coming up. A combination of spins and short ferries are needed to go through a channel full of obstacles. You might then want to fish through a nice-looking run and then turn your back downstream and kick through a long, unproductive piece of slow water. Aim your back downstream only in slow water, never in rapids.

KICKBOAT SAFETY

All watersports are inherently dangerous, so you need to take kickboat safety seriously. There is no watercraft design in which you'll be completely safe if you ignore or don't see upcoming dangers. In 14 years of kickboating, I have never flipped a kickboat, but I know those who have done so and some more than once. Pay attention, keep control and float smart.

Don't ever use a boat designed for lakes, like float tubes, U-tubes, V-tubes or small pontoon boats, on moving water — they lack the buoyancy required for turbulent waters. Don't use appropriately designed river watercraft in water types beyond your skill level. Get off the water if storm systems threaten violent weather.

Basic safety starts by always wearing a Coast Guard-approved flotation vest, especially on rivers. Pay attention to what is going on around you, so a motorboat or rapids don't sneak up on you. Kickboats are designed with portability in mind, so it is much better to portage or line the boat around dangerous water if you are not comfortable with your whitewater skills or if your boat is not designed for serious fast water.

Safety and emergency items to have along include: A life jacket, first-aid kit, mini survival kit, boat repair kit, pump with proper valve adapters, waterproof flashlight, extra fin or oar (or both fins and oars), throw rope, rope knife, a whistle or mirror signaling device, snacks and drinks.

Kickboats are the most fun you can have sitting down if you choose and use them correctly. Think of all the places you can access with this type of watercraft. Happy floats and tight lines.

Larry Tullis *lives in Salt Lake City and is a writer, photographer and fishing guide.*

The kickboat author on Henry's Fork.

Drift Boats and Rafts

By Kory Kapaloski

oats allow for many options. With them you can: carry things you may not want or be able to lug around on foot, fish from a position not possible on foot, fish side by side and simultaneously with others who can share the experience with you, and access areas — and fish — that cannot be reached otherwise. All of these factors make it very popular to view a river from the perspective of a floating boat, and rafts and drift boats are two of the most popular watercraft for this purpose.

Modern rafts became popular after the World War II era as a means to travel rivers that could not be navigated in any other craft. Where wooden boats were once eaten up by large rocks and boulders, canvas and rubber rafts could travel without significant risk of serious damage, many times just bouncing off rocks that would shatter a wooden boat. Rafts also have the advantage of being able to be transported deflated. Before drift boats attained their current level of popularity, rafts were the primary means used to float rivers.

Drift boats have their roots in old European whaling dories, which had very large, high, pointed bows to slice through waves and allow the current to be pushed underneath the boat rather than over the bow. Drift boats retain this design. But while dories were made of wood, modern drift boats are made primarily from aluminum and fiberglass, which offer many advantages over wood. Aluminum boats are durable, heavy-duty craft that allow you to scrape and brush minor rocks without causing serious damage, hold up better to typical wear and tear, and are affected much less by wind because of their weight. Fiberglass boats are lightweight, easy to maneuver and less expensive in construction, and allow for easy repair.

CHOOSING A BOAT

Both drift boats and rafts allow you to accomplish the same goal of floating down a river, but each has very distinct advantages:

❑ Drift boats ride quite high in the water, often drafting as little as four or five inches of water, making them highly maneuverable. Rafts sit much lower in the water, making them much more difficult to maneuver.

❑ Drift boats are made from rigid, unforgiving materials, which can get damaged when going over shallow gravel or rocks. Rafts are made from soft pliable materials, making them much more forgiving when going over these types of obstacles.

❑ Drift boats are typically designed with fishing in mind, allowing anglers to fish from front and rear braces and level platforms in high and dry positions. Rafts are designed more for conquering large rapids and typically don't have platforms to stand on, let alone casting braces, making it much more difficult or even impossible to fish while moving.

❑ Rafts are capable of handling large quantities of gear by piling them and configuring them in any way you need, and they provide much more freedom in where you can pack things. Drift boats have fixed interior structures that allow much less room for equipment and people.

❑ Rafts are deflatable, allowing them to be carried in small spaces and then inflated at the river in any area with bank space. Drift boats require a trailer to carry them and must have a ramp to put in and take out of the water.

❑ Drift boats are stored ready to go so you can drive to the river, put in and get going. Rafts often require inflation and intensive rigging time and knowledge.

❑ Rafts are designed with whitewater pursuits in mind and are capable of handling large rapids. Drift boats equipped for fishing typically don't even have floatation, so technical whitewater can be far more dangerous.

BASIC NAVIGATION

Floating a river can be a way of fishing or simply a method of accessing fishing areas. In order to fish while moving down a river in either a drift boat or a raft, you must have a properly outfitted craft. At the very minimum, there must be an area where you can stand (preferably with a brace to lean against), and an area for someone to row (a rowing frame in a raft). Most modern drift boats are set up with all of these things and require no modification. Rafts are designed without these conveniences and do require modifications. Additional useful equipment for float fishing includes an anchor (which can be very helpful when pulling over to land fish), and a net, which can be essential to getting a fish onboard without injury to allow for a healthy release. If the only goal of floating the river is to access fishing areas and not to fish on the move, this additional equipment isn't necessary.

Rowing for fishing and rowing for access are two very different pursuits. To effectively row for fishing, the person at the oars must be very skilled. His job is to keep the boat moving at the proper speed, in the proper location and at the proper angle for both anglers. When rowing for fishing, the boat must be constantly slowed to at least match the current speed of the water being fished, and must be maneuvered so that the fisher can cast to the desired water. In addition to this, the oarsman must also be aware of rapids, obstacles, other boats and bank anglers. Becoming proficient at rowing for fishing requires much practice and is a sport in and of itself. When rowing simply to access fishing spots, the only things to focus on are maneuvering around major obstacles and through or around rapids, and to avoid other boats and bank anglers.

RIVERCRAFT FLOATING SAFETY

Drift boats and rafts can be very fun, but in certain circumstances can also be very dangerous. As long as you take safety seriously, they can provide you with years of pleasure without major problems. But there are some basic guidelines to follow when floating any river in a drift boat or raft, and they can prevent major disasters.

PHOTO: STEVE SCHMIDT

Know your watercraft and how to use it.

First of all, know your watercraft and how to use it. Most river mistakes (including capsized boats and rock-wrapped rafts) are a result of lack of knowledge and experience. Assuming that you can just "float" down a river, without worrying about obstacles or rapids, is shortsighted to say the least. However, many accidents are caused by this fundamental mistake. At the very minimum, if you are unfamiliar with maneuvering the craft that you intend to use, go out on nonmoving water and get a fundamental knowledge of how the boat works.

The next basic guideline is to know the water that you intend to float. Get an overview of the water you are drifting; if it is above your ability level, take someone who knows the water and is capable of rowing it — or don't go. If you are on unfamiliar water but have good general river experience, talk to someone who knows the water you are drifting and find out about dangerous rapids/obstacles. Before going into dangerous areas, always "scout" the obstacle (look and plan your path extensively before proceeding), getting out if possible. If the rapid seems beyond your ability level, then line the boat (hold a line attached to the boat while walking on or along the bank behind it) or portage the boat through if possible.

Essential safety equipment includes life jackets, a throw bag, a bail bucket and a first-aid kit.

Life jackets should always be considered when floating any river, and they are an essential part of any properly outfitted watercraft. Many rivers even require them to be worn at all times while floating. Although this can seem a nuisance, the rules are there to protect your life.

A throw bag (found at any store that sells rivercraft-related equipment) is simply a coil of rope in a bag designed to be thrown to any person who goes overboard. Many rivers require this, and even if they don't, you should have one on board.

Bail buckets may seem simply like waterfight tools to some people, but they are also essential. Boats in rivers can take on huge amounts of water, making the craft very difficult to maneuver and more prone to capsizing. Any plastic bucket of at least 5 gallons that will hold water will do.

The final piece of equipment is one that you hope never to use, the first-aid kit. Depending on the duration of the trip, the kit should contain fundamental equipment to provide basic first aid and CPR. It is also wise to include major bandaging, splinting and breathing devices. Many very comprehensive kits can be found in outdoor stores.

Remember: It is always better to be prepared and not need things than to wish that you had something you don't.

Kory Kapaloski *is the guide service manager and one of the founders of Trout Bum 2 in Park City, Utah. He has spent eight years guiding on the Green River below Flaming Gorge and a lifetime fishing the great waters of Utah and surrounding states.*

Wading Safety

By Andy Fitzhugh

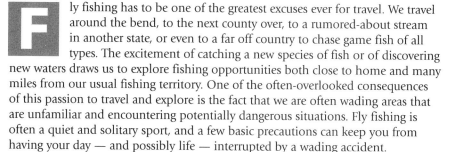ly fishing has to be one of the greatest excuses ever for travel. We travel around the bend, to the next county over, to a rumored-about stream in another state, or even to a far off country to chase game fish of all types. The excitement of catching a new species of fish or of discovering new waters draws us to explore fishing opportunities both close to home and many miles from our usual fishing territory. One of the often-overlooked consequences of this passion to travel and explore is the fact that we are often wading areas that are unfamiliar and encountering potentially dangerous situations. Fly fishing is often a quiet and solitary sport, and a few basic precautions can keep you from having your day — and possibly life — interrupted by a wading accident.

Common sense would tell us that we should never venture out alone, but many times we find ourselves doing just that, especially when fishing is a by-product of a business trip. If you are out alone, make sure you leave your intended destination with someone who will know if you don't return on schedule.

Once you are out on the stream, equipment can make a huge difference. Felt-bottomed shoes are a necessity, and shoes with studs are nice if you are on a particularly slick river. Make sure you purchase good shoes with ankle support.

The days of tight-fitting neoprene waders are coming to an end, and the standard wader on streams today is the lightweight breathable type. The one problem with these waders is that they generally fit loosely and could potentially fill with water if you fall. Therefore it is imperative that you wear a snug-fitting wading belt that will prevent water from filling the legs in the event of a swim.

Finally, a collapsible wading staff is a very good idea, especially if you are not the most sure-footed of waders or if the river is fast and slick.

Equipment can help, but not putting yourself in a bad situation is the best way to avoid swimming. With that in mind, here are some tips:

❑ There are just as many fish on your side of the river; if you don't feel good about crossing, don't try it.

❑ If you do cross, angle from upstream to downstream with your profile to the current. Make sure there are no stumps or snags below you so if you do fall there is nothing to get swept into.

❑ Try to cross at the tail of a pool above a riffle where the water is generally shallower.

❑ Be careful on the bank; many people are injured hopping along the rocky bank before they even get their feet wet.

❑ Be careful of backeddies, which can be deceptively deep, and of bogs along the stream, especially beaver ponds. The mud can act like a vice-grip on your wading shoes.

Finally if you do fall in, don't worry about your rod — you can get a new one. If you can't grab a streamside branch or get back up quickly, orient yourself with your feet downstream and use your arms to reverse dog paddle if you are in deep water. If you have positioned yourself this way and have a wading belt on you should be able to ride out most anything and make it to the bank easily. You may be a little wet or bruised, but you should be able to tell your buddies about how you chased a monster fish through a set of rapids only to have it come off before you could net it and get the all-important picture.

Andy Fitzhugh *is the manager of Western Rivers Flyfisher in Salt Lake City, Utah.*

ARIZONA

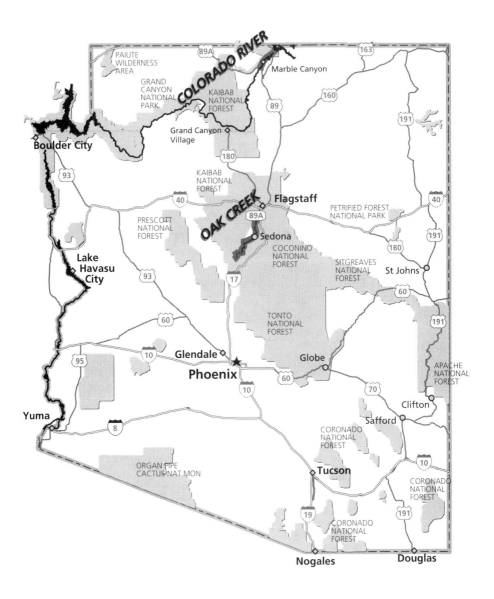

Arizona

rizona is not normally thought of as a state that attracts fly fishers, but it does contain a few wonderful waters. Located far south of most of the Rocky Mountain's trout streams, Arizona rivers can be pleasant and productive to fish when other destinations are buried in snow and ice. If you long for warm weather and fly fishing in the colder months of the year, consider a trip to the Grand Canyon State.

2000 GENERAL SEASON DATES AND BAG & POSSESSION LIMITS

Waters in Arizona are open year-round, unless noted under special regulations.

Species	2000 Daily Bag & Possession Limits
STATEWIDE	
Trout, including char, grayling and salmon	six trout in the aggregate

LICENSE FEES

Fishing License	Age	Fee
RESIDENT		
Lifetime	varies	varies
Season (Class A + trout stamp)	14 and over	$22
Family Season (Class I)	varies	varies
Daily (Class D)	14 and over	$8
Youth Group (Two-day)	up to 17	$25
NONRESIDENT		
Season	14 and over	$48
Four-month (Class B)	14 and over	$22
Five-day (Class C)	14 and over	$18.50
Daily (Class D)	14 and over	$8.00
Season Colorado River only (Class E)	14 and over	$32.50

❏   A valid fishing license is required for any person 14 years or older.
❏   Unlicensed persons under the age of 14 may take half the regular limit of trout.

The commission has initiated a season family fishing license to encourage fishing as a family activity. The cost of the first parent is $22, the cost for the second parent is $17.60, and the cost for each child age 14-17 is $2.

BOATING REGULATIONS

The Arizona Game & Fish Department regulates all boating activities. Boating regulations are published on its web site (*www.gf.state.az.us*), or you can obtain a copy by calling (602) 942-3300.

In Arizona, float tubes are presently not required to carry a personal flotation device (PFD). The rule of thumb is if the watercraft sits above water and has a frame, it is considered a "vessel" and a Coast Guard-approved PFD is required onboard as well as a sound-producing device, such as a whistle or horn. Children under the age of 12 must wear a PFD while boating or rafting.

RESOURCES

Arizona Game & Fish Department
Phone number/s: (602) 942-3300
Web site: www.gf.state.az.us

Fly Fishing in Arizona
Web site: www.azlink.com/~jshannon

Arizona State Parks
Phone number/s: (602) 542-4174
Web site: www.pr.state.az.us

Arizona Office of Tourism
Phone number/s: (602) 230-7733
Web site: www.arizonaguide.com

Bureau of Land Management
Phone number/s: (602) 417-9200
Web site: www.az.blm.gov

U.S. Forest Service
Phone number/s: (520) 527-3600 (Cocino)
Web site: www.fs.fed.us/recreation/states/az.shtml

Colorado River at Lees Ferry

The first Europeans to reach this rugged and inaccessible country were members of the Dominguez-Escalante expedition. They came here in 1776, searching for a route across the Colorado River. Lees Ferry was the single place along the river that offered good access to both banks, but crossing the river was still very difficult until John D. Lee and "Uncle" Tommy Smith arrived in 1873 to build the first ferry boat. They christened her the *Coloredo*, and she became an important link between the southwest and the emerging Mormon communities of southeastern Utah.

The thick, muddy water of those days has been replaced by the clear, emerald green outflow of Glen Canyon Dam, but a person is left feeling that little else has changed. The immensity of the Colorado River in its deep canyon can make a person feel small indeed. The timeless red walls rise more than 1,000 feet straight up from the surging waters of this huge river. The continent's largest and rarest raptor, the California condor, resides here. You may witness these endangered birds soaring on giant wings along the cliff tops.

FISH SPECIES
Rainbow trout

TIP
Keep a careful eye on water levels

HIGHLIGHT
Sight fishing with nymphs in winter

SEASON
Open year-round

A solitary figure is dwarfed by the immense canyon walls.

Colorado: *Lees Ferry to Glen Canyon Dam*

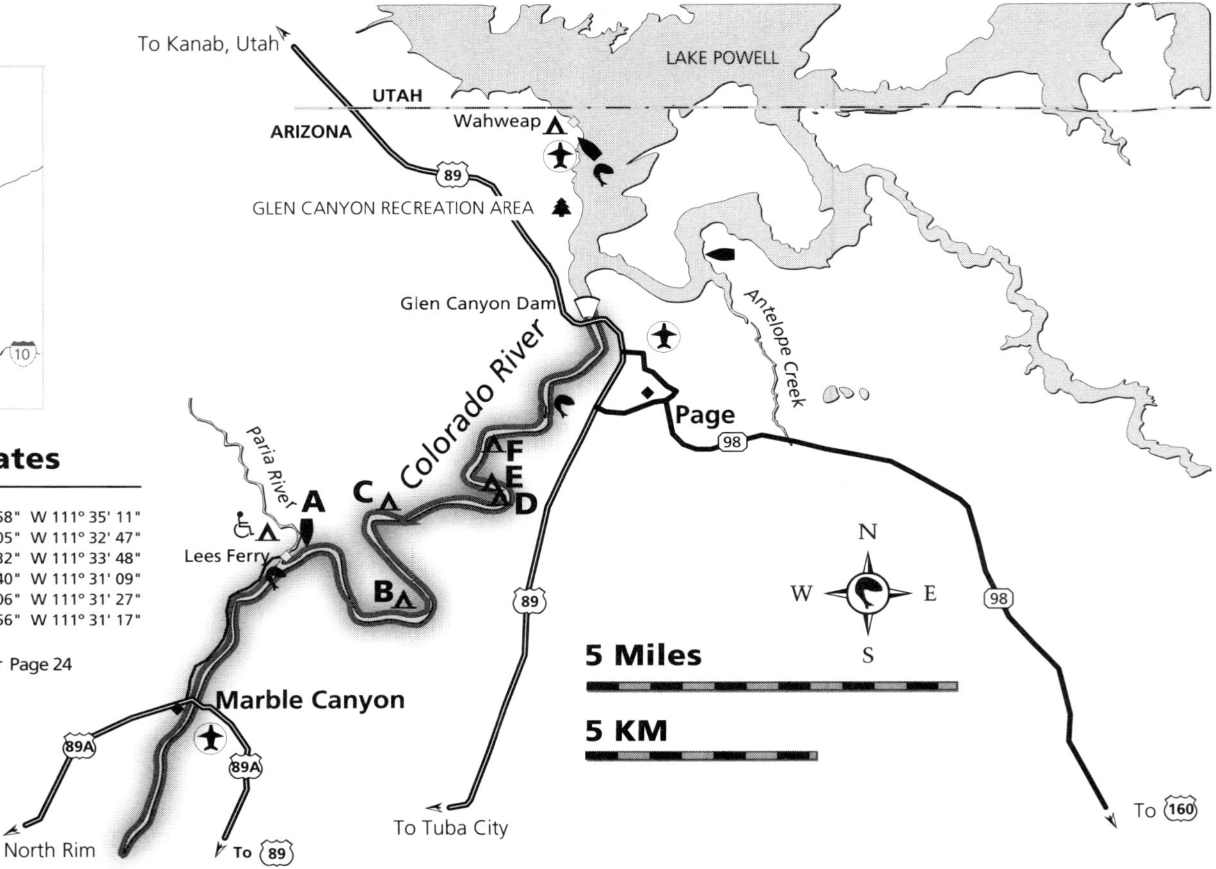

LAKE POWELL

UTAH

ARIZONA

To Kanab, Utah

GLEN CANYON RECREATION AREA

Wahweap

89

Antelope Creek

Page

98

To 160

Glen Canyon Dam

Colorado River

Paria River

Lees Ferry

A

C

F A

E

D

B

89

Marble Canyon

89A

To 89

To Tuba City

To Grand Canyon, North Rim

89A

N E S W

5 Miles

5 KM

St. George, UT

Lees Ferry

Flagstaff

Phoenix

Glendale

Tempe

Yuma

Tucson

40

17

10

8

19

10

GPS Coordinates

A	Lees Ferry Boat Ramp	N 36° 51' 58"	W 111° 35' 11"
B	Three Mile Bar	N 36° 51' 05"	W 111° 32' 47"
C	Six Mile Camp	N 36° 52' 32"	W 111° 33' 48"
D	Eight Mile Bar	N 36° 52' 40"	W 111° 31' 09"
E	Duck Island	N 36° 53' 06"	W 111° 31' 27"
F	Ferry Swale Camps	N 36° 53' 56"	W 111° 31' 17"

Arizona Atlas and Gazetteer Page 24

◣ Boat Launch

▽ Dam

The massive Glen Canyon Dam holds back the waters of Lake Powell. The dam is 300 feet thick at its base and over 700 feet tall. The reservoir of Lake Powell extends for 186 miles and took 17 years to fill completely. Perhaps it is not surprising that a dam of this stature should generate controversy as well as electricity. Some groups advocate draining the reservoir and returning the flooded canyon river to its original state; others resist changing back and look to the future opportunities of technology and power. A proposal to install structures allowing temperature control of waters exiting Glen Canyon Dam has also generated much discussion. The primary purpose would be to improve spawning of the endangered humpback chub and other native species. Colorado River trout are expected to benefit from the warmer waters and increased productivity, but some fear an outbreak of whirling disease could have a serious impact on the fishery.

Bobby Webb with a 20-inch rainbow he caught in mid-January at Lees Ferry.

Whatever your feelings about the dam, its daily operation is a key factor to understanding the habits of fish in the river below. Glen Canyon Dam supplies up to 1.3 million kilowatts of electricity and river flows are dictated, in large part, by power demands. Flows can go from about 8,000 cfs in the morning to 20,000 cfs by afternoon. Keep these fluctuations in mind when wading and make sure you don't get stranded.

Winter is the busiest time of year on the river. Guide boats routinely leave the dock before sunrise to claim prime gravel bars for their clients. As there is not much shallow water suitable for both fly fishers and spawning trout, you may have difficulty finding a good place to fish. Ask other anglers for permission before fishing close to them.

SPECIAL REGULATIONS AND FEES

The Colorado River from Glen Canyon Dam to Marble Canyon Bridge (Lees Ferry):
- ❐ Artificial lures and flies with barbless hooks.
- ❐ The daily limit is two trout under 16 inches.

Vehicle entrance fee for Glen Canyon National Recreation Area is $5 for one to seven days or $15 for an annual permit. Boating permits cost $10 for one to seven days or $20 annually. Do not boat below the cable downstream from the launch ramp. Downstream waters are restricted to those with a Grand Canyon float permit. Rapids begin just downstream.

Entrance and boating fees can be purchased at the self-serve station on the road to Lees Ferry, or call (520) 608-6542 for details.

TACTICS

Beginning in October, Colorado River rainbows move onto the shallow gravel bars in preparation for spawning. Many anglers are drawn to the river at this time for the opportunity to sight fish for these big trout. Good polarized glasses are a must, and the most common rig is a combination of a glo-bug and a midge. Light tippets (5x) and careful casting will improve your chances of hooking these skittish fish in shallow water. Be sure to use enough weight to get down near the bottom and position yourself so that you can get the flies within a foot or less of your quarry. Streamer fishing can also be productive at this time of year. Employ sinking-tip lines and five to six feet of leader tapered down to 3x. If the prime gravel bars are full, you can find fish in deep, slow eddies while you wait for someone to leave.

After spawning, fish will retreat to deeper water and try to regain the energy they expended while procreating. You will find trout in the deeper runs and especially behind gravel bars and below drop-offs. Deep nymphing is productive. Fish are actively feeding and may go out of their way to intercept larger flies. Scud imitations, San Juan worms and midge larvae are effective, as well as traditional patterns like pheasant tails, hare's ears and prince nymphs. Long, extended downstream drifts can be effective at times; just pull extra line from your reel and keep shaking "squiggles" onto the water without letting your line become tight.

When you find fish actively feeding on midges, try a Griffith's gnat with a small midge pupa or emerger on a dropper. Reduce tippet size to 6x and make short, accurate casts to your target. Don't expect trout to move very far for such small food items. Fluorocarbon tippet material can give you an extra edge, and softer action, lighter weight rods can aid in gentle presentations as well as cushioning fragile terminal tackle when you finally connect.

Regular water level fluctuations have led to an unusual fly pattern on this stretch of water. When water levels drop, scuds can be stranded on gravel bars and die. Returning water washes these dead (orange) and floating scuds back into the flow. During rising water, try fishing a floating scud pattern by itself or as a strike indicator.

Hatch Chart

AVAILABILITY

Food Items	J	F	M	A	M	J	J	A	S	O	N	D
Midges	X	X	X	X	X	X	X	X	X	X	X	X
Scuds	X	X	X	X	X	X	X	X	X	X	X	X
Annelid worms	X	X	X	X	X	X	X	X	X	X	X	X
Trout eggs	X	X								X	X	X
Terrestrials							X	X	X			

Insects	Suggested Fly Patterns
Midges	Griffith's gnats (#16-20), grizzly midges (#16-20), zebra midges (#16-20), midge pupae, brown, olive, red and black (#16-22), brassies (#18-22), disco midges (#18-22)
Scuds	olive, tan, pink and orange scuds (#12-16), unbelievables — orange floating scuds (#12-16)
Annelid worms	San Juan worms, orange and red (#12-16), red hots (#18-20)
Trout eggs	pink, orange and yellow glo-bugs (#12-16), bead-head glo-bugs (#12-16), bead eggs (#14-16)
Terrestrials	Dave's hoppers (#8-12), black foam cicadas (#8-12)

If you can stand the summer heat, you can find some explosive dry-fly fishing with terrestrial fly patterns. This approach is most effective when high water reaches up into the tamarisk thickets on the bank. Try grasshoppers and large cicadas.

HOW TO GET THERE

The closest cities with major airports are Phoenix and Las Vegas, both about five hours drive time, or Salt Lake City, which is eight hours by car. Anglers can get commuter flights into Page, Arizona, which is only 45 minutes from the river. Sunrise Air (877-978-6747 or *www.sunriseair.com*) has regular flights from Phoenix and Las Vegas.

From Page, Arizona, go southwest on US 89 24 miles, then turn north onto US 89A and go 14 miles. Turn northeast about 0.3 miles past the bridge. It is about 5.5 miles up this road to Lees Ferry.

To drive up from Phoenix, go north 140 miles on I-17 to Flagstaff. Go northeast about 6 miles on I-40, then take US 89 north for 105 miles. Turn north onto US 89A and travel 14 miles, then turn northeast about 0.3 miles past the bridge. Lees Ferry is about 5.5 miles ahead.

Anglers coming from Las Vegas should take I-15 northeast 130 miles. Go east on SR 9 to Hurricane, Utah, then turn southeast 22 miles on SR 59, which will become SR 389 when you cross the state line into Arizona. Continue east 33 miles to Fredonia, where you will turn east onto US 89A. Drive east 71 miles to Marble Canyon, then turn northeast and go 5.5 miles to Lees Ferry.

ACCESSIBILITY

There are about 15 miles of river from Glen Canyon Dam to Lees Ferry, most of which is carefully guarded by steep cliffs. Shore anglers can only reach about 1 ½ miles of riverbank below the boat ramp, and the best water here is the gravel bar formed where the Paria River (Piute for muddy water) meets the Colorado. The rest of this huge river belongs to boaters.

At Lees Ferry, fly fishers use power boats to reach the river's productive gravel bars.

If you are going to operate a boat here, be sure to exercise caution and consider spending a day with a licensed guide or friend that is intimately familiar with the river. While there are no real rapids, there are shallow areas that can damage propellers and leave boats crippled. Be sure your boat is adequately powered — at least 30 horsepower is recommended — to make its way up the river.

Lee's Ferry Anglers rents power boats that are outfitted for the river. These are 18-foot shallow draft river boats with 50 horsepower jet drives. You must be able to tow the boat to the river (trailer hitch with a 2-inch ball) and have boating experience. Make reservations well in advance of your trip. Current charge is $115 per day plus fuel.

WHEN TO GO

Winter is the most popular season here as anglers come in search of big trout spawning in the shallows. You can count on warmer weather (compared to most other trout fisheries in winter) and a lack of snow. Make sure you are prepared to dress warmly, as many areas of the canyon get very little direct sunlight this time of year.

Early spring is wonderful here as fish begin to feed heavily in this post-spawn period. This is a great place for northern anglers to recover from cabin fever. Technical anglers will enjoy matching wits with trout feeding on the increasing numbers of midges.

Summer is your best choice if you want to cast dry flies to feeding fish, but be sure you are prepared for the heat (up to 110 degrees F). Drifting nymphs through deeper flows and at the bottom of riffles is the most common method employed to hook Colorado River trout during the summer dog days.

Early fall brings more comfortable weather in the canyon. Fishing conditions are much the same as summertime until spawners begin to show up in October.

AREA ATTRACTIONS

This portion of the river is part of the Glen Canyon National Recreation Area, which includes massive Lake Powell. Visitors can enjoy a wide variety of water sports, including houseboating, on this strikingly beautiful reservoir. You can take a break from fishing to see the Navajo Bridge Interpretative Center where US 89A crosses the Colorado River or drive to the Carl Hayden Visitor Center near Page, Arizona, and take a tour of Glen Canyon Dam.

RESOURCES

There are six first-come, first-served designated campsites on the Colorado River. There is no charge for these sites, which have pit toilets. No ground fires are allowed. The other camping alternative is the Lees Ferry campground, also first-come, first serve. It has 51 campsites and flush toilets. If you prefer lodgings, Marble Canyon is just a few miles from the river.

Lodging

MARBLE CANYON

Marble Canyon Lodge
US 89A
P.O. Box 6001
Marble Canyon, AZ 86036
Phone number/s: (520) 355-2225,
toll-free (800) 726-2569

Lee's Ferry Lodge
US 89A
Marble Canyon, AZ 86036
Phone number/s: (520) 355-2231

Cliff Dwellers
US 89A
Marble Canyon, AZ 86036
Phone number/s: (520) 355-2228,
toll-free (800) 433-2543

Tackle Shops and Guide Services

MARBLE CANYON

Marble Canyon Guides
P.O. Box 6032
Marble Canyon, AZ 86036
Phone number/s: (520) 355-2245,
toll-free (800) 533-7339
Web site: www.leesferryflyfishing.com
E-mail: leesferry@aol.com

Lee's Ferry Anglers
N. US 89A, Milepost 541 ½
HC-67 Box 2 Marble Canyon, AZ 86036
Phone number/s: (520) 355-2261,
toll-free (800) 962-9755
Fax: (520) 355-2271
E-mail: anglers@leesferry.com

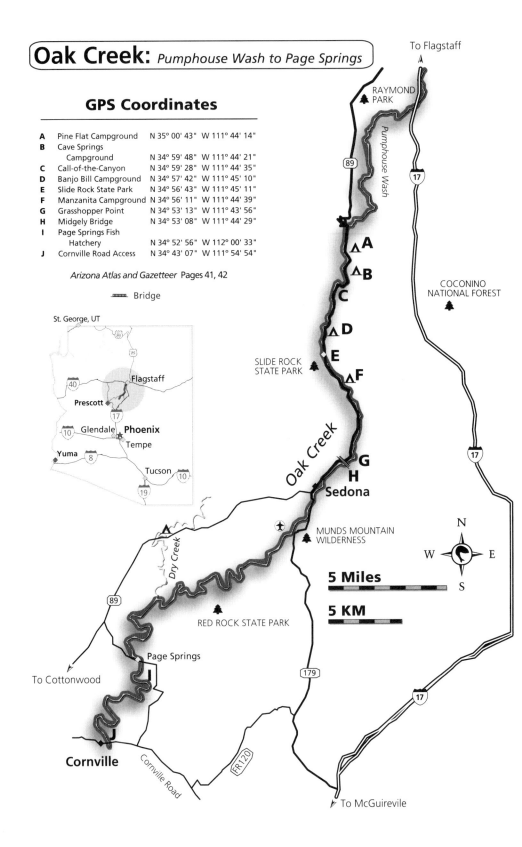

Oak Creek: *Pumphouse Wash to Page Springs*

GPS Coordinates

A	Pine Flat Campground	N 35° 00' 43"	W 111° 44' 14"
B	Cave Springs Campground	N 34° 59' 48"	W 111° 44' 21"
C	Call-of-the-Canyon	N 34° 59' 28"	W 111° 44' 35"
D	Banjo Bill Campground	N 34° 57' 42"	W 111° 45' 10"
E	Slide Rock State Park	N 34° 56' 43"	W 111° 45' 11"
F	Manzanita Campground	N 34° 56' 11"	W 111° 44' 39"
G	Grasshopper Point	N 34° 53' 13"	W 111° 43' 56"
H	Midgely Bridge	N 34° 53' 08"	W 111° 44' 29"
I	Page Springs Fish Hatchery	N 34° 52' 56"	W 112° 00' 33"
J	Cornville Road Access	N 34° 43' 07"	W 111° 54' 54"

Arizona Atlas and Gazetteer Pages 41, 42

▬▬ Bridge

To Flagstaff

RAYMOND PARK

Pumphouse Wash

89

17

COCONINO NATIONAL FOREST

▲A
▲B
C
▲D
E
▲F

SLIDE ROCK STATE PARK

Oak Creek

G
H
Sedona

MUNDS MOUNTAIN WILDERNESS

17

17

N
W   E
S

5 Miles

5 KM

Dry Creek

89

RED ROCK STATE PARK

Page Springs

To Cottonwood

179

J

Cornville

Cornville Road

FR120

To McGuirevile

St. George, UT

Flagstaff

Prescott

17

Glendale   Phoenix
        Tempe

Yuma

Tucson

Oak Creek

FISH SPECIES
Rainbow and brown trout

TIP
Wade with care

HIGHLIGHT
Incredible scenery

SEASON
Open year-round

Oak Creek Canyon is considered one of the most beautiful drives in Arizona. If you plan a trip here for the scenery and ambiance of the canyon, as well as the fishing, you won't be disappointed. From the overlook above the switchbacks on SR 89A, you can appreciate the depth of the canyon that Oak Creek has been carving for more than 10 million years. The cream-colored Coconino Sandstone at the canyon rim gives way to the red Schnebly Hill Formation as you drop farther down to a verdant ribbon of water in this high desert region.

This is small, intimate water in an incredible natural setting. It begins at the confluence of Sterling Canyon and Pumphouse Wash, and the perennial flow originates at Sterling Springs. While very small above the West Fork, Oak Creek steadily increases in size until it reaches a normal flow of about 30 cfs near Sedona. It's not always a small stream, however. Like other desert drainages, Oak Creek is subject to periodic flash floods. Most years it will rise as high as 1,000 cfs, and in 1993 and 1995, it reached 8,000 cfs.

Oak Creek Canyon lies within the Coconino National Forest. The several day-use areas, campgrounds and turnouts make it much easier to get to the river than it is to wade your way up it. The easy access and the popularity of the canyon makes it difficult to get away from others at times.

Most trout in Oak Creek are in the 10- to 14-inch range, but there are fish up to 18 inches. The catch-and-release regulations currently being enforced at the top of the canyon should ensure that more large fish are available to Oak Creek anglers in the future.

SPECIAL REGULATIONS AND FEES

Special regulations apply to the area that spans the confluence between Oak Creek and the West Fork of Oak Creek. The remainder of Oak Creek falls under the statewide daily bag and possession limit of six trout.

West Fork of Oak Creek and Oak Creek itself between Junipine Crossing and Call-of-the-Canyon Crossing:
❏ Catch-and-release only. Trout must be immediately released.
❏ Anglers may use only artificial lures and flies with single barbless hooks.

There is a $5 fee for parking at Call-of-the-Canyon and Grasshopper Point day-use areas.

A certain amount of stealth is required to avoid spooking fish in Oak Creek's calm, clear pools.

TACTICS

This is a small, steep freestone stream with pocket water and many large pools. If you don't find actively rising fish, start working your way upstream with an attractor dry fly like a stimulator or royal Wulff. Using a small bead-head nymph dropper can improve your chances of locating fish.

During the heat of the summer or the cold winter months, expect to find trout at the head of deeper pools, where they will take nymph patterns presented at their level. Small bead-head nymphs fished below a strike indicator can be quite effective, especially when using light (5x) tippet.

When you do find fish rising in Oak Creek's calm, clear pools, use long leaders and concentrate on gentle presentations to avoid spooking fish. A shorter fly-rod that throws a lighter line can be very handy in tight casting situations. Remember to check behind you for backcast room or you may spend much of your time retrieving flies from trees instead of fishing.

HOW TO GET THERE

From Flagstaff, go south on Arizona Route 89A. You will cross Oak Creek in about 15 miles; it is another 12 miles to Sedona.

If you are driving up from Phoenix, take I-17 North about 80 miles to Exit 298, then go north another 14 miles on SR 179 to reach the town of Sedona. From there, turn north on SR 89A to Oak Creek Canyon.

Hatch Chart

AVAILABILITY

Food Items	J	F	M	A	M	J	J	A	S	O	N	D
Blue-winged olives	X	X	X	X	X	X	X	X	X	X	X	X
Black stoneflies	X	X	X	X								
Golden stoneflies					X	X						
Caddisflies					X	X	X	X	X			
Terrestrials						X	X	X	X			

Insects	Suggested Fly Patterns
Blue-winged olives	parachute Adams (#16-20), thorax BWOs (#16-20), pheasant tails (#16-20), hare's ears (#16-20), WD40s (#16-20), RS2s (#16-20)
Black stoneflies	bead-head prince nymphs (#14-16)
Golden stoneflies	yellow stimulators (#14-16), bead-head prince nymphs (#14-16)
Caddisflies	elk-hair caddis, green and tan (#16), yellow stimulators (#8-10), green stimulators (#16-18), sparkle caddis, tan and green (#16), chamois caddis (#16)
Terrestrials	Dave's hoppers (#8-12), fur ants, black (#14-18), deer-hair beetles, black (#14-16)

ACCESSIBILITY

You will find trout in Oak Creek above the town of Sedona in the deep and beautiful Oak Creek Canyon. The water below town gets quite warm and will not support trout year-round. The Page Springs State Fish Hatchery (11 miles southwest of Sedona on SR 89A, then follow the signs) is fed by cool springs, and the water below the hatchery is much larger and cold enough for trout. Many local anglers feel that this is the best section of the river — perhaps due to the added bonus of smallmouth bass. There is public access where Cornville Road crosses Oak Creek.

Oak Creek is steep and rocky, making for challenging wading. Be sure to bring felt-soled boots, and a wading staff is a good idea. You will find some pools too deep to wade and bordered by steep cliffs, necessitating a retreat back to the high-way. There are several of these areas near Slide Rock State Park and above.

Grasshopper Point is a day-use area just two miles north of Sedona. There is a trail going upstream that provides anglers with good access to the water for some distance. You won't make it far downstream before you have to either wade the creek or scramble up to a ledge. Either way you go, you can find some wonderful pools and pocket water. Just one mile downstream, there is a trail from the parking area at Midgely Bridge. A short hike will take you down to the creek. There is no parking fee here, and the stream is well below the highway traffic.

Call-of-the-Canyon day-use area is at the top of the catch-and-release water and just above the confluence of Oak Creek and its West Fork. The popular West Fork Trail leaves from here. The West Fork of Oak Creek is very small, and trout are few and far between. The water gets very low in late summer and very cold in winter. The hike is spectacular, especially in the fall. But expect to work for any fish.

January in Oak Creek can provide a solitary experience.

WHEN TO GO

You can find fish in Oak Creek any month of the year. Fishing conditions are toughest during winter months, but you can have long stretches of the creek to yourself during the week.

Keep in mind that 4 million people visit the area annually. If possible, plan your trip to avoid holidays, and try to schedule fishing for weekdays. The busiest time of year is from May through December, so consider an early spring trip if you prefer solitude.

If you are willing to work around the crowds, the caddis hatches of June and July can provide some of the best dry-fly fishing of the year.

AREA ATTRACTIONS

If you are staying in Flagstaff, stop by the Museum of Northern Arizona, which is known for its exhibits of the indigenous Hopi, Zuni and Navajo tribes.

Walnut Canyon National Monument is just 12 miles east of Flagstaff. A short, hardy hike up a steep set of rugged steps will bring you to cliff dwellings built over 800 years ago by the Pueblo people.

Montezuma Castle National Monument is a remarkably well-preserved example of a Sinagua Indian cliff dwelling and worth a visit. It is 25 miles south of Sedona, just off I-17 at Exit 28. Tuzigoot National Monument, 25 miles southwest of Sedona, near Clarkdale, also features the remains of Sinagua (Spanish for "without water") cliff dwellings.

Sedona's red rock beauty is considered a source of healing energy among people in New Age circles.

Snowbowl Ski Resort is about 15 miles north of Flagstaff and offers skiing and snowboarding in winter, as well as lodgings and outdoor recreation year-round. The Flagstaff Nordic Center has 40 kilometers of groomed cross-country ski trails located in the Coconino National Forest, just seven miles north of Snowbowl Road on US 180.

RESOURCES

There are several U.S. Forest Service campgrounds located in Oak Creek Canyon along SR 89A. These creekside campgrounds in the Coconino National Forest fill up quickly on the weekends. To reserve a campsite at Cave Springs, call the National Recreation Reservation Center toll-free at (877) 444-6777 or reserve online at *http://reserveusa.com*. No trailers are allowed at Bootlegger or Manzanita.

There are many places for visiting anglers to stay in Sedona and Flagstaff, but if you want to walk to the creek, stay in one of the lodgings listed.

Campgrounds

COCONINO NATIONAL FOREST

For more information, call the Sedona Ranger District at (520) 282-4119, or see www.fs.fed.us/r3/coconino/rec_redrock.html.

❑ Bootlegger
❑ Manzanita
❑ Cave Springs
❑ Pine Flat

Lodging

SEDONA

Don Hoel's Cabins
9440 N. SR 89A
Sedona, AZ 86336-9623
Phone number/s: (520) 282-3560,
toll-free (800) 292-HOEL (4635)

Junipine Resort
8351 N. SR 89A
Sedona, AZ 86336
Phone number/s: (520) 282-3375,
toll-free (800) 742-PINE
Web site: www.junipine.com
E-mail: info@junipine.com

Slide Rock Lodge
6401 N. SR 89A
Sedona, AZ 86336
Phone number/s: (520) 282-3531

Tackle Shops / Guide Services

FLAGSTAFF

Babbitt's Fly Fishing Specialists
15 E. Aspen Ave.
Flagstaff, AZ 86001
Phone number/s: (520) 779-3253

SEDONA

Canyon Market at Don Hoel's Cabins
9440 N. SR 89A
Sedona, AZ 86336-9623
Phone number/s: (520) 282-3560,
toll-free (800) 292-HOEL (4635)

Area Attractions

Arizona Snowbowl Ski Resort
Flagstaff Nordic Center
P.O. Box 40
Flagstaff, AZ 86002
Phone number/s: (520) 779-1951
Web site: www.arizonasnowbowl.com
E-mail: info@arizonasnowbowl.com

Montezuma Castle National Monument
PO Box 219
Camp Verde, AZ 86322
Phone number/s: (520) 567-3322

The Museum of Northern Arizona
3101 N. Fort Valley Road
Flagstaff, AZ 86001
Phone number/s: (520) 774-5211
Web site: www.musnaz.org

Slide Rock State Park
P.O. Box 10358
Sedona, AZ 86339
Phone number/s: (520) 282-3034
Web site: ww.pr.state.az.us/parkhtml/slide-rock.html

Tuzigoot National Monument
One Tuzigoot Road
Clarkdale, AZ 86324
Phone number/s: (520) 634-5564

Walnut Canyon National Monument
Walnut Canyon Road #3
Flagstaff, AZ 86004
Phone number/s: (520) 526-3367
Web site: www.nps.gov/waca

COLORADO

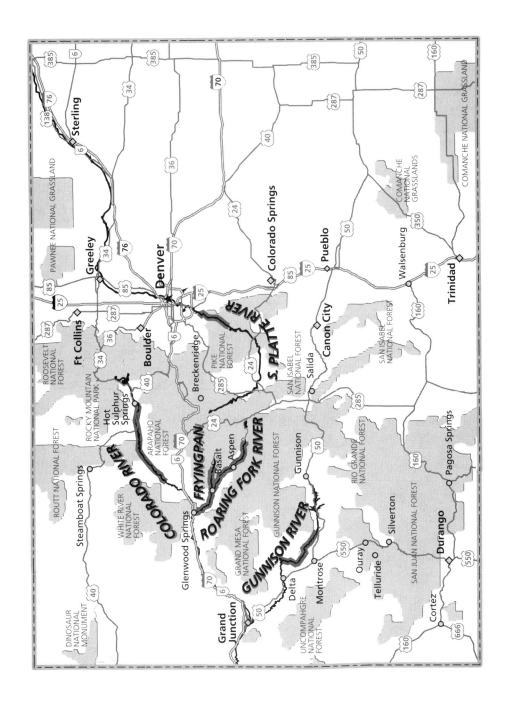

Colorado

olorado has designated several stretches of river as "Gold Medal." These waters are deemed to offer the greatest potential for trophy trout fishing. Not surprisingly, these waters attract the crowds, and special regulations are in effect to protect these stretches of water. Colorado also designates portions of 16 rivers as "Wild Trout Waters." These waters have self-sustaining trout populations, and artificial stocking occurs only in emergencies.

FISHING ACCESS LAWS

All rivers and streams in Colorado belong to the state. Anglers floating any river or stream through private property may not touch the bottom of the river or the riverbank, which are considered the property of the private landowner. Anglers must obtain permission from the landowner to enter private lands.

2000 GENERAL SEASON DATES AND BAG & POSSESSION LIMITS

Waters in Colorado are open year-round, unless noted under special regulations. Colorado uses the Continental Divide as a boundary for its general bag and possession limits for rivers and streams. Anglers are also allowed to keep certain species in addition to the daily general limits. There are no bag limits for whitefish.

The Colorado, Fryingpan, Gunnison and Roaring Fork Rivers all fall west of the Continental Divide. The South Platte River is east of the Continental Divide.

Species	2000 Daily Bag & Possession Limits
EAST OF THE CONTINENTAL DIVIDE	
Rainbow, brown, brook, cutthroat, golden and lake trout, splake, arctic char, grayling, salmon (except kokanee)	eight
WEST OF THE CONTINENTAL DIVIDE	
Rainbow, brown, brook, cutthroat, golden and lake trout, splake, arctic char, grayling, salmon (except kokanee)	two
STATEWIDE	
Brook Trout, eight inches or less	eight, in addition to daily limits
Kokanee Salmon	10

LICENSE FEES

A Colorado Conservation Certificate, free and available at all licensing agents, is required for all fishing licenses. The certificate is good from year to year as long as the information on it remains current.

Fishing License	Age	Fee
RESIDENT		
Season	16 and over	$20.25
Senior Season	64 and over	$10.25
Five-day	16 and over	$18.25
Daily	16 and over	$5.25
NONRESIDENT		
Season	16 and over	$40.25
Five-day	16 and over	$18.25
Daily	16 and over	$5.25

❐   A fishing license is required for people 16 years or older.
❐   Children under 16 do not need a fishing license. The bag limit for youths under 16 is the full daily bag and possession limit. A licensed angler does not need to accompany the youth.

BOATING REGULATIONS

Colorado State Parks regulates all boating activities. Boating regulations are published on its web site (*http://parks.state.co.us/boating*) or you can obtain a copy by calling (303) 791-1954.

In Colorado, float tubes are presently not required to have a PFD on board. However, once an inflatable or kickboat is rigged with oars, it is considered a "vessel" and a Coast Guard-approved PFD is required onboard as well as a sound-producing device, such as a whistle or horn.

RESOURCES

Colorado Division of Wildlife
Phone number/s: (303) 297-1192
Web site: www.dnr.state.co.us/wildlife

Recorded Fishing Information
Phone number/s: (303) 291-7533
Web site: http://wildlife.state.co.us/fishing/fishcond.html

Colorado Stream Flows
Web site: http://dwr.state.co.us/Hydrology/flow_search.asp

Colorado State Parks
Phone number/s: (303) 866-3437
Web site: http://parks.state.co.us

Colorado Travel and Tourism Authority
Phone number/s: (303) 832-6171
Web site: www.colorado.com

Bureau of Land Management
Phone number/s: (303) 239-3600
Web site: www.co.blm.gov

U.S. Forest Service
Phone number/s: (303) 275-5350
Web site: www.fs.fed.us/recreation/states/co.shtml

Colorado River

HIGHLIGHT
Consistent quality fishing

TIP
Start late and fish till dark

FISH SPECIES
Brown and rainbow trout with a few cutthroats

SEASON
Year-round

The Colorado River flows 1450 miles to the Sea of Cortez and passes through the middle of three major deserts on its route. This "Lifeline of the Southwest" is so heavily used that it is divided up into pipelines and irrigation canals, and water no longer reaches the sea for most of the year. Upstream from this intense development, the Colorado begins as a high mountain stream in Rocky Mountain National Park. Although the river has already been impounded before it reaches the beginning of the special regulations at the bottom of Byer's Canyon, this section of the Colorado down to State Bridge retains much of its elemental nature.

While not known for trophy fish, the river offers a large population of trout between 13 and 16 inches. The fly fishing on the Colorado is typified by its consistency. On any given day throughout the summer and fall, moderately skilled anglers are likely to fool several of the river's trout, and most people find a day spent on the Colorado to be simple and satisfying. If you would like to introduce a friend or family member to the joys of fly fishing, then this section of the Colorado River is a good place to start.

SPECIFIC REGULATIONS

From lower boundary of Byer's Canyon, three miles west of Hot Sulphur Springs (US 40 bridge), to Troublesome Creek about five miles east of Kremmling:

❐   Artificial flies or lures only.
❐   All trout must be returned to the water immediately.

TACTICS

Although you may find good fishing in the early morning hours, it is the evening fishing that creates many of the great memories of fishing the Colorado River. Barry Kirkpatrick of Cutthroat Anglers in Silverthorne recommends that anglers begin their day a bit late and plan to stay on the river until dark.

High numbers of moderate-sized trout make fishing this portion of the Colorado River a fairly simple proposition most of the season. Just employ the techniques that work for you on other waters. If you find no active risers, standard nymph fishing with a strike indicator and nine-foot leaders down to 4x or 5x should bring some trout to hand.

During active hatch periods, select a fly that imitates the predominant insect species and tie on tippet that corresponds to the size of your fly. Leaders of nine

Pumphouse is a popular launch site for floaters on the Colorado.

feet are normally sufficient unless you are fishing some of the large, slow pools. Combining a large dry fly (like a hopper) with a bead-head nymph underneath is very effective, especially if you are floating the river.

Streamer fishing can provide good action on the Colorado, and a favorite local technique is to rig up with two different-colored woolly buggers. Tie the first fly to the end of a seven- to nine-foot leader of 3x diameter, then add the second fly to 18 inches of 3x tippet tied to the eye or bend of the first bugger. Weighted streamers combined with floating lines will normally get deep enough to entice trout, and this type of rig expedites a change to nymph or dry-fly fishing.

The steep, rocky water of Byer's Canyon is good habitat for salmonflies. The main hatch will come in late April or early May. The hatch is very sporadic and unpredictable, and normally comes during high water. It is great fun if you can time it right, but you can still benefit from the big bugs at other times. Fishing a girdle bug or yuk bug down in the canyon will usually turn a good number of trout; just be careful getting around in this rugged spot.

HOW TO GET THERE

Visitors can fly into Denver, about a 2 ½-hour drive from Kremmling. There is regular air service into Yampa Valley Regional Airport near Hayden. It is about an hour closer to the river, but most flights will connect through Denver anyway, making the larger airport a better choice for most travelers.

From the Denver airport, head west on I-70 and turn north on SR 9 at Exit 205 near Silverthorne. SR 9 will take you to Kremmling. To fish this stretch of the

Hatch Chart

AVAILABILITY

Food Items	J	F	M	A	M	J	J	A	S	O	N	D
Midges	X	X	X	X	X	X	X	X	X	X	X	X
Blue-winged olives			X	X	X			X	X	X		
Pale morning duns						X	X	X				
Green drakes						X	X					
Red quills						X	X					
Tricos							X	X	X			
Salmonflies						X						
Caddisflies				X	X	X	X	X	X			
Terrestrials							X	X	X			

Colorado (from Hot Sulphur Springs to State Bridge), the town of Kremmling makes a good base. Kremmling is 55 miles southeast of Steamboat Springs on US 40.

ACCESSIBILITY

US 40 follows the section of river from Kremmling to Hot Sulphur Springs, and most of the access is directly off the highway. Byer's Canyon is just downstream from the town of Hot Sulphur Springs. The river is caught between the road and the railroad and runs quickly through this narrow channel, emerging by Beaver Creek in about 2 ½ miles. The river spreads out again, and the Paul F. Gilbert State Wildlife Area, situated in the trees along the river and away from the main road, is a nice day-use area. It is located down the hill from the Colorado Division of Wildlife offices.

The Kemp Unit access is found at the town of Parshall. Head south of US 40 a little over ½ mile on CR 3. It will be a short walk to the river, and you can access the bottom of the Williams Fork as well as the Colorado. Be sure to check the sign in the parking area so you don't inadvertently trespass.

There are two main parking areas in the Breeze Unit. The one to the east has a trout pond that is open to children under 16 or those who are mobility impaired. There are handicap-accessible fishing platforms at the pond and at the river. At Breeze West, it is a bit of a walk down to the river, and you will need to avoid the wetland area to the west from March 15 to July 15. There is also about ¼ mile of public access at the Sunset Bridge site. This stretch from Parshall to Kremmling has limited public access. "Leaving Public Lands" signs are posted upstream and downstream on the river. According to Colorado state law, banks and the bottom of a river are considered private if the adjacent land is private. Fishing beyond these signs requires permission of the private landowners. Many private waters are leased to fishing clubs; be respectful and avoid possible trespass charges.

Downstream from Kremmling, the Blue River enters the Colorado and the river becomes large enough for year-round floating, but you don't want to get on the river until Pumphouse Recreation Site. Gore Canyon is just upstream, and it is

Insects	Suggested Fly Patterns
Midges	Griffith's gnats (#16-22), Adams (#16-22), peacock soft hackles (#16-20), suspender midges (#18-22), brassies (#18-22), midge pupae (#18-22)
Blue-winged olives	parachute Adams (#16-20), thorax BWOs (#16-20), olive comparaduns (#16-20), sparkle duns, olive (#16-20), Quigley cripples, olive (#16-20), CDC emergers, olive (#16-20), Barr emergers (#16-20), pheasant tails (#16-20), hare's ears (#16-20), bead-head pheasant tails (#16-20), bead-head hare's ears (#16-20), WD40s (#18-20), RS2s (#18-20)
Pale morning duns	thorax PMDs (#14-16), cream parachutes (#14-16), cream comparaduns (#16-20), Quigley cripples, cream (#16-20), rusty spinners (#14-16), CDC emergers, cream (#16-20), Barr emergers (#16-18), pheasant tails (#14-16), hare's ears (#14-16), bead-head pheasant tails (#14-16), bead-head hare's ears (#14-16)
Green drakes	green drake Wulffs (#8-12), olive paradrakes (#10-12), olive comparaduns (#10-12), Quigley cripples, olive (#8-12), soft-hackle emergers, olive (#8-12), CDC emergers, olive (#10-14), hare's ear, olive (#10-14), zug bugs (#10-14)
Red quills	H&L variants (#14-16), red quills (#14-16), quill spinners, red (#14-16), rusty spinners (#14-16), pheasant tails (#14-16), hare's ears (#14-16)
Tricos	trico spinners (#18-22), double trico spinners (#18), CDC tricos (#18-22), parachute Adams (#18-22), pheasant tails (#18-20)
Salmonflies	sofa pillows (#6-10), Mac Salmons (#6-10), orange stimulators (#6-10), bullethead salmonflies (#6-10), girdle bugs (#6-10), Bitch Creek nymphs (#6-10), Brook's stone nymphs (#6-10)
Caddisflies	elk-hair caddis (#16-18), partridge caddis (#16-18), CDC elk-hair caddis (#16-18), sparkle caddis (#16-18), X-caddis (#16-18), peeking caddis (#14-16), bead-head peeking caddis (#14-16)
Terrestrials	Dave's hoppers (#8-12), Henry's Fork hoppers (#8-12), fur ants, black (#14-18), CDC ants (#14-18), deer-hair beetles, black (#14-16), hi-vis foam beetles (#14-16)

a very challenging whitewater canyon with Class V rapids. You can walk up into Gore Canyon to wade or fish from shore.

Many floaters launch at Pumphouse, and it is a little over four miles to the next access at Radium. Both recreation sites have campgrounds. There is a day-use fee of $3 per vehicle (or a season pass for $15). Pumphouse is 11 miles south of

Colorado: *Hot Sulphur Springs to Kremmling*

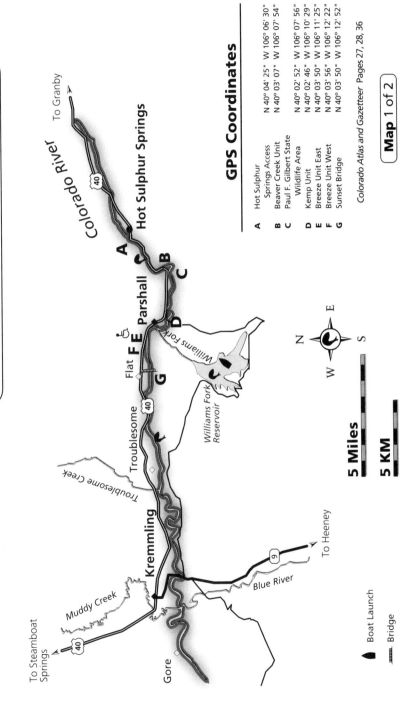

GPS Coordinates

A Hot Sulphur Springs Access	N 40° 04' 25" W 106° 06' 30"
B Beaver Creek Unit	N 40° 03' 07" W 106° 07' 54"
C Paul F. Gilbert State Wildlife Area	N 40° 02' 52" W 106° 07' 56"
D Kemp Unit	N 40° 02' 46" W 106° 10' 29"
E Breeze Unit East	N 40° 03' 50" W 106° 11' 25"
F Breeze Unit West	N 40° 03' 56" W 106° 12' 22"
G Sunset Bridge	N 40° 03' 50" W 106° 12' 52"

Colorado Atlas and Gazetteer Pages 27, 28, 36

Map 1 of 2

Boat Launch

Bridge

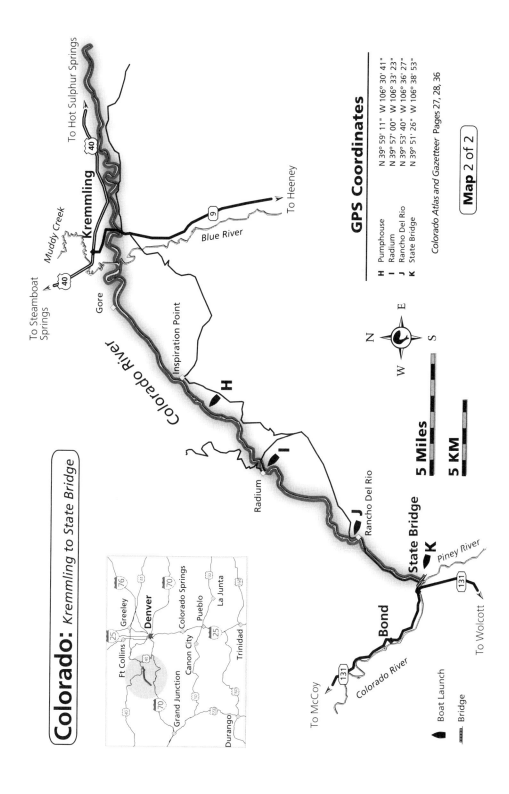

Colorado: *Kremmling to State Bridge*

To Hot Sulphur Springs

To Steamboat Springs

Kremmling

Muddy Creek

40

40

Gore

Colorado River

Inspiration Point

Blue River

9

To Heeney

H

Radium

I

Rancho Del Rio

J

State Bridge

K

Piney River

131

To Wolcott

Bond

Colorado River

131

To McCoy

GPS Coordinates

H   Pumphouse   N 39° 59' 11"   W 106° 30' 41"
I   Radium   N 39° 57' 00"   W 106° 33' 23"
J   Rancho Del Rio   N 39° 53' 40"   W 106° 36' 27"
K   State Bridge   N 39° 51' 26"   W 106° 38' 53"

Colorado Atlas and Gazetteer Pages 27, 28, 36

Map 2 of 2

N   E   S   W

5 Miles

5 KM

Ft Collins   Greeley   76   55

Denver   70

Colorado Springs   70

Pueblo   La Junta

Grand Junction   70   Canon City   25

Durango   Trinidad

Boat Launch

Bridge

Kremmling on Trough Road (County Road 1). To reach Radium, go five miles farther west on Trough Road and turn right on Sheephorn Road (County Road 11). Six miles down the river from Radium is the boat ramp at Rancho Del Rio. There is public access at the bridge, or pay a usage fee at the larger private ramp where you can arrange for shuttle service. The launch area at State Bridge, four miles downstream from Rancho Del Rio, is also private and a fee is charged.

The Colorado River from Pumphouse down to State Bridge has several Class II and III rapids, so be sure your skills and equipment are up to the challenge.

CHECK RIVER FLOWS ON THE WEB
http://nwis-colo.cr.usgs.gov/rt-cgi/gen_tbl_pg

WHEN TO GO

Although the Colorado is open to fishing year-round, cold winter weather will freeze sections of the river, and fishing from December through February is normally quite slow. With March things warm up a bit, and blue-winged olives begin to bring some fish to the river's surface and are the mainstay of fly fishers until run-off begins.

If the water clears and recedes somewhat by June, the salmonfly hatch can give anglers some great fishing opportunities, but it can be sporadic, requiring some good luck to hit it right. The green drakes may be the river's best hatch, and it can start as early as late June. Catch it at its peak and this river can surprise you. Pale morning duns, tricos and caddis keep fish feeding on the surface for much of the summer, and streamer fishing picks up in late September and continues until winter closes back in on the Colorado.

AREA ATTRACTIONS

The Colorado River Headwaters Scenic Byway follows the Colorado River from its headwaters in Rocky Mountain National Park through Kremmling to the historic stage stop at State Bridge on SR 131. Kremmling has a wildlife area where antelope and eagles are regularly spotted. Inspiration Point on Trough Road (County Road 1) overlooks the spectacular Gore Canyon carved by the Colorado River.

RESOURCES

The town of Kremmling makes for a convenient base to fish the upper and middle sections of the Colorado River, but there are limited options for lodging and restaurants. If you prefer a wider range of amenities, you may want to stay in the Silverthorne/Dillon area or Steamboat Springs.

From April to October, you can camp at BLM campgrounds, Pumphouse and Radium. Sites are on a first-come, first-served basis.

Campgrounds

BLM, KREMMLING RECREATION MANAGEMENT AREA

1116 Park Ave.
Kremmling, CO 80459
Phone number/s: (970) 724-3437

❏　Pumphouse — 12 sites
❏　Radium — 4 sites

KREMMLING

Red Mountain RV Park
US 40 & CR 22
Kremmling, CO 80459
Phone number/s: (970) 724-9593

Lodging

HOT SULPHUR SPRINGS

Hot Sulphur Springs Resort
P.O.Box 295
Hot Sulphur Springs, CO 80451
Phone number/s: (970) 725-3306,
toll-free (800)510-6235
Web site: www.hotsulphursprings.com

Riverside Hotel
509 Grand Ave.
Hot Sulphur Springs, CO 80451
Phone number/s: (970) 725-3589

KREMMLING

Cliffside Inn
113 N. 6th
Kremmling, CO 80459
Phone number/s: (970) 724-9620

Eastin Hotel
105 S. 2nd St.
Kremmling, CO 80459
Phone number/s: (970) 724-3261

Elktrout Lodge
1853 County Road 33
P.O. Box 614
Kremmling, CO 80459
Phone number/s:(970) 724-3343

PARSHALL

Bar Lazy J Guest Ranch
447 County Road 3 West
Parshall, CO 80458-8714
Phone number/s: (970) 725-3437

Tackle Shops and Outfitters

DILLON

Summit Guides
P.O. Box 2489
Dillon, CO 80435
Phone number/s: (970) 468-8945
Fax: (970) 468-7845
Web site: www.summitguides.com
E-mail: guides@imageline.com

HOT SULPHUR SPRINGS

Riverside Anglers
Riverside Hotel
509 Grand Ave.
Hot Sulphur Springs, CO 80451
Phone number/s: (970) 725-0025

Parri's Outfitting & Guide Service
P.O. Box 254
Hot Sulphur Springs, CO 80451
Phone number/s: (970) 725-3531
(BLM permittee for Upper Colorado River)

KREMMLING

Elktrout Lodge
P.O. Box 614
1853 County Road 33
Kremmling, CO 80459
Phone number/s: (970) 724-3343
(BLM permittee for Upper Colorado River)

Fishin' Hole Sporting Goods
310 Park Ave.
Kremmling, CO 80459
Phone number/s: (970) 724-9407

SILVERTHORNE

Cutthroat Anglers
400 Blue River Parkway
Silverthorne, CO 80498
Phone number/s: (970) 262-2878,
toll-free (888) 876-8818
Web site: www.fishcolorado.com

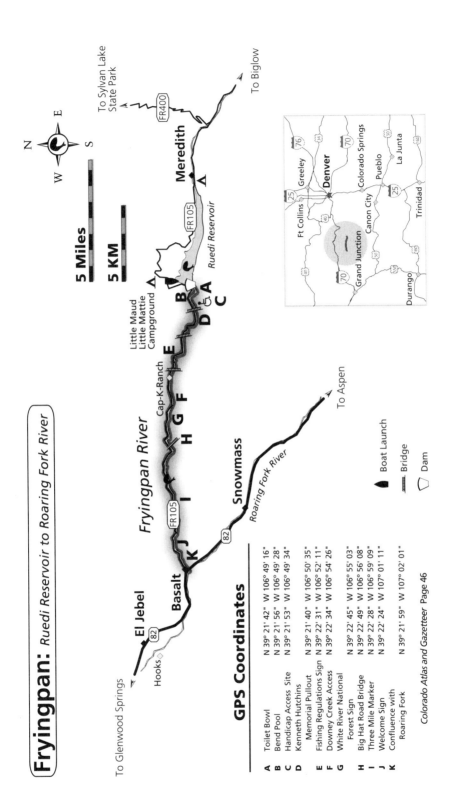

Fryingpan: *Ruedi Reservoir to Roaring Fork River*

To Sylvan Lake State Park

FR400

To Biglow

Meredith

Ruedi Reservoir

FR105

Little Maud
Little Mattie
Campground

Fryingpan River

Cap-K-Ranch

FR105

El Jebel

Basalt

Hooks

Snowmass

Roaring Fork River

82

To Aspen

To Glenwood Springs

5 Miles

5 KM

N
W E
S

Greeley
Ft Collins
76
34
Denver
70
Colorado Springs
Pueblo
La Junta
50
Canon City
25
Grand Junction
70
Trinidad
Durango

Boat Launch

Bridge

Dam

GPS Coordinates

A	Toilet Bowl	N 39° 21' 42" W 106° 49' 16"
B	Bend Pool	N 39° 21' 56" W 106° 49' 28"
C	Handicap Access Site	N 39° 21' 53" W 106° 49' 34"
D	Kenneth Hutchins Memorial Pullout	N 39° 21' 40" W 106° 50' 35"
E	Fishing Regulations Sign	N 39° 22' 31" W 106° 52' 11"
F	Downey Creek Access	N 39° 22' 34" W 106° 54' 26"
G	White River National Forest Sign	N 39° 22' 45" W 106° 55' 03"
H	Big Hat Road Bridge	N 39° 22' 49" W 106° 56' 08"
I	Three Mile Marker	N 39° 22' 28" W 106° 59' 09"
J	Welcome Sign	N 39° 22' 24" W 107° 01' 11"
K	Confluence with Roaring Fork	N 39° 21' 59" W 107° 02' 01"

Colorado Atlas and Gazetteer Page 46

Fryingpan River

HIGHLIGHT
Giant trout below the dam

TIP
Go to heavier tippet after sun drops behind the mountains

FISH SPECIES
Brook, brown, cutthroat and rainbow trout

SEASON
Open year-round

T he Fryingpan is one of Colorado's best producers of truly huge trout. The upper mile of this small river holds quite a few trout that weigh 10 pounds and more. These fish reach prodigious size by eating the Mysis shrimp that are sucked down through Ruedi Dam. Spend a little time watching the water in the Toilet Bowl (the plunge pool at the base of the dam), and you will likely see one of these giants.

Mysis shrimp (*Mysis relicta*) are a species native to lakes in Canada and the Great Lakes region. These freshwater shrimp came into use as a fisheries management tool to bolster the forage base of cold, deep, well-oxygenated waters. These shrimp were planted in Ruedi Lake, but their habit of migrating to deep, dark waters during daylight keeps them from being of any great benefit to the reservoir's trout. They don't live in the river but are washed down through the dam, where they quickly become the targets of hungry trout. Their easy availability and highly nutritious value allow fish to put on serious weight and girth.

Even though the Mysis shrimp are responsible for the Fryingpan's biggest trout, don't assume that this is a one-dimensional fishery. The river is home to an unbelievable variety and quantity of insect life. Visiting anglers can expect some phenomenal hatches (and consequently more anglers). If you would like to avoid the crowds, you will find more room downstream, where there are still some very large trout to be had. For those moments when you can pry your attention away from the Pan's trout, you will find yourself in a stunningly beautiful mountain stream cutting its way through a fiery red canyon. Much of the water is shaded by tall trees. In short, a trip to the Fryingpan can fulfill all of an angler's hopes and dreams for numbers of trout, trophy potential, and a gorgeous place to unwind for a few days with a fly rod in hand.

SPECIFIC REGULATIONS

From Ruedi Dam downstream to Roaring Fork River (14 miles) — Gold Medal Water:
❑ Artificial flies and lures.
❑ All trout, except browns, must be released to the water immediately.
❑ Maximum size limit for brown trout is 14 inches long.

TACTICS

One of the biggest dilemmas for an angler fishing for big trout is which tippet size to use. Dropping down to 6x will improve your chances of hooking the big,

Hatch Chart   AVAILABILITY

Food Items	J	F	M	A	M	J	J	A	S	O	N	D
Mysis shrimp	X	X	X	X	X	X	X	X	X	X	X	X
Midges	X	X	X	X	X	X	X	X	X	X	X	X
Blue-winged olives			X	X				X	X	X	X	
Pale morning duns							X	X				
Green drakes							X	X	X			
Red quills									X	X		
Salmonflies				X								
Yellow sallys							X	X				
Caddisflies				X	X	X	X	X				
Pumpkin caddis									X	X		
Craneflies							X	X	X			

finicky trout but is a serious impediment to landing them. Art Rowell of Frying Pan Anglers recommends that anglers increase their tippet size once the sun drops behind the mountains. Trout are less likely to be bothered by the heavier monofilament, and it can give you that extra edge when trout become more active at dusk. Some anglers are also using fluorocarbon tippet, which is less visible to fish and still allows for a heavier tippet, despite having a thinner diameter of nylon.

With the heavy fishing pressure on the upper Fryingpan, most trout are accustomed to seeing anglers and will tolerate your presence and continue to feed. The trout seem more sensitive to heavy tippets and poor drifts. The major food source from the Toilet Bowl down through the Bend Pool is the Mysis shrimp. The availability of shrimp varies, and you may try other nymph patterns here as well, especially midges. You will not often find the big fish in this area feeding on dry flies. You can greatly improve your chances by sighting a particular fish and concentrating your efforts on it. When you find a big trout holding, you will often be able to drift flies past it for as long as it takes to get a strike. Continue to adjust flies and terminal tackle and keep your offering in front of the trout as much as possible. When sight nymphing, some Fryingpan anglers prefer not to use a strike indicator, but rather keep their eyes focused on the fish. If they see the fish move, flash or open its mouth as their fly comes by, they set quickly before it has a chance to reject their hook. Another trick practiced by some local anglers is to rig two flies in tandem, say a shrimp imitation and a brighter fly like a small glo-bug. They can watch the egg imitation as an underwater strike indicator.

When you move below the Bend Pool into the steeper sections of the river, the noise and rush of the water will cover some mistakes, but getting a good drift can be challenging, as the currents drop, twist and bend around the river's boulders. Nymphing in the larger pools and runs is made easier by employing a strike indicator. If you are fishing smaller pockets, try removing the indicator and adding a little more weight. Fish with your rod elevated and keep the line just tight enough to feel

Insects	Suggested Fly Patterns
Mysis shrimp	live Mysis (#14-18), crystal Mysis (#14-18), litebrite Mysis (#14-18)
Midges	Griffith's gnats (#18-24), Adams (#18-24), midge pupae (#18-24), midge emergers, black and peacock (#18-24), candy canes (#18-24), disco midges (#18-24)
Blue-winged olives	parachute Adams (#18-24), thorax BWOs (#18-22), olive comparaduns (#18-24), sparkle duns, olive (#18-24), Quigley cripples, olive (#18-22), CDC emergers, olive (#18-24), pheasant tails (#18-24), hare's ears (#18-24), bead-head pheasant tails (#18-24), bead-head hare's ears (#18-24), WD40s (#18-24), RS2s (#18-24)
Pale morning duns	yellow quills (#12-16), thorax PMDs (#12-16), PMD parachutes (#12-16), comparaduns (#12-16), Quigley cripples, PMD (#12-16), rusty spinners (#12-16), CDC emergers, cream (#12-16), AK's melon quills (#16-20), pink Cahills (#16-20), pheasant tails (#12-20), bead-head pheasant tails (#12-20)
Green drakes	green drake Wulffs (#8-12), olive paradrakes (#10-12), olive comparaduns (#8-12), Quigley cripples, olive (#8-12), CDC emergers, olive (#8-12), Roy's green drake nymphs (#14-18), hare's ears, olive (#8-12), epoxy-back green drake nymphs (#8-12)
Red quills	H&L variants (#14-16), red quills (#14-16), quill spinners, red (#14-16), rusty spinners (#14-16), pheasant tails (#14-16), hare's ears (#14-16)
Salmonflies	sofa pillows (#6-10), Mac Salmons (#6-10), orange stimulators (#6-10), rubber-legs, black (#6-10), Bitch Creek nymphs (#6-10), Brook's stone nymphs (#6-10)
Yellow sallys	yellow stimulators (#12-16), Flint's stones (#12-16), irresistible stimulators, yellow (#12-16), red fox squirrel nymphs (#14-18)
Caddisflies	elk-hair caddis (#16-20), partridge caddis (#16-20), CDC elk-hair caddis (#16-20), Hemingway caddis (#16-20), parachute caddis (#16-20), X-caddis (#16-20), sparkle pupae (#16-20), peeking caddis (#16-20)
Pumpkin caddis	elk-hair caddis, orange (#12-14), irresistible caddis, orange (#12-14), orange stimulators (#12-14)
Craneflies	Baxter's small yellow craneflies (#16-18), cranefly larvae (#10-14), cone-head crane fly larvae (#10-14)

Stuart Asahina of Salt Lake City has his hands full with one of the legendary Fryingpan trout.

any resistance. This approach works best when you are fishing in close, with no more than three to five feet of fly line past your rod tip.

When fishing dry flies, concentrate your efforts on the slower water next to the bank and behind boulders. You will get better drifts, and fish are more apt to rise in the slower flows. This is especially important during hatches of the river's smaller insects. When big bugs like the green drakes are out, trout are more likely to be found rising in faster lies.

HOW TO GET THERE

Aspen and Denver are the best choices to fly in and rent a car. The Aspen airport is only 18 miles southeast of Basalt and the Fryingpan River. SR 82 will take you straight to Basalt.

From Denver, go west 160 miles on I-70 to Glenwood Springs, take Exit 116, then go south on SR 82; it is 25 miles to Basalt. At Basalt, head east on FR 105, also called Frying Pan Road, which parallels the river.

ACCESSIBILITY

The Fryingpan below Ruedi Dam is easily accessed from Frying Pan Road, which follows the river from the town of Basalt up to the dam. There is a patchwork of private and public lands, but you will find the private sections well-marked, so it is easy to avoid trespassing. In general, the Fryingpan is a steep, small river with a generous sprinkling of boulders and a rocky bottom. Anglers should always use caution when wading, and carrying a staff is a good idea.

The Rocky Fork day-use area is at the dam's base. There are picnic tables, restrooms and a very good handicap-accessible fishing site. This is some of the most popular water on the river, and for good reason. The biggest trout in the river will be found in the first mile below the dam, where Mysis shrimp are readily available. The Toilet Bowl and the Bend Pool just below are the two best spots to land one of the river's giant fish.

The first two miles of river below the dam are public lands and receive at least twice as much pressure as the lower portions of the river. There are many sections of water downstream that are open to the public and will give anglers a greater opportunity for solitude. You are less likely to hook a big fish farther down the river, but you will still find plenty of good fish.

As you move down the river, you will find just over one mile of accessible water in the Folkstad Spring area. It begins at the fishing regulations sign just above Frenchman Creek and continues upstream. Downey Creek enters the Fryingpan at the center of another mile of public water. There are two short accessible sections of about ¼ mile long that are often overlooked. The first is downstream from the White River National Forest sign and the second is downstream from the Big Hat Road Bridge. From the three-mile marker going upstream for 1¾ miles to the Castle View sign is another section of public water. Seven Castles Creek can dump a lot of sediment into the bottom of this section after heavy rains. Just upstream from Basalt, you will see a sign welcoming you to the Fryingpan Valley. There is a mile of public water going upstream from this point, if you are willing to scramble down the steep bank to the river.

CHECK RIVER FLOWS ON THE WEB
http://nwis-colo.cr.usgs.gov/rt-cgi/gen_tbl_pg

WHEN TO GO

The Fryingpan fishes well all year-round, even during the winter months. Pack your neoprene waders and your skis to combine a little fly fishing with a ski trip to one of the nearby resorts. Winter flows are fairly low (between 100 and 200 cfs), and crowds are thin, giving anglers a good chance to sight fish to some of the river's big trout.

The pre run-off period in late March and April can produce some good fishing during blue-winged olive hatches. By early May, the Mother's Day caddis begin to work their way up the river. Run-off usually begins about this time and impedes fishing until it drops, but in very low water years salmonflies can provide good dry-fly fishing.

Insect activity peaks in July and August, with caddisflies, pale morning duns and the much-anticipated green drakes. This is arguably the best fishing of the year, but be prepared to share the river with others. The Fryingpan's reputation draws a lot of anglers, but with good hatches and the high numbers of trout, you may find that it doesn't take a lot of water to keep you deeply engrossed.

Crowds begin to thin out in late September, and red quills and pumpkin caddis begin to appear in good numbers, making the Fryingpan a great option for your last road trip of the season.

AREA ATTRACTIONS

For over 50 years, Aspen has welcomed the music world for nine weeks every summer. From chamber music to contemporary concerts, the Aspen Music Festival offers something for everyone in an atmosphere known for its laid-back style. For a complete schedule of events, check out *www.aspenmusicfestival.com*.

Anglers can find a little more room by moving farther down the canyon.

Glenwood Springs is home to the world's largest outdoor mineral pool. The hot springs pool, held at a comfortable temperature of 90 degrees, is fed by the Yampah Springs, which flow at 3.5 million gallons per day and at a temperature of 112 degrees. Take a dip in the pool or relax in the 104-degree therapy pool. The pool is open daily until 10 p.m.

RESOURCES

Basalt was an old railroad town in the heyday of silver mining in Aspen. When the railroad went bust in 1918, so did Basalt. Situated at the confluence of the Roaring Fork and Fryingpan rivers, Basalt has reinvented itself as a first-class fishing and recreational destination. For a complete list of lodgings, go to *www.basaltonline.com*. Glenwood Springs, a town of 8,000, offers a wide choice of accommodations, which can be viewed on its Chamber of Commerce's web site, *www.glenscape.com*. Aspen and Snowmass Village provide the logistics for a dream summer vacation. During the summer, there are free fly-fishing clinics at Snowmass Village. For lodging and activities in the Aspen/Snowmass area, go to *www.aspen.com*.

Campgrounds

BASALT

Aspen-Basalt Campground
20640 SR 82
Basalt, CO 81621
Phone number/s: (970) 927-3405
E-mail: ABC@sopris.net

MEREDITH

Rocky Mountain Recreation Co.
29088 Frying Pan Road
Meredith, CO 81621
Phone number/s: (970) 927-0532

Lodging

ASPEN/SNOWMASS VILLAGE

Aspen Central Reservations
Phone number/s: toll-free (888) 649-5982
Fax: (970) 925-9008
Web site: www.aspen4u.com
E-mail: info@aspen4u.com

Aspen Lodging Company
747 Galena St.
Aspen, CO 81611
Phone number/s: (970) 925-2260,
toll-free (800) 321-7025
Fax: (970) 925-2264
Web site: www.aspen.com/aspenlodgingco

Aspenwood Condominiums
600 Carriage Way
Snowmass Village, CO 81615
Phone number/s: (970) 923-2711,
toll-free (800) 451-8540
Web site: www.aspendwoodcondos.com
E-mail: info@aspenwoodcondos.com

BASALT

Aspenwood Lodge
220 Midland Ave.
Basalt, CO 81621
Phone number/s: (970) 927-4747,
toll-free (800) 905-6797
Fax: (970) 927-0218
Web site: aspenwoodlodge.com
E-mail: info@aspenwoodbasalt.com

Best Western Apenalt Lodge
157 Basalt Center Circle
Basalt, CO 81621
Phone number/s: (970) 927-3191,
toll-free (877) 379-6476

Tackle Shops and Outfitters

ASPEN/SNOWMASS VILLAGE

Aspen Outfitting Co.
315 E. Dean St.
Aspen, CO 81611
Phone number/s: (970) 925-3406

BASALT

Frying Pan Anglers
123 Emma Road, #100
Basalt, CO 81621
Phone number/s: (970) 927-3441

Taylor Creek Fly Shops
183 Basalt Center Circle
Basalt, CO 81621
Phone number/s: (970) 927-4374

CARBONDALE

Alpine Angling
981 Cowen Drive
Carbondale, CO 81623
Phone number/s: (970) 963-9245
E-mail: flyfish@sopris.net

GLENWOOD SPRINGS

Roaring Fork Anglers
2114 Grand Ave., # B
Glenwood Springs, CO 81601
Phone number/s: (970) 945-0180,
toll-free (800) 781-8120
Web site: www.RFAnglers.com
E-mail: flyfish@sopris.net

Area Attractions

Hot Springs Lodge & Pool
401 N. River
Glenwood Springs, CO 81602
Phone number/s: (970) 945-7131,
toll-free (800) 537-SWIM
Web site: www.hotspringspool.com

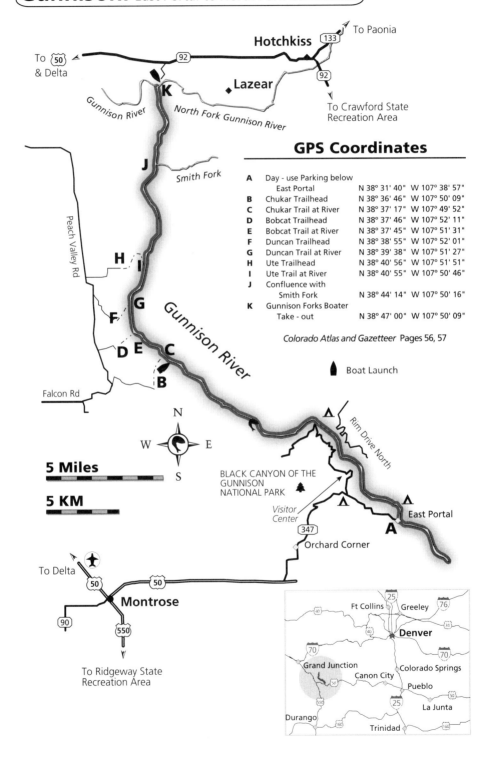

Gunnison: *East Portal to North Fork Confluence*

To Paonia

Hotchkiss

Lazear

To Crawford State
Recreation Area

To 50 & Delta

Gunnison River

North Fork Gunnison River

K

J

Smith Fork

Peach Valley Rd

H I

G

F

D E C

B

Falcon Rd

Gunnison River

GPS Coordinates

A	Day - use Parking below East Portal	N 38° 31' 40"	W 107° 38' 57"
B	Chukar Trailhead	N 38° 36' 46"	W 107° 50' 09"
C	Chukar Trail at River	N 38° 37' 17"	W 107° 49' 52"
D	Bobcat Trailhead	N 38° 37' 46"	W 107° 52' 11"
E	Bobcat Trail at River	N 38° 37' 45"	W 107° 51' 31"
F	Duncan Trailhead	N 38° 38' 55"	W 107° 52' 01"
G	Duncan Trail at River	N 38° 39' 38"	W 107° 51' 27"
H	Ute Trailhead	N 38° 40' 56"	W 107° 51' 51"
I	Ute Trail at River	N 38° 40' 55"	W 107° 50' 46"
J	Confluence with Smith Fork	N 38° 44' 14"	W 107° 50' 16"
K	Gunnison Forks Boater Take - out	N 38° 47' 00"	W 107° 50' 09"

Colorado Atlas and Gazetteer Pages 56, 57

Boat Launch

N
W E
S

5 Miles

5 KM

BLACK CANYON OF THE
GUNNISON
NATIONAL PARK

Rim Drive North

Visitor
Center

East Portal

A

347

Orchard Corner

To Delta

50

50

Montrose

90

550

To Ridgeway State
Recreation Area

Ft Collins Greeley

Denver

Grand Junction

Canon City

Colorado Springs

Pueblo

Durango

La Junta

Trinidad

Gunnison River

HIGHLIGHT
Fishing the remote waters of Black Canyon or the Gunnison Gorge

TIP
Carry a water filter when hiking into the river

FISH SPECIES
Brown, cutthroat and rainbow trout

SEASON
Year-round (but with very limited winter access)

T he Black Canyon of the Gunnison is America's newest national park, yet its dark walls are made up of some the world's oldest rock. While the dark coloring of this ancient schist and gneiss give Black Canyon its somber appearance, it is the hard, resistant nature of the rock that has kept this river canyon so steep and narrow. Nowhere else in North America will you find a gorge that combines the sheer walls, startling depth and narrow channel offered by the Black Canyon of the Gunnison. At a point called "the Narrows," the canyon is 40 feet wide at river level — yet the walls rise 1,700 feet up to the plateau. Above and just below East Portal, the canyon is almost 2,000 feet deep.

This chasm is so imposing that the Ute Indians believed that no one could return from the canyon alive. In September of 1900, William Torrence led a group of men determined to traverse and survey the depths of Black Canyon. The expedition was halted at the "Falls of Sorrow," and the party was forced to retreat. Torrence vowed, "If I get out of this scrape alive, I shall come back." The following year he did exactly that. He and Abraham Lincoln Fellows descended into the canyon with minimal gear — just air mattresses and about 70 pounds of food and equipment. On reaching the Falls of Sorrow, they plunged bodily into the unknown river below. Luck was with them, and they eventually finished their journey and escaped the canyon alive. Much of their equipment was lost or abandoned in their struggle for survival, but they saved Fellows' engineering book with its valuable records.

> *The roar of the water . . . was constantly in our ears. . . . Occasionally a rock would fall . . . , exploding like a ton of dynamite when it struck bottom, making us think our last day had come.*
>
> Abraham Lincoln Fellows, 1901

While much of the Black Canyon is still inaccessible, visitors can drive to the river at East Portal, and there are a half dozen steep routes that provide access from the rim of the canyon to the river. These routes are for the fit and adventurous only. Downstream in the Gunnison Gorge National Conservation Area, access is a bit easier. Anglers can negotiate some more realistic hikes to the river or float down the Class III and IV rapids in search of trout. This section of the Gunnison is a designated Gold Medal fishery, and anglers can expect good numbers of brown trout that average 15 to 17 inches. In the more remote areas, some fish will exceed 24 inches. Rainbow trout numbers have been drastically reduced in recent years by the

Hatch Chart   AVAILABILITY

Food Items	J	F	M	A	M	J	J	A	S	O	N	D
Midges	X	X	X	X	X	X	X	X	X	X	X	X
Blue-winged olives			X	X	X	X	X	X	X			
Pale morning duns						X	X	X	X			
Red quills						X	X	X	X	X		
Tricos								X	X	X		
Yellow sallys						X	X	X				
Golden stoneflies						X	X					
Salmonflies						X						
Caddisflies				X	X	X	X	X	X			
Terrestrials							X	X	X			

effects of whirling disease, but the "bows" that remain are very fat, healthy, strong fish that will delight any angler lucky enough to hook them.

SPECIFIC REGULATIONS AND FEES

From upstream boundary of the Black Canyon of the Gunnison National Park to the North Fork of the Gunnison River — Gold Medal Water and Wild Trout Water:

❏   Artificial flies or lures only.
❏   Brown trout 12-16 inches must be returned to water immediately.
❏   Bag and possession limit for brown trout is four fish, 12 inches or less, or three fish less than 12 inches and one fish 16 inches or longer.
❏   Rainbow trout must be returned to water immediately.

For Black Canyon of the Gunnison National Park, there is a $7 entrance fee valid for seven days and good for both the South and North Entrances or a $15 annual entrance pass. All national park passport passes are honored. Visitors to the Gunnison Gorge Wilderness Area are charged $3 per person for a day-use pass ($15 per year for an annual pass). There is no charge for private walk-in fishing or camping below the Smith Fork.

TACTICS

Your backcountry skills can be more important than fishing technique on this rugged river. This is an arid climate, and summer temperatures can easily reach the high 90s. One of your first considerations should be carrying enough water to get in and out of the canyon safely. Bob Burk of Cimarron Creek recommends carrying a water filter and enough water bottles for the one-way journey in or out. This will cut your water load down to a manageable level. Giardia is in all water sources, including the river. All water must be purified.

When nymphing in the Gunnison, look for trout along current seams and middepth runs. Leaders of nine to 10 feet will reach most trout holding areas;

Insects	Suggested Fly Patterns
Midges	Griffith's gnats (#16-22), Adams (#16-22), brassies (#16-22), suspender midges (#16-22), disco midges (#16-22), midge pupae, brown, red and black (#16-22)
Blue-winged olives	parachute Adams (#14-22), Adams (#14-22), thorax BWOs (#14-22), blue duns (#14-22), olive comparaduns (#14-22), quill duns, olive (#14-22), RS2s (#16-20), pheasant tails (#16-20), hare's ears (#16-20), flashback pheasant tails (#16-20), flashback hare's ears (#16-20), epoxy-back baetis (#16-20)
Pale morning duns	yellow quills (#12-18), thorax PMDs (#12-18), PMD parachutes (#12-18), comparaduns (#12-18), Quigley cripples, cream (#12-18), rusty spinners (#12-18), CDC emergers, cream (#12-18), pheasant tails (#14-18), bead-head pheasant tails (#14-18)
Red quills	H&L variants (#12-16), red quills (#12-16), quill spinners, red (#12-16), rusty spinners (#12-16), pheasant tails (#12-16), hare's ears (#12-16)
Tricos	trico spinners (#20-24), CDC tricos (#20-24), parachute Adams (#20-24), pheasant tails (#20-24)
Yellow sallys	yellow stimulators (#10-14), Flint's stones (#10-14), irresistible stimulators, yellow (#10-14), red fox squirrel nymphs (#10-14)
Golden stoneflies	yellow stimulators (#4-6), prince nymphs (#4-6), bead-head prince nymphs (#8-10), golden stonefly nymphs (#6-10), Bitch Creek nymphs (#6-10), copper Johns (#10-14)
Salmonflies	sofa pillows (#4-8), Mac Salmons (#4-8), orange stimulators (#4-8), bullethead salmonflies (#4-8), girdle bugs, black (#4-8), Bitch Creek nymphs (#4-8), Brook's stone nymphs (#4-8)
Caddisflies	elk-hair caddis (#12-18), partridge caddis (#12-18), CDC elk-hair caddis (#12-18), Hemingway caddis (#12-18), parachute caddis (#12-18), X-caddis (#12-18), sparkle pupae (#14-18), peeking caddis (#14-18)
Terrestrials	Dave's hoppers (#8-12), Henry's Fork hoppers (#8-12), fur ants, black (#14-18), CDC ants (#14-18), deer-hair beetles, black (#14-16), hi-vis foam beetles (#14-16)

For more information on hatch chart and fly patterns, go to Cimarron Creek's web site at *www.cimarroncreek.com.*

tippets are commonly 4x or 5x. A two-nymph setup with a San Juan worm and a woolly bugger works well when dead-drifted in the early season. Later in the year, you may want to combine a light and a dark nymph, or use one bead-head pattern and one unweighted nymph.

You can find trout rising in a variety of water. Prime locations will be along the banks, on current seams and in shallower runs. When floating the river in the Gunnison Gorge, it is hard to beat a hopper with a bead-head nymph dropper in late summer. Cast ahead of the boat at about a 45-degree angle and place your two flies next to the bank or along the edge of eddy lines.

Streamer fishing is very effective at times. Woolly buggers (especially black and peacock), muddler minnows and Clouser minnows are all good choices and can be effectively fished with floating or sink-tip lines.

HOW TO GET THERE

Grand Junction is located on I-70 only 60 miles from Montrose — the gateway community to the Black Canyon of the Gunnison River National Park. There is commercial air service into both towns.

Montrose is located at the junction of US 50 and US 550. To reach the Black Canyon of the Gunnison National Park, take US 50 east eight miles from Montrose, then turn north on SR 347. It is six miles to the South Rim entrance of the park. To reach the North Rim of the park, continue east on US 50 and turn north on SR 92 to Crawford. Follow the signs to North Rim Road (which is unpaved) 11 miles to the park entrance. North Rim Road is closed in the winter.

ACCESSIBILITY

There is very limited access to the river in Black Canyon of the Gunnison. The East Portal Road in the Curecanti National Recreation Area, which shares its western boundary with the park, is the only road access in the canyon to the Gunnison River. It is closed in the winter, and vehicles over 22 feet are prohibited. This is the put-in for Black Canyon, only run by the most advaced kayakers willing to run Class V rapids, portage their boats and rappel down waterfalls. Lives have been lost in the canyon. This is definitely not a canyon for fly fishers to float, but some do launch canoes and float tubes to cross the river. Anglers who cross over to the north bank have access to about five miles of the river going downstream, if they are willing to scramble up and over a ridge. Those who stay on the south bank can walk down about one mile until they are walled off.

From this point downstream, Black Canyon is probably one of the most inaccessible trout streams in America. There are six routes — *not* trails — down to the river, three from the South Rim and three from the North Rim. They are all physically demanding, require good navigational skills and are for the sure-footed only. There are inherent risks in climbing down into this rugged canyon; you must assume responsibility for your own safety. Don't forget the Calamine Lotion, as poison ivy grows along these river access routes. Once you reach the river, you will only be able to fish a limited amount of water (only ¼ mile at Long Draw, and

North Rim River Access Routes

S.O.B. Draw (west of the North Rim campground)

Beware of poison ivy on the route and along the river. River access: 2 miles. Descent: 2 hours; ascent: 4 hours. Distance: 1 ¾ miles. Vertical Drop: 1800 feet. Six river campsites.

Long Draw (northeast of Balanced Rock Overlook)

Beware of 5-foot-tall poison ivy on the route and along the river. River access: ¼ mile. Descent: 1 ½ hours; ascent: 3 hours. Distance: 1 mile. Vertical Drop: 1800 feet. No camping.

Slide Draw (park at Kneeling Camel View)

Loose rocks and extremely steep. River access: ¾ mile. Descent: 1 ½ hours; ascent: 4 ½ hours. Distance: 1 mile. Vertical Drop: 1620 feet. Two river campsites.

South Rim River Access Routes

Gunnison Route (Oak Flats Trail at the Gunnison Point Visitor Center)

Recommended for first inner-canyon hikes. An 80-foot chain is placed to help you get down this 1-mile route. River access: ¾ mile. Descent: 1 ½ hours; ascent: 2 hours. Vertical Drop: 1800 feet. Three campsites and an outhouse.

Tomichi Route (begins at the parking area at the South Rim campground)

Dangerous loose rock and full exposure to sun. River access: ½ mile. Descent: 1 ½ hours; ascent: 4 ½ hours. Vertical Drop: 1960 feet. Two campsites.

Warner Route (splits off from the Warner Nature Trail)

A 2 ½-mile route dropping 2,660 feet to the river. River access: 1 ½ miles. Descent: 2-2 ½ hours; ascent: 4 hours. Overnight camping recommended. Five campsites.

probably not worth the effort). The water is cold even at low flow, limiting wading; wading is not recommended at water levels above 450-500 cfs.

Permits are required to hike into the canyon. They are free and available on a first-come, first-served basis from the South Rim Visitor Center or the North Rim Ranger Station. For more information on permits, call (970) 249-1914, ext. 23.

The Gunnison Gorge Recreation Area begins at the western boundary of the park. Here, the incredible height and sheer steepness of the canyon walls diminish quite a bit, making a hike in a more reasonable proposition. All the trailhead roads branch off of Peach Valley Road, which is a fairly smooth dirt road in dry weather. It becomes impassable when the road gets wet, as do the roads to the trailheads. Driving these roads when wet is risky and can leave them badly rutted for those who will follow you.

The Gunnison Gorge is a great whitewater fishing trip for those with the necessary experience. You can spend up to three nights on the float, fishing water that sees few anglers. But there are many Class III and IV rapids, and you will be far from help if something goes wrong. Don't attempt this trip without good equipment and the necessary experience. You can make this trip with experienced river guides by contacting Gunnison River Expeditions or one of the other licensed outfitters. For more information on floating the Gunnison Gorge, contact the BLM office in Montrose at (970) 240-5300 or go online at *www.co.blm.gov/ubra/gorge.htm*.

The Chukar Trail is the put-in for floaters going into the Gunnison Gorge. The Chukar Road to the trailhead is seven miles long. The last three miles are steep and rough and best left to four-wheel-drive vehicles with high clearance. The trail is a little more than one mile; this is the easiest hike into the river. If you are launching boats here you will either need to carry them to the river or you can have them packed in by horse (see J & Ray Guides & Outfitters). You will get walled out fairly soon both upstream and down.

The road to the Bobcat Trailhead is also four-wheel drive. The trail is 1½ miles, with the last ¼ mile a steep scramble; a length of knotted rope helps you down the steepest part. Cliffs block access to the river upstream, but you can go downstream a good distance.

Duncan Road is the best road into a trailhead on this stretch of the Gunnison. While four-wheel drive is still recommended, you should be able to get in with most vehicles that offer a reasonable amount of clearance. There is a restroom and picnic shelter at the trailhead. This trail is a difficult scramble for the last ½ mile,

Floaters enveloped in the Gunnison's rugged solitude.

but it does put you on the river at some very nice water, and you can move both up and down the river for a good distance.

The Ute Road is another rough one, so ease your way to the trailhead in four-wheel drive. There is a restroom and picnic area at the trailhead and a ranger station where you meet the river. This trail is the longest at 4 ½ miles, but you can access the river after hiking a little over three miles. This stretch of water can be very kind to fly fishers.

The final access to the Gold Medal water of the Gunnison is from the confluence with the North Fork. The road is suitable for all vehicles, and it is only one mile down to the river from SR 92. You will be turning south to the river about seven miles east of Austin. From the confluence, the Smith Fork Trail follows the Gunnison upstream for four miles. This route provides the easiest access to the river in Gunnison Gorge, but you will need to get across the North Fork. It is wade-able much of the year, or you can engage the Gunnison River Pleasure Park (970-872-2525) to ferry you across. Motors are allowed on the Gunnison River up to the Smith Fork. You can arrange to have your boat or raft towed upriver by jet boat, then float back down to the confluence. If you cast streamers on this stretch of the river, you may be surprised by hooking one of the northern pike that live here.

> **CHECK RIVER FLOWS ON THE WEB**
> http://nwis-colo.cr.usgs.gov/rt-cgi/gen_tbl_pg

WHEN TO GO

In winter, the only reliable access is at the confluence with the North Fork. This area can get fairly crowded on winter weekends. The road to the East Portal and the North Rim are closed in winter. South Rim Drive is not plowed and only left open for ski or snowshoe access. The Peach Valley Road and the trails into the Gunnison Gorge may be accessible in dry winters, but don't attempt these roads when they are wet. Even if you manage to get in and out, you will damage the road for others.

The roads into the East Portal and Gunnison Gorge normally open up in April, weather permitting. Once anglers can reach the river, blue-winged olives should be hatching in good numbers to kick off the Gunnison's fishing season. High water usually begins in May, but the river often remains fishable due to its tailwater nature (Blue Mesa Reservoir, Colorado's largest body of water, is upstream). If you are planning to float the gorge, remember that flows above 5,000 cfs make the river very dangerous for boating.

High flows will normally continue into June, but anglers can still find good fishing during the salmonfly hatch, which is closely followed by the giant golden stones. These large insects often spark the best fishing of the year.

Red quills, pale morning duns and yellow sallys keep fish active as the big stonefly hatches fade out. By early September, brown trout brighten up with the foliage and will take woolly buggers and other streamers aggressively. Just don't

PHOTO: RICHARD MUNOZ

One of the Gunnison's fat, healthy rainbows.

wait too long to plan a fall trip to the Gunnison; in many years, early snows can close the roads in October.

Check flows on the Internet or call the BLM hotline at (970) 240-5388 (only operates spring and summer).

AREA ATTRACTIONS

With its dizzying 2,000-foot narrow canyon walls dropping almost vertically to the Gunnison River, the Black Canyon of the Gunnison National Park offers startling views. There are trails above the rim ranging from easy to moderate, but the routes down to the river are not for the faint-hearted.

RESOURCES

There is camping (but no hookups) at the national park on both the South and North Rims for a $10 per night fee. The South Rim campground has two handicap-accessible camping sites. Private campgrounds and lodging are available in the neighboring towns of Cimarron, Montrose and Delta.

For complete listing of campgrounds and lodging outside of the park, contact the Montrose Visitors and Convention Bureau at (800) 873-0244 or Delta County Tourism at (800) 436-3041.

Campgrounds

BLACK CANYON OF THE GUNNISON NATIONAL PARK

❏ South Rim — 102 sites
❏ North Rim — 13 sites

CURECANTI NATIONAL RECREATION AREA

❏ East Portal — 15 sites

HOTCHKISS

Gunnison River Pleasure Park
Leroy Jagodinski
907-2810 Lane
Hotchkiss, CO 81419
Phone number/s: (970) 872-2525,
toll-free (888) 782-7542
Web site: www.troutfisherman.net
E-mail: Cjago270@cs.com
(Also tackle shop)

DELTA

Flying A Motel and RV Park
676 US 50, #13
Delta, CO 81416
Phone number/s: (970) 874-9659

KOA Kampgrounds
1675 SR 92
Delta, CO 81416
Phone number/s: (970) 874-3918

MONTROSE

Black Canyon RV Park & Camp
84348 US 50
Montrose, CO 81220
Phone number/s: (970) 249-1147

Lodging

DELTA

Best Western Inn
903 Main St.
Delta, CO 81416
Phone number/s: (970) 874-9781

Comfort Inn
180 Gunnison River Drive
Delta, CO 81416
Phone number/s: (970) 874-1000

MONTROSE

Black Canyon Motel
1605 E. Main St.
Montrose, CO 80401
Phone number/s: (970) 249-3495

Country Lodge
1624 E. Main
Montrose, CO 80401
Phone number/s: (970) 249-4567
Web site: www.contryldg.com
E-mail: info@countryldg.com

Tackle Shops and Outfitters

MONTROSE

Cimarron Creek
317 E. Main St.
Montrose, CO 81401
Phone: (970) 249-0408
Web site: www.cimarroncreek.com
E-mail: cimcrk@montrose.net

Gunnison River Expeditions
Hank Hotz
19500 US 550
Montrose, CO 81401
Phone number/s: (970) 249-4441,
toll-free (800)-297-4441
Fax: (970) 249-4441
Web site: www.cimarroncreek.com/
FLYFISHING/FF_GRE.html
E-mail: hhotze@gwe.net

Horse Packers

J & Ray Guides & Outfitters
Larry Franks
8310 6400 Road
Montrose, CO 81401
Phone number/s: (970) 323-0115
Web site: www.sportsmandream.com/jray
E-mail: WbarX@aol.com

Area Attractions

Black Canyon of the Gunnison National
Park/Curecanti National Recreation Area
102 Elk Creek
Gunnison, CO 81230
Phone number/s: (970) 641-2337
Web site: www.nps.gov/blca
E-mail: cure_vis_mail@nps.gov

Roaring Fork River

The Roaring Fork Valley is home to one of Trout Unlimited's oldest chapters, named in honor of Ferdinand Hayden, a nineteenth-century explorer who was to become the first director of the U.S. Geological Survey. He believed that some things in nature should be preserved for perpetuity in a time when "progress" meant exploitation. His example is evident here on the Roaring Fork, where the namesake chapter has worked hard to obtain catch-and-release regulations and the "Wild Trout" designation for the upper river near Aspen. One of the founding members of this group of anglers was Chuck Fothergill, considered one of the fathers of Aspen fly fishing and the author of several fishing guidebooks. You can pause for a moment at his memorial in the park just above Upper Woody Bridge, before you walk upstream to fish the river he and so many others helped preserve for those of us to follow.

The Roaring Fork is a steep freestone stream and home to chunky, strong rainbows as well as brown trout. The average fish is 14 to 15 inches, but trout in excess of five pounds are found here. The river offers a wide variety of water types: the high mountain stream up in the White River National Forest, the boulder-strewn whitewater canyon below Aspen, and the wide and powerful river below Carbondale. Visiting anglers can select from a similarly broad range of lodgings in the different towns and resorts of the Roaring Fork Valley, and vacations can be tailored to fit most tastes and pocketbooks.

SPECIFIC REGULATIONS

The Division of Wildlife has designated the stretch from Hallum Lake (in Aspen) downstream to upper Woody Creek bridge as a "Wild Trout water" and it is not stocked. The stretch from Crystal River downstream to the Colorado River is designated as a "Gold Medal water" signifying its trophy trout potential.

From McFarlane Creek downstream to upper Woody Creek Bridge:
- Artificial flies only.
- All fish must be returned to the water immediately.

From upper Woody Creek Bridge to the Colorado River:
- Artificial flies and lures only.
- Minimum size limit for trout is 16 inches.

A beautiful morning on the Roaring Fork between Aspen and Basalt.

TACTICS

When fishing dry flies on the Fork, concentrate on the edges of the river, current seams and the rare slower pools. Trout are more apt to rise for dry flies in areas where less effort is required for them to capture a meal. Imitate the prevailing hatches that you find, but remember that trout often focus their attention on small blue-winged olives even when larger insects are present. Terrestrials are underutilized on the Roaring Fork and can be quite effective. A "hopper and a dropper" works well over the length of the river from Glenwood up to Aspen. Cast them to the banks, midstream eddy lines and on slower pools. Don't overlook ant and beetle patterns, which can also be productive on late summer days.

Nymph fish the deeper pools and pocket water. Strike indicators work well when fishing the longer pools or when fish are suspended just under the surface. There are many short, deep pockets and pools on the upper Roaring Fork. The most effective way to nymph these is without an indicator and with fairly heavy weight, say one or two 3/0 split shot, on the end of a nine- to 12-foot 4x leader. Lob your flies and shot to the head of the pool and let them sink down to the bottom. Lift your rod tip as the nymphs float back to you and keep a tight line to detect strikes.

Art Rowell of Frying Pan Anglers in Basalt believes that the Roaring Fork is an excellent streamer river, especially the lower stretches. Either sink-tip lines or heavily weighted flies on floating lines will take fish. Woolly buggers are the most

Hatch Chart AVAILABILITY

Food Items	J	F	M	A	M	J	J	A	S	O	N	D
Midges	X	X	X	X	X	X	X	X	X	X	X	X
Blue-winged olives		X	X	X	X	X	X	X	X	X	X	
Pale morning duns						X	X	X				
Green drakes							X	X				
Red quills								X	X			
Salmonflies					X	X						
Yellow sallys							X	X				
Caddisflies				X	X	X	X	X	X			
Pumpkin caddis									X	X		
Terrestrials							X	X	X			

popular pattern, but matukas and spruce flies also work well. One reliable local pattern is the autumn splendor. It is a brown woolly bugger with olive-dyed grizzly hackle and yellow rubber-legs.

HOW TO GET THERE

The Pitkin County Airport in Aspen will put you on the ground a stone's throw from the Roaring Fork but flying into Denver will often save money on air-fares. It is a straight shot 140 miles west on I-70 from Denver to Glenwood Springs. Exit 116 on I-70 will take you to SR 82.

From its headwaters just shy of Independence Pass, the Roaring Fork runs along SR 82 through the communities of Aspen, Woody Creek, Snowmass Village, Basalt and Carbondale before it meets the Colorado River at Glenwood Springs.

ACCESSIBILITY

It is 40 miles from Aspen to Glenwood Springs, and the river drops more than 2,000 feet in its rapid plunge toward the Colorado River. SR 82 follows the river for its length but has a surprising amount of commuter traffic. From Snowmass up to Aspen, a string of secondary roads (Lower River Road, Upper River Road and McCain Flats Road) won't get you to your destination any quicker, but they make it easy to find the river access points and may keep your stress level a bit lower.

The upper portion of the river has the best access for wading anglers, and from Aspen down to Basalt, the river is normally gin clear as it tumbles over boulders and cobble rock. Use care when walking on the river's well-polished bottom. Wading staffs and studded boots will help you stay on your feet. From Carbondale downstream, access is limited for shorebound anglers, and anglers who float will normally find more fish.

Independence Pass Road (SR 82) going upstream from Aspen is closed in the winter, so this upper section is best fished after run-off subsides. The White River National Forest boundary is just over two miles southwest of the edge of Aspen.

Insects	Suggested Fly Patterns
Midges	Griffith's gnats (#18-22), Adams (#18-22), midge pupae (#18-22), biot midge emergers (#18-22), candy canes (#18-22), disco midges (#18-22)
Blue-winged olives	parachute Adams (#18-24), thorax BWOs (#18-22), olive comparaduns (#18-24), sparkle duns, olive (#18-24), Quigley cripples, olive (#18-22), CDC emergers, olive (#18-24), pheasant tails (#18-24), hare's ears (#18-24), bead-head pheasant tails (#18-24), bead-head hare's ears (#18-24), WD40s (#18-24), RS2s (#18-24)
Pale morning duns	yellow quills (#12-16), thorax PMDs (#12-16), PMD parachutes (#12-16), comparaduns (#12-16), Quigley cripples, cream (#12-16), rusty spinners (#12-16), CDC emergers, cream (#12-16), AK's melon quills (#16-20), pink Cahills (#16-20), pheasant tails (#12-20), bead-head pheasant tails (#12-20)
Green drakes	green drake Wulffs (#8-12), olive paradrakes (#10-12), olive comparaduns (#8-12), Quigley cripples, olive (#8-12), CDC emergers, olive (#8-12), Roy's green drake nymphs (#14-18), hare's ears, olive (#8-12), epoxy-back green drake nymphs (#8-12)
Red quills	H&L variants (#14-16), red quills (#14-16), quill spinners, red (#14-16), rusty spinners (#14-16), pheasant tails (#14-16), hare's ears (#14-16)
Salmonflies	sofa pillows (#6-10), Mac Salmons (#6-10), orange stimulators (#6-10), rubber-legs, black (#6-10), Bitch Creek nymphs (#6-10), Brook's stone nymphs (#6-10)
Yellow sallys	yellow stimulators (#12-16), Flint's stones (#12-16), irresistible stimulators, yellow (#12-16), red fox squirrel nymphs (#14-18)
Caddisflies	elk-hair caddis (#16-20), partridge caddis (#16-20), CDC elk-hair caddis (#16-20), Hemmingway caddis (#16-20), parachute caddis (#16-20), X-caddis (#16-20), sparkle pupae (#16-20), peeking caddis (#16-20)
Pumpkin caddis	elk-hair caddis, orange (#12-14), irresistible caddis, orange (#12-14), orange stimulators (#12-14)
Terrestrials	Dave's hoppers (#8-12), parachute hoppers (#8-12), Henry's Fork hoppers (#8-12), Turck's tarantulas (#8-12), fur ants, black (#14-18), CDC ants (#14-18), deer-hair beetles, black (#14-16), hi-vis foam beetles (#14-16)

Roaring Fork: *Lost Man Creek to Snowmass*

GPS Coordinates

A	Lincoln Gulch Campground	N 39° 07' 01"	W 106° 41' 42"
B	Weller Campground	N 39° 07' 17"	W 106° 43' 11"
C	White River National Forest Boundary	N 39° 08' 55"	W 106° 46' 50"
D	Confluence with Mc Farlane Creek	N 39° 09' 05"	W 106° 47' 07"
E	North Star Nature Preserve	N 39° 10' 36"	W 106° 47' 46"
F	Henry Stein Park	N 39° 12' 41"	W 106° 50' 24"
G	Upper Woody Creek Bridge	N 39° 15' 31"	W 106° 52' 55"
H	Lower Woody Creek Bridge	N 39° 17' 54"	W 106° 55' 16"
I	Old Snowmass Trail Access	N 39° 19' 57"	W 106° 59' 10"

Colorado Atlas and Gazetteer Pages 35, 45-47

Map 1 of 2

▬▬▬ Bridge

To Twin Lakes Reservoir

Lost Man Creek

Independence

82

A A

B

Difficult Campground

D C A

E

Roaring Fork River

McCain Flats Road

F

Aspen

82

G

Upper River Road

Woody Creek

H

Lower River Road

82

To Glenwood Springs

Snowmass

I

Snowmass Village

N
E
S
W

5 Miles

5 KM

Ft Collins

Greeley

25

76

34

Denver

70

Colorado Springs

90

Grand Junction

70

Canon City

Pueblo

25

La Junta

50

160

Durango

Trinidad

Roaring Fork: *Snowmass to Colorado River*

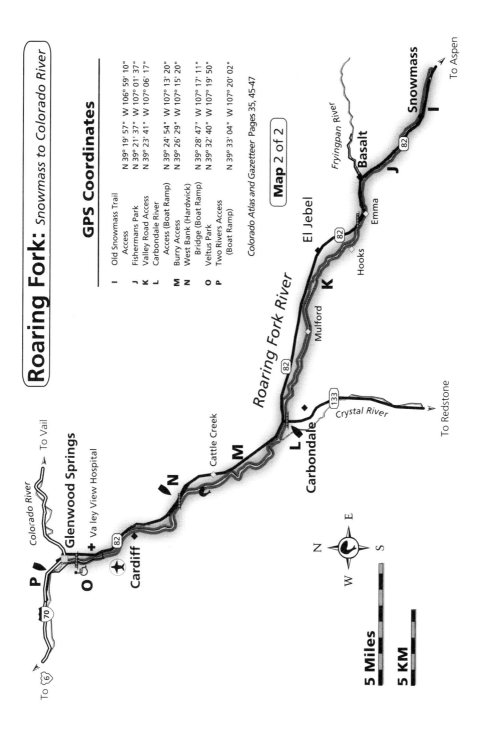

GPS Coordinates

I	Old Snowmass Trail Access	N 39° 19' 57" W 106° 59' 10"
J	Fishermans Park	N 39° 21' 37" W 107° 01' 37"
K	Valley Road Access	N 39° 23' 41" W 107° 06' 17"
L	Carbondale River Access (Boat Ramp)	N 39° 24' 54" W 107° 13' 20"
M	Burry Access	N 39° 26' 29" W 107° 15' 20"
N	West Bank (Hardwick) Bridge (Boat Ramp)	N 39° 28' 47" W 107° 17' 11"
O	Veltus Park	N 39° 32' 40" W 107° 19' 50"
P	Two Rivers Access (Boat Ramp)	N 39° 33' 04" W 107° 20' 02"

Colorado Atlas and Gazetteer Pages 35, 45-47

Map 2 of 2

5 Miles

5 KM

Slaughterhouse Falls on the Roaring Fork.

From this point upstream almost all of the Roaring Fork is on Forest Service lands. It is a mixture of slow meadow water and steep mountain stream. Above Lincoln Gulch campground, the river gets very small.

As you move downstream, you will pass the river's confluence with McFarlane Creek and the next 10 miles or so down to Upper Woody Creek Bridge is the catch-and-release water on the Roaring Fork. Anglers have access to ½ mile of slow meadow water on the North Star Nature Preserve before the river reaches Aspen.

Going downstream from Aspen, the Rio Grande bike path follows the north bank of the Fork for over five miles of spectacularly pretty water. You can leave your vehicle at Henry Stein Park or at the Wilton Jaffe Sr. Park just above Upper Woody Creek Bridge. This is some of the best access on the river, and you are away from the roads and crowds. (You are, however, on the flight path of the jet traffic going in and out of Pitkin County Airport.) This Wild Trout section is some of the most attractive water on the Roaring Fork.

Lower Woody Creek Bridge is on Gerbaz Road, and from this point anglers can fish upstream for two miles on the south bank. From the Old Snowmass Trail access, anglers can follow the foot trail down past the old car body to the river, which is open to anglers for a mile downstream until you reach the Lazy Glen Trailer Park.

From Fishermans Park downstream through the town of Basalt, anglers have access to about three miles of the north bank of the Roaring Fork. There are several turnouts where anglers can park, and access continues downstream to the lower Bypass Bridge below Basalt. There are some unimproved launch ramps through this area, but the river is very steep and technical, with some diversion dams, and only runnable during the high waters of May and June. This section is not recommended for floaters. If you are planning a winter trip, the water below the confluence with the Fryingpan will be slightly warmer.

There is foot access to the river just below the town of El Jebel on Valley Road. Anglers can fish upstream for over a mile on the north bank.

The Carbondale River access is the first good launch site on the Roaring Fork. It is a bit hard to find. From SR 82 eastbound, turn onto Sutank Road about one mile northwest of SR 82's intersection with SR 133 at Carbondale. The boat launch area is just below the Sopris RV Park, so follow the camping signs until you see the turn down to the ramp. This is the most poplar float (eight miles) on the Roaring Fork and can be fished most of the year.

The Burry access is reached from a turnout from SR 82 at the nine-mile marker and gives access to about a mile of the north bank of the Roaring Fork.

The West Bank (Hardwick) Bridge access has a rough boat ramp with limited room to turn around trailers and not much parking. You may want to look at it yourself before floating down. This is the take-out for the popular float coming downstream from Carbondale. If you use it as a launch site, you will have to nego-tiate Cemetery Rapids (Class III). This is a semi-urban float that will take you through the town of Glenwood Springs. The take-out for this float is at Riverside Park at the Roaring Fork's confluence with the Colorado. To get to the Two Rivers access, cross to the north bank of the Colorado River on SR 82, continue to the northwest about one mile, then turn southwest on Devereux Road.

Veltus Park is on Midland Road just south of the 7th Street Bridge in Glen-wood. It has a nicely constructed handicap accessible fishing site, but a four-foot-high railing will make fly casting difficult for many physically challenged anglers.

CHECK RIVER FLOWS ON THE WEB
http://nwis-colo.cr.usgs.gov/rt-cgi/gen_tbl_pg

WHEN TO GO

The Roaring Fork is a year-round fishery; just remember it is a high-altitude freestone river. The water runs very cold in the winter months, but you can find some good midge fishing on warm, sunny afternoons, especially in February and March. Blue-winged olives first appear on the lower river near Glenwood Springs in late March and can take a full month to work their way up the river. These small mayflies are a good warm-up for the river's heaviest hatch, the Mother's Day caddis. Heavy swarms can blanket the lower river beginning in the last week of April, and this hatch moves up to Basalt by the first week of May.

Run-off usually begins in earnest by mid-May and continues through June but is heavily affected by snowpack and weather. Check with local contacts to see how the river is running or check flows on the Internet. Once the high waters recede, the Roaring Fork's best fishing begins with caddis and yellow sallys. These insects are soon joined by the excellent hatch of green drakes, beginning at Glenwood in mid-July and gradually ascending the river into late August.

Streamer fishing heats up early on the Roaring Fork, with aggressive browns (and rainbows) attacking big flies from August until winter arrives in late November.

RESOURCES

The Roaring Fork Valley communities of Glenwood Springs, Carbondale, Basalt, Snowmass Village, Woody Creek and Aspen offer a variety of lodging and attractions. From Glenwood Springs, Aspen is 45 miles to the southeast on SR 82. For more information, go online at www.roaringfork.net.

Summer tourists flock to Aspen, a community of 6,000 year-round residents, and for good reason: the 2 ¼ million-acre White River National Forest has enough recreational opportunities to keep adventurers satisfied, and cultural attractions like the annual summer music festival balance the scales. Look for discounted summer lodging rates after mid-August and into September.

There are four campgrounds along the Roaring Fork River on SR 82 as you head from Aspen toward Independence Pass. Only Difficult campground, with 47 sites, accepts reservations. The other three operate on a first-come, first-served basis and have limited sites (11 and fewer).

Campgrounds

WHITE RIVER NATIONAL FOREST

For reservations, contact the National Reservation System at (877) 444-6777. For more information, contact the Aspen Ranger District at (970) 925-3445.

❏ Difficult
❏ Lincoln Gulch
❏ Lost Man
❏ Weller Family

BASALT

Aspen-Basalt Campground
20640 SR 82
Basalt, CO 81621
Phone number/s: (970) 927-3405
E-mail: ABC@sopris.net

CARBONDALE

Sopris RV Park
640 County Road 106
Carbondale, CO 81623
Phone number/s: (970) 963-0163

Lodging

ASPEN/SNOWMASS VILLAGE

Aspen Central Reservations
Phone number/s: toll-free (888) 649-5982
Fax: (970) 925-9008
Web site: www.aspen4u.com
E-mail: info@aspen4u.com

Aspen Lodging Company
747 Galena St.
Aspen, CO 81611
Phone number/s: (970) 925-2260,
toll-free (800) 321-7025
Fax: (970) 925-2264
Web site: www.aspen.com/aspenlodgingco

Aspenwood Condominiums
600 Carriage Way
Snowmass Village, CO 81615
Phone number/s: (970) 923-2711,
toll-free (800) 451-8540
Web site: www.aspendwoodcondos.com
E-mail: info@aspenwoodcondos.com

BASALT

Aspenwood Lodge
220 Midland Ave.
Basalt, CO 81621
Phone number/s: (970) 927-4747,
toll-free (800) 905-6797
Fax: (970) 927-0218
Web site: aspenwoodlodge.com
E-mail: info@aspenwoodbasalt.com

Best Western Apenalt Lodge
157 Basalt Center Circle
Basalt, CO 81621
Phone number/s: (970) 927-3191,
toll-free (877) 379-6476

CARBONDALE
Crystal River Inn
12954 SR 133
Carbondale, CO 81623
Phone number/s: (970) 963-3902

Thunder River Lodge
179 SR 133
Carbondale, CO 81623
Phone number/s: (970) 963-2543

Tackle Shops and Outfitters

ASPEN
Aspen Outfitting Co
315 E. Dean St.
Aspen, CO 81611
Phone number/s: (970) 925-3406

Outfitters
P.O. Box 6068
Snowmass Village, CO 81615
Phone number/s: (970) 923-5959

BASALT
Frying Pan Anglers
123 Emma Road, #100
Basalt, CO 81621
Phone number/s: (970) 927-3441

Taylor Creek Fly Shops
183 Basalt Center Circle
Basalt, CO 81621
Phone number/s: (970) 927-4374

CARBONDALE
Alpine Angling
981 Cowen Drive
Carbondale, CO 81623
Phone number/s: (970) 963-9245
E-mail: flyfish@sopris.net

GLENWOOD SPRINGS
Roaring Fork Anglers
2114 Grand Ave., Suite B
Glenwood Springs, CO 81601
Phone number/s: (970) 945-0180,
toll-free (800) 781 8120
Web site: www.RFAnglers.com
E-mail: flyfish@sopris.net

Roaring Fork Outfitters
2022 Grand Ave.
Glenwood Springs, CO 81601
Phone number/s: (970) 945-5800

Area Attractions
Aspen Music Festival
2 Music School Road
Aspen, CO 81611
Phone number/s: (970) 925-9042 (tickets)
Fax: (970) 925-8077 (tickets)
Web site: aspenmusicfestival.com

Hot Springs Lodge & Pool
401 N. River
Glenwood Springs, CO 81602
Phone number/s: (970) 945-7131,
toll-free (800) 537-SWIM
Web site: www.hotspringspool.com

South Platte: *Cheesman Dam to North Fork*

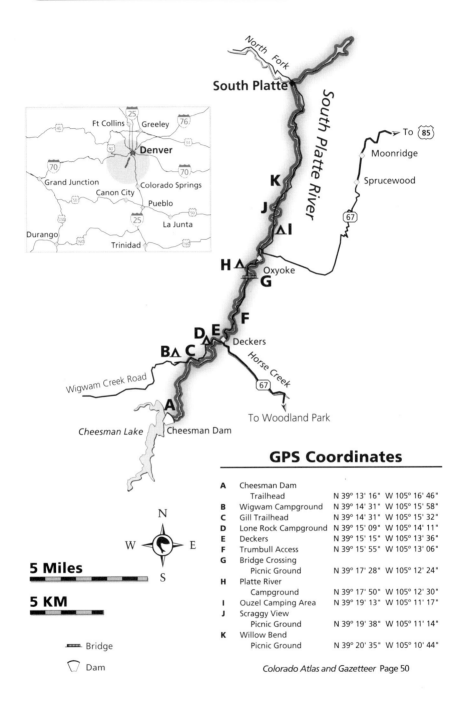

North Fork

South Platte

South Platte River

To 85

Moonridge

Sprucewood

K

J

△**I**

67

H△

Oxyoke

G

F

D E

△

Deckers

B△ **C**

Horse Creek

Wigwam Creek Road

67

A

To Woodland Park

Cheesman Lake Cheesman Dam

Ft Collins Greeley 76

25

Denver

70

Grand Junction 70

Canon City Colorado Springs

Pueblo

Durango La Junta

Trinidad

GPS Coordinates

A	Cheesman Dam Trailhead	N 39° 13' 16"	W 105° 16' 46"
B	Wigwam Campground	N 39° 14' 31"	W 105° 15' 58"
C	Gill Trailhead	N 39° 14' 31"	W 105° 15' 32"
D	Lone Rock Campground	N 39° 15' 09"	W 105° 14' 11"
E	Deckers	N 39° 15' 15"	W 105° 13' 36"
F	Trumbull Access	N 39° 15' 55"	W 105° 13' 06"
G	Bridge Crossing Picnic Ground	N 39° 17' 28"	W 105° 12' 24"
H	Platte River Campground	N 39° 17' 50"	W 105° 12' 30"
I	Ouzel Camping Area	N 39° 19' 13"	W 105° 11' 17"
J	Scraggy View Picnic Ground	N 39° 19' 38"	W 105° 11' 14"
K	Willow Bend Picnic Ground	N 39° 20' 35"	W 105° 10' 44"

N

W ⊕ E

S

5 Miles

5 KM

▥ Bridge

⬠ Dam

Colorado Atlas and Gazetteer Page 50

South Platte River

HIGHLIGHT
Rugged beauty of Cheesman Canyon

TIP
Drop tippets down to 6x

FISH SPECIES
Brown and rainbow trout

SEASON
Year-round

I t is amazing that a river so close to so many anglers has been so well-preserved. A short hike leads to a pristine canyon cut deep into the pink granite, shaded by tall ponderosa pines. Walk in early enough in the morning, and the only human signs will be the twisting trails made by many wader-clad feet and remnant fire rings of winter fly fishers. Cheesman Canyon on the South Platte is close to the Greater Denver Area and Colorado Springs, putting it just over a one-hour drive from more than 1 million potential anglers. As you might expect, the river is heavily fished in this celebrated section. Yet it was the river's popularity that won it so many allies when it was in danger in 1990. The South Platte furnishes 70 percent of Denver's water supply, and growing demand sparked a plan to add another dam to the river and inundate more than 20 miles of Gold Medal trout water. Members of Trout Unlimited and a variety of other environmental groups joined forces to protect this great river from the water developers, ensuring today that we all have the opportunity to cast a line to the trout that call it home.

Cheesman Canyon is ruggedly beautiful, with the clear waters of the South Platte fighting their way through a maze of huge boulders and rock outcroppings. Iridescent, midnight blue Steller's jays flit from pines to boulders, looking for a handout from an angler's lunch. The canyon's rainbows are also very colorful, sporting rosy red-colored cheeks and flanks that make them stand out in the river's flow. You will find plenty of rainbows in the South Platte. The trout population in Cheesman Canyon is estimated at approximately 5,000 per mile with an average size of 14 to 16 inches. Some fish do stretch to 20 inches or more, but an angler will need a large dose of both luck and skill to wrap his or her hands around one of these trophies.

SPECIFIC REGULATIONS AND FEES

The South Platte River Corridor, which extends from Cheesman Dam to Scraggy View picnic ground, is designated Gold Medal water.

From Cheesman Dam downstream to upper Wigwam property line — Gold Medal water:
☐   Artificial flies or lures only.
☐   All fish must be returned to the water immediately.

South Platte River from lower boundary of Wigwam Club to Scraggy View picnic ground — Gold Medal water:

☐ Artificial flies or lures only.
☐ Bag and possession limit for trout is two fish, 16 inches or longer.

South Platte River from Scraggy View picnic ground downstream to dam at Strontia Springs Reservoir:

☐ Bag and possession limit for trout is two fish.

There are three day-use picnic areas along SR 67, north of Deckers, that provide fishing access. There is a $4 per day fee. There are vault toilets but no drinking water available.

☐ Bridge Crossing picnic ground (3 miles north of Deckers on SR 67)
☐ Scraggy View picnic ground (6 miles north of Deckers on SR 67)
☐ Willow Bend picnic ground (7 miles north of Deckers on SR 67)

Hatch Chart   AVAILABILITY

Food Items	J	F	M	A	M	J	J	A	S	O	N	D
Midges	X	X	X	X	X	X	X	X	X	X	X	X
Scuds	X	X	X	X	X	X	X	X	X	X	X	X
Annelid worms	X	X	X	X	X	X	X	X	X	X	X	X
Blue-winged olives			X	X	X				X	X	X	X
Pale morning duns						X	X	X				
Tricos								X	X	X		
Golden stoneflies						X	X	X				
Caddisflies					X	X	X	X	X			
Terrestrials							X	X	X			

TACTICS

These rainbow and brown trout are well-known for their fastidious nature. Whether fishing on the surface or underneath, successful anglers will have to make accurate casts and clean, drag-free drifts with small flies on light tippets just to connect. If you are fishing in one of the boulder-choked areas, landing a good fish can be at least as challenging as getting them to eat. If you are the kind of fly fisher who appreciates this evenly matched chess game, then you will find yourself at home here.

You won't normally find many rising trout in the first 2 ½ miles below Cheesman Dam, so be prepared to nymph if you head into this water. The many deep slots, plunge pools and huge boulders present a great variety of fishing situations. Getting a nymph down to fish with a good drift presents enough different challenges to keep you deeply absorbed for hours. Keep your tippet light; most Cheesman Canyon regulars use 6x. You will need the fine terminal tackle to get some lifelike movement on the tiny nymphs that make up the majority of trout

Insects	Suggested Fly Patterns
Midges	Griffith's gnats (#18-24), grizzly midges (#18-24), double midges (#18-24), suspender midges (#18-24), mercury midges (#18-24), black beauties (#16-24), brassies (#18-24), disco midges (#18-24), biot midges (#18-24)
Scuds	olive, tan, pink, and orange scuds (#12-16)
Annelid worms	San Juan worms, tan and red (#12-16)
Blue-winged olives	parachute Adams (#18-22), thorax BWOs (#18-22), olive comparaduns (#18-22), sparkle duns, olive (#18-22), Quigley cripples, olive (#18-22), CDC emergers, olive (#18-22), Barr emergers (#18-22), pheasant tails (#16-20), hare's ears (#16-20), bead-head pheasant tails (#16-20), bead-head hare's ears (#16-20), WD40s (#18-20), RS2s, gray and olive (#18-22)
Pale morning duns	thorax PMDs (#14-18), cream parachutes (#14-18), cream comparaduns (#14- 28), Quigley cripples, cream (#16-20), rusty spinners (#14-18), CDC emergers, cream (#16-20), Barr emergers (#16-18), pheasant tails (#14-18), hare's ears (#14-18), bead-head pheasant tails (#14-18), bead-head hare's ears (#14-18)
Tricos	trico spinners (#18-22), double trico spinners (#18), CDC tricos (#18-22), parachute Adams (#18-22), pheasant tails (#18-20)
Golden stoneflies	yellow stimulators (#8-12), irresistible stimulators, yellow (#8-12)
Caddisflies	elk-hair caddis (#16-20), partridge caddis (#16-20), CDC elk-hair caddis (#16-20), X-caddis (#16-20), sparkle pupae (#16-18), pulsating caddis (#14-16)
Terrestrials	Dave's hoppers (#8-12), Henry's Fork hoppers (#8-12), fur ants, black (#14-18), CDC ants (#14-18), deer-hair beetles, black (#14-16), hi-vis foam beetles (#14-16)

A South Platte rainbow surrenders after falling for a tiny nymph.

food in this tailwater. Most fish will be caught on size 18 or smaller nymphs. Pat Dorsey's mercury midge and black beauty are effective midge patterns most of the year, although many of the largest trout fall victim to a San Juan worm in tan, buckskin or red.

If you prefer to fish dry flies, head for the first ½ mile of water above the Wigwam Club, or stay on the public water above and below Deckers. Open pools with slower flows encourage trout to feed on the surface. Rich Speer of Flies and Lies in Deckers recommends leaders of at least 10 feet with four to five feet of 6x added to give slack near the fly. Downstream drifts are the most effective. A simple parachute Adams is perhaps the single most effective dry-fly pattern, while a gray RS2 works well when fished in the film.

HOW TO GET THERE

Visiting anglers can fly into Denver or Colorado Springs, both about a 1 ½-hour drive to Deckers. From the Denver airport, you want to get to I-25. Take Pena Boulevard to I-70 West to pick up I-225 South, which will take you to I-25. Take Exit 187, Happy Canyon Road, which intersects US 85. Head west on US 85 to Sedalia. At Sedalia, take SR 67 south all the way to Deckers. It is 72 miles from the airport.

If you're coming from Colorado Springs, head west on US 24 (East Fountain Boulevard). Turn north at Woodland Park onto SR 67, which will lead you to Deckers. It is about 50 miles from the airport.

ACCESSIBILITY

Anglers can hike into the South Platte just below Cheesman Dam. This is a bit more strenuous than hiking into the bottom of the canyon above the Wigwam Club, but you can get away from some of the fishing pressure found downstream. To get to your jumping-off point from Deckers, go southwest almost three miles to FR 211 and follow this narrow, twisty road four miles to the parking area at Cheesman Lake. Load up your pack, hike through the gate, and go south on the road along the lakeshore. Following the signs will keep you on the road all the way down to the river. It is a little over one mile, with the last third being quite steep. Plan on about 30 minutes to get to the river and maybe 40 minutes to walk back out. The trail downstream — there is no access upstream from where you reach the river — is rough and faint, so

The river is exceptionally rugged at the head of Cheesman Canyon just below the dam.

use caution. The river here is full of huge granite boulders with many deep pools and drops in between. If you choose to wade, be extremely careful.

The main access to Cheesman Canyon is by way of the Gill Trail. You can park at the turnout just east of FR 211, but if this area is full, go up to Wigwam campground. You will have to pay the day-use fee, and the walk is slightly longer. The trail to the river is about ½ mile and a little steep to begin with. Stay right at the fence that marks the boundary to the Wigwam Club. When you come within sight of the river, you can drop down and fish the slow, wide pools that are found here in the first ½ mile or so upstream from the Wigwam Club.

As you continue upstream into the canyon, the river gets hemmed in by granite walls and flows over, around and under huge boulders, making for some very interesting water. The trail continues all the way to the dam three miles upstream. If you find the river too crowded for your liking when you reach it, you can generally hike your way up into some solitude. The main trail stays well above the water, so if you are trying to cover ground, always stay on the highest visible trail. Even though the trail doesn't gain much elevation on its way to the dam, it has many

There are slower pools (and more anglers) in Cheesman Canyon just above the Wigwam Club.

ups and downs that are quite steep. The last mile or so to the gauging station below the dam is quite difficult hiking.

The Wigwam Club downstream from the Gill Trail is private and open to members only. The next public access is at Lone Rock campground, which is located right on the river. To access the south bank from the Wigwam Club to Deckers, use Douglas CR 75, which goes west up the river just across from the store. From Deckers down through Trumbull, there is very good access to the river with lots of parking areas and turnouts. Downstream from Trumbull there is a long section of private water, but public access resumes at the Bridge Crossing picnic site. The river is again open to anglers for most of its length down to Scraggy View picnic ground, which marks the end of the Gold Medal water on this stretch of the South Platte. Fishing continues to be quite good down to the confluence with the North Fork.

> **CHECK RIVER FLOWS ON THE WEB**
> http://nwis-colo.cr.usgs.gov/rt-cgi/gen_tbl_pg

WHEN TO GO

You can fish the South Platte and Cheesman Canyon most of the year. It is a good choice for anglers looking for a winter "fish fix," and you can find trout feeding on midges even in the coldest months. Blue-winged olives hatch for six or seven months of the year, and they get started in March. This is the most reliable and long-term mayfly hatch of the season and provides good dry-fly fishing.

The pale morning duns come on at the start of summer as the blue-winged olives fade out, but many fly fishers feel that the river's tricos are the best hatch of the year. Time your visit right and you will find big swarms of these small insects mating then falling to the water, where they are gobbled up by hungry fish. The excitement will last from about 8 to 11 each morning. Small blue-winged olives begin to appear in late summer and carry through to the first snows of winter.

Boulders in Cheesman Canyon make for interesting fishing.

AREA ATTRACTIONS

The Colorado Trail runs from Denver all the way to Durango. It parallels the South Platte from Platte River Reservoir to Strontia Springs Reservoir and then crosses the river near its confluence with the North Fork. This impressive trail runs 500 miles through some of Colorado's most scenic high country, crossing eight mountain ranges and five river systems.

RESOURCES

The fly shop Flies N Lies at Deckers rents fully furnished, kitchen-equipped cabins alongside the river. Just be sure to stop at one of the larger towns on your way to Deckers to pick up food supplies.

Camping in the Pike National Forest offers many options. Buffalo campground near Buffalo Creek is popular with the metro mountain bikers due to its proximity to Denver and the Colorado Trail. Camping sites can be reserved by calling (877) 444-6777.

The South Platte General Forest Area has five campgrounds, all located within a short distance of the town of Deckers on SR 67 and providing easy access to South Platte's Gold Medal trout waters. Open from May 1 through October 31, these smaller campgrounds are all on a first-come, first-served basis. There is trailer camping and drinking water at Wigwam and Lone Rock. The popular Gill Trail, which leads to the Gold Medal stretch of water below Cheesman Dam, leaves from the Wigwam campground.

For those who prefer motels and eating out to camping or cooking your own meals in a cabin, Woodland Park, 23 miles south of Deckers on SR 67, will keep you in comfort and put you within a reasonable drive to the river.

Campgrounds

PIKE NATIONAL FOREST

For more information, call the South Platte Ranger District at (303) 275-5610.

- ❑ Buffalo — 41 sites
- ❑ Lone Rock — 21 sites
- ❑ Osprey — 13 sites
- ❑ Ouzel — 13 sites
- ❑ Platte River — 10 sites
- ❑ Wigwam — 10 sites

BUFFALO CREEK

Buffalo Creek Campground
28718 Redskin Creek Road
Buffalo Creek, CO 80425
Phone number/s: (303) 816-1601

Lodging

DECKERS

Flies N Lies
8570 S. SR 67
Deckers, CO 80135
Phone number/s: (303) 647-2237
Fax: (303) 647-0482
Web site: www.fliesnlies.com
E-mail: DickJohnson1@uswest.net

WOODLAND PARK

Grand View Motel
411 E. US 24
Woodland Park, CO 80863
Phone number/s: (719) 687-2444

Lofthouse Motel
222 E. Henrietta Ave.
Woodland Park, CO 80863
Phone number/s: (719) 687-9187

Tackle Shops and Outfitters

CONIFER

South Platte Angler
10714 US 285, Suite C-206
Conifer, CO 80433
Phone number/s: (303) 838-8687

DECKER

Flies N Lies
8570 S. SR 67
Deckers, CO 80135
Phone number/s: (303) 647-2237
Fax: (303) 647-0482
Web: www.fliesnlies.com
E-mail: DickJohnson1@uswest.net

EVERGREEN

The Blue Quill Angler
1532 Bergen Parkway
Evergreen, CO 80439
Phone number/s: (303) 674-4700,
toll-free (800) 435-5353
Web site: www.bluequillangler.com
E-mail: flyfish@bluequillangler.com

PINE

Hatch Fly Shop Inc.
480 Sioux Trail, # 50
Pine, CO 80470
Phone number/s: (303) 816-0487

IDAHO

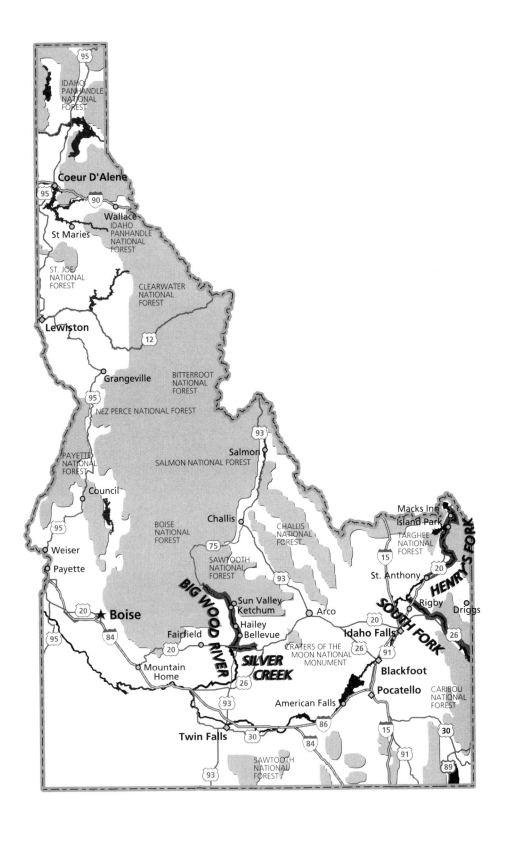

Idaho

 daho has 25,000 miles of fishing streams and more combined public lands and wilderness areas than any state in the lower 48 — almost 70 percent of the state is in public ownership. These impressive statistics mean lots of fly-fishing water in a state best known for its potatoes.

FISHING ACCESS LAWS

In Idaho, Code 36-1601 preserves the public's right to boat and fish on "navigable streams," defined as streams that will float a watercraft.

2000 GENERAL SEASON DATES AND BAG & POSSESSION LIMITS

The general stream fishing season opens the Saturday before Memorial Day and runs through November 30. Be sure to check special regulations in the current proclamation.

The general season for whitefish is extended to include the period from January 1 to March 31. Steelhead and salmon seasons vary as do the regulations that apply. Refer to the current proclamation.

Species	2000 Daily Bag & Possession Limits
STATEWIDE	
Brook trout	10, in addition to the trout limit on any water
Bull trout	None; release immediately
Trout (including brook, brown, cutthroat, golden, lake, rainbow, and sunapee), grayling, trout hybrids, and the landlocked forms of chinook, coho, Atlantic and kokanee (blueback) salmon	six, in the aggregate for all species
Whitefish	50

LICENSE FEES

The state of Idaho has a variable fee system for resident lifetime license certificates. You can buy someone a license before he or she reaches one year of age and pay $551.50 as of the year 2000. From age two through 50, the price is $771.50, and at 51 years of age, the price drops to $441.50. Once you have a lifetime license, you retain it regardless of your residency.

❑   A separate salmon or steelhead permit is required
❑   Valid fishing licenses/permits are required for anyone who fishes, except residents under 14 years.

Fishing License	Age	Fee
RESIDENT		
Lifetime	varies	varies
Season	17 and over	$23.50
Junior Season	14 to 17	$12.50
Daily	14 and over	$10.50
NONRESIDENT		
Season	17 and over	$74.50
Junior Season	14 to 17	$38
Daily	14 and over	$10.50

❐ Nonresidents under 14 may fish without a license if accompanied by the holder of a valid license. Fish taken by the child must be included in the bag limit of the license holder.

❐ Nonresidents under 14 may buy a fishing license and be entitled to an individual bag limit.

❐ Anglers may extend a one-day license at the time of purchase by paying $4 for each consecutive day.

BOATING REGULATIONS

The Idaho State Parks and Recreation regulates all boating activities. Boating regulations are published on its web site (*www.idahoparks.org*), or you can obtain a copy by calling (208) 334-4199.

Float tubes are considered a "vessel" in Idaho. You must have a Coast Guard-approved-PFD and a sound-producing device onboard, such as a whistle or horn.

RESOURCES

Idaho Department of Fish & Game
Phone number/s: (208) 334-3700
Web site: www.state.id.us./fishgame

Current Fishing Conditions
Phone number/s: toll-free (800) ASK-FISH
Web site: http://www2.state.id.us/fishgame/askfish.htm

Idaho River Flows
Web site: www.visitid.org/outdoor/rivers/index.hmtl

Idaho Outfitters and Guides Association
Phone number/s: toll-free (800) 847-4843
Web site: www.ioga.org

The Idaho Recreation and Tourism Initiative
Web site: www.idoc.state.id.us/irti *(useful links)*

Idaho State Parks and Recreation
Phone number/s: (208) 334-4199
Web site: www.idahoparks.org

Idaho Department of Commerce
Phone number/s: (208) 334-2470
Web site: www.idoc.state.id.us

Idaho Division of Tourism Development
Phone number/s: toll-free (800) VISIT-ID
Web site: www.visitid.org

Bureau of Land Management
Phone number/s: (208) 373-4000
Web site: www.id.blm.gov

U.S. Forest Service
Phone number/s: (208) 373-4007
Web site: www.fs.fed.us/recreation/states/id.shtml

RV Idaho
(listing of all public and private campgrounds)
Web site: www.idoc.state.id.us/lasso/infonet/csearch.html

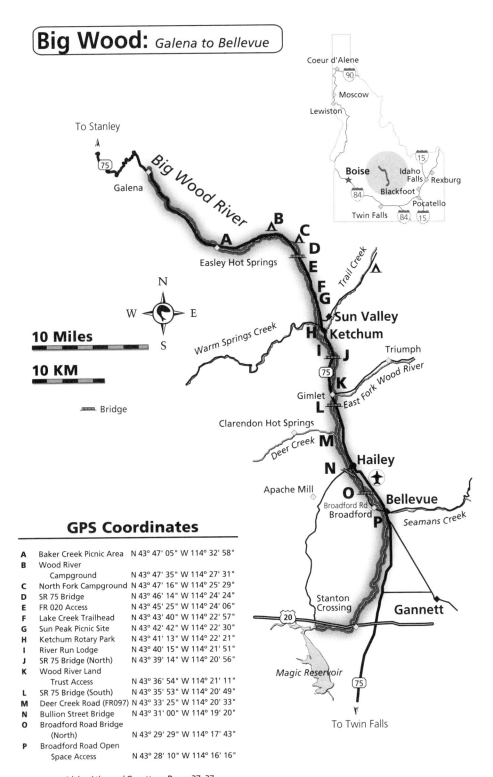

Big Wood: *Galena to Bellevue*

To Stanley

75

Galena

Big Wood River

Easley Hot Springs

A
B
C
D
E
F
G

Trail Creek

Sun Valley
H Ketchum

Warm Springs Creek

I
J Triumph

75

East Fork Wood River

Gimlet
K
L

Clarendon Hot Springs

Deer Creek
M

N Hailey

Apache Mill

O
Broadford Rd
Broadford
P
Bellevue

Seamans Creek

N

W   E

S

10 Miles

10 KM

Bridge

Coeur d'Alene
90
Moscow
Lewiston

Boise
15
Idaho Falls Rexburg
84 Blackfoot
Pocatello
Twin Falls 84 15

Stanton Crossing

20

Gannett

Magic Reservoir

75

To Twin Falls

GPS Coordinates

A	Baker Creek Picnic Area	N 43° 47' 05" W 114° 32' 58"
B	Wood River Campground	N 43° 47' 35" W 114° 27' 31"
C	North Fork Campground	N 43° 47' 16" W 114° 25' 29"
D	SR 75 Bridge	N 43° 46' 14" W 114° 24' 24"
E	FR 020 Access	N 43° 45' 25" W 114° 24' 06"
F	Lake Creek Trailhead	N 43° 43' 40" W 114° 22' 57"
G	Sun Peak Picnic Site	N 43° 42' 42" W 114° 22' 30"
H	Ketchum Rotary Park	N 43° 41' 13" W 114° 22' 21"
I	River Run Lodge	N 43° 40' 15" W 114° 21' 51"
J	SR 75 Bridge (North)	N 43° 39' 14" W 114° 20' 56"
K	Wood River Land Trust Access	N 43° 36' 54" W 114° 21' 11"
L	SR 75 Bridge (South)	N 43° 35' 53" W 114° 20' 49"
M	Deer Creek Road (FR097)	N 43° 33' 25" W 114° 20' 33"
N	Bullion Street Bridge	N 43° 31' 00" W 114° 19' 20"
O	Broadford Road Bridge (North)	N 43° 29' 29" W 114° 17' 43"
P	Broadford Road Open Space Access	N 43° 28' 10" W 114° 16' 16"

Big Wood River

HIGHLIGHT
On a warm winter day, trade your skis for a fly rod

TIP
The Big Wood is southern Idaho's best-kept secret

FISH SPECIES
Predominantly rainbows with a few brook, brown and hybrid cuttbow trout

SEASON
End of May to end of March

rnest Hemingway was a master of understated prose and is considered one of the greatest American writers of the twentieth century. His accomplishments were recognized with both the Pulitzer Prize and the Nobel Prize for Literature. He spent a great deal of time in the Sun Valley area, writing his most financially successful book, *For Whom the Bell Tolls*, in 1940. As an avid fly fisher, he was drawn by the area's rivers, and many of his works reflected his passion for fishing. Suffering from a variety of recurrent physical ailments, he returned to the Big Wood Valley near Ketchum, where he eventually ended his days.

The fine fishing, skiing and other outdoor sports that drew Hemingway to this country are still thriving today. Ketchum and Sun Valley are bustling tourist towns that still offer the same comfort and relaxation they did 50 years ago. The wide variety of restaurants, lodging and recreation opportunities make this area a good choice for a family vacation that includes fly fishing. While nearby Silver Creek has been attracting visitors to the area for years, the Big Wood has remained relatively uncrowded.

It seems no accident that the Big Wood and the more famous Silver Creek are neighbors. They each possess completely different yet complementary characteristics to lure the visiting angler. If Silver Creek is the place where developing fly fishers go to earn their graduate degrees, then the Big Wood is a primary school, where one can learn the basic skills of the sport while getting a few gold stars along the way. The Wood's rainbows are unsophisticated fish living in faster water. Instead of carefully studying each potential meal, they have to decide instantly if something is worth eating. An angler's mistakes and loud movements are often covered by the rushing river, and a day spent on the Big Wood can restore a fly fisher's belief in his or her abilities.

SPECIFIC REGULATIONS AND FEES

From Magic Reservoir flat water upstream to Glendale Diversion:
- ❏ Open Saturday of Memorial Day weekend to November 30.
- ❏ December 1 to March 31: Closed to harvest.

From the Glendale Diversion, approximately three miles below Bellevue, upstream to SR 75 Bridge at milepost 122.2:

❏ Open Saturday of Memorial Day weekend to November 30.

❏ Trout limit: two; none between 12 inches and 16 inches.

❏ December 1 to March 31: Closed to harvest.

From SR 75 Bridge at milepost 122.2 upstream to the mouth of the North Fork:

❏ Open Saturday of Memorial Day weekend to March 31.

❏ Catch-and-release only.

The river is closed to fishing from the first of April to Memorial Day Weekend to protect spawning trout.

TACTICS

The Big Wood is an uncomplicated river where "what you see is what you get." Mayflies make up the bulk of hatch activity, and any reasonable imitation will usually receive a response when trout are feeding on the surface. Jim Santa of Sturtevants says, "Day in and day out, a parachute Adams is the standard dry fly for the Big Wood." Look for trout on current seams and against the banks, and remember that the river's rainbows will hold in very fast water at times.

Nymph fishing can be quite straightforward as well, with prince nymphs and hare's ears reliably producing trout. Fishing with nine-foot leaders down to 4x or 5x and a strike indicator is the preferred method. In the early season, try dead drifting a woolly bugger with a prince nymph trailer.

Streamers also work well in the early season with muddlers and sinkers being favored. A sink-tip line is helpful in getting your fly down to the trout. Local guides

PHOTO: DARREN SUTHERLAND

Keep a low profile and work the current seams on the Big Wood.

Hatch Chart   AVAILABILITY

Food Items	J	F	M	A	M	J	J	A	S	O	N	D
Midges	X	X	X	X	X	X	X	X	X	X	X	X
Blue-winged olives			X	X	X	X	X	X	X	X	X	
Pale morning duns						X	X					
Green drakes						X	X					
Red quills						X	X	X	X	X		
Tricos							X	X	X			
Golden stoneflies						X	X					
Caddisflies						X	X	X	X			
Terrestrials							X	X	X			

Insects	Suggested Fly Patterns
Midges	Griffith's gnats (#16-20), grizzly midges (#16-20), midge pupae, brown, red and black (#16-20)
Blue-winged olives	olive comparaduns (#18-20), parachute Adams (#18-20), thorax BWOs (#18-20), Quigley cripples, olive (#18-20), pheasant tails (#16-20), hare's ears (#16-20), bead-head pheasant tails (#16-20), bead-head hare's ears (#16-20)
Pale morning duns	comparaduns, cream (#16-18), thorax duns, cream (#16-18), cream parachutes (#16-18), sparkle duns (#16-18), Quigley cripples, cream (#16-18), rusty spinners (#16-18), pheasant tails(#16-18), bead-head pheasant tails (#16-18)
Green drakes	green drake Wulffs (#8-12), olive paradrakes (#10-12), olive comparaduns (#10-12), Quigley cripples, olive (#8-12), soft-hackle emergers, olive (#8-12), CDC emergers, olive (#10-14), hare's ears, olive (#10-14), zug bugs (#10-14)
Red quills	H&L variants (#10-16), red quills (#10-16), parachute Adams (#10-16), Adams (#10-16), pheasant tails (#10-16), hare's ears (#10-16)
Tricos	trico poly spinners (#18-22), trico CDC spinners (#18-22), parachute Adams (#18-22), pheasant tails (#18-20)
Golden stoneflies	yellow stimulators (#10-16), prince nymphs (#10-16), bead-head prince nymphs (#10-16), golden stonefly nymphs (#10-16), copper Johns (#10-16)
Caddisflies	elk-hair caddis (#14-18), partridge caddis (#14-18), Goddard caddis (#14-18), stimulators (#14-18)
Terrestrials	Dave's hoppers (#8-12), fur ants, black (#14-18), deer-hair beetles, black (#14-16)

The Big Wood's equivalent of a gold star.

jokingly call one popular pattern the "mortgage maker." It seems that everyone ties it differently, so check with area shops for their version of this effective fly.

HOW TO GET THERE

There is regular air service into Hailey, which will put you on the ground next to the Big Wood. Boise and Idaho Falls have larger airports, and both are about 140 miles from Hailey or about a three-hour drive.

To reach Hailey from Boise, travel southwest 43 miles on I-84, then take Exit 95 at Mountain Home and go east 83 miles on US 20, finally turning north on SR 75.

From Idaho Falls, go west on US 20 for about 130 miles before turning onto SR 75 and driving the last 15 miles north to Hailey. This route will bring you past Craters of the Moon National Monument, which is well worth a visit to those interested in geology.

ACCESSIBILITY

The Big Wood is a steep, free-flowing river, dropping 1,000 feet in the 25 or so miles from the North Fork to Bellevue. This river gains size rather quickly as it moves downstream. Near the confluence with the North Fork, the Big Wood is only a fair-sized mountain stream, yet it gets larger and stronger as it runs through Ketchum. By the time it reaches Hailey, it is a good-sized river and can be difficult to wade across. It runs over cobble rock and can change its course from year to year. There are many islands and side channels, often with steep or loose banks, and thick brush can grow right to the water's edge. Wear sturdy felt-soled wading boots to fish the Big Wood. Wading staffs and studded boots add an extra measure of security.

This is a fairly easy river to access, and the fishing pressure seems to be evenly spread over the major points of entry. Idaho SR 75 follows the river, and anglers can start fishing from any of the bridges where the highway crosses the river. Downstream from Ketchum, there are some side roads that also give access away from the noise and traffic along the highway. There is much private land in this area, but you can walk through as long as you stay below the high-water mark.

North of Ketchum is the Lake Creek trailhead, which has restrooms and a hiking/biking trail that leads up the river and makes it easy to reach some of the delightful pools that can be found on this stretch. Remember that the river is catch-and-release from Ketchum to the North Fork.

WHEN TO GO

Although the Big Wood is a freestone river, there is some good winter fishing. You can plan a ski trip to Sun Valley and squeeze in a little midge fishing on warmer afternoons. The blue-winged olives will usually get started before the ski season ends.

The best fishing occurs as run-off subsides in late June or early July, when you can find green drakes, red quills and golden stones all hatching in unison. Just be prepared for challenging wading as the flow can still be quite strong, even though it may be low and clear enough to fish. Fishing continues strong through the summer.

Sun Valley and Ketchum are popular resort areas in summer and winter, but tourism really slows down in the fall. Visitors can find more lodging options in town at this time as well as more room on the river.

CHECK RIVER FLOWS ON THE WEB
http://idaho.usgs.gov./rt-cgi/gen_tbl_pg

AREA ATTRACTIONS

Sun Valley Resort is one of the premier ski resorts in the country and was the site of the first modern chairlift back in the 1930s. Summer activities include golf, tennis, horseback riding, trap and skeet shooting, indoor and outdoor ice skating, swimming, biking and rollerblading. Like other ski resort towns, Sun Valley offers an array of activities to keep a family with diverse interests content. The Sun Valley Living web site offers listings of food, fun, lodging, nightlife and more. Log onto *www.svliving.com*.

RESOURCES

There is public camping in the Sawtooth National Recreatio Area. To reserve campsites, call the National Recreation Reservation System at (800) 280-CAMP.

Campgrounds

SAWTOOTH NATIONAL RECREATION AREA

For more information, call the Twin Falls Ranger District at (208) 737-3200.

- ❏ Easley
- ❏ North Fork
- ❏ Wood River

For more information, call the Ketchum Ranger District at (208) 622-5371.

- ❏ Federal Gulch

BELLEVUE

Riverside RV Park & Campground
403 Broadford Road
Bellevue, ID 83313
Phone number/s: (208) 788-2020

KETCHUM

Sun Valley RV Resort
106 Meadow Circle
Ketchum, ID 83340
Phone number/s: (208) 726-3429

The Meadows RV Park
13 Broadway Run
Ketchum, ID 83340
Phone number/s: (208) 726-5445

Lodging

BELLEVUE

Come On Inn
Beech and Main St.
Bellevue, ID 83313
Phone number/s: (208) 788-0825

KETCHUM

Lift Tower Lodge
703 S. Main St.
Ketchum, ID 83340
Phone number/s: (208) 726-5163,
toll-free (800) 462-8646
Fax: (208) 726-2614
Web site: http://vestra.net/lifttowerlodge
E-mail: imre@micron.net

Premiere Resorts at Sun Valley
333 S. Main
Ketchum, ID 83340
Phone number/s: (208) 727-4000
Web site: www.premierresortssv.com

Sun Valley Area Reservations
460 Sun Valley Road, # 201
Ketchum, ID 83340
Phone number/s: (208) 726-3660

Sun Valley Resort
One Sun Valley Road
P.O. Box 10
Sun Valley, UD 83353-0010
Phone number/s: (800) 786-8259
Web site: www.sunvalley.com

Tackle Shops and Outfitters

HAILEY

Sturtevants
Main Street and Carbonate
Hailey, ID 83333
Phone number/s: (208) 788-7847

KETCHUM

Lost River Outfitters
171 N. Main
Ketchum, ID 83340
Phone number/s: (208) 726-1706
Web site: www.lostriveroutfitters.com

Silver Creek Outfitters, Inc.
500 N. Main St.
Ketchum, ID 83340
Phone number/s: (208) 726-5282,
toll-free (800) 732-5687
Fax: (208) 726-9056
Web site: www.silver-creek.com
E-mail: silvercreek@flyshop.com

SUN VALLEY

Wood River Outfitters, LLC
P.O. Box 271
Sun Valley, ID 83353
Phone number/s: (208) 725-0666
Fax: (208) 726-2922
E-mail: headwaters@svidaho.net

Henry's Fork of the Snake River

T he Henry's Fork is one of the crown jewels of Rocky Mountain fly fishing. It arises in Island Park from the world's largest caldera, a broad crater-like remnant of a collapsed volcano. Clear, cold spring water makes its way to the surface though channels in the remaining basalt rock and gives birth to the river at Big Springs, which gushes forth nearly ½ million gallons of water per day. The myriad springs and tailwater outflow of two reservoirs gives the Henry's Fork the high quality water that makes for strong and fast-growing trout.

The river's fishing potential was recognized at the turn of the last century. Wealthy, speculative Easterners began buying up the holdings of the area's original homesteaders and incorporated the Island Park Land and Cattle Company in 1902. Many owners were also involved in railroads, and the large tract of land known as the Railroad Ranch was used as a summer resort for its affluent owners. Eventually, the Harriman family of the Union Pacific Railroad became the sole owners. In 1977, the Harrimans donated the ranch to the state of Idaho — under the conditions that it would remain an operating ranch, a bird sanctuary and fly-fishing water only. Harriman State Park would be preserved for the enjoyment of future generations.

In years past, the Henry's Fork has been a battleground with irrigators and environmentalists at odds over water rights and dam operation. Tensions remained high for years, but in 1992, draining of the Island Park Dam caused an estimated 50,000 tons of sediment to be flushed into the most famous water of the river, destroying a huge amount of fish habitat. This sad event became the catalyst that brought the Henry's Fork Foundation and the local irrigation district together in a cooperative element. The Henry's Fork Watershed Council was established to address watershed issues, with consideration of individual interests and mutual respect for all parties. A couple high-water years have helped the river recover from the sedimentation, and the new spirit of cooperative management in the watershed promises a bright future for this fabled river.

The attention the Henry's Fork receives as one of the most famous fly-fishing rivers in the Rocky Mountains is justified. No other river offers such an incredible variety of water in such a short space. There is simple fishing for mostly smaller trout on the river above Island Park Reservoir, "power fishing" with big nymphs and streamers for the Box Canyon's big rainbows, or the difficult and demanding dry-fly fishing for the Railroad Ranch's educated trout. All of this comes in an incredibly scenic package of alpine meadows, with Upper Mesa Falls the glory of

HIGHLIGHT
Landing a trout on the Railroad Ranch section

TIP
Positioning and presentation are everything

FISH SPECIES
Brown, rainbow, also brook and cutthroat trout

SEASON
Varies depending on stretch of water

this area's natural beauty. While the Henry's Fork offers so much by itself, it is in the center of the Rocky Mountain West's best fly fishing, and only a short drive into Yellowstone Park.

SPECIFIC REGULATIONS

From the Old US 20 Bridge (Del Rio Bridge approximately one mile north of St. Anthony) upstream to Ashton Dam:
- Open all year
- No motors.
- Trout limit: two; none under 16 inches.

From Vernon (Fritz) Bridge to Ashton Dam:
- Trout limit: two; none under 16 inches.
- No motors.
- Open Saturday of Memorial Day weekend through November 30.

From Ashton Dam to US 20 (Wendell) Bridge:
- Open year-round.

From US 20 (Wendell) Bridge to Warm River:
- Trout limit: two; none under 16 inches
- No motors.
- Open year-round.

From Warm River to the posted boundary upstream from Riverside campground:
- Trout limit: two; none under 16 inches.
- No motors.
- Open Saturday of Memorial Day weekend through November 30.

From the posted boundary upstream from Riverside campground upstream to Island Park Dam except Harriman State Park:
- Catch-and-release only.
- No motors.
- Open Saturday of Memorial Day weekend through November 30.

Harriman State Park (including East Harriman) except the bird sanctuary:
- Catch-and-release only.
- No motors.
- Open June 15 to September 30.

Harriman Bird Sanctuary (Osborne Bridge upstream to the ranch bridge):
- Catch-and-release only.
- No motors.
- Open June 15 to September 30.

From McCrea Bridge upstream to Macks Inn Bridge:
- ❏ No motors.
- ❏ Open Saturday of Memorial Day weekend through November 30.

From Henry's Lake outlet upstream to and including the head of Big Springs:
- ❏ Closed to fishing.

TACTICS

The upper river near Macks Inn and Coffee Pot Rapids is a good place to acquaint newcomers with the sport of fly fishing. This portion of the Henry's Fork is easy to wade, and thickly forested banks block some of the wind. Even though the area is heavily used for recreation and many trout are harvested, frequent stocking usually means that fish are easily encouraged to eat.

The Box Canyon is a food factory, and its big trout spend most of their time eating larger prey under the water. Stonefly nymphs are the cornerstone of a diet that also includes leeches, sculpins and crayfish, as well as some mayfly and caddis nymphs. Large flies are generally most successful, and sizes 4 to 10 black rubber-

PHOTO: COURTESY OF MIKEY LANGFORD

Mikey Langford and a big hybrid cuttbow from the Henry's Fork, the end result of careful positioning and presentation.

Hatch Chart

AVAILABILITY

Food Items	J	F	M	A	M	J	J	A	S	O	N	D
Midges	X	X	X	X	X	X	X	X	X	X	X	X
Blue-winged olives			X	X	X	X			X	X	X	
Pale morning duns						X	X	X				
Green drakes						X	X					
Flavs						X	X					
Brown drakes						X	X					
Callibaetis							X	X	X			
Gray drakes								X	X			
Mahogany duns								X	X			
Tricos								X	X			
Salmonflies				X	X							
Golden stoneflies						X	X					
Yellow sallys						X						
Caddisflies					X	X	X	X	X	X		
Terrestrials							X	X	X	X		

Insects	Suggested Fly Patterns
Midges	Griffith's gnats (#18-22), grizzly midges (#18-22), Adams (#18-22), midge pupae, cream, red and black (#18-22), brassies (#16-20), serendipities (#18-22), midge emergers, black and peacock (#18-22)
Blue-winged olives	CDC comparaduns, olive (#16-22), parachute Adams (#16-22), thorax BWOs (#16-22), no-hackle duns, olive (#16-22), CDC loopwing emergers, olive (#16-22), Quigley cripples, olive (#16-22), pheasant tails (#16-22), hare's ears (#16-22), WD40s (#16-22), RS2s (#16-22)
Pale morning duns	CDC comparaduns, cream (#16-20), thorax duns, cream (#16-20), cream parachutes (#16-20), sparkle duns (#16-20), no-hackle duns, cream (#16-20), CDC loopwing emergers, cream (#16-20), Quigley cripples, cream (#16-20), rusty spinners (#16-20), pheasant tails (#16-20), hare's ears (#16-20)
Green drakes	olive paradrakes (#10-12), olive comparaduns (#10-12), Quigley cripples, olive (#8-12), soft-hackle emergers, olive (#8-12), CDC emergers, olive (#10-14), hare's ears, olive (#10-14), zug bugs (#10-14)

Insects	Suggested Fly Patterns
Flavs	green drake Wulffs (#14-16), olive parachutes (#14-16), olive comparaduns (#14-16), Quigley cripples, olive (#14-16), olive soft hackle emerger (#14-16), CDC emergers, olive (#14-16), hare's ears, olive (#14-16)
Brown drakes	Lawson's brown paradrakes (#10-14), sparkle duns, brown (#10-14), Quigley cripples, brown (#10-14), hare's ears (#10-14), bead-head hare's ears (#10-14)
Callibaetis	parachute Adams (#14-18), callibaetis thorax duns (#14-18), Quigley cripples, light gray (#14-18), CDC comparaduns, light gray (#14-18), hare's ears (#14-18)
Gray drakes	gray Wulffs (#12-16), parachute Adams (#12-16), gray comparaduns (#12-16), black or gray spinners (#10-12), muskrat nymphs (#14-16), pheasant tails (#14-16), bead-head pheasant tails (#14-16)
Mahogany duns	Harrop's hair-wing duns, brown (#14-16), sparkle duns, brown (#14-16), pheasant tails (#14-16), bead-head pheasant tails (#14-16)
Tricos	trico poly spinners (#18-22), trico CDC spinners (#18-22), parachute Adams (#18-22), pheasant tails (#18-20)
Salmonflies	sofa pillows (#6-10), Mac Salmons (#6-10), orange stimulators (#6-10), bullethead salmonflies (#6-10), rubber-legs, black (#6-10), Bitch Creek nymphs (#6-10), Brook's stone nymphs (#6-10)
Golden stoneflies	yellow stimulators (#8-12), prince nymphs (#8-10), bead-head prince nymphs (#8-10), golden stonefly nymphs (#6-10), Bitch Creek nymphs (#6-10), copper Johns (#10-14)
Yellow sallys	yellow stimulators (#12-16), Flint's stones (#12-16), irresistible stimulators, yellow (#12-16), red fox squirrel nymphs (#14-18)
Caddisflies	elk-hair caddis (#16-18), partridge caddis (#16-18), Hemingway caddis (#16-18), CDC elk-hair caddis (#16-18), CDC caddis (#16-18), sparkle caddis (#16-18), X-caddis (#16-18), peeking caddis (#14-16), bead-head peeking caddis (#14-16), olive serendipities (#14-16)
Terrestrials	Dave's hoppers (#8-12), Lawson's Henry's Fork hoppers (#8-12), fur ants, black (#14-18), CDC ants (#14-18), deer-hair beetles, black (#14-16), hi-vis foam beetles (#14-16)

legs fished deep on a minimum of 3x leader will hook and hold the big trout. Add a bead-head dropper fly like a prince nymph, hare's ear or pheasant tail to cover the bases. Fish the deepest, fastest water you can find. If you can stand in it, fish can hold in it. Bring plenty of flies. If you aren't making periodic sacrifices to the river's basalt rocks, you are probably not fishing deep enough. Fishing streamers early and late in the day can bring some big fish to net.

Once you break out into the smooth water at Last Chance, all the rules change. Fish on the Railroad Ranch have seen it all and are not easily fooled. Many anglers come here to test their skills on what many consider is one of the most challenging pieces of river in the West. You will need long, light leaders, usually 10- to 12-foot tapered leaders, and add two to three feet of 5x tippet. Fly selection is important. Mike Lawson of Henry's Fork Anglers has developed many low-floating patterns specifically for this river. Even these preparations won't guarantee fish. Mikey Langford has spent more than a decade guiding in Island Park and believes that "positioning and presentation are everything on the Railroad Ranch." This means a careful approach, a low profile, a gentle cast and usually a downstream drift. Get it all right and you will be in the hunt for one of the river's most challenging trophies.

Once you drop down into the canyon above the falls, fast-water fishing techniques again come into play. Attractor dry flies like royal Wulffs and stimulators work well, and adding a bead-head dropper nymph will increase an angler's chances for success. Stoneflies thrive in the fast water found here, so try black rubber-legs and prince nymphs under the surface.

PHOTO: STEVE SCHMIDT

Everything comes together for this Henry's Fork angler.

The river between the Lower Falls and Ashton provides consistently good float fishing from early summer to late fall. Slapping big dry salmonfly imitations against the banks is very good in the later days of May. When the salmonfly hatch fades, return to the same attractor dry flies and nymphs that are effective above the falls, or chuck some streamers. Zonkers, muddlers and other baitfish imitations will take some good fish.

Below Ashton Dam, you can expect good midge fishing in the winter months, but caddis are the big draw on this section. Make sure you're on the water in the evenings when the heaviest activity occurs. Accurate casting is important for success during very heavy hatches, or you can swing a swimming caddis to garner extra attention.

HOW TO GET THERE

The two airports closest to the Henry's Fork are West Yellowstone (just over ½ hour) or Idaho Falls (about 1 ½ hours). West Yellowstone only has regular air service from June 1 to September 30, while Idaho Falls has regular flights throughout the year.

Last Chance, Idaho, is the epicenter of fly fishing on the Henry's Fork. To reach it from West Yellowstone, Montana, just hop on US 20 and head southwest about 30 miles. If you are driving up from Idaho Falls and I-15, take US 20 northeast a little over 70 miles.

ACCESSIBILITY

Henry's Fork has its beginning at Big Springs, where you can stop and admire the giant trout that wait under the bridge for handouts. However, you can't fish the Henry's Fork until it is joined by the Henry's Lake Outlet. The section of the river from Big Springs' boat launch downstream to Macks Inn or Upper Coffee Pot campground is a popular canoe trip. There are trout to be had in this section, and the river is mostly slow and relaxing. Many anglers enjoy the short but steep hike down to Coffee Pot rapids, or you can park at Macks Inn or either of the two Coffee Pot campgrounds. Trout are mostly small and there are plenty of brook trout, but in the early season you can find some large rainbows that come up from Island Park Reservoir.

Below Island Park Reservoir is the well-known Box Canyon section of the Henry's Fork. Cold, clear water emerges from the dam and rushes down though the steep, walled canyon in the black volcanic rock. There are many mild rapids and riffles as the Henry's Fork speeds over the rock-strewn riverbed. Rainbows flourish in the fast flow. Anglers can choose between wading or floating the river, and the hard-working guides of the Henry's Fork have developed a hybrid approach that is somewhat of a combination of both. They row clients down the river, and at the best water, jump out to walk the boat slowly downstream, giving their clients a much better opportunity to hook one of the trophy fish that reside here. The Box Canyon float is fairly short, at about three miles if you put in below the dam and take out at the Last Chance boat ramp. During the very busy salmonfly hatch, you

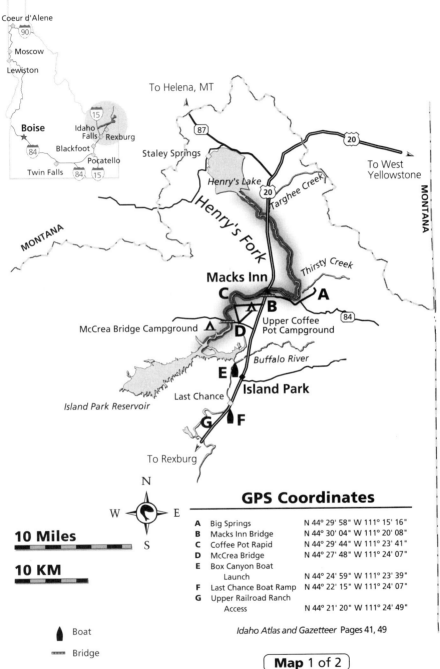

Henry's Fork: *Henry's Lake to Island Park*

Coeur d'Alene
90
Moscow
Lewiston

Boise
Idaho
Falls
Rexburg
Blackfoot
84
Pocatello
Twin Falls
84 15

To Helena, MT

87
20

To West
Yellowstone

Staley Springs

Henry's Lake
20

Targhee Creek

Henry's Fork

MONTANA

MONTANA

Thirsty Creek

Macks Inn
C
B
A

McCrea Bridge Campground
D
Upper Coffee
Pot Campground
84

Buffalo River

E
Island Park

Last Chance

Island Park Reservoir
G F

To Rexburg

WYOMING

N
W E
S

10 Miles

10 KM

GPS Coordinates

A	Big Springs	N 44° 29' 58" W 111° 15' 16"
B	Macks Inn Bridge	N 44° 30' 04" W 111° 20' 08"
C	Coffee Pot Rapid	N 44° 29' 44" W 111° 23' 41"
D	McCrea Bridge	N 44° 27' 48" W 111° 24' 07"
E	Box Canyon Boat	
	Launch	N 44° 24' 59" W 111° 23' 39"
F	Last Chance Boat Ramp	N 44° 22' 15" W 111° 24' 07"
G	Upper Railroad Ranch	
	Access	N 44° 21' 20" W 111° 24' 49"

Idaho Atlas and Gazetteer Pages 41, 49

Boat

Bridge

Map 1 of 2

Henry's Fork: *Island Park to St. Anthony*

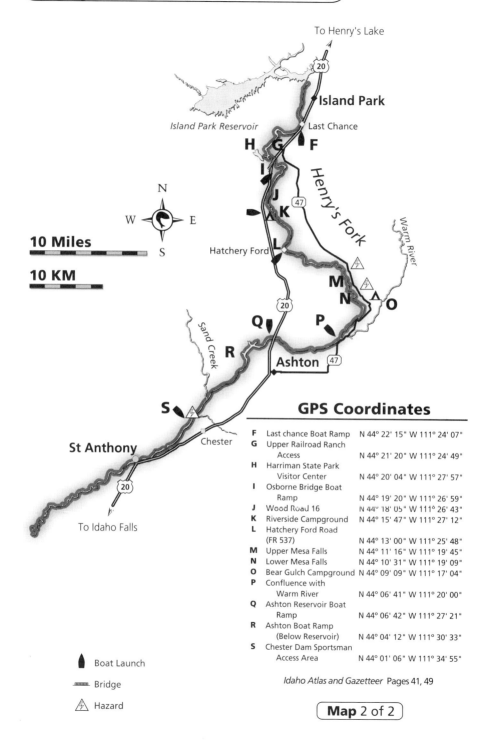

To Henry's Lake

Island Park

Island Park Reservoir

Last Chance

H G F

I

J

47

K

Hatchery Ford

L

Henry's Fork

Warm River

M

N

O

P

20

Q

Sand Creek

R

Ashton 47

S

St Anthony

Chester

To Idaho Falls

20

N
W E
S

10 Miles

10 KM

GPS Coordinates

F	Last chance Boat Ramp	N 44° 22' 15" W 111° 24' 07"
G	Upper Railroad Ranch Access	N 44° 21' 20" W 111° 24' 49"
H	Harriman State Park Visitor Center	N 44° 20' 04" W 111° 27' 57"
I	Osborne Bridge Boat Ramp	N 44° 19' 20" W 111° 26' 59"
J	Wood Road 16	N 44° 18' 05" W 111° 26' 43"
K	Riverside Campground	N 44° 15' 47" W 111° 27' 12"
L	Hatchery Ford Road (FR 537)	N 44° 13' 00" W 111° 25' 48"
M	Upper Mesa Falls	N 44° 11' 16" W 111° 19' 45"
N	Lower Mesa Falls	N 44° 10' 31" W 111° 19' 09"
O	Bear Gulch Campground	N 44° 09' 09" W 111° 17' 04"
P	Confluence with Warm River	N 44° 06' 41" W 111° 20' 00"
Q	Ashton Reservoir Boat Ramp	N 44° 06' 42" W 111° 27' 21"
R	Ashton Boat Ramp (Below Reservoir)	N 44° 04' 12" W 111° 30' 33"
S	Chester Dam Sportsman Access Area	N 44° 01' 06" W 111° 34' 55"

Idaho Atlas and Gazetteer Pages 41, 49

◗ Boat Launch

▭ Bridge

⚠ Hazard

Map 2 of 2

can avoid much of the crowds by putting on early, having lunch in Last Chance, and then launching again in the afternoon. Access is right below Island Park Dam, where there is a boat launch area. Or, park at Box Canyon campground and make the short walk to the river. If you wade the Box Canyon, exercise caution, especially during high-water periods. Wading belts and staffs are recommended for safety.

As the river emerges from the Box Canyon at Last Chance, it changes character dramatically. It spreads out and slows down, becoming a wide, smooth spring creek. The Harriman State Park (Railroad Ranch) begins here and continues on downstream to a point about 2½ miles below Osborne Bridge. These miles of the most famous water on the Henry's Fork can be fairly crowded. It is easily wadeable and well-worn trails make it easy to walk up and down the river. Access points are the parking lot across US 20 and just south of Last Chance, the mailbox about two miles south of Last Chance (one mile walk to the river), and Osborne Bridge. You can also park at the Harriman State Park Visitor Center for a small fee. Some anglers float this section of the river from Last Chance to Osborne Bridge. It is a great way for anglers with limited mobility to experience the Railroad Ranch, but the able-bodied will usually find wading a better option.

Below the state park there is access to another mile or more of slow water at Wood Road 16, and then the gradient increases and the river picks up speed as it enters the deep canyon that contains Upper and Lower Mesa Falls. Osborne Bridge to Riverside campground is a fairly popular float, or if your skills are up to it, you can float from Riverside to Hatchery Ford. This stretch is Class II water with a lot of rocks to be avoided; fishing often takes a back seat to safe navigation. This section

PHOTO STEVE SCHMIDT

Railroad Ranch demands an angler's best presentation skills on its slow, still waters.

PHOTO: COURTESY OF BOB JOHNSON

Bob Johnson with a giant Box Canyon rainbow.

of the river has mostly small fish but can be good during either the salmonfly or golden stonefly hatch. Do not miss the take-out at Hatchery Ford! This is the last take-out before the falls. There is good foot access at Hatchery Ford both upstream and down, but keep in mind that there are dangerous falls downstream.

Upper and Lower Mesa Falls are well worth a visit. Both have view areas where you can pause a moment and feel the power of the falling water as it vibrates up through the soles of your feet. If you are looking for some "extreme fly fishing," then the Cardiac Canyon float might interest you. There is a rough road that leads from the Grandview campground by the Lower Mesa Falls Overlook to the very brink of the canyon. From this point, it is about ¼ mile to the river and the steep trail drops about 600 feet to the water. People really do slide rafts and other watercraft down this steep incline to launch below. This canyon has some good fish and incredible scenery, as well as Class II to III rapids. Floaters should make their first trip down Cardiac Canyon with an experienced guide. You can walk down into this rugged canyon from the Bear Gulch campground.

The take-out for the Cardiac Canyon float is at the confluence with Warm River, which is also the start for a nice float down to Ashton Reservoir. There is good shore access to this section, but the river is quite large after the Warm River joins in, so there is a distinct advantage to floating.

There is one more quality section of river below Ashton Dam. This stretch has the highest density of trout on the Henry's Fork, and there are some very big individuals in the Chester Backwaters. Waders can hike down a short trail between the dam and the first bridge, or you can launch a boat just downstream (east bank) from the bridge on Atchley Road, just three miles west of US 20 at Ashton. The take-out is just above the Chester diversion dam (note: this is the diversion just below the confluence with the Falls River), which you should be very careful to avoid. From this point downstream there are several diversion dams and steep drops. If you wish to float below this point, you should first go with an experienced guide or someone familiar with the river. Public access for waders is limited as well.

> **CHECK RIVER FLOWS ON THE WEB**
> http://idaho.usgs.gov./rt-cgi/gen_tbl_pg

WHEN TO GO

While some of the lower portion of the Henry's Fork is open year-round, most of the river doesn't open until Saturday of Memorial Day weekend. At this time, salmonfly nymphs are beginning to get active, and the hatch of the adult insect begins above Ashton Reservoir and works its way up through the faster sections of the river, reaching the Box Canyon by the first or second week of June most years.

When the Railroad Ranch opens in mid-June, it draws the bulk of angler attention. Hatches are in full swing for the opener, with blue-winged olives, pale morning duns and caddis on hand to greet returning fly fishers. Green drakes quickly follow as do the even larger brown drakes. Green drakes are most important on the upper reaches of the Ranch near Last Chance and usually hatch in greatest numbers from morning through midday. The brown drakes — more of an evening hatch — prefer the slower flows down by the state park visitor center and Osborne Bridge. At this same time, there are heavy hatches of caddis every evening below Ashton Dam.

By July, many anglers move on to other rivers and you can find a little more room on the famous Henry's Fork. Pale morning duns, flavs and the elusive gray drakes can keep things interesting through the end of the month. Callibaetis, tricos and terrestrials fill out the hatch situation for August.

September may well be the best time to fish the Henry's Fork. The Railroad Ranch is uncrowded and weather can be beautiful. Blue-winged olives and the larger mahogany duns will continue to bring trout to the river's surface until the state park closes to fishing at the end of the month. Water levels drop in the Box Canyon, allowing anglers to wade the river effectively and fish big nymphs and streamers to big trout that get aggressive with the cool weather. Fishing here and below the state park continues until the end of November.

AREA ATTRACTIONS

Harriman State Park is a 16,000-acre wildlife reserve on the Henry's Fork that originally belonged to the Harriman family of Union Pacific Railroad fame. The state park and Red Rock Lakes National Wildlife Refuge combine to protect habitat important to the rare and beautiful trumpeter swan, the world's heaviest flying bird. Rescued from near extinction, trumpeters breeding in the Greater Yellowstone ecosystem have grown in number from a low of only 69 birds in 1932 to more than 500 at present.

Visiting anglers stand a good chance of seeing a trumpeter swan while fishing at Harriman park, or you can make the short trip over the pass to the Red Rocks Refuge. Drive up over the Red Rock Pass Road (reach it from SR 87 north of Henry's Lake, then go southwest for 5 ½ miles on Henry's Lake Road). Take binoculars or a spotting scope and perhaps you will get a look at one of these graceful and elegant birds.

RESOURCES

There is abundant camping in the Henry's Fork area or stay at one of the cool, rustic lodges. If you're looking for budget accommodations, head to West Yellowstone, only a ½-hour drive from the Henry's Fork.

Campgrounds

STATE PARK

Henry's Lake State Park
3917 E. 5100 N.
Island Park, ID 83429
Phone number/s: (208) 558-7532
E-mail: hen@idpr.state.id.us

TARGHEE NATIONAL FOREST

For information, call the Ashton Ranger District at (208) 652-7442.

❏ Riverside
❏ Warm River

For camp reservations, call the Island Park District at (208) 558-7301.

❏ Big Springs
❏ Box Canyon
❏ Buffalo Loops
❏ Buttermilk
❏ Flat Rock
❏ Upper Coffee Pot

ISLAND PARK

Snowy River Campground
HC 66 Box 431, 3502 N Hwy. 20
Island Park, ID 83429
Phone number/s: (208) 558-7112,
toll-free (888) 797-3434
Fax: (208) 558-7112
Web site: snowyriver.com
E-mail: marleenb@ida.net

Staley Springs Lodge
HC66 Box 102
Island Park, ID 83429
Phone number/s: (208) 558-7471
Fax: (208) 558-7300
E-mail: staleys@fretel.com

ST. ANTHONY

Sandhills Resort Inc.
865 Redroad
St. Anthony, ID 83445
Phone number/s: (208) 624-4127
Fax: (208) 624-3727
Web site: www.sand-dunes.com
E-mail: sandhills@fretel.com

Lodging

ISLAND PARK/MACKS INN

A-Bar Motel & Supper Club
HC 65 Box 452
Island Park, ID 83429
Phone number/s: (208) 558-7358,
toll-free (800) 286-7358 (reservations only)
Fax: (208) 558-7790
E-mail: abar@fremontnet.com

Aspen Lodge
HC 66 Box 269
Island Park, ID 83429
Phone number/s: (208) 558-7407,
toll-free (800) 755-7407
Fax: (208) 558-7407
Web site: www.idaho4fun.com
E-mail: snow@fremontnet.com

Macks Inn
Pond's Lodge
US 20
Island Park, ID 83429
Phone number/s: (208) 558-7221,
toll-free (888) 731-5153

Village Motel and RV Park
4080 Sawtelle Peak
Island Park, ID 83429
Phone number/s: (208) 558-9366
Fax: (208) 558-9769
Web site: www.outbackrealty.com

Tackle Shops and Outfitters

ST. ANTHONY

Henry's Fork Anglers, Inc.
340 N. 7th E.
St. Anthony, ID 83445
Phone number/s: (208) 624-3590,
toll-free (800) 788-4479
Fax: (208) 624-3595
E-mail: henfork@ida.net

ASHTON

Three Rivers Ranch
1662 SR 47
Ashton, ID 83420
Phone: (208) 652-3750
Web site: www.ThreeRiversRanch.com
E-mail: 3rivers@ida.net

Trouthunter, LLC
HC 66, Box 477
Island Park, ID 83429
Phone number/s: (208) 558-9900
E-mail: trout@fretel.com

ST. ANTHONY

Harrop Flies
33 W. 4th N.
St. Anthony, ID 83445
Phone number/s: (208) 624-3537

WEST YELLOWSTONE

Blue Ribbon Flies
315 Canyon St.
West Yellowstone, MT 59758
Phone number/s: (406) 646-7642

Bud Lilly's Trout Shop
39 Madison Ave.
West Yellowstone, MT 59758
Phone number/s: (406) 646-7630.
toll-free (800) 854-9559
Web site: www.budlillys.com

Area Attractions

Harriman State Park
3489 E. US 20
Island Park, ID 83429
Phone number/s: (208) 558-7368
Fax: (208) 558-7045
E-mail: HAR@idpr.state.id.us

Silver Creek

HIGHLIGHT
Demanding dry-fly fishing with some very large fish present

TIP
Downstream presentations work best

FISH SPECIES
Rainbow and brown trout with a few brookies

SEASON
Varies depending on stretch of water

T here is a verdant oasis flowing past the exposed, dry Timmerman Hills of southern Idaho. Surrounded by high desert, the cold, clear waters of Silver Creek nourish native plant and animal species as well as some exceptional trout. While other watersheds have been sacrificed for development, in effect strangled by those who love them too closely, the unique ecosystem that is Silver Creek is being preserved by an unprecedented partnership. At the urging of Ernest Hemingway's son Jack, the Nature Conservancy purchased the Sun Valley Ranch in 1976 to form the Silver Creek Preserve, which has since expanded to nearly 900 acres. A large tract, to be sure, but not nearly enough to protect a watershed. The whole story includes the landowners of the Silver Creek Valley, who have voluntarily donated conservation easements on 8,500 acres of privately owned lands.

This unity of purpose has preserved the consistent flow of cold, clean spring water into Silver Creek. By preserving riparian habitat, tributary streams stay shaded and cooler. Native grasses and vegetation hold banks together, minimizing sedimentation and allowing natural undercuts to form and shelter trout. Conservation easements prevent future owners from subdividing sensitive areas, protecting this unique green valley from the negative impacts of increased development for generations to come.

Silver Creek begins at the confluence of two spring-fed creeks, Grove and Stalker. There are no streams carrying surface water down from the dry hills above, so the flows are entirely made up of spring water. This flow creates near ideal habitat for the creek's resident rainbows, browns and brooks. Estimates put Silver Creek's trout population at over 5,000 per mile, with some trout in excess of two feet, patiently holding above the weeds as they wait for their next meal to float by.

On many freestone rivers, finding fish is the challenge — but not so on Silver Creek. If you are present during a good hatch, the trout will be self-evident. It is fooling them that can require much of an angler's skill. Once that is accomplished, the fortunate fly fisher is often faced with trying to land a big, strong trout on extremely light tippet amongst the creek's thick aquatic weeds. A problem many of us find as pleasant as it is difficult.

SPECIFIC REGULATIONS AND FEES

The Silver Creek Preserve is open to the public and there is no charge. There is a suggested donation of $5 per day to help cover the preserve's operating budget of around $150,000/year. If you consider what it costs to fish other privately owned (and much smaller) spring creeks, this is one of fly fishing's best bargains.

Lush Silver Creek flows through the dry hills of southern Idaho

Silver Creek and its tributaries:
- No motors.
- All diversion ponds have the same regulations as stream segments.

Downstream from Highway 93:
- Open all year.

From US 93 upstream to the bridge at milepost 187.2 on US 20 west of Picabo:
- Trout limit: two; none between 12 and 16 inches.
- Open Saturday of Memorial Day weekend through November 30.
- Closed to harvest December 1 to February 28.

From the bridge at milepost 187.2 on US 20 west of Picabo upstream to the road right-of-way fence on the west side of Kilpatrick Bridge:
- Catch-and-release only
- No fishing from rafts or boats; float tubes permissible.
- Open Saturday of Memorial Day weekend through November 30.

You might have to share the river with locals on the Silver Creek Preserve.

From the road right-of-way fence on the west side of Kilpatrick Bridge upstream and all waters within The Nature Conservancy Silver Creek Preserve property:
- Fly fishing only.
- Catch-and-release only.
- No fishing from rafts or boats; float tubes permissible.
- Open Saturday of Memorial Day weekend through November 30.

TACTICS

There are many ways to fly fish at Silver Creek, but most anglers journey here to match the prolific hatches with dry flies. It is demanding and challenging fishing, where all of a fly fisher's skills and knowledge can be brought into play. The first order of business is to find some sizeable rising fish. This is fairly easy to accomplish on these rich waters; just check with one of the local shops for the timing of the hatches so that you show up during prime time. For most of the season, there is good activity in midmorning and again at dusk.

Once you have found a good group of risers, you are faced with fly selection. At times the choice of fly is quite apparent, with the majority of trout feeding on one stage of one dominant insect; at other times, anglers can be faced with several insects emerging, mating and laying their eggs in the water. When things are this complicated, pick out a single fish and spend 10 or 15 minutes watching the rise forms carefully. Does the mouth come above the surface of the water while feeding, or just the dorsal fin and tail? If you are close enough, pick out an insect in the drift above and watch as it floats over. Make your best selection after this careful observation and be prepared to change flies frequently. Attach your fly to a long, delicate leader, something like 12 to 14 feet tapered down to 6x or 7x. The new fluorocarbon tippet materials can give you an added advantage.

Take time to get into your best casting position. In most cases, this will be upstream about 40 or 50 feet and slightly off to one side. Cast downstream and slightly across, finishing with your rod held high at 10 to 11 o'clock. Lowering your rod tip from this position will give you slack line for the first 10 feet of your drift. Then, shake slack out of the guides to continue your float. If you are blessed with a take, pause slightly and set the hook by moving the rod to the side and away from the fish. Setting the hook too quickly or directly up will often pull the fly out of a trout's mouth when they feed directly below you. If you are refused or ignored, mend line away from your target fish before lifting it off the water for your next cast. Be persistent; you may accurately present the correct fly dozens of times before receiving your reward.

Heavy weed growth can make nymphing difficult on Silver Creek, but if you choose your water carefully, it can be quite productive. Trout that are very selective on the surface may be a little less cautious underneath. Using a small dry fly with a small nymph as a dropper is the preferred method. If you do elect to use strike indicators, the smallest sizes are recommended. Bead-head nymphs can eliminate the need for split shot and give anglers a slightly more subtle presentation.

Float tube anglers can enjoy the lower portion of the Silver Creek Preserve above Kilpatrick Bridge as well as the water running through the Purdy Ranch. Dry-fly fishing is still the method of choice, but stillwater fly-fishing techniques are also effective. Stripping damselfly nymphs and woolly buggers will produce some good fish, even during midday, when there is little hatch activity. Slow-sinking fly lines work well for this type of fishing, and the new clear intermediate lines can give you an extra edge when seeking these shy, selective trout.

Hatch Chart

AVAILABILITY

Food Items	J	F	M	A	M	J	J	A	S	O	N	D
Midges	X	X	X	X	X	X	X	X	X	X	X	X
Blue-winged olives					X	X			X	X	X	
Pale morning duns						X	X	X	X			
Brown drakes					X	X						
Callibaetis							X	X				
Tricos							X	X				
Mahogany duns									X	X	X	
Damselflies						X	X	X				
Caddisflies						X	X	X	X			
Terrestrials						X	X	X	X			

Persistence pays off for Steve Jackson. This big brown ate a size 16 caddis after the sun dropped below the hills.

PHOTO: RICHARD WINKLER

Insects	Suggested Fly Patterns
Midges	Griffith's gnats, adding a post of white or black poly yarn to aid in strike detection (#20-22), grizzly midges (#20-22), Adams (#20-22), midge pupae, cream, red and black (#18-22), brassies (#16-20), serendipities (#18-22), midge emergers, black and peacock (#18-22)
Blue-winged olives	CDC comparaduns, olive (#18-22), parachute Adams (#18-22), thorax BWOs (#18-22), no-hackle duns, olive (#18-22), CDC loopwing emergers, olive (#18-22), Quigley cripples, olive (#18-22), pheasant tails (#16-20), hare's ears (#16-20), WD40s (#16-20), RS2s (#16-20)
Pale morning duns	CDC comparaduns, cream (#16-18), thorax duns, cream (#16-18), cream parachutes (#16-18), sparkle duns (#16-18), no-hackle duns, cream (#16-18), CDC loopwing emergers, cream (#16-18), Quigley cripples, cream (#16-18), floating nymphs, cream (#16-18), rusty spinners (#16-18), pheasant tails (#16-18), hare's ears (#16-18)
Brown drakes	brown paradrakes (#10-12), sparkle duns, brown (#10-12), Quigley cripples, brown (#10-12), hare's ears (#10-12), bead-head hare's ears (#10-12)
Callibaetis	parachute Adams (#14-16), callibaetis thorax duns (#14-16), Quigley cripples, light gray (#14-16), CDC comparaduns, light gray (#14-16), hare's ears (#14-16)
Tricos	trico poly spinners (#18-22), trico CDC spinners (#18-22), parachute Adams (#18-22), pheasant tails (#18-20)
Mahogany duns	Harrop's hair wing duns, brown (#14-16), sparkle duns, brown (#14-16), pheasant tails (#14-16), bead-head pheasant tails (#14-16)
Damselflies	elk-hair damsels, blue (#12-14), blue foam damsels (#12-14), Marabou damselfly nymphs (#10-14), pheasant tail damselfly nymphs (#10-14)
Caddisflies	CDC caddis, olive, tan and brown (#16-18), CDC caddis, black (#18-20), parachute caddis, olive, tan and brown (#16-18), caddis sparkle pupae, olive, tan and brown (#16-18), partridge caddis (#16-18)
Terrestrials	Dave's hoppers (#10-12), Dave's crickets (#10-12), fur ants, black (#16-20), CDC ants, black (#16-18), deer-hair beetles, black (#14-18), hi-vis foam beetles (#14-18)

Silver Creek: *Picabo to Stalker Creek*

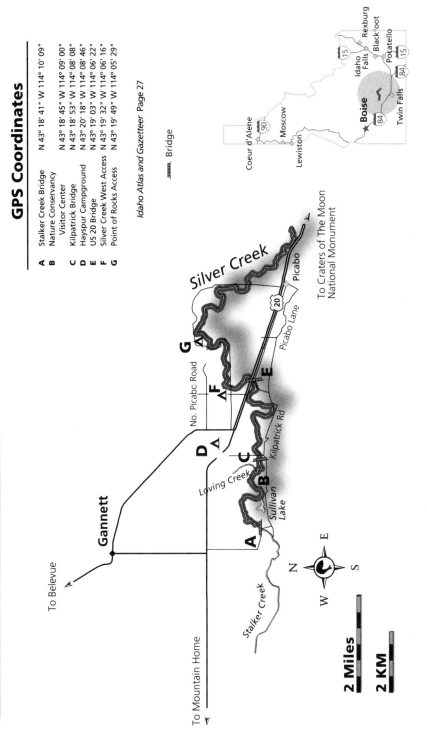

GPS Coordinates

A	Stalker Creek Bridge	N 43° 18' 41" W 114° 10' 09"
B	Nature Conservancy	
	Visitor Center	N 43° 18' 45" W 114° 09' 00"
C	Kilpatrick Bridge	N 43° 18' 53" W 114° 08' 08"
D	Hayspur Campground	N 43° 20' 18" W 114° 08' 46"
E	US 20 Bridge	N 43° 19' 03" W 114° 06' 22"
F	Silver Creek West Access	N 43° 19' 32" W 114° 06' 16"
G	Point of Rocks Access	N 43° 19' 49" W 114° 05' 29"

Idaho Atlas and Gazetteer Page 27

━━━ Bridge

HOW TO GET THERE

There is regular air service into the Friedman Memorial Airport in Hailey, or anglers can fly into either Boise or Idaho Falls, which are both about 120 miles from Hailey.

To reach the Nature Conservancy Visitor Center on Silver Creek from Hailey, go south about 15 miles on SR 75 until you reach US 20. Turn east and drive 7 ½ miles to Kilpatrick Road, then turn south. You will cross Kilpatrick Bridge and reach the visitor center in about 2 ½ miles.

From Boise, go southeast about 40 miles on I-84, then turn east onto US 20. Drive about 90 miles to reach Kilpatrick Road (7 ½ miles east of the junction with SR 75). Turn south on Kilpatrick Road and follow it around to the west to reach the visitor center (2 ½ miles). From Idaho Falls, go west 120 miles on US 20, then turn south on Kilpatrick Road, about four miles west of the town of Picabo.

ACCESSIBILITY

The Nature Conservancy's Silver Creek Preserve encloses most of the first two miles of Silver Creek, as well as Sullivan Lake and portions of Stalker Creek and Loving Creek. There are several access points and trails that make it easy and convenient for anglers to get around. People also canoe through the preserve, but fishing is not permitted from boats, rafts or canoes. Fishing from float tubes is permitted from a point just above the "S-turns" to the Kilpatrick Bridge.

Float tubes are the best way to fish the lower portion of the Silver Creek Preserve.

Below Kilpatrick Bridge, Silver Creek enters the Purdy Ranch. Anglers can float through this area but must stay in the water to avoid trespassing. Again, fishing is not permitted from boats, rafts or canoes, but it is allowed from float tubes. It is a fairly long and weedy float down to the bridge at US 20, and you must portage around the small dam.

From US 20 downstream, fly fishers can again walk the banks as Silver Creek enters public lands in about ½ mile. There are two access points, West and Point of Rocks, with about 1 ½ miles of the creek between them. Both sites allow camping. Since firewood is scarce, campers should bring their own or rely on fuel stoves for cooking.

WHEN TO GO

Many anglers circle Memorial Day weekend on their calendars to signify Silver Creek's opening, which usually coincides with its notorious brown drake hatch. The best fishing during this hatch of oversized mayflies is usually found down by Silver Creek West and Point of Rocks. This is primarily an evening hatch, so plan your schedule to be in the water at least an hour before the sun sets. Brown drakes will continue into June. Caddis hatches can also be important at this time.

July brings hot weather to the desert country of southern Idaho, and Silver Creek's hatches heat up as well. By the end of the month, pale morning duns, tricos and callibaetis can all be found in good numbers and make for interesting fishing. Terrestrials like black ants can work well in a variety of situations and will often take some fish when you just can't seem to figure out exactly what the fish are eating. The best times to be on the water are midmorning and sunset. Oppressive heat and minimal trout activity can make afternoon fishing difficult. You may be better off taking a nap or tying flies in preparation for the evening rise.

Fishing continues good through August, as long as you concentrate on the productive morning and evening fishing. Larger terrestrials like grasshoppers or crickets really come into their own at this time. September and October bring mahogany dun mayflies and a resurgence of caddisflies and blue-winged olives.

AREA ATTRACTIONS

Craters of the Moon National Monument is about 30 miles east of Picabo and preserves 83 square miles of stunning volcanic features. Eruptions that occurred here as recently as 2,000 years ago have left behind an incredible post-apocalyptic landscape. If you feel adventurous, you can explore some of the undeveloped caves left by retreating lava flows. A good light and a helmet are recommended. Use caution and do not enter caves alone. There is a visitor's center, a seven-mile driving loop through the monument with many trails, and a campground for those who want to linger and explore this unique geologic area.

Sun Valley Resort has been voted the number one ski resort by *Ski* magazine. Summer activities include golf, tennis, horseback riding, trap and skeet shooting, ice skating indoors and out, swimming, biking and rollerblading. There is also easy access to fine dining and many shopping opportunities, making this a good option for family trips that include fishing.

RESOURCES

It is about a one-hour drive to Silver Creek from Ketchum/Sun Valley, so if fishing is your main focus, you will want to stay closer, say at Bellevue or Hailey. Fishing is often best during midmorning and late evening, and staying close to the creek makes it easier to take advantage of prime fishing times.

Hayspur, Point of Rocks and Silver Creek West all offer primitive camping on a first-come, first-served basis. Hayspur is closest to the Nature Conservancy section of Silver Creek.

Campgrounds

BELLEVUE

Riverside RV Park & Campground
403 Broadford Road
Bellevue, ID 83313
Phone number/s: (208) 788-2020

Lodging

BELLEVUE

Come On Inn
114 N. Main
Bellevue, ID 83313
Phone number/s: (208) 788-0825

High Country Motel
765 Main St.
Bellevue, ID 83313
Phone number/s: (208) 788-2050,
toll-free (800) 692-2050
Fax: (208) 726-1789
Web site: http://vestra.net/
highcountrymotel
E-mail: ahkoffler@svidaho.com

KETCHUM

Lift Tower Lodge
703 S. Main St.
Ketchum, ID 83340
Phone number/s: (208) 726-5163,
toll-free (800) 462-8646
Fax: (208) 726-2614
Web site: vestra.net/lifttowerlodge
E-mail: imre@micron.net

Premiere Resorts at Sun Valley
333 S. Main
Ketchum, ID 83340
Phone number/s: (208) 727-4000
Web site: www.premierresortssv.com

Sun Valley Area Reservations
460 Sun Valley Road, #201
Ketchum, ID 83340
Phone number/s: (208) 726-3660

Tackle Shops and Outfitters

BELLEVUE

Idaho Angling Service
208 David St. Picabo
Bellevue, ID 83313
Phone number/s: (208) 788-9709
Fax: (208) 788-0232
Web site: www.anglingservices.com
E-mail: info@anglingservices.com

HAILEY

Sturtevants
P.O. Box 830
Main Street and Carbonate
Hailey, ID 83333
Phone number/s: (208) 788-7847

KETCHUM

Silver Creek Outfitters, Inc.
500 N. Main St.
Ketchum, ID 83340
Phone number/s: (208) 726-5282,
toll-free (800) 732-5687
Fax: (208) 726-9056
Web site: www.silver-creek.com
E-mail: silvercreek@flyshop.com

SUN VALLEY

Wood River Outfitters, LLC
P.O. Box 271
Sun Valley, ID 83353
Phone number/s: (208) 725-0666
Fax: (208) 726-2922
E-mail: headwaters@svidaho.net

Area Attractions

Craters of the Moon National Monument
US 20
Arco, ID 83213
Phone number/s: (208) 527-3257
Web site: www.nps.gov/crmo

Sun Valley Resort
One Sun Valley Road
P.O. Box 10
Sun Valley, ID 83353-0010
Phone number/s: (800) 786-8259
Web site: www.sunvalley.com

South Fork of the Snake River

I daho's South Fork of the Snake River is one of the best wild cutthroat fisheries in America. Its Yellowstone cutthroat are as beautiful as they are willing to intercept a fly fisher's feathered offerings. The large population of less-than-selective trout can often generate an angler's most productive fishing day of the season. This is not to say that the river doesn't become difficult at times, but once South Fork cutthroat get into the surface-feeding mode, you can often find large groups of feeders at every gravel bar. For every trout that snubs you, there is another who will not. Cutthroat average 14 to 16 inches here, but browns do occasionally grow much larger — late fall produces a fish or two in excess of 10 pounds most years. The South Fork was home to the 26-pound Idaho state record brown trout.

HIGHLIGHT
Sublime dry-fly fishing

TIP
Must bring a portable toilet to camp on the river between Conant and Byington

FISH SPECIES
Great cutthroat fishery with some rainbows and browns

SEASON
Varies depending on stretch of water

The largest threat to the river's native cutthroat is their close relatives, the rainbow trout. Since 1986, rainbows and their hybrids have risen from 1 percent of the total trout numbers up to 27 percent in 1997, indicating that they have the potential to completely replace the native species as they have on the adjacent Henry's Fork of the Snake. The fishing regulations allow for fairly generous limits of rainbows; you will be helping to maintain the river's precarious balance if you harvest a few.

The canyon section of the South Fork is one of the last great overnight float trips in the West that does not require a permit. The scenery of the area matches the grand scale of this powerful river that often exceeds 20,000 cfs when full of spring's bountiful flows. Just west of the Tetons, the South Fork cuts between 9,000-foot peaks as it emerges from Palisades Dam and drops in to the big, wide canyon below rolling fields of grain.

Although the South Fork is easy to reach, it retains a wild character that belies its location. The largest winter roost of bald eagles can be found along the river, as well as nesting peregrine falcons, and plenty of moose along the banks. This author will always recall one late-season day, floating the South Fork with two favorite companions. We slid the boat in close to the bank to retrieve a fly just as two young mountain lions stood up in the brush not 40 feet away. They calmly moved off, their dappled sides blending into the broken light under the autumn cottonwoods.

SPECIFIC REGULATIONS AND FEES

From the mouth of the South Fork of the Snake River upstream to the water measuring cable near Heise:
- ❏ Trout limit: six; only two cutthroat or brown trout in the aggregate. None under 16 inches.
- ❏ Open all year.

From the water-measuring cable near Heise upstream to Palisades Dam:
- ❏ Trout limit: six; only two cutthroat or brown trout in the aggregate. None under 16 inches.
- ❏ Open Saturday of Memorial Day weekend through November 30. There is a parking fee of $3 per day at Palisades Dam, Conant and Byington.

TACTICS

Although the South Fork is best known for its dry-fly fishing, if you arrive before the salmonfly hatch in July, be prepared to fish underneath. Streamer fishing can be effective for floaters, casting big flies like the super X or yuk bugs under the brush and as close to the banks as possible. Short 7 ½-foot leaders will help with accuracy, while 2x or 3x tippet will allow you to retrieve many of the flies that will inevitably get caught in the brush. If you get tired of pounding the banks, stop at the gravel bars and dead drift small bead-head nymphs. You will take whitefish as well as trout with this approach.

Cutthroat in the South Fork average about 14 to 16 inches.

Once the adult salmonflies are present, cast sofa pillows up close to the river's edge. Some anglers prefer bullethead salmonfly patterns like the Mac Salmon, which can be skipped in underneath overhanging brush. Golden stoneflies and yellow sallys are often present at this time as well and may be more effective than the bigger salmonflies when you find fish rising in side channels or below gravel bars.

As summer progresses, pale morning duns become more important, and you may experience several overlapping hatches. Shaun Lawson of South Fork Lodge recommends fishing an attractor fly at times like these. Try renegades or humpies of about the same size as the bugs on the water. Casting large stimulators or Dave's hoppers works well for floaters later in the summer, particularly if they add small dry flies or bead-head nymphs to a two-foot dropper.

If you are looking for one of the South Fork's huge brown trout, break out the big streamers and head for the upper river in the late fall. Heavily weighted streamers from six to eight inches long can get the interest of the river's monsters.

HOW TO GET THERE

The airport at Idaho Falls is very close to the South Fork, at about thirty minutes drive time to the lower river near Twin Bridges or a one-hour drive to the upper river and the Spring Creek access. From Idaho Falls take US 26 northeast. To go to Twin Bridges, turn north in about 15 miles on SR 29, then stay right to get on Archer Road in Ririe, reaching the river in about three miles. If you are going to the upper river near Spring Creek access, stay on US 26 northeast for about 40 miles from Idaho Falls.

Fish concentrate at the river's gravel bars.

Hatch Chart   AVAILABILITY

Food Items	J	F	M	A	M	J	J	A	S	O	N	D
Midges	X	X	X	X	X	X	X	X	X	X	X	X
Blue-winged olives					X	X				X	X	
Pale morning duns							X	X	X			
Yellow sallys							X	X	X			
Golden stoneflies						X	X					
Salmonflies							X					
Caddisflies							X	X	X			
Terrestrials							X	X	X			

Insects	Suggested Fly Patterns
Midges	Griffith's gnats (#16-20), grizzly midges (#16-20), bead-head midges, various colors (#14-18), midge emergers (#20-26)
Blue-winged olives	parachute Adams (#16-20), thorax BWOs (#16-20), olive comparaduns (#16-20), sparkle duns, olive (#16-20), Quigley cripples, olive (#16-20), CDC emergers, olive (#16-20), pheasant tails (#16-20), hare's ears (#16-20), bead-head pheasant tails (#16-20), bead-head hare's ears (#16-20)
Pale morning duns	thorax PMDs (#14-16), cream parachutes (#14-16), cream comparaduns (#16-20), Quigley cripples, cream (#16-20), rusty spinners (#14-16), CDC emergers, cream (#16-20), pheasant tails (#14-16), hare's ears (#14-16), bead-head pheasant tails (#14-16), bead-head hare's ears (#14-16)
Yellow sallys	yellow stimulators (#10-14), yellow seducers (#10-14), elk-hair caddis, yellow (#10-14), yellow humpies(#10-14), prince nymphs (#10-14)
Golden stoneflies	yellow stimulators (#6-10), irresistible stimulators, yellow (#6-10), prince nymphs (#8-12), bead-head prince nymphs (#8-12), golden stonefly nymphs (#8-12), copper Johns (#8-12)
Salmonflies	sofa pillows (#6-10), Mac Salmons (#6-10), orange stimulators (#6-10), black rubber-legs, (#6-10), Bitch Creek nymphs (#6-10) Brook's stone nymphs
Caddisflies	elk-hair caddis (#16-18), partridge caddis (#16-18), CDC elk-hair caddis (#16-18), sparkle caddis(#16-18), X-caddis (#16-18), peeking caddis (#14-16), chamois caddis (#14-16)
Terrestrials	Dave's hoppers (#8-12), Henry's Fork hoppers (#8-12), club sandwich (#8-12), fur ants, black (#14-18), CDC ants (#14-18), deer-hair beetles, black (#14-16), hi-vis foam beetles (#14-16)

The canyon section of the South Fork makes for a great overnight float trip.

ACCESSIBILITY

The South Fork is a huge river, especially when flows peak in June and July. Floating is by far the best way to access the river, and wading is not practical until flows drop below 8,000 cfs. If you come to the South Fork without a boat, your best bet is to wait until flows drop after mid-September. The best water for wade fishing will be found near Falls Creek on the river's south side, or around Wolf Flats on the north bank.

While the sheer size of the South Fork limits shorebound anglers, a drift boat or raft gives anglers the freedom to explore this expansive river. While fairly easy to float, the big water deserves respect. Beware of tree hazards in the river that can block off side channels. The first 10 miles of the South Fork from Palisades Dam down to Spring Creek is easy for floaters to access, with half a dozen launch sites and roads on both sides of the river. US 26 parallels the north side while FR 058 (Snake River Road) closely follows the south bank. This section of the river is the most crowded, and it also produces some of the larger fish.

The next launch site two miles downstream from Spring Creek is Conant Valley, which is a large, new facility with paved lots and a large concrete ramp capable of launching larger powerboats. This launch area is on the river's south side and is the normal put-in for the remote and scenic canyon section of the South Fork. To camp overnight in the canyon, you are required to carry a portable toilet and fill out a float permit. This stretch of the South Fork is the most remote, with the next access 14 miles downstream at Cottonwood. If you float from Conant to Cottonwood, the shuttle is very long, as you must cross the river downstream near Heise then drive back upstream on dirt roads. The next access downstream is Wolf Flats, also on the north. Byington comes next — another new, large facility like Conant and just a short distance from US 26 on the river's south bank. Anglers looking for a two- or three-day float with a night or two spent camping on the river will enjoy floating from Conant to Byington (about 25 miles). The Cottonwood to Wolf Flats float (seven miles) works well for people who want to camp on the river and do their own shuttles for several day-floats.

As you go downstream from Byington, the river becomes more hazardous, and you should float with an experienced person before trying it on your own. Several diversion dams pull water from the river. They are relatively easy to avoid but are potentially very dangerous to the unwary. The Great Feeder Diversion Dam is about two miles below Byington on the south bank; the Reid Canal Diversion is three miles downstream from the Twin Bridges launch on the north bank. These are the two most hazardous diversions, but all dams should be given wide berth. The lower portion of the river is also more prone to being blocked in places with large, downed trees. This lower section of the river has more brown trout, with the river's best potential for a real trophy early in the season. Many of these fish will move up above the canyon to spawn in the fall. Boat launches on the lower river include Heise Bridge (south bank), Twin Bridges (south bank) and Lorenzo (US 20 bridge north bank).

Palisades Creek (Timberwolf), Conant and Byington all have docks with handicap-accessible ramps to allow mobility-challenged anglers to board boats on the river. The docks are not appropriate for fishing.

CHECK RIVER FLOWS ON THE WEB
http://idaho.usgs.gov./rt-cgi/gen_tbl_pg

WHEN TO GO

Good blue-winged olive and midge fishing begins in March and continues through April below Heise. Water typically comes up in May and then, hopefully, recedes somewhat by early July. The salmonflies get things kicked off in the first week of July and are followed up by golden stoneflies and yellow sallys. PMDs quickly join the scene and, along with grasshoppers, keep fish at the surface most of the summer. The fast, easy dry-fly fishing of summer often becomes more challenging by August.

Fall brings the return of blue-winged olives. Most of the river's big brown trout move to the upper stretches as waterfowl begin their autumn migrations overhead. Golden late summer days have a special appeal as you cast a line with the knowledge that snow is soon to come.

AREA ATTRACTIONS

Fall Creek Falls is located off SR 26 on Snake River Road. The falls spill from a height of 60 feet into the Snake River over an outcropping of travertine. There are no developed viewing points.

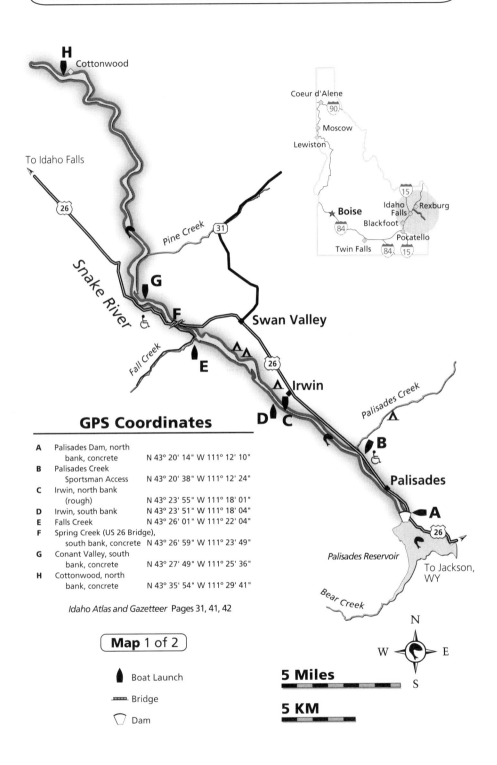

South Fork Snake: Palisades Reservoir to Cottonwood

H Cottonwood

To Idaho Falls

Coeur d'Alene

Moscow

Lewiston

Boise

Idaho Falls

Rexburg

Blackfoot

Pocatello

Twin Falls

Pine Creek

Snake River

G

F

Swan Valley

Fall Creek

E

Irwin

D **C**

Palisades Creek

B

Palisades

Palisades Reservoir

To Jackson, WY

Bear Creek

GPS Coordinates

A Palisades Dam, north
    bank, concrete — N 43° 20' 14" W 111° 12' 10"
B Palisades Creek
    Sportsman Access — N 43° 20' 38" W 111° 12' 24"
C Irwin, north bank
    (rough) — N 43° 23' 55" W 111° 18' 01"
D Irwin, south bank — N 43° 23' 51" W 111° 18' 04"
E Falls Creek — N 43° 26' 01" W 111° 22' 04"
F Spring Creek (US 26 Bridge),
    south bank, concrete — N 43° 26' 59" W 111° 23' 49"
G Conant Valley, south
    bank, concrete — N 43° 27' 49" W 111° 25' 36"
H Cottonwood, north
    bank, concrete — N 43° 35' 54" W 111° 29' 41"

Idaho Atlas and Gazetteer Pages 31, 41, 42

Map 1 of 2

⬤ Boat Launch

▭ Bridge

⬠ Dam

5 Miles

5 KM

N
W   E
S

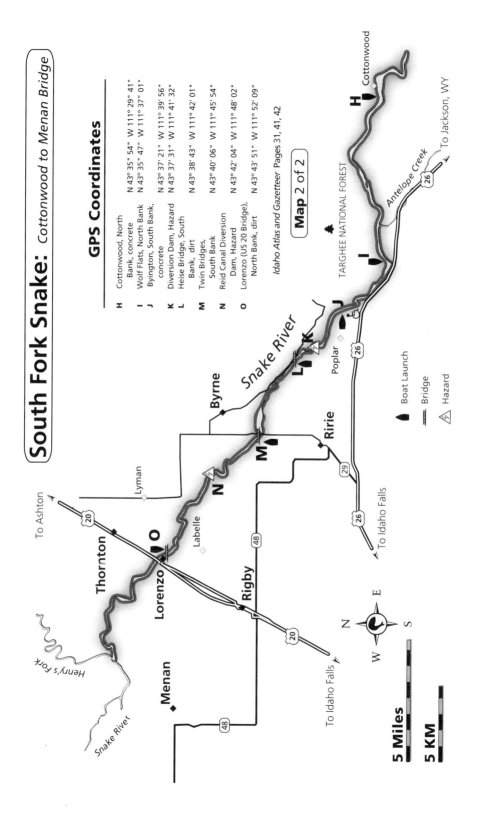

South Fork Snake: *Cottonwood to Menan Bridge*

GPS Coordinates

H Cottonwood, North
Bank, concrete   N 43° 35' 54" W 111° 29' 41"

I Wolf Flats, North Bank N 43° 35' 47" W 111° 37' 01"

J Byington, South Bank,
concrete   N 43° 37' 21" W 111° 39' 56"

K Diversion Dam, Hazard N 43° 37' 31" W 111° 41' 32"

L Heise Bridge, South
Bank, dirt   N 43° 38' 43" W 111° 42' 01"

M Twin Bridges,
South Bank   N 43° 40' 06" W 111° 45' 54"

N Reid Canal Diversion
Dam, Hazard   N 43° 42' 04" W 111° 48' 02"

O Lorenzo (US 20 Bridge),
North Bank, dirt   N 43° 43' 51" W 111° 52' 09"

Idaho Atlas and Gazetteer Pages 31, 41, 42

Map 2 of 2

Boat Launch

Bridge

Hazard

5 Miles

5 KM

RESOURCES

There are several places to lodge along the South Fork, but if you prefer a larger town, Idaho Falls is relatively close.

Campgrounds

TARGHEE NATIONAL FOREST

For reservations, call the Palisades Ranger District at (208) 523-1412.

- ❑ Bear Creek
- ❑ Big Elk Creek
- ❑ Falls
- ❑ McCoy Creek
- ❑ Palisades Creek
- ❑ Table Rock

Lodging

DRIGGS

Teton Valley Lodge
379 Adams Rd
Driggs, ID 83422
Phone number/s: winter (208) 354-8124, summer (208) 354-2386, toll-free (800) 455-1182
E-mail: jpehrson@pdt.net

IRWIN

The Lodge at Palisades Creek
P.O. Box 70
Irwin, ID 83428
Phone number/s: (208) 483-2222
Fax: (208) 483-2227

SWAN VALLEY

Sandy Mite Fly Shop & Café
3333 Swan Valley Highway
Swan Valley, ID 83449
Phone number/s: (208) 483-2609
(Also shuttle service)

Tackle Shops and Outfitters

IDAHO FALLS

Hyde Outfitters
1520 Pancheri
Idaho Falls, ID 83402
Phone number/s: (208) 529-4343, toll-free (800) 444-4933
E-mail: jeff@hydeboats.com

RIRIE

Heise Expeditions
5116 Heise Road
Ririe, ID 83443
Phone number/s: (208) 538-7453, toll-free (800) 828-3984
Fax: (208) 538-6039
Web site: www.srv.net/~heise/heise_expeditions.html
E-mail: heise@srv.net

SWAN VALLEY

Drifters of the South Fork
Box 148
Swan Valley, ID 83449
Phone number/s: (208) 483-2722, toll-free (800) 490-1201
Fax: (208) 483-2722
Web site: www.CatchOurDrift.com
E-mail: drifters@CatchOurDrift.com

South Fork Lodge
40 Conant Valley Loop
Swan Valley, ID 83449
Phone number/s: (208) 483-2112, toll-free (800) 483-2110
Fax: (208) 483-2121
Web site: www.southforklodge.com
E-mail: southforklodge@earthlink.net
(Also lodging)

MONTANA

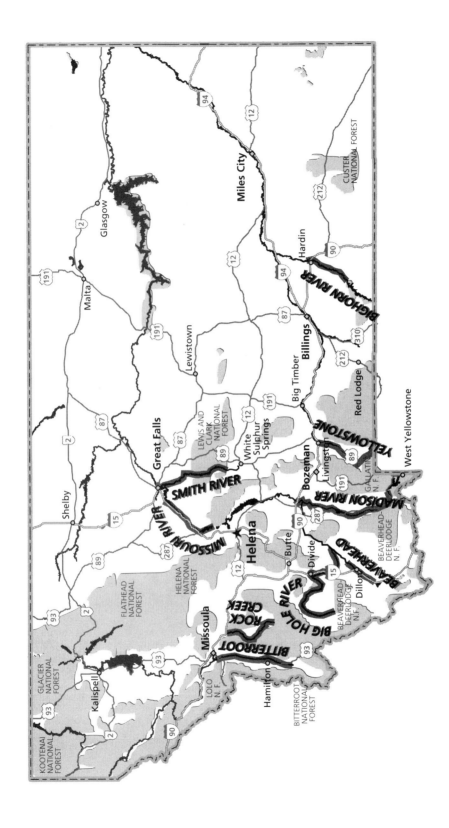

Montana

No other state seems to appreciate visiting fly fishers more than Montana. The clearest symbol of this is the familiar hook and fish road sign that clearly marks hundreds of public fishing access sites in Montana. Angler-friendly stream access laws keep most waters open to the public and even many small towns boast a fly shop or two. Of course, all this would mean nothing if there weren't some good rivers, and Montana has been especially blessed with many of the country's best trout streams.

FISHING ACCESS LAWS

Under the Montana Stream Access Law, anglers are required to stay within the ordinary high-water marks. Anglers can wade in a stream, walk along the streambank below the high-water mark, or float. The law does not give anglers the right to enter private lands bordering streams or to cross private lands to gain access to streams. An angler may enter private land only with the permission of the landowner or when the landowner has failed to post a no-trespassing notice. However, it is the responsibility of the angler to find out if private lands are posted.

2000 GENERAL SEASON DATES AND BAG & POSSESSION LIMITS

In Montana, general seasons and daily bag and possession limits are governed by three districts: Western, Central and Eastern. In the Western and Central fishing districts, the general season opens the third Saturday in May and continues through November 30, except where special regulations apply. In the Eastern Fishing District, all waters are open year-round, except where special regulations apply.

The waters covered in this book that fall under the Western Fishing District are Bitterroot River and Rock Creek. Armstrong's/DePuy Spring Creek, Beaverhead, Big Hole, Bighorn, Madison, Missouri, Nelson Spring Creek, Smith and Yellowstone River in Paradise Valley fall under the Central Fishing District.

Species	2000 Daily Bag & Possession Limits
WESTERN FISHING DISTRICT — RIVERS AND STREAMS	
Combined trout limit, including the following in any combination: brown, cutthroat, golden, rainbow and grayling	five, only one fish over 14 inches
Brook trout	20
Bull trout	none
Lake trout	10
Salmon	20
Whitefish	100
CENTRAL FISHING DISTRICT — RIVERS AND STREAMS	
Combined trout limit, including the following in any combination: brown, golden, rainbow	five, only one fish over 18 inches
Cutthroat trout and grayling	none; must be immediately released
Brook trout	20
Bull trout	none
Lake trout	three
Salmon	10
Whitefish	100

LICENSE FEES

A $4 conservation license is required to fish in Montana. Beginning March 2000, anglers will need to provide their social security number as well. Season licenses are valid from March 1 through the end of February.

Fishing License	Age	Fee
RESIDENT		
Season	15 to 61	$17
Senior Season	62 and over	$4
Youth Season	12 to 14	$4
NONRESIDENT		
Season	15 and over	$45
Two-day	15 and over	$15

❏ No license is required for resident anglers under the age of 12. Legal limits and regulations apply.

❏ No license is required for nonresident anglers under the age of 15 if accompanied by an adult with a valid Montana license. The combined fish limit for the two anglers cannot exceed the legal limit for one licensed angler.

❏ For a nonresident angler under the age of 15 to catch the legal limit, the youth must purchase a fishing license.

BOATING REGULATIONS

Montana Fish, Wildlife & Parks regulates all boating activities. Boating regulations are published on its web site (*www.fwp.state.mt.us*), or you can obtain a copy by calling (406) 444-2535.

In Montana, float tubes are presently not required to carry a PFD. However, once an inflatable or kickboat is rigged with oars, it is considered a "vessel" and a Coast Guard-approved PFD is required onboard as well as a sound-producing device, such as a whistle or horn. Children under the age of 12 must wear a PFD while boating or rafting.

RESOURCES

Montana Fish, Wildlife & Parks
Phone number/s: (406) 444-2535
Web site: www.fwp.state.mt.us

Montana Streamflow Conditions
Web site: http://montana.usgs.gov/rt-cgi/gen_tbl_pg

Fishing Outfitters Association of Montana
Phone number/s: (406) 763-5436

Montana Outfitters and Guides Association
Phone number/s: (406) 449-3578

Travel Montana
Phone number/s: toll-free (800) VISIT-MT
Web site: www.visitmt.com

Bureau of Land Management
Phone number/s: (406) 896-5000
Web site: www.mt.blm.gov

U.S. Forest Service
Phone number/s: (406) 329-3511
Web site: www.fs.fed.us/recreation/states/mt.shtml

Armstrong's/DePuy Spring Creek

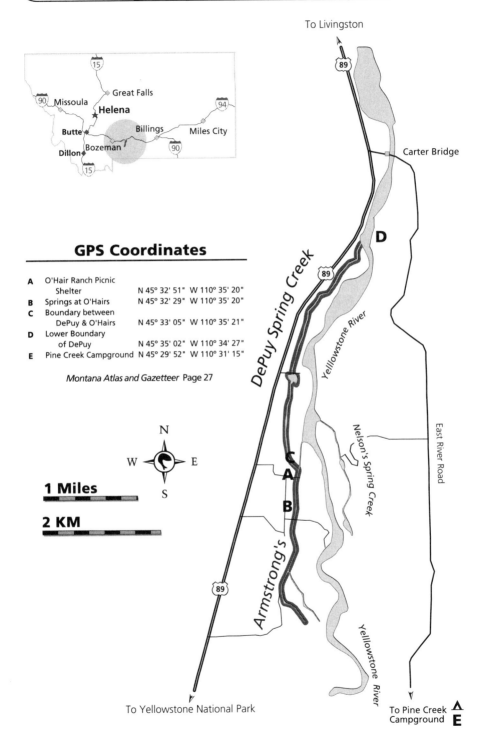

To Livingston

Carter Bridge

89

DePuy Spring Creek

D

Yellowstone River

Nelson's Spring Creek

East River Road

GPS Coordinates

A O'Hair Ranch Picnic
       Shelter   N 45° 32' 51" W 110° 35' 20"
B Springs at O'Hairs   N 45° 32' 29" W 110° 35' 20"
C Boundary between
       DePuy & O'Hairs   N 45° 33' 05" W 110° 35' 21"
D Lower Boundary
       of DePuy   N 45° 35' 02" W 110° 34' 27"
E Pine Creek Campground N 45° 29' 52" W 110° 31' 15"

Montana Atlas and Gazetteer Page 27

N
W — E
S

1 Miles

2 KM

C
A

B

Armstrong's

89

Yellowstone River

Great Falls
Missoula
Helena
Butte
Bozeman
Dillon
Billings
Miles City

15
90
94
90
15

To Yellowstone National Park

To Pine Creek
Campground E

Armstrong's / DePuy Spring Creek

FISH SPECIES
Browns and rainbows with a few cutthroat trout

TIP
Fish fine tippets down to 7x

HIGHLIGHT
Matching the prolific hatches

SEASON
Open year-round

The Armstrong/O'Hair family has looked after Armstrong's Spring Creek for four generations. Owen Taylor Armstrong arrived in Paradise Valley in 1877, the year after Custer and the Seventh Cavalry were destroyed at the Battle of Little Bighorn 150 miles to the east. The mules he brought with him proved to be a great temptation for the Crow tribe across the river, so he exchanged them for oxen to reduce tension with his native neighbors.

Armstrong's Spring Creek used to dump directly into the Yellowstone River about 1 ½ miles below its source. In 1958, it was diverted into Little Trail Creek and became known as DePuy Spring Creek, creating the unusual situation where the same flow of water is known by two different names. DePuy Spring Creek today is still a bit of an odd juxtaposition of different elements. The creek has the rich and manicured look of an English chalk stream, complete with three angler huts and comfortable benches along its length, and the main house is a classic southern mansion replete with massive white columns — all of this set against the rugged backdrop of the Absaroka Range that borders Paradise Valley.

Both streams were adversely affected in the spring of 1996, when heavy run-off in the Yellowstone River broke over into the spring creeks and began to create a new channel for itself. Both landowners worked together to install $800,000 worth of riprap and diking, and by Thanksgiving of that year, a levee had been constructed and the river was forced back into its old channel. This new levee survived even heavier flooding in 1997, but DePuy Spring Creek was still heavily impacted, requiring more expensive efforts to hold the Yellowstone at bay.

The spring creeks have healed and will flourish again behind their protective earthworks. The clear spring waters flow through a pastoral setting while the resident trout gain size and strength with their deliberate feeding on the prolific aquatic insects. The current threat to these waters is litigation that may call for the removal of the protective dikes. If this takes place, the Yellowstone will likely swallow up these unique angling destinations and the famous spring creeks will only exist in the memories of the lucky fly fishers who knew them.

SPECIAL REGULATIONS AND FEES

Both properties are open year-round. All trout must be released and only fly fishing is allowed.

The upper 1 ½ miles of Armstrong's Spring Creek is found on the O'Hair Ranch. They charge a variable rate throughout the year, approximately what you see

Drake keeps both eyes on the monster rainbow that his friend Scott Lane landed on a fine day at DePuy Spring Creek.

listed. They do adjust the rates at times depending on weather and other considerations. The O'Hair Ranch is limited to 12 rods per day. For reservations, call (406) 222-2979.

November 15 to February 28	$30/rod/day
March 1 to March 31	$40/rod/day
April 1 to April 15	$50/rod/day
April 15 to September 30	$75/rod/day
October 1 to November 15	$50/rod/day

DePuy has about three miles of spring creek as well as a large pond. They restrict access to 16 rods per day; reservations can be made by phone at (406) 222-0221 or by fax at (406) 222-5506. Their fees are listed below:

October 15 to April 14	$35 /rod/day
April 15 to June 14	$75/rod/day
June 15 to September 14	$100/rod/day
September 15 to October 14	$75 /rod/day

TACTICS

The real drawing card is dry-fly fishing during hatch periods. These fish can be highly selective and very sensitive to any shortcomings in your drift. Check with local shops for up-to-date hatch information. The locals can help you select flies that match the size, color and stage of insect that is most effective. Take the time to catch and observe insects on the stream. Then, once you have found a feeding fish that you want to pursue, watch carefully for clues to what the fish is feeding on. Can you see sips for mayfly duns, or is there only a dorsal fin and tail that breaks the surface as the fish takes emergers just below the surface? "Buzz" Basini of Spring Creek Specialists Fly Shop recommends mayfly emerger and dun patterns that incorporate CDC feathers to provide flotation but still allow flies to ride naturally on the surface.

Rig up with long leaders and light tippets during most hatch conditions — this will mean leaders of at least 12 feet and tippet tapered down to 6x or even 7x. Adding a few feet of tippet can improve your drift by increasing slack at the end of your leader.

Your best approach will normally be a downstream presentation. This allows your fly to float over the fish before your leader, plus you can cast well above your target fish and still maintain a good drift. Anglers who pay careful attention to detail will be rewarded. Keep false casts to a minimum and be sure they are not made over the head of your quarry.

A day at the spring creek can delight or discourage. If you make a reservation at either Armstrong's or Depuy, be sure your skills are up to the challenge or consider hiring a guide.

Nymphing is also popular on the spring creeks. Rig up with longer leaders of 10 to 12 feet with fine (5x or 6x) tippet. Suspend nymphs under a dry fly with a reasonable amount of flotation or the smallest sizes of strike indicators. Keep weight to the minimum needed to reach the depth at which fish are feeding. In most situations, only a very small amount of weight is needed. Small bead-head nymphs sink effectively and cause only slight disturbance when cast carefully.

Smaller diameter tippets will allow for a better sink rate without adding weight.

Many Yellowstone trout move up into the spring creeks to spawn and are especially vulnerable to anglers while spawning in the shallow riffle areas. Anglers have to decide for themselves how much they are willing to disrupt the activities of these fish. If you do opt to fish to spawners, consider the following guidelines:

- ❑ Do not walk on spawning beds. These will be shallow depressions with lighter-colored gravel.
- ❑ Use tackle heavy enough to allow you to land and release fish quickly.
- ❑ Limit the amount of time you spend disturbing these fish. Remember, spawners here are helping to repopulate the Yellowstone River as well as the spring creeks.

Dick's Pond at DePuy is becoming increasingly popular with float tubing anglers. In addition to the spring creeks' regular hatches, expect to find callibaetis and damselfly activity in this stillwater fishery. Anglers can strip woolly buggers and nymphs under the surface on sinking or sink tip lines, or try to anticipate cruising "gulpers" and cast a dry fly into their path.

HOW TO GET THERE

Visitors from out of the area can fly into either Bozeman, which is 26 miles west of Livingston on I-90, or Billings, 120 miles to the east on I-90.

From I-90, take Exit 333 at Livingston, Montana, and go south 5.2 miles on US 89 to reach the entrance to DePuy. If you are headed to the O'Hair Ranch, it is one mile farther south on O'Hair Lane.

Opposites attract: The classic southern architecture of the DePuy mansion amid the rugged Absarokas.

Hatch Chart   AVAILABILITY

Food Items	J	F	M	A	M	J	J	A	S	O	N	D
Midges	X	X	X	X	X	X	X	X	X	X	X	X
Blue-winged olives			X	X	X			X	X	X	X	X
Pale morning duns						X	X	X				
Sulphurs						X	X	X	X			
Caddisflies					X	X	X	X	X			
Terrestrials							X	X	X			

Insects — Suggested Fly Patterns

Midges

Griffith's gnats, adding a post of white or black poly yarn to aid in strike detection (#20-22), grizzly midges (#20-22), Adams (#20-22), midge pupae, cream, red and black (#18-22), brassies (#16-20), serendipities (#18-22), midge emergers, black and peacock (#18-22)

Blue-winged olives

CDC comparaduns, olive (#18-22), parachute Adams (#18-22), thorax BWOs (#18-22), no-hackle duns, olive (#18-22), CDC loopwing emergers, olive (#18-22), Quigley cripples, olive (#18-22), pheasant tails (#16-20), hare's ears (#16-20), WD40s (#16-20), RS2s (#16-20)

Pale morning duns

CDC comparaduns, cream (#16-18), thorax duns, cream (#16-18), cream parachutes (#16-18), sparkle duns (#16-18), no-hackle duns, cream (#16-18), CDC loopwing emergers, cream (#16-18), Quigley cripples, cream (#16-18), floating nymphs, cream (#16-18), rusty spinners (#16-18), pheasant tails (#16-18), hare's ears (#16-18)

Sulphurs

CDC comparaduns, cream (#20-22), thorax duns, cream (#20-22), cream parachutes (#20-22), sparkle duns, cream (#20-22), no-hackle duns, cream (#20-22), CDC loopwing duns, cream (#20-22), Quigley cripples, cream (#20-22), cream or tan spinners (#20-22), pheasant tails (#20-22), hare's ears (#20-22)

Caddisflies

CDC caddis, olive, tan and brown (#16-18), CDC caddis, black (#18-20), parachute caddis, olive, tan and brown (#16-18), caddis sparkle pupae, olive, tan and brown (#16-18), partridge caddis (#16-18)

Terrestrials

Dave's hoppers (#10-12), Dave's crickets (#10-12), fur ants, black and cinnamon (#16-20), CDC ants, black and cinnamon (#16-18), deer-hair beetles , black (#14-18), hi-vis foam beetles (#14-18)

If you are driving up from Yellowstone Park and the town of Gardiner, Montana, go north on US 89. It is 46 miles to O'Hair's and 47 to DePuy.

ACCESSIBILITY

It is quite easy for visiting anglers to get around on the spring creeks, and handy facilities make your day more comfortable. O'Hair's has parking with a picnic shelter and restroom centrally located on the creek, as well as benches overlooking the water. DePuy's has a road that follows almost the entire length of the creek. There are three strategically located huts (with nearby outhouses) where fly fishers can escape the weather, and benches to relax on while waiting for the hatch to get going. The DePuy ranch also offers the most in terms of variety of water. There are riffles, slow runs, deep holes and the large pond (Dick's) near the main house.

WHEN TO GO

Winter may bring slower fishing to the spring creeks, but they are much better than surrounding waters at that time of year. You can easily get a reservation with short notice and can still find some good hatches. Even insects that normally hatch in midsummer, like pale morning duns, can appear on the odd winter day. Big rainbows begin to move into the creeks to spawn in January and continue through April.

Blue-winged olives appear in March as harbingers of spring, and many great days can result. Careful water management keeps the water low and clear even when run-off is in full swing.

Summer is the time when anglers can expect a couple different hatches during the day as well as terrestrial fishing, but it is very hard to get a reservation during summer. Try to book at least six months in advance for July dates.

Angler numbers and daily rates both decline in the fall, despite the large browns that move into the creek as the spawning urge takes over. Cottonwoods turn yellow and the warm, golden light of autumn turns the Paradise Valley into a vision of wonder that can sustain fly fishers through the long months of winter.

AREA ATTRACTIONS

Yellowstone National Park is just 40 miles south. In 1872, 2.2 million acres were set aside as the earth's first national park. Yellowstone is a geothermal hot spot and contains more geysers and hot springs than the rest of the world combined.

RESOURCES

Lodgings in Livingston are plentiful, and it is a short drive to the spring creek. If you're looking to rough it, try the Pine Creek campground in the Gallatin National Forest. This campground has handicap-accessible campsites.

Campgrounds

GALLATIN NATIONAL FOREST

For more information, call the Livingston Ranger District at (406) 222-1892.

❏   Pine Creek

LIVINGSTON

Livingston-Paradise Valley KOA
163 Pine Creek Road
Livingston, MT 59047
Phone number/s: (406) 222-0992,
toll-free (800) KOA-2805
Fax: (406) 222-5911
Web site: www.koa.com
E-mail: liv.koa@ycsi.net

Yellowstone's Edge RV Park
3501 US 89 South
Livingston, MT 59047
Phone number/s: (406) 333-4036

Lodging

LIVINGSTON

Jumping Rainbow Ranch
110 Jumping Rainbow Road
Livingston, MT 59047
Phone number/s: (406) 222-5425

Comfort Inn
114 Loves Lane
Livingston, MT 59047
Phone number/s: (406) 222-4400

Blue Winged Olives
5157 US 89 South
Livingston, MT 59047
Phone number/s: (406) 222-8646

Pine Creek Lodge
2495 E. River Road
Livingston, MT 59047
Phone number/s: (406) 222-3628

PRAY

Chico Hot Springs Lodge
One Old Chico Road
Pray, MT 59065
Phone number/s: (406) 333-4933
Fax: (406) 333-4694

Tackle Shops and Guide Services

LIVINGSTON

Dan Bailey's Fly Shop
209 W. Park St.
Livingston, MT 59047
Phone number/s: (406) 222-1673,
toll-free (800) 356-4052
E-mail: dan@danbailey.com

Spring Creek Specialist Fly Shop
(on the creek at DePuy)
2742 E. River Road
Livingston, MT 59047
Phone number/s: (406) 222-5664
E-mail: basini@mcn.net

Yellowstone Angler
P.O. Box 629
5256 US 89 South
Livingston, MT 59047
Phone number/s: (406) 222-7130
Fax: (406) 222-7153
Web site: www.yellostoneangler.com
E-mail: staff@yellowstoneangler.com

Beaverhead River

I n a state that is famous for its trout fishing, there is one small river that stands out as one of the best trophy trout streams in Montana. The Beaverhead gets its water from Clark Canyon Reservoir, which is both the river's blessing and curse. While the reservoir provides high quality water and moderates temperatures throughout the year, its main purpose is to control flows for the benefit of downstream water users. This means that during drought conditions, winter flows can drop to extremely critical levels. This has created boom and bust cycles on the Beaverhead, as the river's trout population can build up to phenomenal levels with a few good water years, only to get knocked back down when precipitation is scarce.

HIGHLIGHT
Cranefly hatch in late summer
TIP
Fish small nymphs
FISH SPECIES
Rainbow, cutthroat and brown trout
SEASON
Open from the third Saturday in May to November 30

While the Beaverhead is booming at the moment, it appears there could be trouble on the horizon. An electro-shocking survey in 1999 revealed 275 fish per mile exceeding 20 inches. The river currently supports nearly two tons of brown trout per mile. The difficulty lies in the drought experienced in the summer of 2000. Dick Oswald, Fisheries Management Biologist for the Dillon area of Region 3, expects that the combination of low winter flows and a very high trout biomass may create problems for the Beaverhead in the winter of 2000/2001. Some mortality is expected in fish above 18 inches, with trout beginning the 2001 season in poor condition. While this sounds like bad news, it is part of the natural cycle of the Beaverhead. In the longer term, a minor reduction in trout numbers may allow the river to produce more of the 6- to 8-pound fish that it has in the past, provided the immediate future holds several good water years.

TACTICS

There are two schools of thought on how to nymph the Beaverhead. The traditional approach is to rig up a tapered leader of nine-foot 5x, add about a foot and a half of 5x tippet to the eye of your top nymph, and tie on your point fly. One BB shot above the top fly is usually about right — but adjust to the conditions. Use an indicator five feet above the split shot. Think small nymphs. Most fish will be taken on bugs sizes 18 to 22. Wide-gaped hooks like the Tiemco 2488 will improve your percentage of hookups. Favorite patterns are olive pheasant tails, hare's ears, red serendipities and red disco midges. Thin, sparse nymphs are best. This style of nymphing will produce hookups, but getting these big, hot fish to the net is difficult on the best of days, and a series of lost fish can be frustrating.

The Beaverhead stands out as one of Montana's best trophy trout streams.

Nick St. George of Watershed Adventures in Dillon recommends that anglers fish slightly larger nymphs (size 14 to 18) and tie them to the new 3x fluorocarbon tippet, which is rated at 6-pound test, yet less visible than nylon monofilament tippets. Size 3/0 split shot will get flies down to the fish in the deeper, faster runs. Fluorocarbon tippet is quite slick, which causes the split shot to slide, so place it immediately above a knot. This type of heavier rig will still get results, and it gives fly fishers a more realistic chance to land big fish.

These fish see a lot of flies in the course of a season, so they get very drift sensitive. Mending is critical, especially later in the season. If you are fishing with a partner who is catching fish on the same setup that leaves you skunked, then perhaps your mending needs attention.

If you find feeding fish during the blue-winged olive or pale morning dun hatches, your best bet is to pull close to the bank to fish to these risers. Use nine- to 12-foot leaders tapered down to 5x or even 6x. Most fish will be along the eddy lines where an upstream cast is often the best approach. Fish here are unbelievably strong and landing them on light tippets and small flies is no easy task. Be sure to enjoy the fish you hook as well as the ones you land.

The cranefly hatch is the most exciting event of the year on the Beaverhead. If you are fortunate enough to be here when it happens, try fishing big brown spiders or even big elk-hair caddis (size 6-12). Cast them to the bank downstream and let them swing out into the current. Be prepared for explosive takes and up your tippet size to 3x.

Streamers can be quite productive at times, allowing anglers the advantage of using heavy (2x) tippets and large, strong hooks. Variations on the yellow yummy work well and are usually weighted heavily enough to sink quickly without having to resort to sinking or sink-tip lines.

HOW TO GET THERE

There is regular air service into Butte and Bozeman. Butte is an hour and Bozeman is about a 2½-hour drive to the stretch of the Beaverhead below Clark Canyon Dam. It is about a 5½-hour drive from the Salt Lake City International Airport, where traveling anglers may find more reasonable fares.

From Butte take I-15 and go south about 80 miles to Exit 44 near Clark Canyon Dam. If you are coming from Bozeman, take I-90 West 70 miles then go south on I-15 85 miles to Exit 44. From Salt Lake City, it is about 330 miles north on I-15.

ACCESSIBILITY

The river above Barrett's Diversion (about the first 16 miles below the dam) is the most popular section and holds the highest density of big trout. This stretch is narrow with a fairly fast flow, and its banks are heavily overgrown with willows. These factors make floating the river challenging, but it is still much more effective than wading. There are also some float-through gates across the river from October to May.

There are a half-dozen launch points, but you will want to stay above Grasshopper Creek during high water as it can cloud the river. Smaller watercraft are much easier to navigate down this tight, serpentine braided river. Smaller float boats like South Fork skiffs, small rafts under 12 feet, or the new pontoon boats are well suited to this river, but a capable person at the oars can get down the river without mishap in drift boats. Most of the boat ramps on the river are small and/or rough — High Bridge and Tash are particularly bad, and there is no ramp at the dam access. Look at your launch and retrieval points in advance and be organized so that you clear ramps quickly and make room for others.

The first few miles of river below the dam have an abundance of food but very little habitat, so don't expect to find a lot of fish here. The fish you do connect with will likely be good ones. If you come to the Beaverhead on a trophy hunt, you will want to spend some time on this challenging stretch.

High Bridge to Henneberry is the most productive section of the river and the most popular float. The take-out at Henneberry comes up quick on the right just above the bridge. Several of the bridges on the river are fairly low. You should be able to fit underneath except at the highest flows, so check with local shops in advance for water levels and make sure people and rods get low enough to clear. If you are looking for a short evening float, try putting in at Buffalo Bridge and floating down to High Bridge.

Caution: If you are going to take out at the ramp at Barrett's Park, it is directly above a diversion dam. Don't miss it. It is best to take a look before you float.

Hatch Chart AVAILABILITY

Food Items	J	F	M	A	M	J	J	A	S	O	N	D
Midges	X	X	X	X	X	X	X	X	X	X	X	X
Blue-winged olives			X	X	X	X	X	X	X			
Pale morning duns					X	X	X					
Tricos								X	X			
Yellow sallys				X	X							
Mother's Day caddis				X	X							
Caddisflies						X	X	X				
Craneflies								X	X			
Terrestrials							X	X	X			

Insects	Suggested Fly Patterns
Midges	Griffith's gnats (#18-22), grizzly midges (#18-22), midge pupae, red and black (#18-22), midge emergers, black and peacock (#18-22), disco midges (#18-22)
Blue-winged olives	parachute Adams (#16-20), thorax BWOs (#16-20), pheasant tails (#18-22), hare's ears (#18-22), WD40s (#18-22), RS2s (#18-22)
Pale morning duns	thorax PMDs (#14-16), cream parachutes (#14-16), rusty spinners (#14-16), pheasant tails (#14-16), hare's ears (#14-16)
Tricos	trico spinners (#18-22), CDC tricos (#18-22), commander whiteheads (#18-22)
Yellow sallys	yellow stimulators (#14-18), yellow sallys (#14-18), red fox squirrel nymphs (#16-18)
Mother's Day caddis	elk-hair caddis, olive (#14-16), Goddard caddis (#14-16), Hemingway caddis (#14-16), soft hackles, olive (#14-16), sparkle pupae, olive (#14-16), X-caddis (#14-16), peeking caddis (#12-14), CK nymphs (#12-14)
Caddisflies	elk-hair caddis (#16-18), partridge caddis (#16-18), iris caddis, gray, yellow and chartreuse (#16-18)
Craneflies	elk-hair caddis (#12-14), brown spiders (#6-12), adult craneflies (#6-12), cranefly larvae, cream and brown (#8-12)
Terrestrials	Dave's hoppers (#8-12), parachute hoppers (#8-12), Henry's Fork hoppers (#8-12), fur ants, black (#14-18), deer-hair beetles, black (#14-16)

Beaverhead: Clark Canyon Reservoir to Dillon

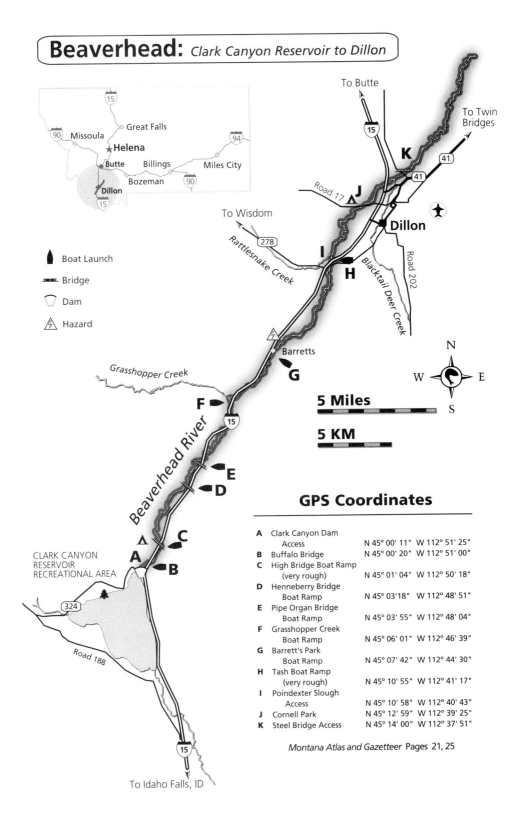

Boat Launch
Bridge
Dam
Hazard

To Butte
To Twin Bridges
To Wisdom

Road 17
Rattlesnake Creek
Blacktail Deer Creek
Road 202

Dillon

K
J
I
H
G
F
E
D
C
A
B

Barretts

Grasshopper Creek

Beaverhead River

CLARK CANYON RESERVOIR RECREATIONAL AREA

Road 324
Road 188

To Idaho Falls, ID

Great Falls
Missoula
Helena
Butte
Billings
Miles City
Bozeman
Dillon

N W E S

5 Miles

5 KM

GPS Coordinates

A	Clark Canyon Dam Access	N 45° 00' 11" W 112° 51' 25"
B	Buffalo Bridge	N 45° 00' 20" W 112° 51' 00"
C	High Bridge Boat Ramp (very rough)	N 45° 01' 04" W 112° 50' 18"
D	Henneberry Bridge Boat Ramp	N 45° 03'18" W 112° 48' 51"
E	Pipe Organ Bridge Boat Ramp	N 45° 03' 55" W 112° 48' 04"
F	Grasshopper Creek Boat Ramp	N 45° 06' 01" W 112° 46' 39"
G	Barrett's Park Boat Ramp	N 45° 07' 42" W 112° 44' 30"
H	Tash Boat Ramp (very rough)	N 45° 10' 55" W 112° 41' 17"
I	Poindexter Slough Access	N 45° 10' 58" W 112° 40' 43"
J	Cornell Park	N 45° 12' 59" W 112° 39' 25"
K	Steel Bridge Access	N 45° 14' 00" W 112° 37' 51"

Montana Atlas and Gazetteer Pages 21, 25

PHOTO: BRAD CUTLER

This brown trout fell for a small nymph fished on 3x fluorocarbon tippet. Using heavier, less visible tippet gives anglers a better chance to land the fish they hook.

Water is siphoned off at Barrett's Diversion, so wading anglers will find the river from here to Dillon much more manageable. Lower flows can lead to warmer water, so early morning or late evening are the most productive times to fish once the summer heat sets in. Don't expect as many large fish as in the upper river, but these trout are less "educated," and anglers can find more room to themselves on this overlooked stretch.

CHECK RIVER FLOWS ON THE WEB
http://montana.usgs.gov./rt-cgi/gen_tbl_pg

WHEN TO GO

Winter fishing on the Beaverhead is normally slow with the river closed above the Pipe Organ Bridge. Nymphing provides the best fishing this time of year, and you will probably be able to find a little more room on the river at this time.

The popular upper section of the Beaverhead opens on the third Saturday of May, and you can expect some company if you plan a trip at this time. During low water years, the river can run around 700 cfs through June and early July, which

A guide can improve your chances of landing the Beaverhead's tough trout.

makes for some good sight fishing. As irrigation demands increase, flows go up to 1,000 cfs or more, making both wading and floating more challenging.

August brings the cranefly hatch, which provides some of the river's best dry-fly fishing. Hoppers also begin to be effective at this time and work well into mid-September. With the fall weather, the big browns of the Beaverhead get more aggressive, and streamer fishing can be the method of choice for itinerant fly fishers looking for a real trophy trout to close out their season.

AREA ATTRACTIONS

Take a step back in time at Bannack State Park, which preserves the ghost town that was Montana's first territorial capital. You can watch reenacted gunfights or take a ride on a stagecoach. The town of Bannack sprang up after gold was discovered along Grasshopper Creek in 1862, and the population quickly grew to over 3,000. The people moved on when the gold ran out, but more than 50 historic buildings remain along Main Street.

RESOURCES

The town of Dillon offers both camping and lodging for the visiting angler and provides a central base to points upstream and downstream of the Beaverhead.

Campgrounds

DILLON

KOA Kampgrounds
735 W. Park St.
Dillon, MT 59725
Phone number/s: (406) 683-2749

Countryside RV Park
2505 Sawmill Road
Dillon, MT 59725
Phone number/s: (406) 683-9860

Hunter Beaverhead Marina (RV Park)
1225 Mt. Highway 324
Dillon, MT 59725
Phone number/s: (406) 683-5556

Lodging

DILLON

Montana High Country Tours
1036 E. Reeder St.
Dillon, MT 59725
Phone number/s: (406) 683-4920

Comfort Inn of Dillon
450 N. Interchange
Dillon, MT 59725
Phone number/s: (406) 683-6831,
toll-free (800) 442-4667

Super 8 Motel
550 N. Montana St.
Dillon, MT 59725
Phone number/s: (406)-683-4288,
toll free (800) 800-8000

Guest House Inn and Suites
580 Sinclair St.
Dillon, MT 59725
Phone number/s: (406) 683-6831,
toll-free (800) 214-8378

Tackle Shops and Guide Services

DILLON

Frontier Anglers
680 N. Montana St.
Dillon, MT 59725
Phone number/s: (406) 683-5276

Montana High Country Tours
1036 E. Reeder St.
Dillon, MT 59725
Phone number/s: (406) 683-4920,
(406) 834-3469
Web site: www.mhct.com
E-mail: montana@mhct.com

Watershed Adventures
610 N. Montana St.
Dillon, MT 50725
Phone number/s: (406) 683-6660,
toll-free (800) 753-6660
Web site: www.watershedadventures.com

Area Attractions

Bannack State Park
4200 Bannack Road
Dillon, MT 59725
Phone number/s: (406) 834-3413
Web site:http://206.58.213.251/bannack
E-mail:bannack@montana.com

Big Hole River

 ewis and Clark were the first explorers to reach the Big Hole and named it the Wisdom River in 1805, but it was the name applied by trappers to the Big Hole Valley that eventually stuck. This is a large, free-flowing river system. It is born in the outflow of Skinner Lake and runs over 150 miles before it mixes with the rich waters of the Beaverhead near Twin Bridges to form the Jefferson. Its character changes greatly throughout its course from steep mountain streams and slow-flowing meadow runs to surging whitewater canyons.

Chief Joseph lead his Nez Percé tribe into Big Hole country during what is considered one of the most brilliant military retreats in American history. In August of 1877, Colonel John Gibbons and the Seventh Infantry attacked the Nez Percé camp at dawn in what would become known as the Battle of the Big Hole. Chief Joseph, called Thunder Rolling Down the Mountain among his people, eventually escaped with his band, only to be forced to surrender just short of the Canadian border in October of that year. He is remembered best for the words he spoke to Colonel Nelson Miles upon his surrender:

I am tired…It is cold and we have no blankets…
My heart is sick and sad.
From where the sun now stands I will fight no more forever.

The Big Hole is not as wild as it was in those days, yet it still harbors the last riverine population of grayling in the lower 48 states. These beautiful and graceful fish were once spread throughout the upper Missouri River system and were even referred to as a separate species, *Thymallus montanus*, although they are now included in *Thymallus articus*. Their outstanding feature is a high, proud dorsal fin. It rises from their blue-gray backs and is edged in mauve with a wider blue band below and colored with spots ranging from orange-red to emerald green. These fish are voracious insect eaters and could have been created just to delight fly fishers. They also take nymphs well, but if there is any kind of hatch, you can expect to find them feeding on adults. Just be sure to treat them like the rare and delicate creatures they are. Use barbless flies and release them with care.

In addition to the grayling, there are rainbow, cutthroat, brown and brook trout as well as the ubiquitous mountain whitefish, giving fly fishers the opportunity to catch six different species of game fish in a single day of fishing.

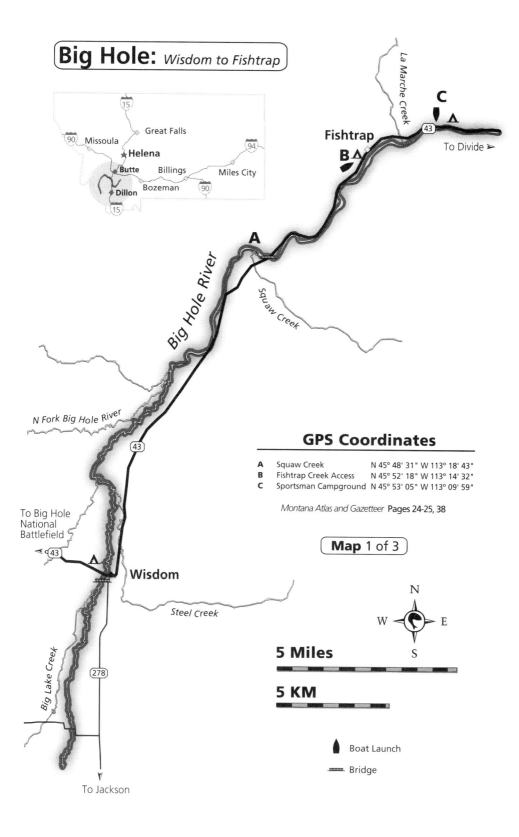

Big Hole: *Wisdom to Fishtrap*

Great Falls
Missoula
Helena
Butte
Billings
Dillon
Bozeman
Miles City

La Marche Creek

C

Fishtrap

B

To Divide ➤

43

A

Squaw Creek

Big Hole River

N Fork Big Hole River

43

To Big Hole
National
Battlefield

43

Wisdom

Steel Creek

Big Lake Creek

278

To Jackson

GPS Coordinates

A Squaw Creek   N 45° 48' 31" W 113° 18' 43"
B Fishtrap Creek Access   N 45° 52' 18" W 113° 14' 32"
C Sportsman Campground   N 45° 53' 05" W 113° 09' 59"

Montana Atlas and Gazetteer **Pages 24-25, 38**

Map 1 of 3

N
W   E
S

5 Miles

5 KM

Boat Launch

Bridge

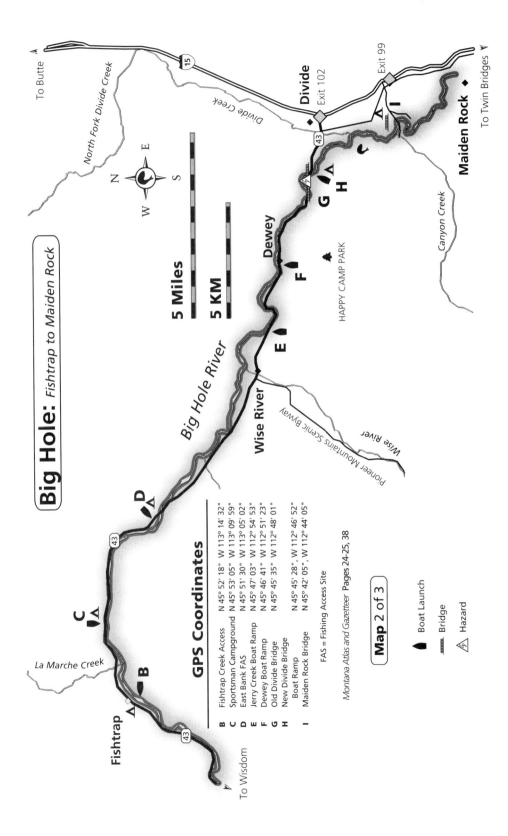

Big Hole: *Fishtrap to Maiden Rock*

To Butte ▲

North Fork Divide Creek

Divide Creek

15

Divide ◆
Exit 102

Exit 99

43

Maiden Rock ◆
To Twin Bridges ▼

Canyon Creek

HAPPY CAMP PARK

Dewey

Wise River

Pioneer Mountains Scenic Byway

Wise River

Big Hole River

43

D ▲

C ▲

B

La Marche Creek

Fishtrap ▲

43

To Wisdom ▲

N E S W

5 Miles

5 KM

GPS Coordinates

B	Fishtrap Creek Access	N 45° 52' 18"	W 113° 14' 32"
C	Sportsman Campground	N 45° 53' 05"	W 113° 09' 59"
D	East Bank FAS	N 45° 51' 30"	W 113° 05' 02"
E	Jerry Creek Boat Ramp	N 45° 47' 03"	W 112° 54' 53"
F	Dewey Boat Ramp	N 45° 46' 41"	W 112° 51' 23"
G	Old Divide Bridge	N 45° 45' 35"	W 112° 48' 01"
H	New Divide Bridge		
	Boat Ramp	N 45° 45' 28",	W 112° 46' 52"
I	Maiden Rock Bridge	N 45° 42' 05",	W 112° 44' 05"

FAS = Fishing Access Site

Montana Atlas and Gazetteer Pages 24-25, 38

Map 2 of 3

🛥 Boat Launch

▦ Bridge

⚠ Hazard

Big Hole: *Maiden Rock to Twin Bridges*

GPS Coordinates

I	Maiden Rock Bridge	N 45° 42' 05"	W 112° 44' 05"
J	Maiden Rock FAS	N 45° 39' 38"	W 112° 42' 02"
K	Salmon Fly FAS	N 45° 37' 33"	W 112° 41' 19"
L	Brownes Bridge FAS	N 45° 32' 49"	W 112° 41' 36"
M	Glen FAS	N 45° 28' 02"	W 112° 40' 00'
N	Notch Bottom Access	N 45° 26' 21"	W 112° 33' 48"
O	Pennington Bridge	N 45° 30' 07"	W 112° 26' 23"
P	High Road	N 45° 32' 51"	W 112° 22' 03"

FAS = Fishing Access Site

Montana Atlas and Gazetteer Pages 24, 25

Map 3 of 3

Boat Launch

Bridge

5 Miles

5 KM

SPECIAL REGULATIONS

The following special regulations are in effect on the Big Hole River.

Entire river and tributaries:
❏ Catch-and-release for grayling and cutthroat trout.

Headwaters to Dickie Bridge:
❏ Extended whitefish season and catch-and-release for trout from December 1 to the third Saturday in May with maggots and/or artificial lures only.

Dickie Bridge to Divide Dam (Butte Water Diversion):
❏ Artificial lures only.
❏ Extended whitefish season and catch-and-release for trout from December 1 to the third Saturday in May with maggots and/or artificial lures only.

Divide Dam to Melrose Bridge:
❏ Combined trout limit: four trout, three under 13 inches and one over 22 inches. All trout between 13 and 22 inches must be released.
❏ Artificial lures only.
❏ Closed to all fishing December 1 to the third Saturday in May.

Melrose Bridge to mouth:
❏ Extended whitefish season and catch-and-release for trout from December 1 to the third Saturday in May with maggots and/or artificial lures only.

Tributaries upstream from Divide Dam:
❏ Open entire year for brook trout.

The Big Hole's brown trout will chase down big streamers like the yellow yummy.

TACTICS

If your purpose is to catch one of the trophy browns that inhabit the Big Hole, be prepared to fish streamers. Standard patterns like woolly buggers and zonkers are effective and a fly called the yellow yummy can be very effective. Yummies are usually tied in larger sizes and are basically woolly buggers with lots of weight or lead eyes and rubber-legs. While the all-yellow version of the yummy works well in the brown-tinted water of the Big Hole, don't be afraid to try brown and olive yummies with yellow rubber-legs. Streamers should be cast right to the banks with floating lines and then stripped out about 10 feet before being thrown right back to the edge. Expect fish in slower pockets and eddies. The middle section of the river between Wise River and Melrose probably holds the greatest numbers of large fish.

When a hatch is in progress on the Big Hole, fish are often not extremely particular about specific patterns, but Steve Bielenberg of Watershed Fly Fishing Adventures recommends that dry-fly fishers be willing to fish patterns a size or two smaller than they might otherwise consider on a typical freestone river. Parachute patterns with an orange post are easier to detect when there is foam on the water.

The Big Hole tends to run reasonably clear and fishable, even when water levels are very high. This quality makes it a much better choice than most rivers if you are planning a fishing trip to coincide with the annual salmonfly hatch. Check with local shops to see where the hatch is best along the river as it moves upstream. If you are a little ahead of the hatch, try big nymph imitations, either dead-drifted or stripped. Once the large adults become the target of hungry fish, cast sofa pillows or other imitations right next to the banks, where the clumsy, first-time fliers often crash into the water.

HOW TO GET THERE

If you are traveling to the Big Hole by air, Butte, Missoula and Bozeman all have regular air service and are nearly equidistant from the town of Melrose on the Big Hole.

Anglers flying into Missoula can pick up a rental car and head east on I-90 about 120 miles before turning south onto I-15. It is another 28 miles south to Exit 93 at Melrose. If you fly into Helena, just get on I-15 and drive south 100 miles. From Bozeman, take I-90 west 70 miles, then go south on I-15 36 miles to Exit 93 to reach Melrose.

ACCESSIBILITY

I-15 and its frontage road provide the best access to the lower part of the river between Divide and Glen. From Wisdom to Divide, SR 43 follows the river and there are well-spaced fishing access sites until you reach Squaw Creek, about 25 miles downstream from Wisdom. It is difficult to access the river around Wisdom.

The Big Hole is rugged, steep in places, and not as easy for wading anglers to fish as some other rivers. Floating allows anglers to cover large stretches of water efficiently, especially when water levels are high and fish have been pushed into the banks.

The diversion dam below the old Divide Bridge has claimed several lives in the past. Be sure to avoid it.

Be sure to watch for diversion dams while floating the river — some can look like side channels from above. There is also a large and dangerous diversion at Divide, below the old Divide Bridge and above the new bridge. This hazard doesn't look very intimidating from above but has claimed several lives in the past. You can portage around, but a safer bet is to take out at old Divide Bridge or Dewey. The gradient of the Big Hole increases when you reach Wise River, and floaters need to be prepared to avoid rocks and other river hazards. After the river leaves the canyon above Melrose, you can expect to find fallen trees or "sweepers" in the river. Choose channels carefully when the river braids and keep your attention focused on the river as well as your fishing.

It is difficult to cover much water when wading the Big Hole, but anglers will find some of the best shore access at Maiden Rock Bridge in the canyon. Or, if you like the lower river, the Burma Road southwest of Pennington Bridge follows some sections of the river.

WHEN TO GO

Winter is slow on the Big Hole as there are no dams to release warmer water into the river. There is an extended whitefish season on much of the river (not from the Divide Dam to the Melrose Bridge). Fishing for whitefish can be good, but this opportunity will likely appeal to few anglers.

Early spring can be surprisingly good on the Big Hole, as run-off can be late to arrive and streamer fishing is often very good, even when water conditions are less than ideal. The river sees little angler activity in the early season, so you can find a little more room to yourself. If you have the good fortune to catch the Mother's

Hatch Chart　　AVAILABILITY

Food Items	J	F	M	A	M	J	J	A	S	O	N	D
Blue-winged olives				X	X				X	X	X	
Pale morning duns						X	X	X				
Tricos							X	X				
Golden stoneflies					X	X	X					
Salmonflies						X						
Mother's Day caddis				X	X							
Caddisflies						X	X	X				
Terrestrials							X	X	X			

Insects	Suggested Fly Patterns
Blue-winged olives	parachute Adams (#16-20), thorax BWOs (#16-20), pheasant tails (#16-20), hare's ears (#16-20), WD40s (#16-20), RS2s (#16-20)
Pale morning duns	thorax PMDs (#14-20), cream parachutes (#14-20), rusty spinners (#14- 20), pheasant tails (#14-18), hare's ears (#14-18)
Tricos	trico spinners (#18-22), thorax tricos (#18-22), parachute Adams (#18-22), pheasant tails (#18-20)
Golden stoneflies	yellow stimulators (#8-12), prince nymphs (#8-10), bead-head prince nymphs (#8-10), golden stonefly nymphs (#6-10), Bitch Creek nymphs (#6-10)
Salmonflies	sofa pillows (#6-10), Mac Salmons (#6-10), orange stimulators (#6-10), rubber-legs, black (#6-10), Bitch Creek nymphs (#6-10), Brook's stone nymphs
Mother's Day caddis	elk-hair caddis, olive (#14-16), Goddard caddis (#14-16), Hemingway caddis (#14 16), soft hackles, olive (#14-16), sparkle pupae, olive (#14-16), X-caddis (#14-16), peeking caddis (#12-14), CK nymphs (#12-14)
Caddisflies	elk-hair caddis (#16-18), partridge caddis (#16-18), CDC elk-hair caddis (#16-18), sparkle caddis (#16-18), X-caddis (#16-18), peeking caddis (#12-14), CK nymphs (#12-14)
Terrestrials	Dave's hoppers (#8-12), fur ants, black (#14-18), CDC ants (#14-18), deer-hair beetles, black (#14-16), hi-vis foam beetles (#14-16)
Streamers	yellow yummies (#2-4), woolly buggers, yellow, olive, ginger and black (#6-10), woolhead sculpins, black, brown and olive (#6-10), zonkers, olive, white and copper (#6-10)

Grayling, once widely distributed throughout the West, are still found in the Big Hole. Treat them like the rare, delicate creatures they are.

Day caddis hatch at its peak, you won't soon forget it. Weather and water can vary greatly at this time of year, so check with a local contact before you go.

June brings the much-heralded salmonfly hatch to the Big Hole and the large numbers of anglers that come with the bugs. The big flies bring big fish to the surface. If you delay your trip until July or August, you can still find a variety of good hatches, and fishing pressure will have dispersed to the other famous rivers in the region. Remember that water gets diverted for irrigation, and you can find the river too low to float with hard-bottomed boats as early as mid-July. If you plan to float later in the season, rafts and kick boats are a better choice.

When the nights turn crisp and leaves turn gold along the Big Hole, it is time to break out your streamer rod and big flies in search of aggressive browns. Their fall coloring can rival the foliage and there is nothing like coming in out of the cold at the end of a day on the water. The autumn months will also bring blue-winged olives to the surface of the river, and Indian summer afternoons can make for the kind of memories that help an angler survive the colder months.

CHECK RIVER FLOWS ON THE WEB
http://montana.usgs.gov./rt-cgi/gen_tbl_pg

AREA ATTRACTIONS

The Big Hole National Battlefield is 10 miles west of Wisdom on SR 43. You can stand upon the same ground where Chief Joseph and the Nez Percé faced Colonel John Gibbons and the Seventh Infantry. The entrance fee is $2 per person, and there is a small museum with Nez Percé artifacts.

RESOURCES

There is camping at most fishing access sites on the river for $5 per night. Sites are first-come, first-served. The towns of Melrose and Wise River both have limited accommodations, so book before you go.

Campgrounds

DILLON
KOA Kampgrounds
735 W. Park St.
Dillon, MT 59725
Phone number/s: (406) 683-2749

Lodging

MELROSE
Sportsman Motel
N. Main St.
Melrose, MT 59743
Phone number/s: (406) 835-2141

WISE RIVER
Craig Fellin's Big Hole River Outfitters
Box 156
Wise River, MT 59762
Phone number/s: (406) 832-3252
E-mail: wsr3252@montana.com

Sundance Lodge
4000 Lamarche Creek Road
Wise River, MT 59762
Phone number/s: (406) 689-3611
Fax: (406) 689-3605

Tackle Shops and Guide Services

DILLON
Watershed Fly Fishing Adventures
610 N. Montana St.
Dillon, MT 59725
Phone number/s: (406) 683-6660,
toll-free (800) 753-6660
Web site: www.watershedadventures.com

MELROSE
Sunrise Fly Shop
US 91 North
Melrose, MT 59743
Phone number/s: (406) 835-3474
Fax: (406) 835-3475

WISDOM
Conover's General Store
SR 43
Wisdom, MT 59761
Phone number/s: (406) 689-3272

WISE RIVER
Troutfitters
62311 Mt. SR 43
Wise River, MT 59762
Phone number/s: (406) 832-3212

Area Attractions
Big Hole National Battlefield
SR 43
Wisdom, MT 59761
Phone number/s: (406) 689-3155

Bighorn River

FISH SPECIES
Rainbow and brown trout

TIP
Look for fish concentrated at gravel bars

HIGHLIGHT
Good numbers of big trout

SEASON
Open year-round

 George Armstrong Custer was one of the most flamboyant and controversial figures in late 19th-century America. During the Civil War, this "Boy General" became the youngest U.S. officer, at the age of 23, to ever reach the rank of Brigadier General. His volatile career ended in one of the most complete military defeats in U.S. history — yet it was this debacle that earned him his place in popular history.

Treaty violations in the sacred Black Hills became a rallying point for native tribes frustrated by the changing policies of the federal government in the summer of 1876. Arapaho, Sioux and Cheyenne gathered together near the Bighorn River in perhaps the largest single alliance of Plains Indians ever amassed. When Lt. Colonel Custer and his Seventh Cavalry came upon this large village on the morning of June 25, he divided his troops into three separate forces and ordered an attack without waiting for reinforcement. The attack was poorly coordinated and Major Marcus Reno and his men were driven back before Custer and his men reached the village. With no other opposition, the Indian forces fell upon Custer and his 210 troops and they were soon enveloped. Horses were shot and their bodies arranged to shield the beleaguered men, but to no avail. Within an hour all were dead.

> *On fame's eternal camping-ground,*
> *Their silent tents are spread,*
> *And glory guards with solemn round*
> *The bivouac of the dead.*

(Inscription from a plaque at Little Bighorn Battlefield National Monument)

While the Battle of the Little Bighorn was the greatest victory achieved by the Plains Indians, it was to be their last. The country demanded retribution for the death of this popular war hero, whose legend had grown much larger with his death. Within a year, the Sioux nation and their allies had been defeated and the Black Hills were thrown open to settlers. The nomadic lifestyle of the Plains Indians had been brought to an end.

The Bighorn flows through the rolling hills of what is now the Crow Indian Reservation. Yellowtail Dam is named after this tribe's famous chairman, Robert Yellowtail. The reservoir it created is more than 70 miles long and as deep as 400 feet — providing a year-round supply of cold water to the river below. The Bighorn is a very productive river with a high density of trout that grow at a phenomenal rate. The majority of the trout here are rainbows that average 16 to 18 inches; they are strong and well-built. There are also good numbers of brown trout. This big water delivers up some trophy fish approaching 10 pounds every year.

The wide-open landscape of the Bighorn as it emerges from Yellowtail Dam.

Although the Bighorn derives its water from the Rocky Mountains, the blue ribbon water below Yellowtail flows out into the beginning of the plains, and the river bottom is heavily farmed. Summer temperatures can run well into the 90s under a relentless sun. There is no nightlife in Fort Smith and limited dining options. Most anglers who visit the Bighorn spend the bulk of their time on the water with one thought in their mind: trout. This great river seldom disapoints.

SPECIAL REGULATIONS AND FEES

The Bighorn River is located in the Bighorn Canyon National Recreation Area, which requires a daily or annual recreation pass if you're planning to have your rig shuttled to one of the take-out areas. You can purchase the pass at the Yellowtail Dam Visitor's Center in Fort Smith. An annual pass is $30 per year ($15 for Golden Age/Access passport visitors) and a 24-hour pass is $5 per vehicle ($2.50 for Golden Age/Access passport holders).

Afterbay Dam to cable 600 feet downstream and downstream from Bighorn Fishing Access Site.
- ❑ Open entire year.
- ❑ May use live nongame bait fish.
- ❑ Combined trout limit: five trout, only one over 18 inches and only one rainbow trout.

Cable 600 feet below Afterbay Dam to Bighorn Fishing Access Site.
- ❑ Open entire year
- ❑ Catch-and-release for rainbow trout.
- ❑ Artificial lures only.
- ❑ Combined trout limit: five brown trout, only one over 18 inches.

Fish concentrate in small areas on the Bighorn and shore access is limited. Anglers use boats primarily as transportation to the best fishing spots.

TACTICS

Though known for its consistent dry-fly fishing, there are times when you will not find active hatches and few fish working the surface. Fishing nymph patterns can be very productive, if you fish them in the correct areas. Trout tend to concentrate on the downstream edge of riffles and deeper water just downstream from the riffles. An effective way to hook these fish is to cast about 15 to 20 feet above these drop-offs and allow your nymph to dead drift across the bottom edge of the riffle and down to the deeper water behind. Expect takes in the shallows or especially when your fly crosses the lip of the drop-off. Keep in mind that the river's rainbows will hold and feed in some surprisingly fast water.

If dry-fly fishing is your thing, look for slightly slower water. Some of the best areas will be where side channels either leave or rejoin the main channel. Summer fishing during the PMD hatch can be great with trout feeding on emerging duns during midday followed by a heavy spinnerfall from evening until dark. Be sure to carry spinner patterns for this event. The black caddis hatch picks up as the pale morning duns start to fade, and the best activity will again be found at dusk when they return to the river to lay their eggs. Try dark patterns and don't be afraid to let them sink below the surface. Tricos put in their appearance at the end of summer and heavy spinnerfalls of this tiny mayfly can really get the trout going. While leaders of nine feet and 5x tippets may work for the PMDs and caddis, you may have to extend out to 12 feet and 6x once finicky fish settle in on tricos.

Note: If you find rising fish in fairly slow water, they may be golden-eye shad, which will often take dry flies. Some anglers enjoy catching a few of these willing fish along with the Bighorn's trout.

Hatch Chart

Food Items	J	F	M	A	M	J	J	A	S	O	N	D
Midges	✗	✗	✗	✗	✗	✗	✗	✗	✗	✗	✗	✗
Annelid worms	✗	✗	✗	✗	✗	✗	✗	✗	✗	✗	✗	✗
Blue-winged olives				✗	✗				✗	✗		
Pale morning duns							✗	✗				
Tricos							✗	✗				
Little yellow stoneflies							✗	✗				
Caddisflies							✗	✗	✗			
Terrestrials							✗	✗	✗	✗		

AVAILABILITY

Insects	Suggested Fly Patterns
Midges	Griffith's gnats (#16-22), Adams (#16-22), midge pupae, brown, red, olive, cream and black (#18-22), serendipities (#18-22), palomino midges (#18-22), brassies (#16-20)
Annelid worms	San Juan worms, orange, brown and red (#12-16), two-tone worms, red and brown (#12-16)
Blue-winged olives	parachute Adams (#16-20), thorax BWOs (#16-20), olive comparaduns (#16-20), Quigley cripples, olive (#16-20), CDC emergers, olive (#16-20), pheasant tails (#16-20), hare's ears (#16-20), bead-head pheasant tails (#16-20), bead-head hare's ears (#16-20)
Pale morning duns	thorax PMDs (#14-16), cream parachutes (#14-16), cream comparaduns (#16-20), Quigley cripples, cream (#16-20), rusty spinners (#14-16), CDC emergers, cream (#16-20), pheasant tails (#14-16), hare's ears (#14-16), bead-head pheasant tails (#14-16), bead-head hare's ears (#14-16)
Tricos	trico spinners (#18-20), CDC tricos (#18-20), parachute Adams (#18-20), pheasant tails (#18-20)
Little yellow stoneflies	yellow stimulators (#14-16), elk-hair caddis, tan and yellow (#14-16), red fox squirrel nymphs (#12-14), golden stonefly nymphs (#12-14)
Caddisflies	elk-hair caddis (#16-18), Hemingway caddis (#16-18), partridge caddis (#16-18), CDC elk-hair caddis (#16-18), sparkle pupae, black and tan (#16-18), X-caddis (#16-18), peeking caddis (#14-16)
Terrestrials	Dave's hoppers (#8-12), Henry's Fork hoppers (#8-12), fur ants, black (#14-18), CDC ants (#14-18), deer-hair beetles, black (#14-16), hi-vis foam beetles (#14-16)

Bighorn: *Yellowtail Dam to St. Xavier*

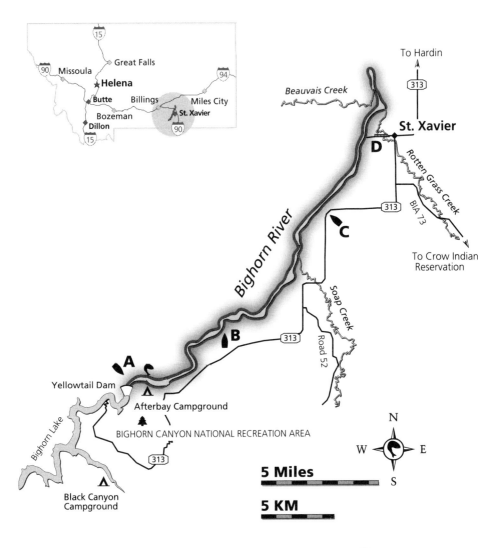

GPS Coordinates

A	Afterbay FAS	N 45° 19' 01" W 107° 55' 16"
B	Three Mile FAS	N 45° 20' 39" W 107° 52' 37"
C	Bighorn FAS	N 45° 25' 00" W 107° 47' 20"
D	St. Xavier Bridge FAS	N 45° 27' 40" W 107° 44' 57"

FAS = Fishing Access Site

Montana Atlas and Gazetteer Page 31

Map 1 of 2

 Boat Launch

Dam

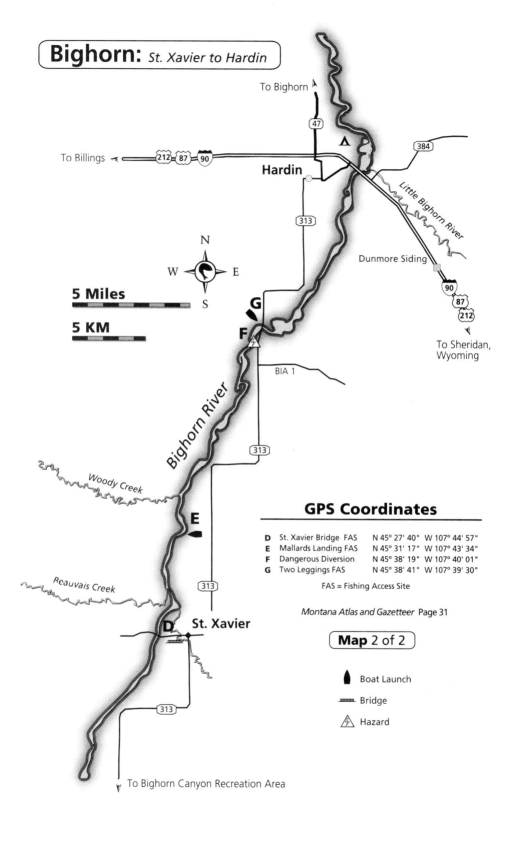

Bighorn: *St. Xavier to Hardin*

To Bighorn

47

To Billings 212 87 90

Hardin

384

Little Bighorn River

313

Dunmore Siding

90
87
212

To Sheridan, Wyoming

N
W E
S

5 Miles

5 KM

G

F

BIA 1

313

Bighorn River

Woody Creek

313

E

Reauvais Creek

313

GPS Coordinates

D St. Xavier Bridge FAS   N 45° 27' 40"   W 107° 44' 57"
E Mallards Landing FAS   N 45° 31' 17"   W 107° 43' 34"
F Dangerous Diversion   N 45° 38' 19"   W 107° 40' 01"
G Two Leggings FAS   N 45° 38' 41"   W 107° 39' 30"

FAS = Fishing Access Site

Montana Atlas and Gazetteer Page 31

Map 2 of 2

D St. Xavier

Boat Launch

Bridge

Hazard

To Bighorn Canyon Recreation Area

Del DeSpain of Bighorn Fly & Tackle Shop says, "Streamer fishing can be unreal." Floating lines are sufficient to reach the fish if you use heavily weighted patterns. Large yellowish streamers (#4-8) are most effective and include the yellow yummy or Bighorn bugger. The Bighorn special, similar to the Platte River special, is also popular. Tapered leaders of nine-foot 3x will work well, and they can be quickly converted for nymph fishing by adding 4x tippet.

HOW TO GET THERE

The nearest airports with regularly scheduled service are Billings, Montana, and Sheridan, Wyoming. It takes about two hours to drive the 90 miles from Billings to Afterbay Dam. Take I-90 East about 45 miles to Exit 497 at Hardin, then get on SR 313 and go south 45 miles to Fort Smith.

Time and distance from Sheridan are about the same; just take I-90 North about 50 miles to Exit 530 at Lodge Grass, then go west 6.3 miles on SR 463. Turn northwest onto BIA Road 73 (Good Luck Road and Rotten Grass Road) for about 20 miles to SR 313. Head southwest 16 miles to reach Fort Smith.

Catch-and-release only for rainbow trout from the cable 600 feet below Afterbay Dam to Bighorn fishing access site.

ACCESSIBILITY

The most popular water on the Bighorn is the first 13 miles below Afterbay Dam. There is limited access as it flows through mostly private and Crow Reservation lands. Shorebound anglers are required to stay below the high-water mark to avoid trespass and will find it difficult to reach much of the prime water.

Some of the best access for waders is around the islands at the Lind (Three Mile) Access Site or downstream from the Afterbay boat launch.

Like many big Western rivers, the Bighorn is best accessed by floating. Drift boats, kickboats, rafts, canoes and kayaks all work well, as most anglers use their craft for transportation and get out to fish. The river is easy to navigate, and there are relatively few hazards. Stay clear of the old cement wall in the river less than one mile below the dam. Drift boats can be rented from several of the tackle shops and outfitters in Fort Smith for those who want to row the river on their own.

The highest section of the river is from just below Afterbay Dam down to Lind (Three Mile), which is 3.8 miles downstream. This may seem like a very short float, but if you spend quite a bit of time out of the boat, you can easily fill up a day. This stretch of the river probably has the highest density of both fish and anglers.

Some of the fish in this area show the effects of careless handling. Please follow good catch-and-release practices and leave trout in good condition for the future.

The float from Lind (Three Mile) to Bighorn is 8.3 miles and makes for a full day of fishing. There are lots of gravel bars and places to get out along this segment, but if you spend much time out of the boat, it can be quite late before you reach the take-out. If you are staying in Fort Smith, this may be a good move as there is not much evening entertainment in this small town.

From Bighorn down to Mallards Landing is 8.9 miles. This section of the river is similar to the upper river but has more slow water. Although there are fewer fish down here, they are also bigger and "less educated." This length of river is a good choice for those looking for a little more solitude.

From Mallards Landing down to Two Leggins there is another 10.7 miles of river. While this section is rumored to hold some big fish, it is not recommended as it includes a dangerous diversion dam. Some anglers do float their boats over this obstacle, but a mishap could have dire consequences. If you do decide to float through here, look at the dam beforehand and provide for safety measures.

CHECK RIVER FLOWS ON THE WEB
http://montana.usgs.gov./rt-cgi/gen_tbl_pg

WHEN TO GO

The Bighorn is an excellent year-round fishery, and you can find good fishing in any month. Nymphs are the ticket to winter success, but midges will take Bighorn trout on the surface from December through March. Blue-winged olives can be abundant in April and May and will bring fish up in good numbers, especially on overcast or stormy days. The Bighorn is usually devoid of significant hatches in June and early July, but angler numbers are also a bit lower and nymph fishing can be very productive.

From late July into September, the dry-fly fishing is at its best — but the Bighorn is at its hottest and most crowded time of the year. You can experience some great PMD, trico and caddis hatches as long as you are willing to share the river with others. Don't forget long-sleeved shirts and wide-brimmed hats to protect you from the sun. You will also want to wear neoprene waders if you are going to spend much time in the water. The Bighorn usually stays a very cold 40 to 50 degrees even during the summer heat.

With the arrival of October, temperatures moderate and caddis and trico fishing can continue well into the cooler weather. Streamer fishing reaches its peak at this time.

For daily fishing updates on the Bighorn, go online at *www.bighornfly.com*.

AREA ATTRACTIONS

Little Bighorn Battlefield National Monument is the site of the June 25, 1876 battle between the United States Army's Seventh Cavalry and several bands of Sioux, Cheyenne and Arapaho. Popularly known as "Custer's Last Stand," you can view this historic battlefield and visit the graves of the soldiers buried here. A

The Battle of Little Bighorn marked the end of the nomadic lifestyle of the Plains Indians.

monument to the Indian warriors who also lost their lives in this famous battle is in the planning stages.

Located just off Exit 510 on I-90 at Crow Agency, it is a 2½-hour round-trip drive for anglers staying in Fort Smith. There is an entrance fee of $6 per vehicle or $3 per person for pedestrians.

RESOURCES

Fort Smith has limited lodgings — some of the fly shops offer simple accommodations — and there is one restaurant near Yellowtail Dam and another cafe down the road at the Bighorn RV Park. Fishing is this town's entertainment. If you want to enjoy an alcoholic beverage, be sure to bring it with you. No alcohol is sold on the reservation.

If you are planning to camp, you'll want your rig to have air conditioning in the summer. The Afterbay public campground is first-come, first-served and does not have showers. For more information on the facilities in Bighorn Canyon National Recreation Area, check its web site at *www.nps.gov/bica.*

Campgrounds

BIGHORN CANYON NRA
❐ Afterbay Campground
(adjacent to Yellowtail Dam)

FORT SMITH
Bighorn RV Park
P.O. Box 305
Fort Smith, MT 59035
Phone number/s: (406) 666-2460
Restaurant, showers, fishing guides, shuttles and boat rentals.

YELLOWTAIL
Cottonwood Camp
(near Lind Access)
P.O. Box 7667
Yellowtail, MT 59035
Phone number/s:(406) 666-2391
Cabins, laundromat and convenience store. Guides and boat rentals available.

Lodging

FORT SMITH
Big Horn River Lodge
P.O. Box 7756
Fort Smith, MT 59035
Phone number/s: (406) 666-2368

Bighorn Angler Motel
577 Parkdale Court
Fort Smith, MT 59035
Phone number/s: (406) 666-2233

Forrester's Bighorn River Resort
P.O. Box 7595
(1 mile north of Fort Smith)
Fort Smith, MT 59035
Phone number/s: (406) 666-9199,
toll-free (800) 665-3799
Fax: (406) 666-9197

Bighorn Fly & Tackle Shop — Motel
Parkdale Trailer Park #5
Fort Smith, MT 59035
Phone number/s: (406) 666-2253

HARDIN
Eagle Nest Lodge
P.O. Box 509
Hardin, MT 59034
Phone number/s: (406) 665-3711
Fax: (406) 665-3712
Web site: www.eaglenestlodge.com

Tackle Shops and Guide Services

FORT SMITH
Big Horn Trout Shop
577 Parkdale Court
Fort Smith, MT 59035
Phone number/s: (406) 666-2375

Bighorn Angler
577 Parkdale Court
Fort Smith, MT 59035
Phone number/s: (406) 666-2233

Bighorn Fly & Tackle Shop
P.O. Box 7597
Fort Smith, MT 59035
Phone number/s: (406) 666-2253
Fax: (406) 666-2553
Web site: www.bighornfly.com
E-mail: info@bighornfly.com

also: Bighorn Fly & Tackle Shop
485 S. 24th St. W.
Billings, MT 59102
Phone number/s: (406) 656-8257

also: Bighorn Fly & Tackle Shop
1426 N. Crawford Ave.
Hardin, MT 59034
Phone number/s: (406) 665-1321,
toll-free (888) 665-1321

Fort Smith Flyshop
P.O. Box 7872
Fort Smith, MT 59035
Phone number/s: (406) 666-2550

Area Attractions
Little Bighorn Battlefield National Monument
P.O. Box 39
Crow Agency, MT 59022
Phone number/s: (406) 638-2621

Bitterroot River

T he year 2000's "Summer of Fire" burned more than 6 million acres across the United States, and the Bitterroot National Forest was one of the hardest-hit areas, with over 350,000 acres of the 1.6 million-acre forest going up in flames. While this sounds pretty disastrous, the fire never reached the main stem of the Bitterroot and was confined to the river's tributaries. And even as fire-fighters worked to extinguish the last flames, vigorous efforts were made to rehabilitate damaged areas and reduce the potential for erosion.

The East Fork of the Bitterroot near Sula was the site of some of the most intense fire; other tributary streams were affected as well. The fallout is that the Bitterroot will be more likely to muddy after rains or snow melt in the short run. The long-term outlook is positive. Ash from the fires is expected to raise nitrogen levels in the river, possibly increasing productivity in the stream for a time. The East Fork and other tributaries are all part of a healthy aquatic system and are expected to recover within a year or so.

The Bitterroot Valley is growing fast; towns like Florence and Stevensville act as bedroom communities for the larger city of Missoula. Once you get on the river, it is surprising how little of this growth is obvious from the water. Perhaps most importantly, fish populations appear to be doing well. While the Bitterroot does not have the very high density of trout of some other rivers, their average size is around 14 to 16 inches, and the number of trout reaching 20 inches has been on the rise, especially downstream from Hamilton. Thus far, the Bitterroot has remained free from whirling disease, and the river's rainbows are fit and strong. Hook a big 'bow here and the final outcome will be hotly contested.

SPECIAL REGULATIONS

One mile downstream of Darby Bridge to Star Falls on the East Fork :
- ❏ Catch-and-release for cutthroat trout.
- ❏ Three rainbow or brown trout, one over 14 inches.
- ❏ Extended whitefish season and catch-and-release for trout open December 1 to the third Saturday in May with aquatic insects, maggots and/or artificial lures only.

The river can be a place of calm and quiet in the fast-growing Bitterroot Valley.

Tucker Crossing to Florence Bridge and one mile downstream from Darby to Como Bridge:
- ❏ Catch-and-release for all trout.
- ❏ Artificial lures only.
- ❏ Extended whitefish season and catch-and-release for trout open December 1 to the third Saturday in May with aquatic insects, maggots and/or artificial lures only.

Como Bridge to Tucker Crossing:
- ❏ Catch-and-release for cutthroat trout.
- ❏ Three rainbow or brown trout, one over 14 inches.
- ❏ Extended whitefish season and catch-and-release for trout open December 1 to the third Saturday in May with aquatic insects, maggots and/or artificial lures only.

Tucker Crossing to Florence Bridge:
- ❏ Catch-and-release for trout.
- ❏ Artificial lures only.
- ❏ Extended season for whitefish and catch-and-release for trout open December 1 to the third Saturday in May with aquatic insects, maggots and/or artificial lures only.

Florence Bridge to mouth of the Bitterroot:
- ❏ Catch-and-release for cutthroat trout.
- ❏ Three rainbow or brown trout, one over 14 inches.
- ❏ Extended season for whitefish and catch-and-release for trout open December 1 to the third Saturday in May with aquatic insects, maggots and/or artificial lures only.

Hatch Chart — AVAILABILITY

Food Items	J	F	M	A	M	J	J	A	S	O	N	D
Midges	X	X	X	X	X	X	X	X	X	X	X	X
Gray drakes			X	X								
Blue-winged olives			X	X	X				X	X		
Pale morning duns						X	X	X	X			
Green drakes							X	X				
Flavs							X	X				
Tricos								X	X			
Mahogany duns								X	X	X		
Skwala stoneflies			X	X								
Salmonflies				X	X							
Caddisflies				X	X	X	X					
Terrestrials								X	X	X		

TACTICS

If you come to fish the famous skwala hatch, the first order of business will be dressing warmly. Even though the Bitterroot is at lower elevation than most of Montana's great trout rivers, it can still be quite cold. You will find the best fishing in the early afternoons when the air temperature is at its peak. The nymphs migrate to the edges to crawl out to hatch, so keep your flies in close to the banks. Trout seem to be quite willing to rise to these first big insects of the year, so don't hesitate to try an olive stimulator if you see an adult skwala or two on the water.

The gray drakes come on just as the skwala hatch is fading. They are a species of Ameletus, and unlike most mayflies, the nymphs are strong swimmers and crawl out on rocks to hatch. Because of this habit, nymphs are much more important than the adults. Fish the nymphs with some movement or even stripped at the end of the drift.

From March through August, there are large insects of one species or another available to the Bitterroot's trout. They get accustomed to snatching big meals from the river's surface and are often vulnerable to large attractor flies like stimulators and Wulffs, especially as the water drops in the summer. The last hour of evening can be the best fishing of the day, often bringing pale morning duns and caddis back to the river for an orgy of egg-laying.

Grasshoppers are important trout food in late summer, and anglers can take a couple different approaches to fishing them. A Dave's hopper with a bead-head dropper is very effective, especially when fished along the banks. You can also fish a Turck's tarantula, dead-drifted as a hopper and stripping it in at the end of the float. Use heavy tippets of about 3x with this aggressive approach.

Insects	Suggested Fly Patterns
Midges	Griffith's gnats (#16-22), Adams (#16-22), midge pupae, gray, cream, brown and black (#18-22), brassies (#18-22)
Gray drakes	parachute Adams (#14-16), gray comparaduns (#14-16), pheasant tails (#14-16), hare's ears (#14-16), bead-head pheasant tails (#14-16), bead-head hare's ears (#14-16)
Blue-winged olives	parachute Adams (#16-20), thorax BWOs (#16-20), olive comparaduns (#16-20), Quigley cripples, olive (#16-20), CDC emergers, olive (#16-20), pheasant tails (#16-20), hare's ears (#16-20), bead-head pheasant tails (#16-20), bead-head hare's ears (#16-20)
Pale morning duns	thorax PMDs (#14-16), cream parachutes (#14-16), cream comparaduns (#16-20), Quigley cripples, cream (#16-20), rusty spinners (#14-16), CDC emergers, cream (#16-20), pheasant tails (#14-16), hare's ears (#14-16), bead-head pheasant tails (#14-16), bead-head hare's ears (#14-16)
Green drakes	green drake Wulffs (#8-12), olive paradrakes (#10-12), olive comparaduns (#10-12), Quigley cripples, olive (#8-12), soft-hackle emergers, olive (#8-12), CDC emergers, olive (#10-14), hare's ears, olive (#10-14), zug bugs (#10-14)
Flavs	parachute Adams (#14-16), olive comparaduns (#14-16), Quigley cripples, olive (#14-16), CDC emergers, olive (#14-16), hare's ears, olive (#14-16), bead-head hare's ears, olive (#14-16)
Tricos	trico spinners (#18-22), CDC tricos (#18-22), parachute Adams (#18-22), pheasant tails (#18-20)
Mahogany duns	March browns (#14-16), parachute hare's ears (#14-16), brown comparaduns (#14-16), CDC emergers (#14-16), rusty spinners (#14-16), pheasant tails (#14-16), bead-head pheasant tails (#14-16)
Skwala stoneflies	olive stimulators (#6-10), bullethead skwalas (#6-10), girdle bugs, brown (#6-10), yuk bugs, brown (#6-10)
Salmonflies	sofa pillows (#6-10), Mac Salmons (#6-10), orange stimulators (#6-10), rubber-legs, black (#6-10), Bitch Creek nymphs (#6-10), Brook's stone nymphs
Caddisflies	elk-hair caddis (#14-18), partridge caddis (#14-18), CDC elk-hair caddis (#14-18), sparkle pupae (#14-18), X-caddis (#16-18), peeking caddis (#14-16), bead-head caddis (#14-16)
Terrestrials	Dave's hoppers (#8-12), Henry's Fork hoppers (#8-12), Turck's tarantulas (#6-8), fur ants, black (#14-18), CDC ants (#14-18), deer-hair beetles, black (#14-16), hi-vis foam beetles (#14-16)

HOW TO GET THERE

Missoula has regularly scheduled air service and is the best jumping-off point for out-of-town anglers. Drive south from Missoula on US 93, which follows the Bitterroot for its entire length.

Visitors to the Bitterroot Valley who are driving up from the south can either take I-15 to I-90 to reach Missoula, or leave I-15 25 miles north of Idaho Falls at Exit 143 and take SR 28 136 miles northwest to Salmon, Idaho. It is about 90 miles north on US 93 from Salmon to the town of Hamilton on the Bitterroot River.

ACCESSIBILITY

US 93 provides anglers with access to the Bitteroot. It follows the river from Missoula to where the Bitterroot joins its East and West Forks near Hannon Memorial fishing access site. The large number of public access points make it easy for visiting anglers to find a place to get on the water, but remember that most land bordering the river is private. Anglers are required to stay below the high-water mark to avoid trespass when the river crosses private lands. Some good access for shore anglers will be found at Stevensville Bridge, Bell Crossing, Bass Creek, Poker Joe and Chief Looking Glass.

Like many big western rivers, anglers who float the river will cover much more water and will likely be more successful. In general, the river is easy to float, but there are some hazardous diversion dams in the Hamilton area that you will need to portage. The river changes from year to year, and large trees can block even major channels, so stay vigilant and assume responsibility for your own safety on the water. Drift boats work well on the Bitterroot at higher water levels, but rafts are a better choice when flows are low. The highest two float sections — four miles from Hannon Memorial to Darby Bridge and seven miles from Darby Bridge down to Wally Crawford — are quite popular due to the greater number of trout in this area, and you can avoid the diversion dams downstream. Any of the floats from Blodgett Park (stay in the west channel to avoid diversions) to Florence can be quite good, as more restrictive regulations have helped fishing to rebound in this section. The float from Stevensville Bridge to Florence Bridge is about 10 miles. Most of this float is quite pretty — except for the section where the bank is stabilized by old car bodies — and flows along the edge of the Lee Metcalf National Wildlife Refuge.

Don't write off the urban fishery as the Bitterroot flows through Missoula; while it may not be the most aesthetically appealing, you can still find good fish, especially near Fort Missoula.

There are launch areas at the following points:

❑ Hannon Memorial fishing access site
❑ Darby Bridge — Small launch next to private bridge. Hard to turn around.
❑ Wally Crawford fishing access site — Improved boat ramp, two diversion dams before Anglers Roost.
❑ Anglers Roost — Private unimproved ramp, no charge for use. One diversion dam before Blodgett Park.

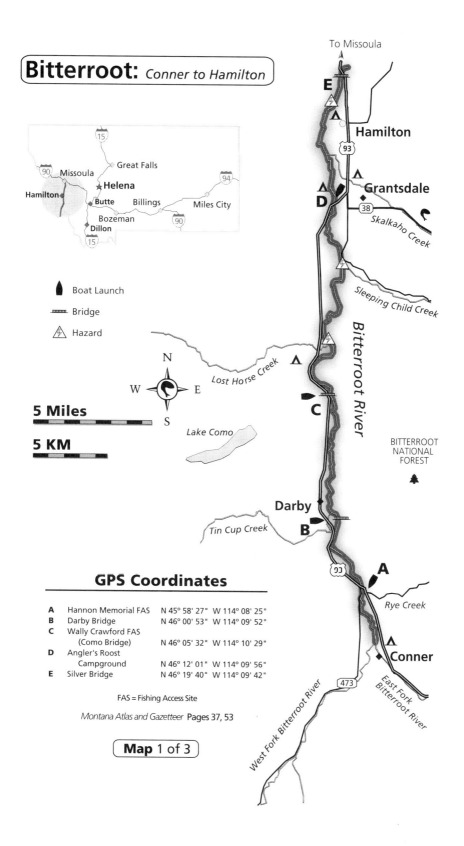

Bitterroot: *Conner to Hamilton*

To Missoula

E

Hamilton

93

D — Grantsdale

38

Skalkaho Creek

Sleeping Child Creek

Bitterroot River

BITTERROOT
NATIONAL
FOREST

Lost Horse Creek

C

Boat Launch

Bridge

Hazard

N
W — E
S

5 Miles

5 KM

Lake Como

Darby

B

Tin Cup Creek

A

Rye Creek

Conner

93

473

West Fork Bitterroot River

East Fork Bitterroot River

Inset map:

15

Great Falls

90 Missoula

94

★Helena

Hamilton

Butte   *Billings*

Miles City

Bozeman   90

Dillon

15

GPS Coordinates

A	Hannon Memorial FAS	N 45° 58' 27"	W 114° 08' 25"
B	Darby Bridge	N 46° 00' 53"	W 114° 09' 52"
C	Wally Crawford FAS		
	(Como Bridge)	N 46° 05' 32"	W 114° 10' 29"
D	Angler's Roost		
	Campground	N 46° 12' 01"	W 114° 09' 56"
E	Silver Bridge	N 46° 19' 40"	W 114° 09' 42"

FAS = Fishing Access Site

Montana Atlas and Gazetteer **Pages 37, 53**

Map 1 of 3

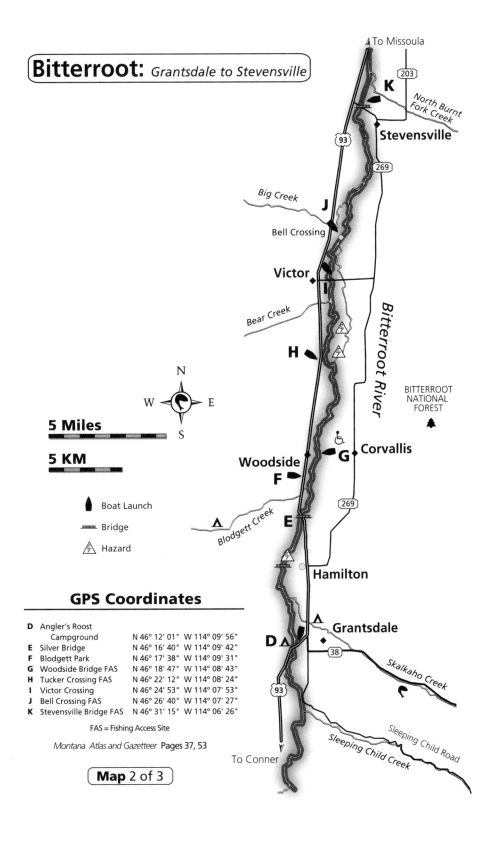

Bitterroot: *Grantsdale to Stevensville*

To Missoula

203

K

North Burnt Fork Creek

93

Stevensville

269

Big Creek

J

Bell Crossing

Victor

I

Bear Creek

H

Bitterroot River

BITTERROOT
NATIONAL
FOREST

N
W **E**
S

5 Miles

5 KM

Corvallis

G

Woodside

F

Boat Launch

Bridge

Hazard

Blodgett Creek

E

269

Hamilton

GPS Coordinates

D Angler's Roost
    Campground   N 46° 12' 01" W 114° 09' 56"
E Silver Bridge   N 46° 16' 40" W 114° 09' 42"
F Blodgett Park   N 46° 17' 38" W 114° 09' 31"
G Woodside Bridge FAS N 46° 18' 47" W 114° 08' 43"
H Tucker Crossing FAS N 46° 22' 12" W 114° 08' 24"
I Victor Crossing   N 46° 24' 53" W 114° 07' 53"
J Bell Crossing FAS   N 46° 26' 40" W 114° 07' 27"
K Stevensville Bridge FAS N 46° 31' 15" W 114° 06' 26"

FAS = Fishing Access Site

Montana Atlas and Gazetteer **Pages 37, 53**

D

Grantsdale

38

Skalkaho Creek

93

Sleeping Child Road

Sleeping Child Creek

To Conner

Map 2 of 3

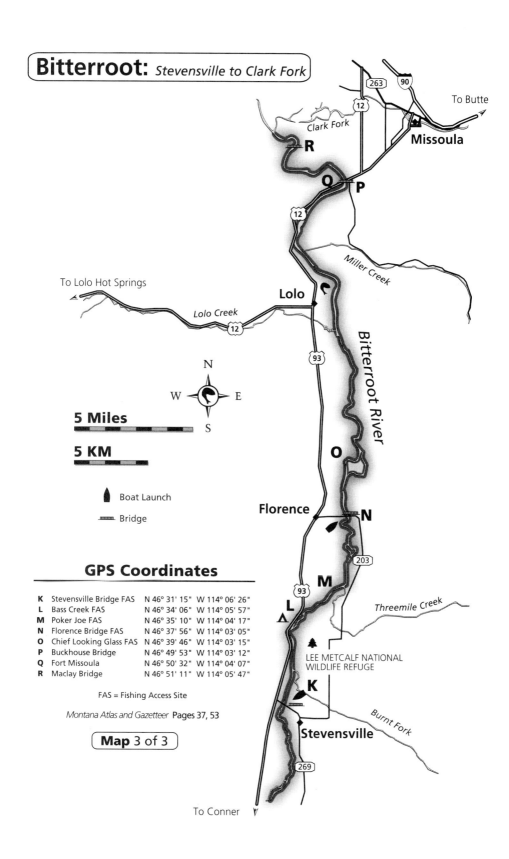

Bitterroot: *Stevensville to Clark Fork*

263
90

To Butte

12

Clark Fork

R

Q **P**

12

Missoula

Miller Creek

To Lolo Hot Springs

Lolo Creek

12

Lolo

93

Bitterroot River

N
E
W
S

5 Miles

5 KM

O

Florence

N

203

Boat Launch

Bridge

M

93

Threemile Creek

L

GPS Coordinates

K	Stevensville Bridge FAS	N 46° 31' 15"	W 114° 06' 26"
L	Bass Creek FAS	N 46° 34' 06"	W 114° 05' 57"
M	Poker Joe FAS	N 46° 35' 10"	W 114° 04' 17"
N	Florence Bridge FAS	N 46° 37' 56"	W 114° 03' 05"
O	Chief Looking Glass FAS	N 46° 39' 46"	W 114° 03' 15"
P	Buckhouse Bridge	N 46° 49' 53"	W 114° 03' 12"
Q	Fort Missoula	N 46° 50' 32"	W 114° 04' 07"
R	Maclay Bridge	N 46° 51' 11"	W 114° 05' 47"

FAS = Fishing Access Site

Montana Atlas and Gazetteer **Pages 37, 53**

Map 3 of 3

LEE METCALF NATIONAL
WILDLIFE REFUGE

K

Burnt Fork

Stevensville

269

To Conner

- ❏ Blodgett Park
- ❏ Woodside Bridge fishing access site — Steep improved ramp. Take west channel; east channel has two diversion dams.
- ❏ Tucker (West) Crossing fishing access site — Improved ramp.
- ❏ Victor Crossing
- ❏ Bell Crossing
- ❏ Stevensville Bridge fishing access site
- ❏ Florence Bridge fishing access site
- ❏ Kelly Island

WHEN TO GO

The Bitterroot is one of the best choices for early season fly fishing in western Montana. The hatch of large skwala stoneflies kicks off the season around mid-March, and this hatch provides good fishing for as long as six weeks, if high water doesn't shut it down early. The skwalas lure a lot of fly fishers out of the house for a taste of spring, so expect plenty of company if you plan a trip to the Bitterroot during this period.

PHOTO: JOHN McCOLGAN

Elk head for cover: Intense fire on the East Fork of the Bitterroot in the summer of 2000.

Like other freestone rivers, run-off on the Bitterroot can vary a great deal, but the water will normally come up in May and recede by late June. There is usually plenty of hatch activity from salmonflies, mayflies and caddis whenever the river is clear enough to fish. As the river settles into summer flows in July, keep your eyes open for big green drakes. August fishing is propped up by tricos and grasshoppers, but water levels can get very low during this period.

Angler numbers really dwindle as autumn approaches in September, and fall can be the best time of year to fish the Bitterroot. By October, you may have the river to yourself as you cast blue-winged olives or mahogany duns to the season's last rising trout.

> **CHECK RIVER FLOWS ON THE WEB**
> http://montana.usgs.gov./rt-cgi/gen_tbl_pg

RESOURCES

There has been quite a bit of growth in the Bitterroot Valley, and commuter traffic gets heavier the closer one gets to Missoula. If you are looking for a relaxing vacation, try staying upriver in Hamilton, or better yet in Darby, which is an attractive, small town that caters to tourists.

Campgrounds

HAMILTON

Angler's Roost Campground
815 US 93 South
Hamilton, MT 59840
Phone number/s: (406) 363-1268

Bitterroot Family Campground
1744 US 93 South
Hamilton, MT 59840
Phone number/s: (406) 363-2430

Lodging

HAMILTON

Angler's Lodge
815 US 93 South, #B
Hamilton, MT 59840
Phone number/s: (406) 363-0980

Best Western Inn
409 S. 1st St.
Hamilton, MT 59840
Phone number/s: (406) 363-2142

Comfort Inn
1113 N. 1st St.
Hamilton, MT 59840
Phone number/s: (406) 363-6600

Skalkaho Lodge
1380 Skalkaho Hwy
Hamilton, MT 59840
Phone number/s: (406) 363-3522

CORVALIS

Teller Wildlife Refuge
1292 Chaffin Road
Corvalis, MT 59828
Phone number/s: toll-free (800) 343-3707

DARBY

Triple Creek Ranch
5551 W. Fork Stage Road
Darby, MT 59829
Phone number/s: (406) 821-4600
Fax: (406) 821-4666
Web site: www.triplecreekranch.com

Tackle Shops and Guide Services

HAMILTON

River Bend Fly Fishing
103 State St.
Hamilton, MT 59840
Phone number/s: (406) 363-4197

VICTOR

Blackbird's Fly Shop & Lodge
1754 US 93 North
Victor, MT 59875
Phone number/s: (406) 642-6375

MISSOULA

Grizzly Hackle International Fishing
215 W. Front St.
Missoula, MT 59802
Phone number/s: (406) 721-8996,
toll-free (800)-297-8996
Web site: www.grizzlyhackle.com
E-mail: info@grizzlyhackle.com

Madison River below Hebgen Lake

FISH SPECIES
Rainbow and brown trout

TIP
Fish streamer with a nymph trailer

HIGHLIGHT
Miles and miles of constant riffle

SEASON
Open year-round on some sections

On August 17, 1959, several families had just settled in for the night at the Rock Creek campground when an incredible shaking and rumbling began. It was the initial jolt of the Hebgen Lake earthquake, and before it was over, 26 people would be buried by a slide of 80 million tons of rock and debris that formed the dam now known as Quake Lake. Montana is one of the most seismically active states in the U.S., and this was the largest quake in Montana's history. Travelers can now visit the Madison River Canyon Earthquake Area to witness the power and scale of our world's evolution.

Just as the shifting plates of the earth's crust have left their mark on the Madison River, so has the Madison helped shape the direction of the sport of fly fishing. Ray Bergman wrote of his experiences on this river in his seminal work *Trout* back in 1938. Joe Brooks honed his fishing craft in these waters and *Ernest Schwiebert's Nymphs* is drawn, in part, from his adventures in pursuit of Madison River trout. For many, the Madison River is synonymous with fly fishing in the American West.

The Madison again came to public attention in 1994, when whirling disease was linked to a dramatic crash of the river's rainbow trout population. This finding sparked the widespread testing of Montana waters, and whirling disease has since been discovered at more than 70 other sites. Since then, rainbow trout have staged a strong comeback in the Madison, reaching respectable levels in 1999, while brown trout are at a high point. Now is a good time to take advantage of improving fish populations and plan a trip to this renowned trout fishery.

SPECIAL REGULATIONS

Hebgen Lake to Quake Lake:
- Open entire year.
- Standard limits apply.

Quake Lake outlet Lyon Bridge:
- Open the third Saturday in May through the end of February.
- Catch-and-release for trout.
- Artificial lures only.
- Closed to fishing from boats.

Hank Kiley enjoys early-season solitude on the Madison River.

Lyon Bridge to McAtee Bridge:

❑ Open the third Saturday in May through the end of February.
❑ Catch-and-release for trout.
❑ Artificial lures only.

McAtee Bridge to Varney Bridge:

❑ Open entire year.
❑ Catch-and-release for trout.
❑ Artificial lures only.

Varney Bridge to Ennis Bridge:

❑ Open entire year.
❑ Catch-and-release for rainbow trout.
❑ Limit: five brown trout; only one over 18 inches

Ennis Bridge to Ennis Lake:

❑ Open the third Saturday in May through the end of February
❑ Catch-and-release for rainbow trout.
❑ Limit: five brown trout; only one over 18 inches.
❑ Closed to fishing from boats.

Ennis Dam to mouth:

❑ Open all year.
❑ Standard limits apply.

Hatch Chart

Food Items		AVAILABILITY										
	J	F	M	A	M	J	J	A	S	O	N	D
Midges	X	X	X	X	X	X	X	X	X	X	X	X
Blue-winged olives				X	X				X	X		
Pale morning duns							X	X				
Green drakes						X	X					
Golden stoneflies						X	X					
Salmonflies						X	X					
Caddisflies					X	X	X	X	X	X		
Terrestrials							X	X	X			

TACTICS

Wading anglers can benefit from the tactics employed by their float-fishing counterparts. Most floaters row down the side of the river and cast their flies right to the bank, where the greatest number of fish are normally found. The shoreline offers shallow water and slower current, as well as concentrating the insects that trout prey upon. When the stoneflies migrate to the river's edge, they can stimulate a feeding binge that continues as newly hatched bugs fall back into the river as they test their wings. Grasshoppers are another trout food that will most often be available only where the thin water meets the banks. Waders can either work up the edge and cast upstream, or wade out into the river as far as current and water depth allow and then work imitations into the slow pockets along the shore.

In the extensive riffle water of the Madison, a fish's vision is limited and the river's voice covers much of the noise that anglers make. These conditions allow fly fishers to get close to their quarry, which is a blessing in the fast water as trout are often reluctant to move far from the calmer water to snatch a meal from the stronger flow.

Streamer fishing on the Madison can be very effective in both the spring and fall. Chris Eaton of Eaton Outfitters recommends adding a size 12 or 14 nymph behind streamer patterns. This will give anglers a chance to hook up with those fish that are interested in the bigger fly but lack the resolution to attack the larger offering.

From Warm Springs below Beartrap Canyon down to Black's Ford, there are good numbers of fish and access sites. Fishing can be rewarding as long as you avoid this stretch in the heat of summer. The biggest fish in this section gain size by feeding on the prolific crayfish. Try casting imitations of these crustaceans, or use simple woolly buggers or woolheads to give a reasonable impression of the resident mudbugs.

HOW TO GET THERE

There is regular air service to Bozeman, and Delta/Skywest has service into West Yellowstone Airport from June 1 to September 30. West Yellowstone is right

Insects	Suggested Fly Patterns
Midges	Griffith's gnats (# 16-22), Adams (#16-22), midge pupae, red, cream, brown and black (#18-22), brassies (#16-20)
Blue-winged olives	parachute Adams (#16-20), thorax BWOs (#16-20), olive comparaduns (#16-20), Quigley cripples, olive (#16-20), olive CDC emergers (#16-20), pheasant tails (#16-20), hare's ears (#16-20), bead-head pheasant tails (#16-20), bead-head hare's ears (#16-20)
Pale morning duns	thorax PMDs (#16-20), cream parachutes (#16-20), cream comparaduns (#16-20), Quigley cripples, cream (#16-20), rusty spinners (#16-20), CDC emergers, cream (#16-20), pheasant tails (#14-18), hare's ears (#14-18), bead-head pheasant tails (#14-18), bead-head hare's ears (#14-18)
Green drakes	green drake Wulffs (#14-16), olive paradrakes (#14-16), olive comparaduns (#14-16), Quigley cripples, olive (#14-16), soft-hackle emergers, olive (#14-16), CDC emergers, olive (#14-16), hare's ears, olive (#14-16), zug bugs (#14-16)
Golden stoneflies	yellow stimulators (#4-8), Madam Xs (#4-8), prince nymphs (#8-10), bead-head prince nymphs (#8-10), golden stonefly nymphs (#4-8), Bitch Creek nymphs (#4-8), copper Johns (#8-10)
Salmonflies	sofa pillows (#4-8), Mac Salmons (#4-8), orange stimulators (#4-8), girdle bugs, black (#4-8), yuk bugs, black, olive and brown (#4-8), Bitch Creek nymphs (#6-10), Brook's stone nymphs (#4-8)
Caddisflies	elk-hair caddis (#14-18), partridge caddis (#14-18), CDC elk-hair caddis (#14-18), sparkle caddis (#14-18), X-caddis (#14-18), peeking caddis (#12-16), CK nymphs (#12-16)
Terrestrials	Dave's hoppers (#8-12), Henry's Fork hoppers (#8-12), fur ants, black (#14-18), CDC ants (#14-18), deer-hair beetles, black (#14-16), hi-vis foam beetles (#14-16)
Streamers	woolly buggers, olive, black and brown (#4-8), bead-head woolly buggers, olive, black and brown (#4-8), muddler minnows (#4-8), spruce flies, light and dark (#4-8), zonkers, copper, olive and gold (#4-8)

CHECK RIVER FLOWS ON THE WEB
http://montana.usgs.gov./rt-cgi/gen_tbl_pg

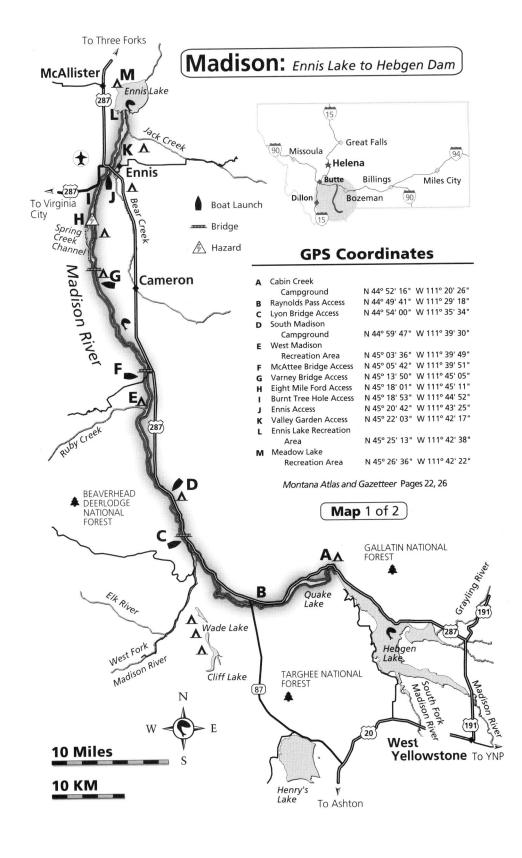

Madison: *Ennis Lake to Hebgen Dam*

Boat Launch

Bridge

Hazard

GPS Coordinates

A	Cabin Creek Campground	N 44° 52' 16" W 111° 20' 26"
B	Raynolds Pass Access	N 44° 49' 41" W 111° 29' 18"
C	Lyon Bridge Access	N 44° 54' 00" W 111° 35' 34"
D	South Madison Campground	N 44° 59' 47" W 111° 39' 30"
E	West Madison Recreation Area	N 45° 03' 36" W 111° 39' 49"
F	McAttee Bridge Access	N 45° 05' 42" W 111° 39' 51"
G	Varney Bridge Access	N 45° 13' 50" W 111° 45' 05"
H	Eight Mile Ford Access	N 45° 18' 01" W 111° 45' 11"
I	Burnt Tree Hole Access	N 45° 18' 53" W 111° 44' 52"
J	Ennis Access	N 45° 20' 42" W 111° 43' 25"
K	Valley Garden Access	N 45° 22' 03" W 111° 42' 17"
L	Ennis Lake Recreation Area	N 45° 25' 13" W 111° 42' 38"
M	Meadow Lake Recreation Area	N 45° 26' 36" W 111° 42' 22"

Montana Atlas and Gazetteer Pages 22, 26

Map 1 of 2

10 Miles

10 KM

Madison: *Three Forks to Ennis Lake*

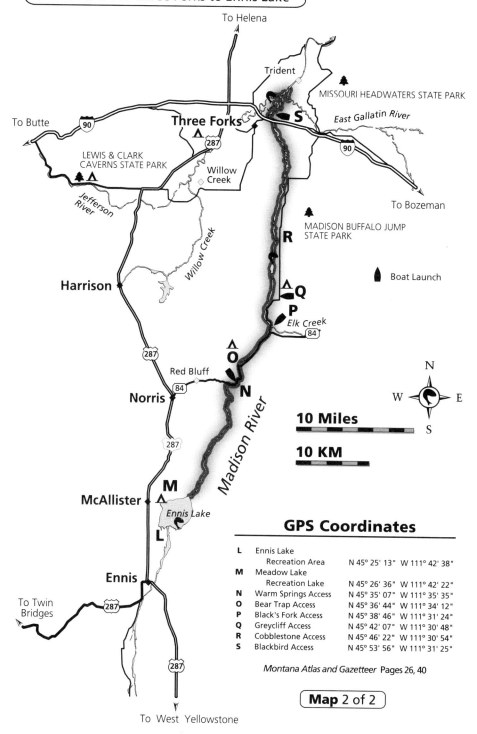

To Helena

Trident

MISSOURI HEADWATERS STATE PARK

To Butte

90

Three Forks

287

East Gallatin River

90

LEWIS & CLARK
CAVERNS STATE PARK

Willow
Creek

S

To Bozeman

Jefferson River

Willow Creek

MADISON BUFFALO JUMP
STATE PARK

R

Boat Launch

Harrison

Q

P

Elk Creek

84

287

O

Red Bluff

84

N

Norris

Madison River

287

N

W   E

S

10 Miles

10 KM

M

McAllister

Ennis Lake

L

Ennis

To Twin
Bridges

287

287

GPS Coordinates

L	Ennis Lake	
	Recreation Area	N 45° 25' 13" W 111° 42' 38"
M	Meadow Lake	
	Recreation Lake	N 45° 26' 36" W 111° 42' 22"
N	Warm Springs Access	N 45° 35' 07" W 111° 35' 35"
O	Bear Trap Access	N 45° 36' 44" W 111° 34' 12"
P	Black's Fork Access	N 45° 38' 46" W 111° 31' 24"
Q	Greycliff Access	N 45° 42' 07" W 111° 30' 48"
R	Cobblestone Access	N 45° 46' 22" W 111° 30' 54"
S	Blackbird Access	N 45° 53' 56" W 111° 31' 25"

Montana Atlas and Gazetteer Pages 26, 40

Map 2 of 2

To West Yellowstone

PHOTO: STEVE SCHMIDT

The long, uninterrupted riffles of the Madison provide good habitat for stoneflies and big trout.

on US 287, which follows the Madison from Hebgen Lake down to Ennis Lake. From Bozeman, go west on US 191 about eight miles, then go west on SR 84 (Norris Road) another 17 miles until you reach the Madison below Beartrap Canyon. SR 84 connects with US 287 at Norris.

ACCESSIBILITY

Access is quite varied on the Madison as it makes its way from West Yellowstone to Three Forks. The short section of river below Hebgen Dam is often overlooked. It holds good numbers of fish both early and late in the season when fish come up from Quake Lake to spawn. It has the consistent temperature and flow of a tailwater and is open all year. There is parking next to the river just above where Beaver Creek enters the Madison.

The slide section at Raynolds Pass is a wild landscape of surging whitewater that intimidates many. This area can be fished if great care is exercised. Fish will be found only in the slower water behind rocks and against the bank. They have only a moment to decide if a fly is edible as it rushes past them and will take most anything that resembles food if it seems obtainable.

The Madison differs from most other Rocky Mountain rivers in that there are two sections that don't permit anglers to fish from a boat: nearly 20 miles of water from the Quake Lake outlet to Lyons Bridge and another six-mile section from Ennis Bridge to Ennis Lake. This restriction effectively reserves the two sections, which offer widely different types of fishing, for wading anglers.

The "Fifty Mile Riffle" of the Madison runs from Raynolds Pass down to a section just above Varney Bridge, and it is just as the name implies — one long, uninterrupted riffle. The water is highly oxygenated, helping to support the large population of stoneflies, including the giant salmonflies. If you float from Lyons Bridge, there are two low bridges downstream that can give you trouble. Drift boats may not fit under at flows above 3,000 cfs (as measured on the gauge at Kirby Ranch near Cameron). The float from McAtee to Varney is quite manageable if you're prepared to dodge a few rocks, but the water is wide open and not recommended in high winds.

From Varney Bridge to Ennis Lake, the river is extensively braided, full of islands and separated by smaller channels. There are lots of deep undercut banks and slower pools. Sharp bends and fallen trees make this section a challenge to row. While trout numbers are generally lower here, there are some very large brown trout in residence and anglers can easily spend many happy hours in this extensive network of water. If you float down from Varney, be sure to stay in the right-hand channel when the river splits about one mile below the bridge.

Beartrap Canyon begins below Ennis Dam, and the river regains some of the fury it exhibits at the Quake Lake outlet. Anglers can walk up the riverbank from below or a short way down from the dam. Beartrap Canyon should not be floated by any but the most experienced boaters, but it does hold some big trout. The Tackle Shop in Ennis has a permit for Beartrap and two guides, Todd and J.T. France, that grew up rowing the canyon with their father. If you are up for a Class IV whitewater adventure as well as some good fishing, this might be the trip for you.

Things calm down markedly as the canyon opens up at Warm Springs, and the river is very floatable from here down to Three Forks. Several access sites make it easy for wading anglers to fish around the islands and flats found through this relatively low gradient section of the Madison.

WHEN TO GO

The salmonfly hatch in late June and early July is by far the most popular event of the year for Madison River fly fishers. While this hatch has the potential to produce unforgettable fishing, high water or bad weather can greatly reduce success. Conditions can be especially disappointing to anglers who have traveled a long distance expecting a dry-fly fishing frenzy, only to experience a crowded river under less than ideal conditions.

Rick Hansen, the owner of Madison Valley Ranch, prefers to fish the shoulder months of April, May and October. Anglers can find good fishing with blue-winged olives, caddis and stonefly nymphs in the early season, and October is streamer time on the Madison with the year's best chance to land a trophy-sized brown moving up out of one of the lakes. The braids above Ennis Lake can be very good at this time or get on the river above Quake Lake.

The water below Beartrap Canyon gets very warm in the summer, but can fish very well during the Mother's Day caddis hatch in early May or again in fall as water temperatures cool.

The river between McAtee and Varney is wide open and wind can be a problem.

The Madison is a great caddis river, and these prolific insects— along with golden stoneflies and grasshoppers — keep trout well-fed throughout the summer. Plan your fishing for early morning or late evening as fishing is usually slow during the heat of the day.

AREA ATTRACTIONS

The Madison holds a large population of mountain whitefish. If you enjoy good smoked fish, stop by Restvedt & Son Meat Market (on US 287 in Ennis by the fly-fisher statue) and for $2 they will exchange cleaned whitefish for smoked.

Virginia City is just 15 miles west of Ennis. This well-preserved gold town and former Territorial Capital was the site of controversy in the Civil War, as both the North and South were in desperate need of the gold produced here to support their war efforts.

Today visitors can walk down streets much the same as they were in the late 1800s, and many original structures are still standing and contain artifacts from that era. You can take a guided tour of the old Victorian town, or catch one of the shows at the Opera House. Visit Virginia City on the web at *www.virginiacity.com* for more information.

RESOURCES

West Yellowstone and Ennis are good bases for fishing the Madison River below Hebgen Lake, and both towns offer plenty of amenities.

Campgrounds

ENNIS

Elkhorn Store & RV
69 Mt. Highway 287 North
Ennis, MT 59729
Phone number/s: (406) 682-4273

Ennis RV Village
Ennis, MT 59729
Phone number/s: (406) 682-5272

WEST YELLOWSTONE

KOA Kampgrounds
US 20
West Yellowstone, MT 59758
Phone number/s: (406) 646-7606

Madison Arm Resort & Marina
716 Electric (South Shore, Hebgen Lake)
West Yellowstone, MT 59758
Phone number/s: (406) 646-9328

Camper Corner
P.O. Box 351
Ennis, MT 59729
Phone number/s: (406) 682-4514,
toll-free (800) 755-3474
Web site: www.campercorner.com
E-mail: trtfishr@3rivers.net

Lodging

CAMERON

Slide Inn
Route 50
Cameron, MT 59720
Phone number/s: (406) 682-4804

ENNIS

Fan Mountain Inn
204 N. Main St.
Ennis, MT 59729
Phone number/s: (406) 682-5200

Madison Valley Ranch
P.O. Box 351
Ennis MT 59729
Phone number/s: toll-free (800) 755-3474
Web site: www.madisonvalleyranch.com
E-mail: trtfishr@3rivers.net

Rainbow Valley Motel
1 mile south of US 287
Ennis, MT 59729
Phone number/s: (406) 682-4264

WEST YELLOWSTONE

Stage Coach Inn
209 Madison Lane
West Yellowstone, MT 59758
Phone number/s: (406) 646-7381
Web site: www.yellowstoneinn.com

Three Bear Lodge & Restaurant
217 Yellowstone Ave.
West Yellowstone, MT 59758
Phone number/s: (406) 646-7353

Tackle Shops and Guide Services

ENNIS

Eaton Outfitters
P.O. Box 351
Ennis MT 59729
Phone number/s: toll-free (800) 755-3474
E-mail: trtfishr@3rivers.net

Madison River Fishing Co.
109 Main St.
Ennis, MT 59729
Phone number/s: (406) 682-4293,
toll-free (800) 227-7127
Web site: www.mrfc.com

Tackle Shop
127 Main St.
Ennis, MT 59729
Phone number/s: (406) 682-4263

WEST YELLOWSTONE

Bud Lilly's Trout Shop
39 Madison Ave.
West Yellowstone, MT 59758
Phone number/s: (406) 646-7801,
toll-free (800) 854-9559
Web site: www.budlillys.com

Madison River Outfitters
117 Canyon St.
West Yellowstone, MT 59758
Phone number/s: (406) 646-9644,
toll-free (800) 646-9644
Web site: www.flyfishingyellowstone.com

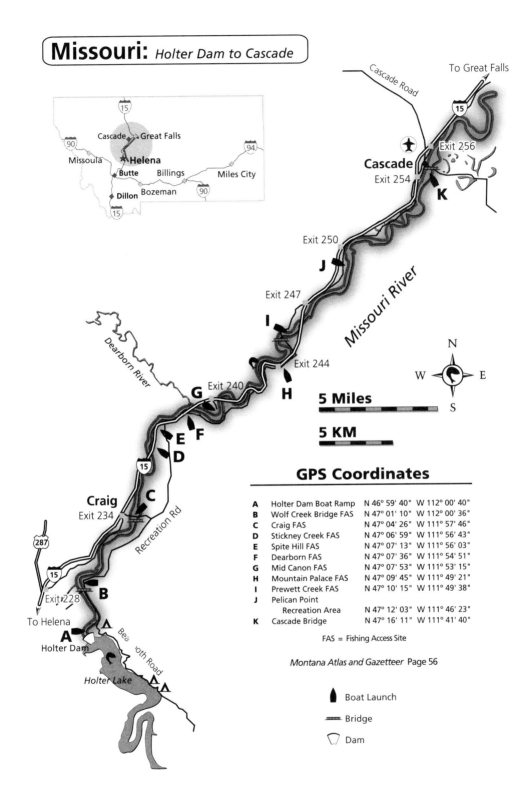

Missouri: *Holter Dam to Cascade*

To Great Falls

Cascade Road

Exit 256

Cascade
Exit 254

K

Exit 250

J

Exit 247

I

Missouri River

Exit 244

Exit 240

G

H

Dearborn River

E **F**

D

Craig
Exit 234

C

Recreation Rd

287

15

Exit 228 **B**

To Helena

A

Holter Dam

Bea 'oth Road

Holter Lake

N

W — E

S

5 Miles

5 KM

GPS Coordinates

A	Holter Dam Boat Ramp	N 46° 59' 40"	W 112° 00' 40"
B	Wolf Creek Bridge FAS	N 47° 01' 10"	W 112° 00' 36"
C	Craig FAS	N 47° 04' 26"	W 111° 57' 46"
D	Stickney Creek FAS	N 47° 06' 59"	W 111° 56' 43"
E	Spite Hill FAS	N 47° 07' 13"	W 111° 56' 03"
F	Dearborn FAS	N 47° 07' 36"	W 111° 54' 51"
G	Mid Canon FAS	N 47° 07' 53"	W 111° 53' 15"
H	Mountain Palace FAS	N 47° 09' 45"	W 111° 49' 21"
I	Prewett Creek FAS	N 47° 10' 15"	W 111° 49' 38"
J	Pelican Point		
	Recreation Area	N 47° 12' 03"	W 111° 46' 23"
K	Cascade Bridge	N 47° 16' 11"	W 111° 41' 40"

FAS = Fishing Access Site

Montana Atlas and Gazetteer Page 56

Boat Launch

Bridge

Dam

Inset map

15

Cascade · Great Falls

Missoula Helena

Butte Billings

Dillon Bozeman Miles City

90

94

90

15

Missouri River

FISH SPECIES
Rainbow and brown
trout

TIP
Fish the structure,
such as islands and
riffles

HIGHLIGHT
Exceptionally strong,
acrobatic rainbows

SEASON
Open year-round

In 1803, President Thomas Jefferson sent instructions to Meriwether Lewis and the newly formed Corps of Discovery "to explore the Missouri River, & such principal stream of it." Thus began American expansion into the western country acquired in the Louisiana Purchase, as well as one of the greatest journeys of discovery in American history.

The Missouri is one of America's largest rivers, flowing over 23,000 miles from its origin, near Three Forks, Montana, to a confluence with the Mississippi. In its course it drains one-sixth of the United States. It arises from three great trout rivers, the Gallatin, the Madison, and the Jefferson, then flows into Canyon Ferry Reservoir and Holter Lake, where sediments settle out and the rich water is cooled until it emerges from the dam, reborn as a giant spring creek. The 34 miles of river from Holter Dam to Cascade offers excellent conditions for fly fishers and is the stretch of river covered by this guide.

The Missouri River below Holter Dam has many qualities that recommend it to the traveling angler. It is easily reached by air and followed in its course by a modern interstate freeway. Its tailwater nature grants a long season, and there are several places to lodge and access the river along its banks. These factors may attract anglers for a first visit, but it is the magnificent trout that live here that will draw them back. Rainbows are predominant in the Missouri, making up about 80 percent of the trout caught. These fish are big, well-proportioned and very strong. Expect them to take to the air multiple times when hooked and be mentally prepared to lose some. Treasure every tough and determined fighter you are able to bring to net.

The numbers of large trout are as high as they have ever been on the Missouri. A 1999 population study by Montana Fish, Wildlife & Parks revealed nearly 4,500 rainbows (over 10 inches) per mile of river between Holter Dam and Craig, and the study noted that these fish were in extremely good condition. While there are some long-term concerns about how whirling disease will impact this incredible fishery, there is no better time than the present to plan a trip to the Missouri.

SPECIAL REGULATIONS

Holter Dam to Cascade Bridge:

❏ Combined trout limit: three rainbow trout, only one over 16 inches; one brown trout, 22-inch minimum.

Holter Dam abutment and spillway structures below the dam:

☐ Closed entire year.

TACTICS

The Missouri below Holter Dam is sometimes called the world's largest spring creek, and you can expect the trout here to behave accordingly. Difficult drifts to large "pods" of rising trout on current seams can keep fly fishers engrossed for hours. Frequent strong winds will often force anglers to keep leaders down to nine feet, but you will want to extend out to 12 feet when conditions allow. Reducing tippet size down to 6x will increase your number of hookups, but it takes a soft rod and a careful touch to land these hot fish. Jerry Lappier of Missouri River Trout Shop and Lodge recommends that fly fishers concentrate their efforts in areas of structure such as riffles and islands. Pay special attention to areas where side channels reenter the main channel of the river below islands.

On the Missouri, expect to find large pods of fish when they are actively rising. Pods are usually made up of fish of the same size and species. If the first one or two fish you hook out of a pod is a whitefish, they are probably all whitefish, and you will want to move on. The Missouri is known for its large numbers of fish in the 14- to 18-inch range, but anglers can find larger fish. These giants are often solitary bank feeders and can be very difficult to approach. The last side channel above Craig (on the west side) may hold some of these larger fish, but can be difficult to float through.

Try to schedule your fishing day so that you are on the water and ready when hatches are in full swing. Tricos will hatch in the early morning hours with a spinnerfall just before noon, while both pale morning duns and caddis begin in late afternoon and usually peak at dusk.

This is big water, and streamer fishing can help anglers cover more area. This is especially beneficial when fishing below Craig where fish numbers are lower. Either

Concentrate on the river's structure. Fish congregate near islands and riffles.

Hatch Chart

AVAILABILITY

Food Items	J	F	M	A	M	J	J	A	S	O	N	D
Midges	X	X	X	X	X	X	X	X	X	X	X	X
Annelid worms	X	X	X	X	X	X	X	X	X	X	X	X
Blue-winged olives				X	X			X	X	X	X	
Pale morning duns						X	X	X				
Tricos							X	X	X			
Caddisflies						X	X	X	X			
Flying ants					X	X						
Grasshoppers							X	X	X			

Insects	Suggested Fly Patterns
Midges	Griffith's gnats (#16-22), Adams (#16-22), cream, brown, and black midge pupae (#18-22), brassies (#16-20), serendipities (#16-22)
Annelid worms	San Juan worms, orange and red (#12-16)
Blue-winged olives	parachute Adams (#16-22), thorax BWOs (#16-22), olive comparaduns (#16-22), Quigley cripples, olive (#16-22), olive CDC emergers (#16-22), lightning bugs (#14-18), pheasant tails (#16-22), hare's ears (#16-22), bead-head pheasant tails (#16-22), bead-head hare's ears (#16-22)
Pale morning duns	thorax PMDs (#16-18), cream parachutes (#16-18), cream comparaduns (#16-20), Quigley cripples, cream (#16-20), rusty spinners (#16-18), CDC emergers, cream (#16-20), pheasant tails (#14-16), hare's ears (#14-16), bead-head pheasant tails (#14-16), bead-head hare's ears (#14-16)
Tricos	trico spinners (#18-22), CDC tricos (#18-22), parachute Adams (#18-22), pheasant tails (#18-20)
Caddisflies	elk-hair caddis (#16-18), partridge caddis (#16-18), CDC elk-hair caddis, olive and brown (#16-18), Hemingway caddis (#16-18), sparkle caddis, olive and brown (#16-18), sparkle pupae, olive and brown (#16-18), X-caddis, olive and brown (#16-18), peeking caddis (#14-16), CK nymphs (#14-16)
Flying ants	fur ants, black (#14-18), flying ants (#14-16), CDC ants (#14-18), winged-foam ants (#14-18)
Grasshoppers	Dave's hoppers (#6-10), Henry's Fork hoppers (#6-10)

Float fishers are at an advantage when it comes to covering water on this big river, especially when the river rises above 7,000 cfs.

high density sink tips or full sink lines will let fly fishers work the deeper water more effectively. Expect to find trout along rocky riprap banks. While streamer fishing can be productive much of the year, September and October will be the best months for this approach.

HOW TO GET THERE

Anglers from outside the area will find regularly scheduled flights into Great Falls and Helena. Both cities are located on I-15, which parallels the quality water of the Missouri. From Helena, go northeast or drive southwest from Great Falls. Exits 226, 234, 240, 244, 247, 250 and 254 will allow anglers to reach Recreation Road (old US 91), which is the main access route to the river.

ACCESSIBILITY

The combination of Recreation Road and nearly a dozen fishing access sites make this section of the Missouri very accessible to floaters. There are good launch facilities and several small campgrounds. From Holter Dam to Craig, fly fishers will find the best dry-fly fishing as well as the highest density of both trout and anglers. If you want a break from the crowds, there are more than 25 miles of good fishing water from Craig to Cascade. The Craig Fishing Access Site is particularly handy, as it is a comfortable day float from Holter Dam and just across the tracks from the Trout Shop Lodge and Café and Hooker's Bar. It is also a good launch site if you want to float down to Mid Canon and get away from some of the traffic found up above.

Fish concentrating features like riffles and islands, which are spaced widely apart on this very large river. Driving, instead of walking, is sometimes the best way to access the next stretch of water. Float fishers have a definitive advantage — especially when the river rises above about 7,000 cfs. The river is very easy to navigate, and drift boat rentals are available for anglers that don't bring a boat with them.

Anglers who fish the Missouri by wading will find a good number of turnouts along the upper river between Holter Dam and Craig. The best of these will typically be associated with islands and side channels and can fill up quickly when the season is in full swing.

Consider getting an early start if you want to fish in these areas. Access for shore anglers and waders tends to diminish as you go downstream from Craig.

If you float the Missouri from Prewett Fishing Access Site to Pelican Point, you will encounter Halfbreed Rapids. Take time to look it over and be sure your skills and craft are adequate before you commit.

The Missouri River rainbows are big and well-proportioned.

WHEN TO GO

The spring creek nature of the Missouri below Holter Dam and its relatively low elevation (below 4,000 feet) make it a good choice for Montana anglers looking for some diversion in the colder months of the year. The weed beds decrease greatly over the winter, which makes for good nymphing conditions, and early spring puts the rainbows in a romantic frame of mind. San Juan worms and midge pupae are effective in this early season, and the locally popular lightning bug will take fish before the blue-winged olives begin to appear in late April.

Once Missouri River rainbows turn their attention to dry flies in May, they tend to keep looking up and fly fishers can expect good dry-fly fishing all day long during the summer. During July and August, there are good hatches of both pale morning duns and caddis, and observant anglers will find a wide variety of fishing opportunities.

In fall, when many anglers have turned their attention to other concerns, the blue-winged olives return to the Missouri. Weather can be surprisingly mild, trout focus on dry flies, and the river is quiet and empty.

CHECK RIVER FLOWS ON THE WEB
http://montana.usgs.gov./rt-cgi/gen_tbl_pg

AREA ATTRACTIONS

Charles M. Russell — Montana's famous artist of the West — had his home and studio in Great Falls, which is now a museum. Admission is $4 for adults, $3 for seniors, and $2 for students. It is open in the summer from 9 a.m. to 6 p.m. Monday through Saturday and from 12 to 5 p.m. on Sunday. Winter hours are Tuesday through Saturday, 10 a.m.to 5 p.m., Sunday 1to 5 p.m.

RESOURCES

Most of the fishing access sites have primitive camping available on the river, but there are a fairly limited number of campsites.

There are two handicap-accessible campsites at Holter Dam Recreation Area just below the dam.

Campgrounds

HELENA

Lincoln Road RV Park
850 W. Lincoln Road
Helena, MT 59602
Phone number/s: (406) 458-3725

Helena Campground
5820 N. Montana Ave.
Helena, MT 59602
Phone number/s: (406) 458-4714

Lakeside Resort & Marina
5295 York Road
Helena, MT 59602
Phone number/s: (406) 227-6076

Lodging

CRAIG

Missouri River Trout Shop and Lodge
110 Bridge St.
Craig, MT 59648
Phone number/s: (406) 235-4474,
toll-free (800) 337-8528

WOLF CREEK

Bungalow Bed & Breakfast
2020 US 287
Wolf Creek, MT 59648
Phone number/s: (406) 235-4276

Holter Lake Lodge
1350 Beartooth Road
Wolf Creek, MT 59648
Phone number/s: (406) 235-4331

Tackle Shops and Guide Services

CRAIG

Missouri River Trout Shop and Lodge
110 Bridge St.
Craig, MT 59648
Phone number/s: (406) 235-4474,
toll-free (800) 337-8528

HELENA

Cross Currents
326 N. Jackson Ave.
Helena, MT 59601
Phone number/s: (406) 449-2292,
toll-free (888) 434-7468
Fax: (406) 449-2293
Web site: www.crosscurrents.com

WOLF CREEK

Montana River Outfitters
515 Recreation Road
Wolf Creek, MT 59648
Phone number/s: (406) 235-4350

Area Attractions

CM Russell Museum and Library
400 13th St. N.
Great Falls, MT 59401
Phone number/s: (406) 727-8787

Nelson's Spring Creek

FISH SPECIES
Browns and rainbows
with a few cutthroats

TIP
Slow, stealthy
approach will get you
in range of feeders

HIGHLIGHT
Delicate dry-fly fishing
to selective trout

SEASON
Open year-round

The Yellowstone area is home to many great rivers and some of the best trout fishing in the country, and yet diminutive Nelson's Spring Creek still stands out as some of the best water the area has to offer. The native limestone is responsible for the rich alkalinity of the clear water welling to the surface at Blue Spring, the major source of water for the ranch. Temperatures are in the 50s year-round and can support good hatches on the coldest days.

The legendary Joe Brooks was especially fond of this spring creek, spending five summers in an old bunkhouse on its bank with his wife Mary in the 1950s. Over the years, simple word of mouth has made Nelson's Spring Creek Ranch world-renowned, and anglers now travel great distances to try their skills on this challenging water.

Helen and Edwin Nelson are fourth generation Montanans and own and operate Nelson's Spring Creek Ranch. Their good stewardship is evident everywhere you look. Strategically placed trees and rocks add a great deal of holding water for the resident trout, and a pond adds stillwater opportunities for guests. On the advice of Joe Brooks, they opened it to the public for fee fishing in 1960, and restricted ranch waters to catch-and-release only, a very far-sighted move at that time.

Though the creek is small in size and only about ¾ of a mile long, the Nelson family controls angler impact by limiting usage to six rods per day, ensuring that everyone can find some good water. A small motel on the property is very comfortable and a short stroll from the creek. If you are out at dawn, you may see sandhill cranes feeding in the early morning light.

SPECIAL REGULATIONS AND FEES

Fishing is on the private land of the Nelson family and is strictly catch-and-release and fly fishing only. Nelson's is open year-round. Rod fee is $75 per day from April 1 to November 1 and $25 per day the remainder of the year. With a limit of six rods per day, make your reservation well in advance — as much as six months to one year for prime summer fishing. For reservations, call (406) 222-2159.

TACTICS

Dry-fly fishers come from far and wide to test their skills against the selective trout that live in these rich waters. In most cases, the angler must do everything right to encourage a fish to take an imitation. You may have to "force feed" fish by making drift after drift right over the feeding lane. Long leaders of 12 to 14 feet are the order of the day and they should taper down to 6x or 7x. In some difficult drift situations, adding an extra two feet of tippet that does not straighten out on the cast can give you some much-needed slack where it is most important. Feeding fish will refuse flies with the slightest drag, so your position, the shape of your cast and mending are key. Downstream drifts will give you the best chance in most situations, especially when the summer weed growth creates dozens of small current seams across a few feet of flow. When met with refusal, shift your position or the shape of your cast (try reach casts, steeple casts or throw in some squiggles). You can often find yourself happily rooted in one place, changing your drift, your flies or your rig while the hours slip by.

While dry-fly fishing is what draws most anglers to Nelson's, nymph fishing can still be very effective. For best results, continue to use long leaders of 10 to 12 feet with fine (6x) tippets. Either use very small strike indicators or suspend your nymph under a dry fly with a reasonable amount of flotation. In most situations, only a very small amount of weight is needed. Adding a small bead-head to your flies gives a reasonable sink rate and makes only a slight plunk when cast. For an even softer presentation of nymphs, try rubbing Soft Lead into the knots of a hand-tied leader or use one of the sinking leader dressings that help get your tippet through the surface tension.

During nonhatch periods, try fishing woolly buggers or other small streamers. They are especially effective when stripped along the front of the many logs set into the streambed. Don't ignore the thin water along the banks; sizable fish only need a few inches to feel secure if there is cover over their heads.

PHOTO: STEVE SCHMIDT

Nelson's Spring Creek has slow water with logs and boulders creating secure lies for trout.

Hatch Chart   AVAILABILITY

Food Items	J	F	M	A	M	J	J	A	S	O	N	D
Midges	X	X	X	X	X	X	X	X	X	X	X	X
Blue-winged olives			X	X	X			X	X	X	X	X
Pale morning duns						X	X	X				
Sulphurs						X	X	X	X			
Caddisflies				X	X	X	X	X				
Terrestrials							X	X	X			

Insects	Suggested Fly Patterns
Midges	Griffith's gnats (#20-22) — add a post of white or black poly yarn to aid visibility, grizzly midges (#20-22), Adams (#20-22), midge pupae, cream, red and black (#18-22), brassies (#16-20), serendipities (#18-22), midge emergers, black and peacock (#18-22)
Blue-winged olives	CDC comparaduns, olive (#18-22), parachute Adams (#18-22), thorax BWOs (#18-22), no-hackle duns, olive (#18-22), CDC loopwing emergers, olive (#18-22), Quigley cripples, olive (#18-22), pheasant tails (#16-20), hare's ears (#16-20), WD40s (#16-20), RS2s (#16-20)
Pale morning duns	CDC comparaduns, cream (#16-18), thorax duns, cream (#16-18), cream parachutes (#16-18), sparkle duns (#16-18), no-hackle duns, cream (#16-18), CDC loopwing emergers, cream (#16-18), Quigley cripples, cream (#16-18), floating nymphs, cream (#16-18), rusty spinners (#16-18), pheasant tails (#16-18), hare's ears (#16-18)
Sulphurs	CDC comparaduns, cream (#20-22), thorax duns, cream (#20-22), cream parachutes (#20-22), sparkle duns, cream (#20-22), no-hackle duns, cream (#20-22), CDC loopwing duns, cream (#20-22), Quigley cripples, cream (#20-22), spinners, cream and tan (#20-22), pheasant tails (#20-22), hare's ears (#20-22)
Caddisflies	CDC caddis, olive, tan and brown (#16-18), CDC caddis, black (#18-20), parachute caddis, olive, tan and brown (#16-18), caddis sparkle pupae, olive, tan and brown (#16-18), partridge caddis (#16-18)
Terrestrials	Dave's hoppers (#10-12), Dave's crickets (#10-12), fur ants, black and cinnamon (#16-20), CDC ants, black and cinnamon (#16-18), deer-hair beetles, black (#14-18), hi-vis foam beetles (#14-18)

PHOTO: COURTESY OF BUZZ BASINI

Buzz Basini of Spring Creek Specialist poses with one of the creek's larger trout.

HOW TO GET THERE

Visitors can fly into either Bozeman, which is 26 miles west of Livingston on I-90, or Billings, 120 miles to the east on I-90.

From I-90, take Exit 333 at Livingston, Montana, and go south 3.5 miles on US 89, then turn onto East River Road (SR 540) and cross Carter's Bridge over the Yellowstone River. It is about 3.7 miles to the turnoff to Nelson's Spring Creek Ranch.

If you are driving up from Yellowstone National Park and the town of Gardiner, Montana, go north 37 miles on US 89 to Mill Creek Road. Turn and head east for about one mile, then turn north onto East River Road (SR 540). The entrance to Nelson's is 11 miles north.

ACCESSIBILITY

The Nelsons have placed a picnic shelter and an outhouse near the center of the creek, and short trails give anglers easy access to the water. There are also a few duck blinds that make a good spot to sit out a rainstorm.

The upper water is typical slow spring creek water with logs and boulders adding varied fishing situations and secure lies for the trout. The pond in the center is home to some large fish that may require all the patience an angler possesses just to get a take. Below the pond, the water is faster and flows over riffles. The trout in this lower water are a little more approachable as the faster water helps cover loud steps and blurs an angler's silhouette. Careful drifts are still important, but there is a slightly greater margin for error.

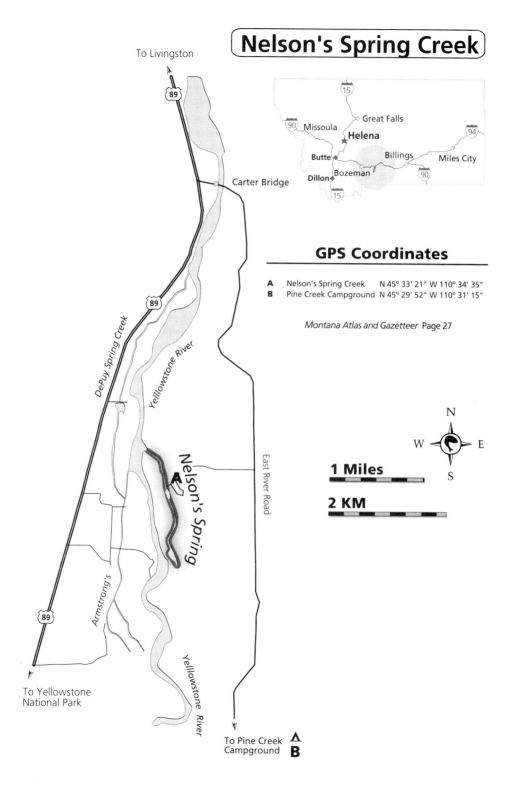

Nelson's Spring Creek

To Livingston

89

Carter Bridge

DePuy Spring Creek

Yelllowstone River

Nelson's Spring

A

East River Road

Armstrong's

89

To Yellowstone
National Park

Yellowstone River

To Pine Creek
Campground B

15

Great Falls

90

Missoula

Helena

94

Butte

Billings

Miles City

Dillon

Bozeman

90

15

GPS Coordinates

A   Nelson's Spring Creek   N 45° 33' 21" W 110° 34' 35"
B   Pine Creek Campground   N 45° 29' 52" W 110° 31' 15"

Montana Atlas and Gazetteer Page 27

N

W   E

S

1 Miles

2 KM

WHEN TO GO

Every day on Nelson's is another day in "paradise," but each season has its attractions. Winter days when the ranch is covered in soft snow, you can find midges mixed in with the steam rising off the creek. The 50-degree water keeps Nelson's fishing through the winter when most other area waters (except Armstrong's/ DePuy Spring Creek) are cold and frozen.

Winter in Paradise Valley. Fifty-degree water keeps Nelson's fishable year-round.

Rainbows bent on pro-creation can be found in the creek in early spring, and the blue-winged olives provide the first mayfly activity of the new year.

Summer brings the best hatches to Nelson's, and of course, the fly fishers are there to meet them. If you expect to fish the creek at this time, call for reservations six months to one year in advance or check in for cancellations.

When the nights cool down and the leaves begin to turn, look for spawn-minded browns to move from the Yellowstone River up to the calm waters of the creek. Try casting streamers for these big, aggressive fish, or fish blue-wings in the golden days of an Indian summer.

AREA ATTRACTIONS

With Yellowstone National Park only 40 miles south, the park and its rivers are worth a visit.

RESOURCES

Nelson's Spring Creek Ranch has three efficiency rooms on the property. For reservations, call (406) 222-2159. The rooms are very comfortable, you can prepare your own meals, and better still, you can wake up within walking distance of the creek. Otherwise, stay in the town of Livingston, where you can either camp or lodge.

The Pine Creek campground in the Gallatin National Forest is nine miles south of Livingston on US 89 and located off of Pine Creek Road. Seventeen of the campsites are handicap-accessible.

Campgrounds

GALLATIN NATIONAL FOREST

For more camping information, call the Livingston Ranger District at (406) 222-1892.

❏ Pine Creek

LIVINGSTON

Livingston-Paradise Valley KOA
163 Pine Creek Road
Livingston, MT 59047
Phone number/s: (406) 222-0992,
toll-free (800) KOA-2805
Fax: (406) 222-5911
Web site: www.koa.com
E-mail: liv.koa@ycsi.net

Yellowstone's Edge RV Park
3501 US 89 South
Livingston, MT 59047
Phone number/s: (406) 333-4036
Fax: (406) 333-4052

Lodging

LIVINGSTON

Blue Winged Olives
5157 US 89 South
Livingston, MT 59047
Phone number/s: (406) 222-8646

Comfort Inn
114 Loves Lane
Livingston, MT 59047
Phone number/s: (406) 222-4400

Jumping Rainbow Ranch
110 Jumping Rainbow Road
Livingston, MT 59047
Phone number/s: (406) 222-5425

Pine Creek Lodge
2495 E. River Road
Livingston, MT 59047
Phone number/s: (406)-222-3628

Tackle Shops and Guide Services

LIVINGSTON

Dan Bailey's Fly Shop
209 W. Park St.
Livingston, MT 59047
Phone number/s: (406) 222-1673,
toll-free (800) 356-4052
E-mail: dan@danbailey.com

Spring Creek Specialist Fly Shop
(on the creek at DePuy)
2742 E. River Road
Livingston, MT 59047
Phone number/s: (406) 222-5664
E-mail: basini@mcn.net

Yellowstone Angler
5256 US 89 South
Livingston, MT 59047
Phone number/s: (406) 222-7130
Fax: (406) 222-7153
E-mail: staff@yellowstoneangler.com
Web site: www.yellowstoneangler.com

Rock Creek

Rock Creek was home to a brief mining boom in the 1890s before its rugged canyon became a hideout for horse thieves and other ruffians. Progress finally reached Rock Creek in 1926 when the Forest Service built a road and several campgrounds along the creek. The present-day visitor is left with the impression that not much has changed since then. The narrow road still winds its way between trees and rocks, and the creek's trout-rich water still tumbles down the forested canyon to lose itself in the Clark Fork near Clinton.

This blue ribbon fishery still contains the high density of trout that brought it fame back in the 1950s. The creek has had its ups and downs, but the enforcement of special regulations, which prevent harvest of rainbow and cutthroat trout, has brought it back to its former glory. Anglers can expect to find plenty of trout in the 12- to 16-inch range, and there are still fish of 18 inches or more. The real excitement comes in June with the *Pteronarcys* emergence. Tony Reinhardt of the Grizzly Hackle states, "Rock Creek has one of the best salmonfly hatches in Montana." And there are many anglers who would agree. When it is really on, a team of fly fishers in a raft can hook 50 or more trout in a single day.

HIGHLIGHT
One of the best salmonfly hatches in Montana

TIP
Nymph for the big fish

FISH SPECIES
Brown, cutthroat and rainbow trout with brook and bull trout present

SEASON
Year-round

SPECIFIC REGULATIONS

Rock Creek (near Clinton) from its mouth to the confluence of the East and West Forks:

- Three brown trout, none over 12 inches.
- Catch-and-release for cutthroat and rainbow trout.
- Artificial lures only, except anglers 12 years of age and younger may use bait.
- Extended season for whitefish and catch-and-release for trout from December 1 to third Saturday in May with aquatic insects, maggots and/or artificial lures only.
- Closed to fishing from boats July 1 through November 30.

TACTICS

To be successful on Rock Creek, you will have to adapt your approach to the water levels and prevailing hatches. During the high-water salmonfly hatch, heavy tackle is the order of the day. Keep leaders short — at about seven feet. Tippet of 3x or heavier is not overkill. If you own a strong 6-weight rod, you will want to bring it to handle the big nymphs and dry flies. If you are nymph fishing, use large yarn

Rock Creek is steep and boulder-choked near Dalles campground.

indicators and enough weight to reach the fish. Vary split shot from size BB to 3/0 depending on the water you are fishing, and remember that the nymphs migrate to the riverbanks prior to emerging. The hatch will gradually move its way up river, progressing about four or five miles per day. If you're ahead of the main emergence, fish nymphs, switching to dry flies once a good number of adults are present. Whether floating or wading, use caution when dealing with the river's powerful flow at this time.

During lower flows, switch to longer, lighter leaders: nine foot and 4x or 5x should suit most situations. The combination of a dry fly with a dropper can work very well during many of Rock Creek's major hatches. Try an olive stimulator with a bead-head prince dropper during the early skwala hatch, or a brown sparkle dun with a pheasant tail trailer when March browns are on the water (Note: It is not clear if this insect is a true March brown — *Rhithrogena* — or possibly a member of Siphlonuridae, the family that includes the gray drakes). A yellow stimulator trailed by a prince nymph or copper John is very effective during summer months; just be prepared to hook as many whitefish as trout. Trout will tend to concentrate in the creek's deeper water once flows decline.

When water gets low, especially in late August and September, you may be required to lengthen leaders out to 12 feet. Tippets of 5x or 6x will fool more trout, especially on the low, still pools. Small mayfly patterns or caddis are the rule, unless fish are keyed into the spruce moths.

Stoneflies make up the largest portion of trout food in Rock Creek. Skwala, golden stonefly and salmonfly nymphs are present year-round, and all the nymphs are reasonably similar. The venerable prince nymph does a good job of imitating all of these bugs and may be the single best fly for Rock Creek over the course of the year. The addition of a bead-head makes the prince even more effective. The smaller stonefly nymphs can be dead drifted on nine-foot 4x leaders with a strike indicator during low-water periods.

Hatch Chart   AVAILABILITY

Food Items	J	F	M	A	M	J	J	A	S	O	N	D
Midges	X	X	X	X	X	X	X	X	X	X	X	X
March browns			X	X								
Blue-winged olives				X	X				X	X	X	
Pale morning duns						X	X	X				
Skwala stoneflies			X	X	X							
Golden stoneflies						X	X	X				
Salmonflies						X	X					
Caddisflies						X	X	X	X	X	X	
Spruce moths								X				
Terrestrials							X	X	X			

HOW TO GET THERE

Missoula International Airport is about 10 miles west of town and has regular air service on a year-round basis. Rock Creek is a 20-minute drive from Missoula. Head east on I-90 to Exit 126, where Clark Fork and Rock Creek meet. FR 102 (Rock Creek Road) parallels the river south until Rock Creek meets the confluence of the West and East Forks at SR 38.

If you find yourself in the Hamilton area, you can drive over the scenic Skalkaho Highway. The road is mostly unpaved and winds its way up over the pass. It is only open from June through October.

ACCESSIBILITY

It is very simple for anglers to gain access to Rock Creek. Just get onto FR 102 (Rock Creek Road) and you can follow the creek for over 40 miles from its confluence with the Clark Fork right up to where Rock Creek proper begins at the confluence of its Middle and West Forks. Rock Creek runs almost entirely through lands administered by the U.S. Forest Service, and there are many fishing access sites, campgrounds and innumerable turnouts where anglers can get to the water. Only about 10 percent of Rock Creek is under private ownership, so respect private property where it exists; there is plenty of room to fish without trespassing.

There is a downside to the easy accessibility on Rock Creek. It can be quite crowded during peak periods, but the road up the canyon (FR 102) does its part to dissuade the faint of heart. If you drive up from I-90, the pavement ends in about nine miles, and the road gets quite interesting from that point. It is very narrow and rough in places, making the posted speed limit of 30 mph superfluous. There is one section where the road is very narrow with a steep drop below that includes a very tight and unexpected hairpin turn. You will see trailers and small RVs on the road, but you may want to drive the road in a regular vehicle before you attempt to bring a trailer or RV into one of the camping areas. If you access Rock Creek from Philipsburg and SR 348, you will find a paved road to the creek and an improved gravel road as you travel north for about the first 10 miles to Puyear Ranch.

Insects	Suggested Fly Patterns
Midges	Griffith's gnats (#16-22), Adams (#16-22), black gnats (#16-20), midge pupae, cream, brown, and black (#14-22), brassies (#16-20), bead-head midge pupae (#16-20)
March browns	sparkle duns, brown (#12-16), Harrop's hair-wing duns, brown (#12-16), Quigley cripples (#12-16), parachute hare's ears (#12-16), pheasant tails(#12-16), bead-head pheasant tails (#12-16)
Blue-winged olives	parachute Adams (#16-22), thorax BWOs (#16-20), olive comparaduns (#16-22), Quigley cripples, olive (#16-20), CDC emergers, olive (#16-22), pheasant tails (#16-20), hare's ears (#16-20), bead-head pheasant tails (#16-20), bead-head hare's ears (#16-20)
Pale morning duns	thorax PMDs (#14-16), cream parachutes (#14-16), cream comparaduns (#16-20), Quigley cripples, cream (#16-20), rusty spinners (#14-16), CDC emergers, cream (#16-20), pheasant tails (#14-16), hare's ears (#14-16), bead-head pheasant tails (#14-16), bead-head hare's ears (#14-16)
Skwala stoneflies	olive stimulators (#6-10), stonefly nymphs, brown (#6-10), girdle bugs, black and brown (#6-10), yuk bugs, black and brown (#6-10), Kauffman's brown stones (#6-10), bead-head prince nymph (#8-12)
Golden stoneflies	yellow stimulators (#4-8), bead-head prince nymphs (#8-12), golden stonefly nymphs (#4-8), copper Johns (#10-14)
Salmonflies	sofa pillows (#2-8), Mac Salmons (#2-8), orange stimulators (#6-10), girdle bugs (#2-10), yuk bugs (#2-10), bead-head prince nymphs (#8-12), Brook's stone nymphs (#6-10)
Caddisflies	elk-hair caddis (#14-18), partridge caddis (#14-18), CDC elk-hair caddis (#14-18), sparkle pupae (#14-18), X-caddis (#16-18), peeking caddis (#14-16), bead-head caddis (#14-16)
Spruce moths	light elk-hair caddis (#12-14), stimulators (#12-14)
Terrestrials	Dave's hoppers (#10-12), Dave's crickets (#10-12), fur ants, black (#16-20), CDC ants, black (#16-18), deer-hair beetles, black (#14-18), hi-vis foam beetles (#14-18)

Suspension bridge at the Welcome Creek trailhead.

The float season on Rock Creek is fairly short and may be curtailed by low water before the July 1 cutoff. Check flows before you go. There are no improved launch ramps on Rock Creek. It is a fairly small and narrow body of water for floating, and this fast-flowing creek drops an average of over 30 feet per mile. Rafts are the best float craft for anglers on this creek, but drift boats are used as well. Most floaters use the river from Gillies Bridge down to Harry's Flat campground or from Fire Ring (unofficial launch) down to Elkhorn, another unofficial launch site, just above Elkhorn Ranch. From Harry's Flat down past Dalles campground, the creek is very steep and boulder-choked and should be avoided by floaters. The lower four miles of Rock Creek below Elkhorn Ranch can be blocked by downed trees and is generally not a good place to float either. Whatever section you decide to float, look it over before you launch and check with local sources for hazards, as river conditions can vary a great deal. Though mostly Class II rapids, there is little opportunity to stop and things can happen quickly. It is a good idea to float with a guide or knowledgeable friend before attempting this river on your own.

Once the water drops, usually in July, you will find Rock Creek quite wadeable. Remember that the bottom is mainly cobble rock with larger boulders, and much of it is coated with mud and algae. Some pools are waist deep and higher, and flows can be quite powerful. Wade with care. Studded boots and a staff are both good insurance against a nasty fall.

The fires of 2000 avoided Rock Creek for the most part. The west bank was burned for a mile or two and crossed the river in the microburst area. This may cause some extra color in the river during run-off or after heavy rains, but otherwise the river should be relatively unaffected.

Like its neighbor the Bitterroot, Rock Creek does have ticks along its banks. Wearing waders is a good preventative for tick bites, or tuck long pants into wading socks if you wade wet in the heat of summer. If you can't resist the urge to wade in shorts, be sure to examine yourself at the end of the day for these disease-carrying hitchhikers.

WHEN TO GO

Although Rock Creek is open year-round, it is a freestone river and winter water temperatures will be quite low, and access via the Rock Creek Road can be difficult. The season really gets started in March, when both skwalas and March browns start to hatch. Fishing either nymph or dry-fly versions of these insects can be very productive and is a great way to shake off a bad case of cabin fever.

Late May normally brings the high waters of spring to Rock Creek, and the much-anticipated salmonfly hatch usually begins during mid-June. Floating is the most productive way to fish at this time, and high flows allow anglers to cover as much as 20 miles of river in a single day. The river's salmonfly hatch is no secret, so expect some crowding, especially if you are competing for space with other shore-bound anglers.

Beginning in July, Rock Creek becomes quite wadeable, and a summer day spent knee-deep in this beautiful tree-shrouded creek is the kind of experience that can take a weight off the most heavily burdened fly fisher. Caddis, golden stoneflies and pale morning duns keep things active until the spruce moths appear in August. An elk-hair caddis or other light-colored fly tied with a down wing in size 12 will effectively imitate these moths. Fishing during this period is often good at first light and continues into late morning.

Low, clear water can slow fishing in the autumn months, but streamers will take some nice brown trout at this time, and blue-winged-olives lure some fish to the surface on cool fall days. Large orange caddis put in an appearance as the weather cools, and some anglers report success fishing size 8 to 10 caddis pupae.

> **CHECK RIVER FLOWS ON THE WEB**
> http://montana.usgs.gov./rt-cgi/gen_tbl_pg

AREA ATTRACTIONS

Philipsburg was the site of Montana's first silver mine in the late 1800s and is now designated as a national historic district. You can shop for sapphires gleaned from the surrounding hills, or try your hand at mining garnets at Philipsburg's Sapphire Gallery. Walk through the town's Victorian-era business district, or visit some of the nearby ghost towns.

RESOURCES

If fishing is your focus, then camp in one of the many campgrounds where you can walk down to the river. If you prefer to stay indoors, the Hogback Homestead, a restored 1920s cabin available for rent through the U.S. Forest Service, is not only the prettiest place to stay on the creek, but it is close to some very good water as well. Book early; reservations for summer begin March 1 and winter reservations begin September 1.

If you are looking for more amenities, it is only a short drive from the quaint historic town of Philipsburg to the upper portion of Rock Creek.

Rock Creek: *Middle / West Confluence to Harry's Flat*

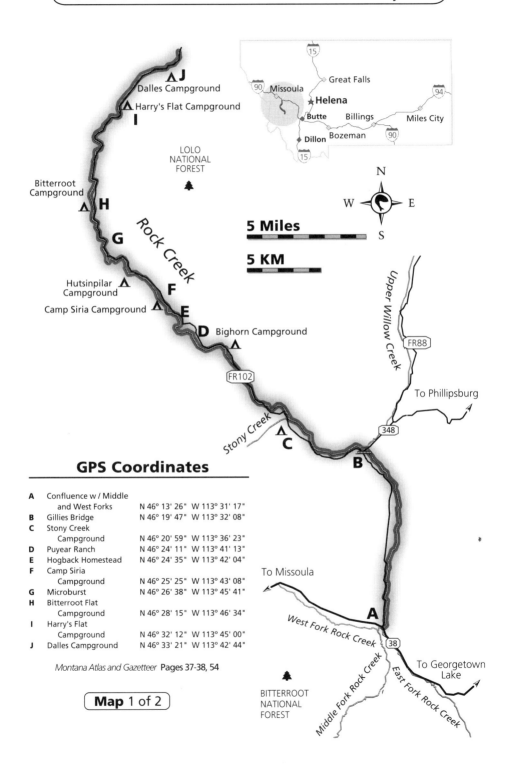

J Dalles Campground

Harry's Flat Campground
I

LOLO
NATIONAL
FOREST

15
90 Missoula Great Falls
★ **Helena**
Butte Billings
Bozeman
Dillon
15
94
Miles City
90

Bitterroot
Campground
H

G

Rock Creek

Hutsinpilar
Campground **F**

Camp Siria Campground **E**

D Bighorn Campground

FR102

N
W E
S

5 Miles

5 KM

Upper Willow Creek

FR88

To Phillipsburg

348

Stony Creek
C

B

GPS Coordinates

A	Confluence w / Middle and West Forks	N 46° 13' 26" W 113° 31' 17"
B	Gillies Bridge	N 46° 19' 47" W 113° 32' 08"
C	Stony Creek Campground	N 46° 20' 59" W 113° 36' 23"
D	Puyear Ranch	N 46° 24' 11" W 113° 41' 13"
E	Hogback Homestead	N 46° 24' 35" W 113° 42' 04"
F	Camp Siria Campground	N 46° 25' 25" W 113° 43' 08"
G	Microburst	N 46° 26' 38" W 113° 45' 41"
H	Bitterroot Flat Campground	N 46° 28' 15" W 113° 46' 34"
I	Harry's Flat Campground	N 46° 32' 12" W 113° 45' 00"
J	Dalles Campground	N 46° 33' 21" W 113° 42' 44"

Montana Atlas and Gazetteer **Pages 37-38, 54**

To Missoula

West Fork Rock Creek

A

38

To Georgetown
Lake

BITTERROOT
NATIONAL
FOREST

Middle Fork Rock Creek

East Fork Rock Creek

Map 1 of 2

Rock Creek: *Stony Creek to Clark Fork*

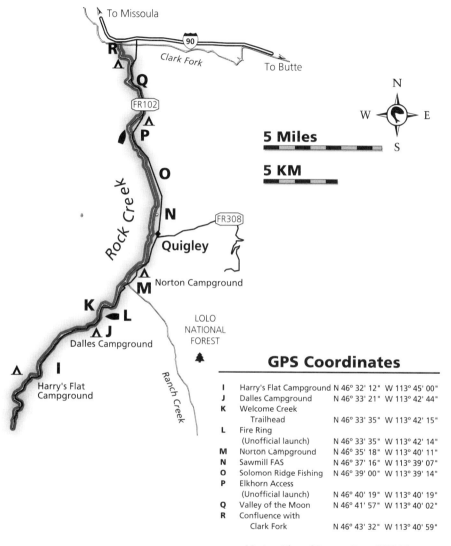

To Missoula

90

Clark Fork

To Butte

R

Q

FR102

P

O

N

FR308

Quigley

M

Norton Campground

K

L

J

Dalles Campground

I

Harry's Flat Campground

Ranch Creek

Rock Creek

LOLO NATIONAL FOREST

N
W · E
S

5 Miles

5 KM

GPS Coordinates

I	Harry's Flat Campground	N 46° 32' 12" W 113° 45' 00"
J	Dalles Campground	N 46° 33' 21" W 113° 42' 44"
K	Welcome Creek Trailhead	N 46° 33' 35" W 113° 42' 15"
L	Fire Ring (Unofficial launch)	N 46° 33' 35" W 113° 42' 14"
M	Norton Campground	N 46° 35' 18" W 113° 40' 11"
N	Sawmill FAS	N 46° 37' 16" W 113° 39' 07"
O	Solomon Ridge Fishing	N 46° 39' 00" W 113° 39' 14"
P	Elkhorn Access (Unofficial launch)	N 46° 40' 19" W 113° 40' 19"
Q	Valley of the Moon	N 46° 41' 57" W 113° 40' 02"
R	Confluence with Clark Fork	N 46° 43' 32" W 113° 40' 59"

Montana Atlas and Gazetteer **Pages 37-38, 54**

Map 2 of 2

Boat Launch

Campgrounds

LOLO NATIONAL FOREST

For more information, call the Lolo National Forest at (406) 329-3750.

- ☐ Bitterroot Flat — 15 sites
- ☐ Dalles — 10 sites
- ☐ Harry's Flat— 18 sites
- ☐ Norton — 10 sites

MISSOULA

KOA Kampgrounds
3450 Tina Ave.
Missoula, MT 59808
Phone number/s: (406) 549-0881

Hogback Homestead on Rock Creek.

Lodging

LOLO NATIONAL FOREST

Hogback Homestead
Missoula Ranger District, Bldg 24
Fort Missoula
Missoula, MT 59804
Phone number/s: (406) 329-3814
Web site: www.fs.fed.us/r1/lolo/
rec-rentals/hogback.html

CLINTON

Chalet Bearmouth
I-90, Exit 138
Clinton, MT 59825
Phone number/s: (406) 825-9950

Elkhorn Guest Ranch
408 Rock Creek Road
Clinton, MT 59825
Phone number/s: (406) 825-3220

PHILIPSBURG

Inn at Philipsburg
1005 W. Broadway St.
Philipsburg, MT 59858
Phone number/s: (406) 859-3959
Web site: www.theinn-philipsburg.com
(Also RV Park and camping)

Tackle Shops and Outfitters

CLINTON

Rock Creek Fisherman's Mercantile
73 Rock Creek Road
Clinton, MT 59825
Phone number/s: (406) 825-6440

MISSOULA

Grizzly Hackle International Fishing
215 W. Front St.
Missoula, MT 59802
Phone number/s: (406) 721-8996,
toll-free (800) 297-8996
Web site: www.grizzlyhackle.com
E-mail: info@grizzlyhackle.com

The Kingfisher
926 E. Broadway St.
Missoula, MT 59802
Phone number/s: (406) 721-6141,
toll-free (888) 542-4911
Web site: www.kingfisherflyshop.com

Missoulian Angler
401 S. Orange St.
Missoula, MT 59801
Phone number/s: (406) 728-7766

PHILIPSBURG

Big M Outfitters
3528 Mt. Highway 1
Philipsburg, MT 59858
Phone number/s: (406) 859-3746
Web site: www,bigmoutfitters.com

Under Wild Skies Lodge
1181 Moose Lake Road
Philipsburg, MT 59858
Phone number/s: (406) 859-3000

Smith River

HIGHLIGHT
Wild trout in a very scenic canyon

TIP
Plan trip well in advance

FISH SPECIES
Brown and rainbow trout

SEASON
Open year-round

Every western fly fisher should try to float the Smith at least once. The best water is between Camp Baker and Eden Bridge, a 59-mile remote canyon stretch. The best way to see the river is a three- to five-day float trip, camping along the way. While the fishing and scenery are both superb, it is the total experience that will be remembered for a lifetime — hours spent quietly floating and fishing, setting up camp at the end of the day, and the soft voice of the river singing you to sleep. Each dawn you will awake to the promise of another day fishing on the ribbon of water just outside your tent.

The North and South Forks of the Smith converge about four miles west of White Sulphur Springs. Camp Baker, where most floaters begin, is located at the confluence of the Smith River and Sheep Creek. In 1869, this was the site of a U.S. Army Fort that provided protection for miners and settlers traveling from White Sulphur Springs westward to the gold fields near Diamond City.

There are summer homes and lodges along the Smith now, but much of the canyon still looks and feels as it must have at the beginning of the last century. The river is often constrained by high cliffs as it forces its way through the Little Belt Mountains, but there are many open meadows and tall stands of pine as well. Large numbers of Canada geese nest here, and floaters can see a variety of water-fowl and wildlife on their journey, including the occasional black bear.

SPECIAL REGULATIONS AND FEES

From the confluence of Rock Creek to Eden (Huntsberger) Bridge:

❏ Artificial lures only.
❏ Combined trout limit: three trout under 13 inches and one trout over 22 inches. All trout between 13 and 22 inches must be released.
❏ Extended whitefish season and catch-and-release for trout open from December 1 to the third Saturday in May.
❏ Children under the age of 12 may fish with bait.

Floating the Smith River between Camp Baker and Eden Bridge is by permit only. Montana Fish, Wildlife & Parks (MFWP) limits the river to nine groups per day, with a maximum group size of 15 people. Potential floaters must enter the permit lottery by February 1 of the year they want to float. Contact the Great Falls MFWP office at (406) 454-5861 or on the web at *www.fwp.state.mt.us* for further details. There is a fee for all floaters over the age of 12: $15 for Montana residents and $35 for nonresidents. The fee is reduced to half in April and October, and there is no fee from November to March.

Hatch Chart   AVAILABILITY

Food Items	J	F	M	A	M	J	J	A	S	O	N	D
Midges	X	X	X	X	X	X	X	X	X	X	X	X
Annelid worms	X	X	X	X	X	X	X	X	X	X	X	X
Blue-winged olives				X	X							
Pale morning duns						X	X					
Brown drakes						X	X					
Skwala stoneflies				X	X							
Salmonflies					X	X						
Golden stoneflies						X	X					
Caddisflies						X	X	X	X			
Terrestrials							X	X	X			

If you don't have experience putting together a river trip or just want to relax while someone else takes care of all the details, contact one of the licensed outfitters that regularly lead trips down the river. Licensed guides and permittees provide the food and camping gear and will row the raft so that you can concentrate on catching fish.

TACTICS

With nearly 60 miles to float in four or five days, expect to do most of your fishing while you make river miles toward your next camp. If you are new to fly fishing from a boat on moving water, here are some of the basics. For most situations, you will want to cast at about a 45-degree angle in front of the boat and toward the shoreline. Both dry flies and streamers should be cast in very close to the bank. There are times when getting within one foot of shore catches fish and two feet out does not. If you are dead-drifting nymphs, you will need to visually estimate depth and try to cast to water deep enough to allow your fly to drift just above the bottom. The person at the oars should keep rowing slowly and steadily back upstream, adjusting the distance of the boat to the bank and slowing down the boat to allow the anglers to work the water more effectively

The Smith is home to large stoneflies, including skwalas, salmonflies and golden stones. Smith River fish gain weight by dining on the large bugs, but shallow, rocky water can make dead-drift nymphing difficult. Try fishing yuk bugs or woolly buggers on sink-tip lines. These patterns give fish the impression of a stonefly nymph. Fly fishers can cover a lot of prime water, especially the slow water and eddies right next to the bank and along the many cliff faces.

Trout can concentrate at the mouths of feeder creeks at certain times of the year, making these areas a good bet for a place to get out and wade. Be sure you understand and abide by Montana's stream access laws if you decide to fish up any of these side canyons — stay below the ordinary high-water mark.

Insects	Suggested Fly Patterns
Midges	Griffith's gnats (#16-22), Adams (#16-22), midge pupae, cream, brown, and black (#18-22), brassies (#16-20)
Annelid worms	San Juan worms, orange and red (#12-16)
Blue-winged olives	parachute Adams (#16-20), thorax BWOs (#16-20), olive comparaduns (#16-20), Quigley cripples, olive (#16-20), CDC emergers, olive (#16-20), pheasant tails (#16-20), hare's ears (#16-20), bead-head pheasant tails (#16-20), bead-head hare's ears (#16-20)
Pale morning duns	thorax PMDs (#14-16), cream parachutes (#14-16), cream comparaduns (#16-20), Quigley cripples, cream (#16-20), rusty spinners (#14-16), CDC emergers, cream (#16-20), pheasant tails (#14-16), hare's ears (#14-16), bead-head pheasant tails (#14-16), bead-head hare's ears (#14-16)
Brown drakes	parachute hare's ears (#12-16), brown Wulffs (#12-16), brown paradrakes (#12-16), pheasant tails (#12-14), hare's ears (#12-14), bead-head pheasant tails (#12-14), bead-head hare's ears (#12-14)
Skwala stoneflies	olive stimulators (#6-10), stonefly nymphs, brown (#6-10), girdle bugs, black and brown (#6-10), yuk bugs, black, brown and olive (#6-10), woolly buggers, black, brown and olive (#6-10)
Salmonflies	sofa pillows (#6-10), Mac Salmons (#6-10), orange stimulators (#6-10), girdle bugs, black, (#4-8), Bitch Creek nymphs (#4-8), Brook's stone nymphs (#4-8)
Golden stoneflies	yellow stimulators (#8-12), prince nymphs (#8-12), bead-head prince nymphs (#10-12), golden stonefly nymphs (#8-12), copper Johns (#8-12)
Caddisflies	elk-hair caddis (#14-18), partridge caddis ((#14-18), CDC elk-hair caddis (#14-18), sparkle caddis (#16-18), X-caddis (#16-18), peeking caddis (#12-14), CK nymphs (#12-14)
Terrestrials	Dave's hoppers (#8-12), Henry's Fork hoppers (#8-12), fur ants, black (#14-18), CDC ants (#14-18), deer-hair beetles, black (#14-16), hi-vis foam beetles (#14-16)

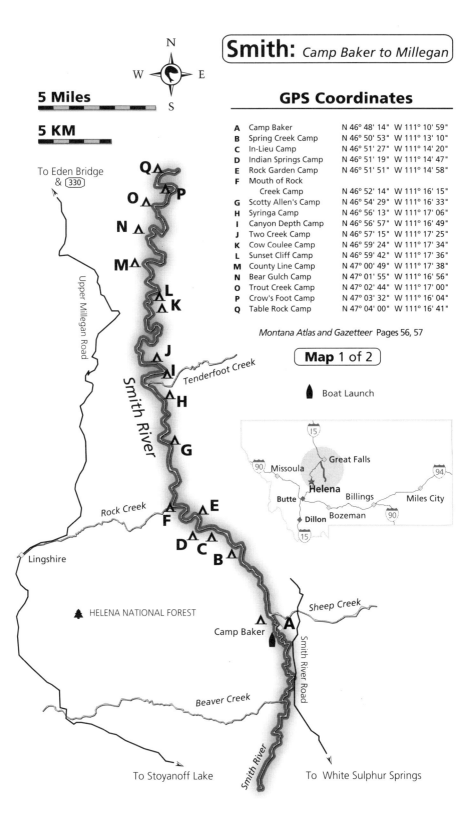

Smith: *Camp Baker to Millegan*

GPS Coordinates

A	Camp Baker	N 46° 48' 14"	W 111° 10' 59"
B	Spring Creek Camp	N 46° 50' 53"	W 111° 13' 10"
C	In-Lieu Camp	N 46° 51' 27"	W 111° 14' 20"
D	Indian Springs Camp	N 46° 51' 19"	W 111° 14' 47"
E	Rock Garden Camp	N 46° 51' 51"	W 111° 14' 58"
F	Mouth of Rock Creek Camp	N 46° 52' 14"	W 111° 16' 15"
G	Scotty Allen's Camp	N 46° 54' 29"	W 111° 16' 33"
H	Syringa Camp	N 46° 56' 13"	W 111° 17' 06"
I	Canyon Depth Camp	N 46° 56' 57"	W 111° 16' 49"
J	Two Creek Camp	N 46° 57' 15"	W 111° 17' 25"
K	Cow Coulee Camp	N 46° 59' 24"	W 111° 17' 34"
L	Sunset Cliff Camp	N 46° 59' 42"	W 111° 17' 36"
M	County Line Camp	N 47° 00' 49"	W 111° 17' 38"
N	Bear Gulch Camp	N 47° 01' 55"	W 111° 16' 56"
O	Trout Creek Camp	N 47° 02' 44"	W 111° 17' 00"
P	Crow's Foot Camp	N 47° 03' 32"	W 111° 16' 04"
Q	Table Rock Camp	N 47° 04' 00"	W 111° 16' 41"

Montana Atlas and Gazetteer Pages 56, 57

Map 1 of 2

Boat Launch

To Eden Bridge & 330

Upper Millegan Road

Smith River

Tenderfoot Creek

Rock Creek

Lingshire

HELENA NATIONAL FOREST

Camp Baker

Smith River Road

Sheep Creek

Beaver Creek

To Stoyanoff Lake

Smith River

To White Sulphur Springs

Great Falls

Missoula

Helena

Butte

Billings

Miles City

Dillon

Bozeman

Smith: *Millegan to Eden Bridge*

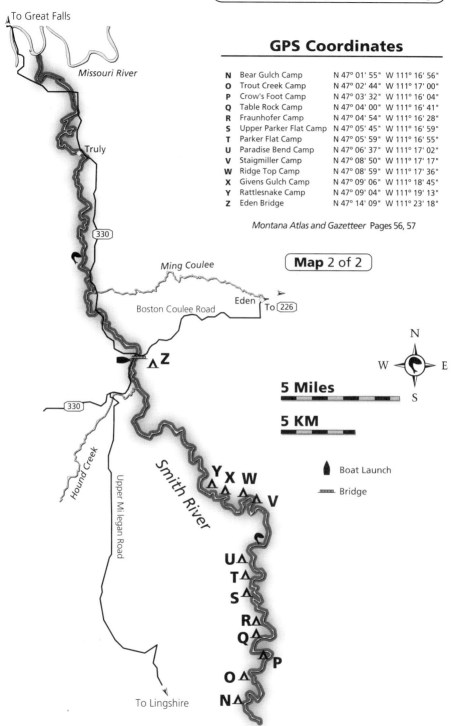

To Great Falls

Missouri River

Truly

330

Ming Coulee

Boston Coulee Road

Eden To 226

330

Hound Creek

Upper Millegan Road

Smith River

Y X W
V

U
T
S
R
Q
P
O
N

Z

GPS Coordinates

N	Bear Gulch Camp	N 47° 01' 55"	W 111° 16' 56"
O	Trout Creek Camp	N 47° 02' 44"	W 111° 17' 00"
P	Crow's Foot Camp	N 47° 03' 32"	W 111° 16' 04"
Q	Table Rock Camp	N 47° 04' 00"	W 111° 16' 41"
R	Fraunhofer Camp	N 47° 04' 54"	W 111° 16' 28"
S	Upper Parker Flat Camp	N 47° 05' 45"	W 111° 16' 59"
T	Parker Flat Camp	N 47° 05' 59"	W 111° 16' 55"
U	Paradise Bend Camp	N 47° 06' 37"	W 111° 17' 02"
V	Staigmiller Camp	N 47° 08' 50"	W 111° 17' 17"
W	Ridge Top Camp	N 47° 08' 59"	W 111° 17' 36"
X	Givens Gulch Camp	N 47° 09' 06"	W 111° 18' 45"
Y	Rattlesnake Camp	N 47° 09' 04"	W 111° 19' 13"
Z	Eden Bridge	N 47° 14' 09"	W 111° 23' 18"

Montana Atlas and Gazetteer Pages 56, 57

Map 2 of 2

N
W E
S

5 Miles

5 KM

Boat Launch

Bridge

To Lingshire

A float trip by raft is the best way for most anglers to experience the remote waters of the Smith River.

HOW TO GET THERE

If you are arriving by air, check the regularly scheduled flights into Great Falls or Helena. Great Falls is closer to the take-out at Eden Bridge, and Helena is a little closer to Camp Baker, depending on your choice of routes.

To reach the take-out at Eden Bridge from Great Falls, go southwest on I-15 to Exit 270 at Ulm, then go southeast on SR 330 18 miles to Eden Bridge. If driving up from Helena, take I-15 northeast about 60 miles to Exit 254, go into Cascade and turn east onto SR 330. Go east 19 miles to reach Eden Bridge.

To reach Camp Baker from Helena, go east on US 12 for 74 miles to White Sulphur Springs, turn west at the center of town, and go northwest on SR 360 for 16 miles. Turn north on Smith River Road and then follow the signs about nine miles to Camp Baker. If driving from Great Falls to Camp Baker, go southeast 17 miles on US 87, then south about 47 miles on US 89 into White Sulphur Springs. Leave town going northwest on SR 360, then turn north onto Smith River Road. The route to Camp Baker is well-marked.

To go from Camp Baker to Eden Bridge, go south on Smith River Road about nine miles, then west on SR 360, which will bend north and become SR 330, then Cottonwood Creek Road, then CR 360 (Lingshire Road). It finally becomes Upper Millegan Road when it enters Cascade County and brings you to SR 330, about 2 ½ miles south of Eden Bridge. This route is mostly gravel, takes about two hours to drive, and should be avoided in wet weather.

ACCESSIBILITY

The main access to the Smith is by floating the 59 miles from Camp Baker to Eden Bridge. Water levels are very important. You will need 150 cfs (measured at the gauge two miles below Camp Baker) to make your way down in canoes; rafts require 250 cfs; drift boats should have 350 cfs or more. Most anglers will be best served by rafts with rowing frames that can be effectively positioned by the person at the oars, draw relatively little water, and can survive the inevitable encounters with rocks in this relatively small river. There are two Class II/III rapids about 49 miles into the float (just above and below Givens Gulch and Rattlesnake camps). Be advised that canoes have been wrecked here before. If you are not confident in your ability to negotiate these

Anglers lucky enough to draw a permit can float nearly 60 miles of the Smith River.

passages safely, be prepared to line your craft down the edge. There is also an easily avoided diversion dam about three miles downstream from the rapids.

Expect to camp a minimum of two nights, with three or four nights being the optimal length. From June 10 to July 10, floaters are restricted to a maximum of four nights stay on the river once they launch. There are 27 boat camps between Camp Baker and Eden Bridge with 52 campsites. River rangers will help you select available sites at the start of your trip. Of the 118 miles of shoreline on this float, only 26 miles is public. Respect private property and reduce your impact on others by moving quickly through summer-home areas.

Arrange for a shuttle before your trip begins. The cost is reasonable and it ensures that your trip will have a happy conclusion.

If you want to experience the remote waters of the Smith River without camping, check out Deep Creek Outfitters and the Heaven on Earth Ranch. They are located on the banks of the Smith about midway between Camp Baker and Eden Bridge. There are warm, comfortable accommodations as well as a nine-hole golf course. Floaters can arrange to spend a night during early and late season (they are usually full during summer), or treat yourself to a full week of fishing and golf.

Indian Springs on the Smith.

WHEN TO GO

The correct timing of a trip on the Smith will depend on two factors: water level and permit availability. Water normally rises to floatable levels in April and falls off by about mid-June. However, each year is different, so watch flows closely before your trip and be sure your chosen craft is suitable to the water levels at that time. In some years, flows can increase to floatable levels in September once irrigation ends. Check flows on the web or call the USGS office in Great Falls at (406) 441-2081.

Late April and early May trips can give an extra measure of peace and solitude, but there is a greater likelihood of inclement weather. Both skwalas and blue-winged olives can be present at this time and should stimulate good fishing if the water remains reasonably clear.

If you feel lucky, try to hit the Smith for the salmonfly hatch in late May or early June. If you can get a permit and find water clear enough to fish, it can be incredible.

Golden stones begin to show in late June, and you can also find brown drakes on the lower reaches of the river as the water clears up and becomes more fishable.

If the water rises to floatable levels in September, expect success with grasshopper and blue-winged olive patterns.

Note: If you don't get a permit in the regular lottery in February, you can call the office in Great Falls at (406) 454-5861 to check for cancellations or other open dates. If that fails and you are willing to take a chance, you can go to Camp Baker with your gear and wait for an opening.

> **CHECK RIVER FLOWS ON THE WEB**
> http://montana.usgs.gov./rt-cgi/gen_tbl_pg

RESOURCES

On the river there are 27 boat camps with 52 campsites. Make reservations for campsites at Camp Baker before you begin your trip. Camping is also allowed at Eden Bridge.

Campgrounds

GREAT FALLS

KOA Kampgrounds
1500 51st St. S.
Great Falls, MT 59405
Phone number/s: (406) 727-3191

Missouri Meadows Campground
3012 Lower River Road
Great Falls, MT 59405
Phone number/s: (406) 452-0408

WHITE SULPHUR SPRINGS

Conestoga Campground
815 8th Ave. W.
White Sulphur Springs, MT 59645
Phone number/s: (406) 547-3890

Lodging

GREAT FALLS

Best Western Inn
1700 Fox Farm Road
Great Falls, MT 59404
Phone number/s: (406) 761-1900

ULM

Deep Creek Outfitters
Heaven on Earth Ranch
c/o Gary and Vi Anderson
P.O. Box 270
Ulm, MT 59485
Phone number/s: (406) 866-3316
E-mail: dpcreek@initco.net

WHITE SULPHUR SPRINGS

Forest Green Resort
2129 US 89 North
White Sulphur Springs, MT 59645
Phone number/s: (406) 547-3496

Spa Hot Springs Motel
202 Mayn Road
White Sulphur Springs, MT 59645
Phone number/s: (406) 547-3366

Tackle Shops and Guide Services

ENNIS

Blast & Cast Outfitters
P.O. Box 824
Ennis, MT 59729
Phone number/s: (406) 682-4420
blstcst@3rivers.net

GREAT FALLS

Montana River Outfitters
923 10th Ave. N.
Great Falls, MT 59401
Phone number/s: (406) 761-1677,
toll-free (800) 800-8218
Fax: (406) 452-3833
(Raft, canoe and equipment rentals available)

HELENA

Big Sky Expeditions
2125 Euclid Ave.
Helena, MT 59601
Phone number/s: (406) 442-2630

WHITE SULPHUR SPRINGS

Headwaters Angling
P.O. Box 645
White Sulphur Springs, MT 59645
Phone number/s: toll-free (888) 246-3759

Shuttle Services

GREAT FALLS

Jody and Caroline Cox
Millegan Route
Great Falls, MT 59405
Phone number/s: (406) 866-3522,
toll-free (888) 813-0137

WHITE SULPHUR SPRINGS

Castle Mountain Sports
PO Box H
White Sulphur Springs, MT 59645
Phone number/s: (406) 547-2330
(Raft, canoe and equipment rentals available)

Think Wild Enterprises
Box 446
White Sulphur Springs, MT 59645
Phone number/s: (406) 547-3792

Yellowstone River in Paradise Valley

G old was discovered at Emigrant Gulch in Paradise Valley in the 1860s, and Yellowstone City became a boomtown. The nearby town of Chico was named after a popular miner in 1868, the same year its mail service was established. In 1900, a miner's boarding house was expanded to include a hotel now known as Chico Hot Springs Resort. The Park Branch of the Northern Pacific Railway ran from Livingston to Gardiner at that time and delivered such famous guests as President Teddy Roosevelt and artist Charles Russell to the resort.

FISH SPECIES
Rainbow, cutthroat and brown trout

TIP
Try a hopper and a dropper

HIGHLIGHT
Mother's Day caddis in early May

SEASON
Open year-round

There has been no gold mining in Paradise Valley since the 1940s, but the Yellowstone River remains one of America's great treasures. It is the longest undammed river in the lower 48 states, running 678 miles from its source in Wyoming until it loses itself in the wide waters of the Missouri near Sidney, Montana. It emerges from Yellowstone National Park at Gardiner, Montana, and enters Paradise Valley about 15 miles downstream. The river writhes and twists across its flood plain and periodically gouges out new channels when full with spring run-off.

The river's wandering ways has brought it into conflict with those who live along its banks. Flooding in 1996 and 1997 has sparked a surge in the construction of dikes and riprap to protect homes and property. When riverside trees and plants are replaced by hard-surfaced riprap, water velocity increases and slow water pockets that provide rest and shelter for trout are eliminated. This has prompted American Rivers to place the Yellowstone on its list of America's 10 most endangered rivers.

While the future holds many questions for the Yellowstone, the river still holds its fair share of trout. Anglers will find good numbers of native cutthroat from Gardiner downstream. Yankee Jim Canyon is rumored to hold big browns in its deep and powerful flow, and you can expect a nice mix of rainbows, browns and cutthroats as the river makes its way down through Paradise Valley.

SPECIAL REGULATIONS

Yellowstone National Park Boundary to Emigrant Bridge:
❑ Catch-and-release for cutthroat trout.
❑ Open entire year.

Emigrant Bridge to Pine Creek Bridge:
❑ Catch-and-release for cutthroat trout.
❑ Artificial lures only.

Emigrant Peak stands tall above theYellowstone near Chico Hot Springs.

- ❏ Combined trout limit: five brown and rainbow trout, four under 13 inches and one over 22 inches.
- ❏ All brown and rainbow trout between 13 and 22 inches must be released.
- ❏ Extended whitefish season and catch-and-release for trout from December 1 to the third Saturday in May.

Pine Creek Bridge to mouth of Clarks Fork:
- ❏ Catch-and-release for cutthroat trout.
- ❏ Open entire year.

TACTICS

Tailor your approach to the hatches in progress when you are on the river. If it is the Mother's Day caddis, you can expect bugs everywhere, but the water will normally be high and fish will tend to feed in whatever slow water they can find. They will take nymphs that imitate caddis larvae in the mornings and then switch to adults by midafternoon when the number of hatching insects peak.

Salmonflies migrate to the edge of the river to crawl out, hatch and make their first experimental flights. That is where you will find the fish, right on the banks — gorging on the bounty of the giant *Pteronarcys.*

Once the large golden stoneflies begin to appear in July, Mitch Hurt of Far & Fine Guide Service in Livingston likes to fish a bead-head prince nymph as a dropper underneath a Dave's hopper. This combination imitates the big Acronuria adults as well as a grasshopper, while the prince passes for the nymph.

An effective approach utilized by local anglers is dead drifting a large trude pattern, such as the H & L trude or Rio Grande trude. Once the big dry fly reaches

Hatch Chart   AVAILABILITY

Food Items	J	F	M	A	M	J	J	A	S	O	N	D
Midges		X	X	X								
Blue-winged olives			X	X					X	X		
Pale morning duns							X	X				
March browns			X	X	X							
Gray drakes							X	X	X			
Green drakes						X	X					
Salmonflies						X	X					
Golden stoneflies							X	X				
Mother's Day caddis				X	X							
Caddisflies						X	X	X	X			
Terrestrials							X	X	X			

the end of its drift, let it swing then strip it back in against the current. Cutthroats seem especially prone to attacking the bright trudes on the move.

Wherever you find banks with both deep water and structure, you will find fish. During high water and strong flows look for trout in the inside bends where currents slow down. Once the water drops, you will find more fish against the banks on the outside bends.

HOW TO GET THERE

Anglers arriving by air can fly into Bozeman, Montana, which is 26 miles west of the Yellowstone River at Livingston. Cody, Wyoming, also has regular air service for visitors who would like to reach the Yellowstone River in Montana by driving through Yellowstone National Park, a distance of about 130 miles.

From Bozeman, go east 26 miles on I-90 to Exit 333 at Livingston. Head south on US 89 to follow the Yellowstone. From Cody, go west 50 miles to the East Entance of Yellowstone National Park. Go west 26 miles on East Entrance Road, then turn north onto Grand Loop Road and travel 49 miles to Mammoth Hot Springs. Turn north onto North Entrance Road, which becomes US 89 at the park boundary. It is only about five miles from Mammoth Hot Springs to Gardiner and the Yellowstone River in Montana. The Grand Loop follows the Yellowstone River through the Park, so expect incredible scenery and slow traffic during summer months. This route closes for the winter in October and some roads don't open until mid-June, so check with Yellowstone National Park Visitor Services at (307) 344-2115 or on the web at *www.nps.gov/yell/planvisit* before you plan your trip.

ACCESSIBILITY

Access to this section of the Yellowstone is greatly facilitated by US 89, which runs along the river from Gardiner to Livingston. East River Road allows anglers to reach the east bank of the Yellowstone from Carter's Bridge to the bottom of

Insects	Suggested Fly Patterns
Midges	Griffith's gnats (#16-22), Adams (#16-22), midge pupae, cream, brown and black (#18-22), brassies (#16-20)
Blue-winged olives	parachute Adams (#16-20), thorax BWOs (#16-20), olive comparaduns (#16-20), Quigley cripples, olive (#16-20), CDC emergers, olive (#16-20), pheasant tails (#16-20), hare's ears (#16-20), bead-head pheasant tails (#16-20), bead-head hare's ears (#16-20)
Pale morning duns	thorax PMDs (#14-16), cream parachutes (#14-16), cream comparaduns (#16-20), Quigley cripples, cream (#16-20), rusty spinners (#14-16), CDC emergers, cream (#16-20), pheasant tails (#14-16), hare's ears (#14-16), bead-head pheasant tails (#14-16), bead-head hare's ears (#14-16)
March browns	parachute hare's ears (#14-16), brown comparaduns (#14-16), pheasant tails (#14-16), hare's ears (#14-16), bead-head pheasant tails (#14-16), bead-head hare's ears (#14-16)
Gray drakes	gray Wulffs (#12-16), parachute Adams (#12-16), gray comparaduns (#12-16), spinners, black and gray (#10-12), muskrat nymphs (#12-14), pheasant tails (#12-14)
Green drakes	green drake Wulffs (#8-12), olive paradrakes (#10-12), olive comparaduns (#10-12), Quigley cripples, olive (#8-12), hare's ears, olive (#10-14), zug bugs (#10-14)
Salmonflies	sofa pillows (#6-10), Mac Salmons (#6-10), orange stimulators (#6-10), rubber-legs, black (#6-10), Bitch Creek nymphs (#6-10), Brook's stone nymphs (#6-10)
Golden stoneflies	yellow stimulators (#8-12), prince nymphs (#8-10), bead-head prince nymphs (#8-10), golden stonefly nymphs (#6-10), Bitch Creek nymphs (#6-10), copper Johns (#10-14)
Mother's Day caddis	elk-hair caddis, olive (#14-16), Goddard caddis (#14-16), Hemingway caddis (#14-16), sparkle pupae, olive (#14-16), X-caddis (#14-16), peeking caddis (#12-14)
Caddisflies	elk-hair caddis (#16-18), partridge caddis (#16-18), CDC elk-hair caddis (#16-18), sparkle caddis (#16-18), X-caddis (#16-18), peeking caddis (#12-14), CK nymphs (#12-14)
Terrestrials	Dave's hoppers (#8-12), Henry's Fork hoppers (#8-12), fur ants, black (#14-18), CDC ants (#14-18), deer-hair beetles, black (#14-16), hi-vis foam beetles (#14-16)
Streamers	woolly buggers, olive, black and brown (#4-8), muddler minnows (#4-8), spruce flies, light and dark (#4-8)

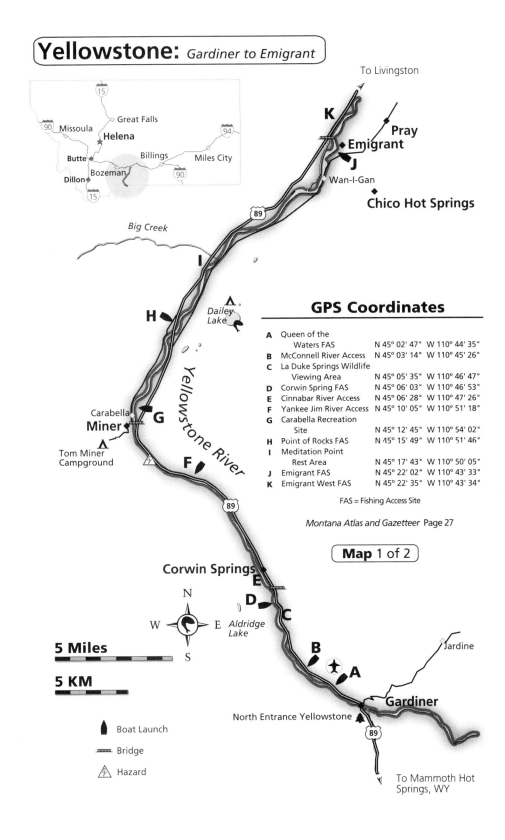

Yellowstone: *Gardiner to Emigrant*

To Livingston

K

Pray

Emigrant

J

Wan-I-Gan

Chico Hot Springs

Great Falls

Missoula

Helena

Billings

Butte

Miles City

Bozeman

Dillon

Big Creek

I

Dailey Lake

GPS Coordinates

A	Queen of the Waters FAS	N 45° 02' 47"	W 110° 44' 35"
B	McConnell River Access	N 45° 03' 14"	W 110° 45' 26"
C	La Duke Springs Wildlife Viewing Area	N 45° 05' 35"	W 110° 46' 47"
D	Corwin Spring FAS	N 45° 06' 03"	W 110° 46' 53"
E	Cinnabar River Access	N 45° 06' 28"	W 110° 47' 26"
F	Yankee Jim River Access	N 45° 10' 05"	W 110° 51' 18"
G	Carabella Recreation Site	N 45° 12' 45"	W 110° 54' 02"
H	Point of Rocks FAS	N 45° 15' 49"	W 110° 51' 46"
I	Meditation Point Rest Area	N 45° 17' 43"	W 110° 50' 05"
J	Emigrant FAS	N 45° 22' 02"	W 110° 43' 33"
K	Emigrant West FAS	N 45° 22' 35"	W 110° 43' 34"

FAS = Fishing Access Site

Montana Atlas and Gazetteer Page 27

Map 1 of 2

H

Carabella

Miner

G

Tom Miner Campground

F

Yellowstone River

Corwin Springs

E

D

C

N

W ⟡ E

S

Aldridge Lake

5 Miles

5 KM

B

Jardine

A

Gardiner

North Entrance Yellowstone

89

⬦ Boat Launch

⬛ Bridge

⚡ Hazard

To Mammoth Hot Springs, WY

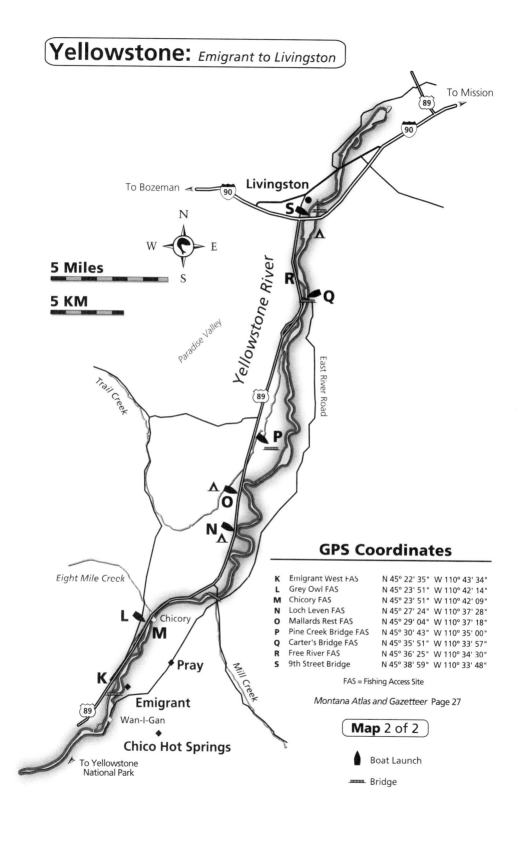

Yellowstone: *Emigrant to Livingston*

To Mission

To Bozeman

Livingston

S

R

Q

Yellowstone River

Paradise Valley

East River Road

Trail Creek

P

O

N

Eight Mile Creek

L

Chicory

M

K

Pray

Mill Creek

Emigrant

Wan-I-Gan

Chico Hot Springs

To Yellowstone
National Park

N
W E
S

5 Miles

5 KM

GPS Coordinates

K	Emigrant West FAS	N 45° 22' 35"	W 110° 43' 34"
L	Grey Owl FAS	N 45° 23' 51"	W 110° 42' 14"
M	Chicory FAS	N 45° 23' 51"	W 110° 42' 09"
N	Loch Leven FAS	N 45° 27' 24"	W 110° 37' 28"
O	Mallards Rest FAS	N 45° 29' 04"	W 110° 37' 18"
P	Pine Creek Bridge FAS	N 45° 30' 43"	W 110° 35' 00"
Q	Carter's Bridge FAS	N 45° 35' 51"	W 110° 33' 57"
R	Free River FAS	N 45° 36' 25"	W 110° 34' 30"
S	9th Street Bridge	N 45° 38' 59"	W 110° 33' 48"

FAS = Fishing Access Site

Montana Atlas and Gazetteer Page 27

Map 2 of 2

Boat Launch

Bridge

Adult salmonfly flanked by a Mac Salmon (left) and a sofa pillow; both are good flies to try when the hatch is on.

Yankee Jim Canyon. There are a good number of public access points along the river and they are well-spaced.

As is true of most big western rivers, floating anglers have a large advantage over their wading counterparts on much of the Yellowstone between Gardiner and Livingston. Floating works well from McConnell down to Corwin Springs. You can expect good numbers of native cutthroat in this section. Yankee Jim Canyon has powerful Class III rapids and can be dangerous. There are several turnouts along US 89 through the canyon, and it is safer to fish carefully from the edge than to launch a boat here. Carabella Recreation Site is below the fury of Yankee Jim and at the top of Paradise Valley. The river is fairly gentle and easy to float from here all the way down to Livingston. Some of the best braids and gravel bars can be found between Pine Creek Bridge and Carter's Bridge.

If you would like to sample the fishing on the Yellowstone and don't have the use of a boat or raft, you will be able to get around on the river anywhere from Point of Rocks down to Carter's Bridge. Mallards Rest Fishing Access Site has camping and good access for anglers working upstream.

CHECK RIVER FLOWS ON THE WEB
http://montana.usgs.gov./rt-cgi/gen_tbl_pg

WHEN TO GO

The pre run-off season on the Yellowstone can be a good cure for a long winter. Good fishing with midges and blue-winged olives can begin in March, and weather can be fine — just don't forget to pack lots of warm clothing.

The rewarding Mother's Day caddis starts at the end of April or first of May. The catch is that the river is usually high and dirty by the time the hatch gets going, so anglers need a flexible schedule and an alternate plan — such as Armstrong's and Nelson's spring creeks.

The salmonfly hatch can be hampered by high, dirty water as well, so it pays to keep track of flow levels as your trip date approaches. Anglers can check flows on the web or call a local shop. Plan your trip for the optimal period around the very end of June or the first week of July. If water conditions are too extreme, you can shift to nearby tailwaters like the Missouri, Madison or Bighorn.

Summer brings the best water conditions, but heavy storms in Yellowstone Park can put the river out for a few days. The big golden stoneflies, grasshoppers, gray drakes and caddis are the smorgasbord presented to Paradise Valley trout during the long days of summer. Anglers can expect a variety of interesting fishing opportunities.

The first frosty nights of fall will turn the cottonwoods golden to match the fine fall sunshine. Streamer fishing comes into its own, and you will find fewer anglers on the water to share the glory of an autumn sunset in Paradise.

The Chico Hot Springs Resort is listed on the National Register of Historic Places.

AREA ATTRACTIONS

Unwind after a hard day of fishing at the historic Chico Hot Springs Resort. You can stay in the romantic turn-of-the-century hotel, listed on the National Register of Historic Places, or soak in the spring-fed hot pools renowned for their restorative powers since the early 1900s. There is great dining and live music in the Chico Saloon on summer weekends.

RESOURCES

The Pine Creek campground in Gallatin National Forest has handicap-accessible campsites.

On the Yellowstone, there are handicap-accessible restrooms at Carter's Bridge, Emigrant, Grey Owl, Meditation Point, Carabella, Yankee Jim, Cinnabar and McConnell access sites.

Campgrounds

GALLATIN NATIONAL FOREST

For more information, call the Gardiner Ranger District at (406) 848-7375.

❐ Tom Miner
❐ Eagle Creek

For more information, call the Livingston Ranger District at (406) 222-1892.

❐ Pine Creek

GARDINER

Rocky Mountain Campground
14 Jardine Road
Gardiner, MT 59030
Phone number/s: (406) 848-7251

Yellowstone RV Park & Camp
117 US 89 South
Gardiner, MT 59030
Phone number/s: (406) 848-7496

LIVINGSTON

Livingston-Paradise Valley KOA
163 Pine Creek Road
Livingston, MT 59047
Phone number/s: (406) 222-0992,
toll-free (800) KOA-2805
Fax: (406) 222-5911
Web site: www.koa.com
E-mail: liv.koa@ycsi.net

Yellowstone's Edge RV Park
3501 US 89 South
Livingston, MT 59047
Phone number/s: (406) 333-4036

Lodging

EMIGRANT

Mountain Sky Guest Ranch
460 Big Creek Road
Emigrant, MT 59027
Phone number/s: (406) 333-4911

Point of Rocks Lodge
2017 US 89 South
Emigrant, MT 59027
Phone number/s: (406) 333-4361
Fax: (406) 848-7222

GARDINER

Best Western Inn
US 89 West
Gardiner, MT 59030
Phone number/s: (406) 848-7311

LIVINGSTON

Comfort Inn
114 Loves Lane
Livingston, MT 59047
Phone number/s: (406) 222-4400

Pine Creek Lodge
2495 E. River Road
Livingston, MT 59047
Phone number/s: (406)-222-3628

PRAY

Chico Hot Springs Lodge
P.O. Drawer D
Old Chico Road
Pray, MT 59065
Phone number/s: (406) 333-4933
Fax: (406) 333-4694

Tackle Shops and Guide Services

GARDINER

Park's Fly Shop
202 2nd St. South
Gardiner, MT 59030
Phone number/s: (406) 848-7314

LIVINGSTON

Dan Bailey's Fly Shop
209 W. Park St.
Livingston, MT 59047
Phone number/s: (406) 222-1673,
toll-free (800) 356-4052
Web site: www.danbailey.com
E-mail: dan@danbailey.com

Yellowstone Angler
P.O. Box 629
5256 US 89 South
Livingston, MT 59047
Phone number/s: (406) 222-7130
Fax: (406) 222-7153
Web site: www.yellowstoneangler.com
E-mail: staff@yellowstoneangler.com

NEW MEXICO

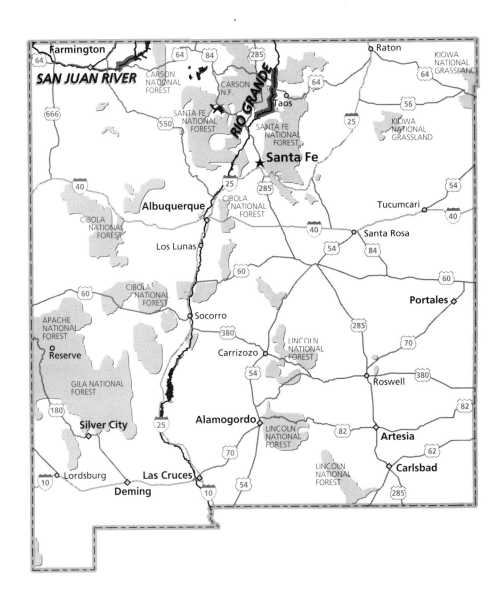

New Mexico

ew Mexico is a state rich in cultural treasures that include Anasazi ruins and present-day pueblos that take you back in time. While much of the state is arid, New Mexico's mountainous north holds some rich trout waters. The San Juan River attracts anglers year-round, and the Rio Grande is an excellent winter fishery. Those who visit the "Land of Enchantment" will find many reasons to return.

FISHING ACCESS LAWS

In New Mexico, you must obtain written permission before entering private lands, including streambeds. Much of New Mexico's public land is mixed with privately owned land. By law, if private land blocks access to public land, the angler must seek another access or receive landowner permission to cross.

2000 GENERAL SEASON DATES AND BAG & POSSESSION LIMITS

The daily bag limit is five per day and 10 in possession for trout and salmon. Only two cutthroat trout may be included in the daily bag and possession limit.

Special trout waters in New Mexico have either reduced bag limits — the possession limit is the same as daily bag limit — or are catch-and-release. Stretches of the Rio Grande and San Juan River are designated special trout waters.

Species	2000 Daily Bag & Possession Limits
STATEWIDE	
Rainbow, brown, brook and lake trout and kokanee salmon	five of any combination; 10 in possession
Cutthroat trout	two; two in possession

LICENSE FEES

The season fishing license is valid beginning April 1 and expires on March 31st. Seniors 70 years of age and over who are residents of New Mexico may fish for free. All fishing licenses include trout validation.

Anglers over age 12 and under 70 are also required to have a Wildlife Habitat Stamp to fish on all U.S. Forest Service and BLM lands in New Mexico. The cost for the stamp is $5 for residents and nonresidents alike.

❏   All persons 12 years or older must carry a current New Mexico fishing license.

Fishing License	Age	Fee
RESIDENT		
Season	14 to 65	$17.50
Senior Season	65 to 70	$5
Junior Season	12 to 14	$5
Five-day	12 and over	$16
Daily	12 and over	$8
NONRESIDENT		
Season	12 and over	$39
Junior Season	12 to 14	$18.50
Five-day	12 and over	$16
Daily	12 and over	$8

BOATING REGULATIONS

New Mexico State Parks regulates all boating activities. Boating regulations are published on its web site (*www.emnrd.state.nm.us/nmparks*), or you can obtain a copy by calling (888) 667-2757.

All vessels must carry proper safety equipment, including PFDs for each person onboard and a sound-producing device. Under New Mexico boating laws, a flotation assist device may be worn instead of a PFD by anglers using a float tube.

RESOURCES

New Mexico Department of Fish & Game
Phone number/s: (505) 827-7905,
toll-free (800) 862-9310
Web site: www.gmfish.state.nm.us

New Mexico River Flows
Web site: http://nm.water.usgs.gov/rt-cgi/gen_tbl_pg

New Mexico State Parks
Phone number/s: toll-free (888) 667-2757
Web site: www.emnrd.state.nm.us/nmparks

New Mexico Department of Tourism
Phone number/s: toll-free (800) 733-6396 ext. 0643
Web site: www.newmexico.org

Bureau of Land Management
Phone number/s: (505) 438-7400
Web site: www.nm.blm.gov

U.S. Forest Service
Phone number/s: (505)758-6200 (Carson)
Web site: www.fs.fed.us/recreation/states/nm.shtml

Rio Grande

HIGHLIGHT
Mother's Day caddis
hatch in early April

TIP
Camp on the river in the
Wild River Recreation Area

FISH SPECIES
Browns, rainbows, Rio
Grande cutthroats and
a few cuttbow hybrids

SEASON
Open year-round, but
only recommended from
October through April

I n 1968, Congress created the National Wild and Scenic Rivers System and declared that "... certain selected rivers of the Nation which ... possess outstandingly remarkable scenic, recreational ... or other similar values, shall be preserved in free-flowing condition, and that they ... shall be protected for the benefit and enjoyment of present and future generations."

The Rio Grande in northern New Mexico so clearly embodied these qualities that it became one of the first rivers to be so protected. You'll be able to see why if you hike down into the gorge in the Wild Rivers Recreation Area. The sparse vegetation at the canyon rim gives way to ponderosa pine and lush vegetation along the river, and clear, cold springs rise up from the black basalt to join the river's flow.

The Rio Grande is the fifth-longest river in North America, running 1,900 miles from its source in the San Juan Mountains to the Gulf of Mexico. Much of the river's course is through arid lands; it is the life-giving water of the river that has made human habitation in the region possible. Large pueblos were located up and down the Rio Grande flood plain when Coronado arrived in the area in 1540. These ancestors of New Mexico's present day Pueblo Indians used the Rio Grande for irrigation, and the practice continues to affect the river today.

The Rio Grande is used for irrigation in the San Luis Valley in southern Colorado. A portion of this irrigation water is returned to the river, burdened with the sediments picked up in the fields. This irrigation return increases the Rio Grande's turbidity downstream in New Mexico and keeps the river cloudy and unappealing through most of the summer. Fishing really comes around in October when the river clears up.

In the fall, anglers can find good numbers of rainbows in the 12- to 14-inch range, with brown trout running slightly larger. You can expect some of either species to reach 18 inches or more, and the remote waters of the Rio Grande still produce some trophy fish that can run to 26 inches or more.

SPECIFIC REGULATIONS

The Rio Grande from the Colorado state line downstream to the Taos Junction Bridge is Special Trout Water:

❏ Anglers may keep only three trout, only two of which may be cutthroat trout.
❏ All gila trout must be released immediately.

A lone fly fisher probes the pocket water of the Rio Grande in the Wild Rivers
Recreation Area near Big Arsenic Springs.

TACTICS

Fly fishers will find that the Rio Grande is not really a float-fishing river. There
are many difficult rapids of Class IV or harder, and when the water is high enough
to float, it is usually quite off-color. Anglers should concentrate on the edges of the
river and pocket water. This is especially true during higher water periods. The Rio
Grande has cut a deep gorge down through the black basalt, and the river is full of
large boulders that provide cover for trout and create deep holes as the river flows
over and around them. Use caution when wading.

The Rio Grande has several good hatches, but nothing quite compares to the
first caddis emergence of the year. John Rainey of Los Rios Anglers says, "Our
Mother's Day caddis is a hatch of biblical proportions, sometimes blotting out the
sky." Although called the Mother's Day caddis, the big event comes early to the Rio
Grande compared to other Rocky Mountain rivers. The hatch normally begins
around the first of April and ends sometime between April 12 to 16. The incredible
number of insects can make it difficult to catch fish during this hatch. To improve
your chances, be sure that you have good imitations in the correct sizes and select a
single rising fish as your target.

While caddisflies are the single most important group of insects on the Rio
Grande, there are multiple hatches much of the year, and trout don't usually get
selective. Attractor patterns like the Rio Grande king and Rio Grande trude often
work well on the river's opportunistic fish. You don't have to limit yourself to standard "dead drift" presentations with these flies either. At the end of your drift, let

Hatch Chart — AVAILABILITY

Food Items	J	F	M	A	M	J	J	A	S	O	N	D
Midges	X	X	X	X	X	X	X	X	X	X	X	X
Blue-winged olives			X	X	X				X	X	X	
Brown stoneflies		X	X	X								
Caddisflies					X	X	X	X	X	X		
Mother's Day caddis					X							
Terrestrials						X	X	X	X	X		
Attractors							X	X	X	X	X	
Streamers	X	X	X	X					X	X	X	X

Insects	Suggested Fly Patterns
Midges	Griffith's gnats (#16-22), grizzly midges (#16-22), double midges (#16-22), Adams (#16-22), suspender midges (#16-22), biot midge pupae (#16-22), brassies (#16-22), palomino midges (#16-22), disco midges (#16-22)
Blue-winged olives	parachute Adams (#16-20), thorax BWOs (#16-20), olive comparaduns (#16-20), Quigley cripples, olive (#16-20), CDC emergers, olive (#16-20), pheasant tails (#14-18), hare's ears (#14-18), bead-head pheasant tails (#14-18), bead-head hare's ears (#14-18)
Brown stoneflies	little brown stone adults (#12-14), black stimulators (#12-14), prince nymphs (#10-14), Brook's stone nymphs (#10-14), little brown stone nymphs (#10-14), peacock stone nymphs (#10-14)
Caddisflies	elk-hair caddis (#12-18), partridge caddis (#12-18), CDC elk-hair caddis (#12-18), sparkle caddis (#12-18), X-caddis (#12-18), peeking caddis (#12-16), pulsating caddis (#12-16)
Mother's Day caddis	elk-hair caddis, olive (#16-18), Goddard caddis (#16-18), Hemingway caddis (#16-18), soft-hackle caddis, olive (#16-18), sparkle pupae, olive (#16-18), X-caddis (#16-18), peeking caddis (#16-18)
Terrestrials	Dave's hoppers (#8-12), Henry's Fork hoppers (#8-12), fur ants, black (#14-18), CDC ants (#14-18), deer-hair beetles, black (#14-16), hi-vis foam beetles (#14-16)
Attractors	Rio Grande trudes (#8-12), Rio Grande kings (#8-12)
Streamers	woolly buggers, olive, black and brown (#6-10), rabbit-strip leeches (#6-10), muddler minnows (#6-10), spruce flies, light and dark (#6-10)

them swing and then strip them in. Aggressive trout will often charge the fast-moving fly.

Prince nymphs and other similar peacock-bodied nymph patterns account for many of the trout caught on this river. They can be fished on a traditional nymph setup with a nine-foot leader and 4x or 5x tippet and a strike indicator, but they are also very effective when combined with dry flies or streamers. A "hopper and a dropper" rig is an efficient setup for searching the water, especially when that dropper fly is a size 12 to 14 bead-head prince nymph.

Fishing streamer patterns allows anglers to cover water quickly. The combination of a floating line and a weighted streamer will give you the necessary control to probe a variety of pockets, runs and riffles effectively. This approach is the best way to fish many of the river's boulder-choked stretches where getting a drift is either difficult or impossible. Don't be afraid to get your streamers down deep. You may lose some flies, but you will also find more fish. Perhaps that trophy trout is waiting for you in the deep dark of a Rio Grande pool.

HOW TO GET THERE

The Taos municipal airport is eight miles northwest of Taos on US 64. It is serviced twice daily by Rio Grande Air, or visitors can fly into Santa Fe (a two-hour drive) or Albuquerque (three-hour drive time). To reach Taos from Albuquerque, go northeast about 60 miles on I-25 and take Exit 282. Proceed north for 28 miles on US 84, then go northeast 45 miles on SR 68.

To reach the river south of Taos, take SR 68 south to Pilar. From Pilar to Velarde, SR 68 south parallels the Rio Grande. To access the river north of Pilar, take CR 570.

The Wild and Scenic National Recreation Area is north of Taos. Head north on US 64 to scenic SR 552, which will take you past the small town of Questa, about 20 miles north of Taos. A few miles north of Questa, take SR 378. This is a loop road that passes the town of Cerro and parallels about four miles of the river. There are four campgrounds along the river, but no road access. The river is reached by a short hike.

ACCESSIBILITY

The Wild Rivers Recreation Area is located on SR 378, just 11 miles southwest of SR 522 and the town of Cerro. This national recreation area provides anglers with access to the most scenic portions of the Rio Grande River Gorge. There are three main trails that lead down into the gorge; all reach the river in about one mile and drop about 750 feet in elevation. These trails all connect with a trail that follows the river for more than three miles from north of Big Arsenic Springs to the south bank of the Red River. There are four camping areas in the gorge near the river, so you can fall asleep with the sound of the "Great River" in your ears. You can also hike to the river from the Chiflo Overlook, or walk down to the Red River from El Aguaje, then follow the Red to the Rio Grande. Remember this is arid desert country — be sure to carry enough water.

Rio Grande: *Wild Rivers Recreation Area to Velarde*

GPS Coordinates

A	Chiflo Overlook	N 36° 44' 27"	W 105° 40' 50"
B	Big Arsenic Springs Trailhead	N 36° 40' 29"	W 105° 40' 52"
C	Little Arsenic Springs Trailhead	N 36° 40' 00"	W 105° 40' 51"
D	La Junta Point Trailhead	N 36° 39' 27"	W 105° 41' 07"
E	El Aguaje	N 36° 49' 00"	W 105° 40' 20"
F	Cebollo Mesa Trailhead	N 36° 38' 33"	W 105° 41' 34"
G	John Dunn Bridge	N 36° 32' 07"	W 105° 42' 31"
H	Manby Hot Springs Trailhead	N 36° 30' 44"	W 105° 43' 04"
I	Taos Junction Campground	N 36° 20' 09"	W 105° 44' 11"
J	Petaca Campground	N 36° 18' 26"	W 105° 46' 02"
K	Arroyo Hondo Campground	N 36° 17' 50"	W 105° 46' 25"
L	Orilla Verde Campground	N 36° 17' 33"	W 105° 46' 52"
M	Pilar Campground	N 36° 17' 09"	W 105° 47' 12"
N	Quartzite Recreation Site	N 36° 15' 55"	W 105° 47' 43"
O	County Line River Access	N 36° 13' 48"	W 105° 51' 22"

New Mexico Atlas and Gazetteer Page 16

Bridge

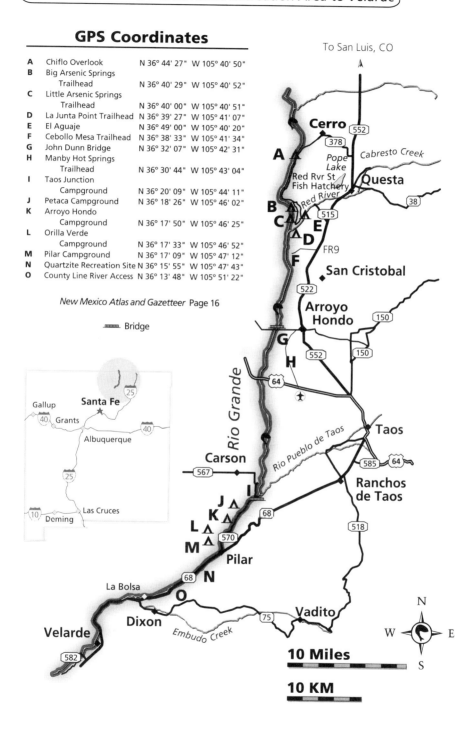

There is very little access to the Taos Box section of the Rio Grande.

The trail from Cebollo Mesa also links up with the trails in the Wild Rivers Recreation Area, except that the footbridge over the Red River is currently in need of repair, and you may have to wade across. To reach this trailhead from SR 522 near the tiny town of Lama, turn west on FR 9 and follow the main road for three miles to the trailhead. Many anglers feel that the best water on the river is downstream from the confluence with the Red River, but molybdenum mining upstream on the Red has damaged the river in the past and may continue to have a negative affect.

There is very little access in the rugged canyon as it approaches Taos, and the aesthetic qualities that most of us associate with trout rivers are greatly diminished. You can drive to the river at the John Dunn Bridge. From Arroyo Hondo drive west on B 005. Stick to the main dirt road and follow it down into the arroyo. You will reach the river in about 2½ miles and can fish up or down the river from this point.

Another access point is just downstream at Manby Hot Springs. From B 005, 1½ miles west of Arroyo Hondo, take the left fork just before the main road drops down into the arroyo. Follow this twisted and rutted road south and west a little over two miles to a graveled parking area at the canyon rim. It is a short 15-minute hike down a rocky but moderate slope trail to the hot springs on the river. Be prepared to see naked bodies soaking in the hot springs or basking on the riverbank. An alternate and smoother route is to turn northwest onto the dirt road just west of the entrance to the Taos Municipal Airport. It is about 4.5 miles on the unmarked and winding dirt road.

The Rio Grande finally breaks out of its inaccessible gorge at the Orilla Verde Recreation Area. There are five campgrounds along the river, and most have a launch site for rafts as well. From Pilar, drive north on SR 570 or take SR 567 east from Taos Junction. Anglers can also access the river downstream from Pilar from turnouts and river access sites along SR 68. There are many riffles, runs and pools along this stretch where anglers can walk down to the river and cast a line. Streamer fishing in this area can produce the occasional northern pike, especially in late winter and early spring.

WHEN TO GO

The Rio Grande fishes best from October, when the water clears up, until late April, when run-off raises the river and clouds its waters. Fall offers good streamer fishing and the best chance for a truly big trout. With winter comes some fine midge fishing. Visitors have a great opportunity to combine downhill skiing at one of the five area resorts with some technical and rewarding dry-fly fishing.

Springtime brings the Rio Grande's best hatch, the Mother's Day caddis. In spite of its name, this hatch usually occurs during the first two weeks of April. Run-off often begins by early May; once the water gets clouded, it stays that way until midfall due to irrigation returns. The Rio Grande will not normally fish well during the summer months. If you are planning some trout fishing in the Taos area at this time, you will want to contact the local shops for information on fishing some of the Rio Grande's tributary streams. These include Rio Costilla, Red River, Rio Hondo and Rio Pueblo.

> **CHECK RIVER FLOWS ON THE WEB**
> http://nm.water.usgs.gov/rt-cgi/gen_tbl_pg

AREA ATTRACTIONS

Taos is rated as one of the top art destinations in America. The landscape and lively culture have been inspiring artists for decades. The Taos Fall Arts Festival draws contemporary talent together to exhibit their work for two weeks beginning in late September and running into October. There are a variety of other events and activities to coincide with when the Rio Grande fishes its best. For more information, contact the Taos County Chamber of Commerce at (800) 732-8267.

Manby Hot Springs next to the Rio Grande attracts the crowds.

RESOURCES

The charming town of Taos offers a central base for fishing the upper and lower stretches of the Rio Grande. Lodging ranges from the economical to the extravagant. Contact Taos Central Reservations at (800) 821-2437 for complete lodging information or go online at *www.newmexicom.com* or *www.taoschamber.com*.

Camping in developed BLM campsites in the Rio Grande Wild and Scenic National Recreation Area or in the Carson National Forest is another option for anglers.

Campgrounds

CARSON NATIONAL FOREST

For more information, call the Questa Ranger District at (505) 586-0520.

❏ Cebolla Mesa

Lodging

QUESTA

Sangre de Cristo Motel
SR 522 and SR 38
Questa, NM 87556
Phone number/s: (505) 586-0300

Kachina Motel
2306 SR 522
Questa, NM 87556
Phone number/s: (505) 586-0640

TAOS

Brooks Street Inn B&B
119 Brooks St.
Taos, NM 87571
Phone number/s: (505) 758-1489,
toll-free (800) 758-1489
E-mail: brooks@taos.newmex.com

Inn on La Loma Plaza
315 Ranchitos Road
Taos, NM 87571
Phone number/s: (505) 758-1717,
toll-free (800) 530-3040
Web site: www.taoswebb.com/laloma

Kachina Lodge and Casino
413 Paseo del Pueblo Norte
Taos, NM 87571
Phone number/s: (505) 758-2275,
toll-free (800) 522-4462
Fax: (505) 758-9207
Web site: www.kachinalodge.com

Sun God Lodge
919 Paseo del Pueblo Sur
Taos, NM 87571
Phone number/s: (505) 758-3162
Fax: (505) 758-1716
Web site: www.sungodlodge.com
E-mail: sungod@laplaza.org

Tackle Shops and Outfitters

TAOS

Los Rios Anglers
226 Paseo Del Pueblo Norte, Suite C
Taos, NM 87571
Phone number/s: (505) 758-2798
Web site: www.losrios.com
E-mail: fish@losrios.com

Taylor Streit Fly Fishing Service
P.O. Box 2759
Taos, NM 87571
Phone number/s: (505) 751-1312

QUESTA

Outpost
59 Red River Hwy
Questa, NM 87556
Phone number/s: (505) 586-1289

San Juan River

f your angling dreams are about catching big rainbows on tiny flies, this may be your river. Many consider the San Juan River to be one of the best rainbow trout fisheries in the United States. Fish average an impressive 17 to 18 inches along the four-mile quality water section of the San Juan — which is home to a staggering 80,000 trout. There are so many fish that every type of water gets utilized on this river, and visitors can find a wide variety of fly-fishing challenges. With some coaching from a guide or knowledgeable friend, even novice anglers can expect to catch some good fish on nymphs during most seasons. If you are up for more difficult situations, spend your time casting tiny dry flies to big, selective trout on the still backwaters.

FISH SPECIES
Rainbow, cutthroat, cuttbows and brown trout

TIP
Carry dollar bills to pay day-use fee

HIGHLIGHT
Really big trout

SEASON
Open year-round

Angler densities can be nearly as impressive as fish densities, so be prepared to adjust your ideas of stream etiquette if you are accustomed to less-crowded rivers. San Juan fly fishers are more sociable than you might expect. They are usually willing to share information as well as the water. The braided nature of the river and the abundance of fish allow the San Juan to accommodate more anglers than other waters of similar size. These trout are not very skittish. If someone else moves through your area, be patient. The fish will generally resume feeding in short order.

The San Juan did not become a trout fishery until after the impoundment of Navajo Lake in 1962. The reservoir can store up to 1.7 million acre-feet of water, which is drawn from below the thermocline of this deep (maximum depth 300 feet) reservoir. Water leaving the dam is consistently in the low 40 degrees year-round, providing a very stable environment for the trout and the insect life they feed upon. The New Mexico Department of Game and Fish recognized the potential of this emerging trout fishery and instituted special regulations on the upper river in 1966.

SPECIAL REGULATIONS AND FEES

From the dam downstream 3.75 miles:
❑ Artificial flies and lures with single barbless hooks only.

From the dam to the cable 0.25 mile downstream:
❑ Catch-and-release only.

From the cable 0.25 mile from the dam, downstream 3.5 miles:
❑ Anglers may keep one fish over 20 inches.

The San Juan fishes well even in the dead of winter; just don't expect to be alone.

If boating on the San Juan, you must wear a life jacket; no motorized watercraft is allowed.

There is a day-use fee of $4 for parking, or you can purchase an annual permit from the Navajo State Park Game and Fish office at Navajo Lake for $20.

TACTICS

The most popular and effective technique to catch San Juan trout is nymph fishing, often with very tiny — size 20-26 — flies. Hooking and landing fish on such small flies is challenging. Reduce tippet size to match your fly. Expect to do much of your nymphing here with 5x. Use smaller, more sensitive strike indicators and just enough weight to reach the fish. Fine-diameter tippet will allow flies to sink faster and does a better job of transmitting the "feel" of light bites. If you tie your own flies, try hooks with a short shank, wide gape and straight eye (like the Tiemco 2488) to tie tiny nymphs.

Stealth is the key to catching trout on many waters, but on the San Juan it is accurate casting that counts most. Fish are harder to spook, but they will generally not move very far for tiny imitations. When you spot a fish, get in close enough to put every cast directly into the feeding lane.

Carry a landing net — the larger, the better. Landing strong, active rainbows on tiny flies is difficult at best. As more trout are released, anglers can help ensure that there will be other fish that live long enough to entertain others. The New Mexico Department of Game and Fish has estimated that 99 percent of fish here have already been caught and released.

Hatch Chart   AVAILABILITY

Food Items	J	F	M	A	M	J	J	A	S	O	N	D
Midges	X	X	X	X	X	X	X	X	X	X	X	X
Blue-winged olives			X	X	X					X	X	X
Pale morning duns						X	X	X	X			
Caddisflies					X	X						
Annelid worms	X	X	X	X	X	X	X	X	X	X	X	X
Trout eggs										X	X	X
Leeches	X	X	X	X	X	X	X	X	X	X	X	X
Terrestrials							X	X	X			

Insects	Suggested Fly Patterns
Midges	Griffith's gnats (#16-22), grizzly midges (#16-22), midge pupae, gray, cream, brown, red and black (#20-26), midge emergers, black and peacock (#20-26)
Blue-winged olives	parachute Adams (#18-20), thorax BWOs (#18-20), pheasant tails (#18-20), hare's ears (#18-20), WD40s (#18-20), RS2s (#18-20)
Pale morning duns	thorax PMDs (#14-16), cream parachutes (#14-16), rusty spinners (#14-16), pheasant tails (#14-16), hare's ears (#14-16)
Caddisflies	elk-hair caddis (#16-18), partridge caddis (#16-18)
Annelid worms	San Juan worms, orange and red (#12-16), red hots (#18-20)
Trout eggs	pink, orange and yellow glo-bugs (#12-16), bead-head glo-bugs (#12-16), bead eggs (#14-16)
Leeches	woolly buggers, black and olive (#8-12), bunny leeches, black, purple and olive (#8-12)
Terrestrials	Dave's hoppers (#8-12), fur ants, black (#14-18), deer-hair beetles, black (#14-16)

Finding a stretch of water to yourself can be more challenging than hooking the trout that inhabit the San Juan.

HOW TO GET THERE

From Farmington, New Mexico, go east 26 miles on US 64, then northeast 13 miles on SR 511.

From Durango, Colorado, go southeast seven miles on US 160. Go southeast 25 miles on SR 172, which will become SR 511 at the New Mexico state line. Continue south another 20 miles to the San Juan River.

For anglers arriving by air, you can usually get lower fares by flying into Albuquerque International Airport, then drive the four hours to the river in a rental car. There are airports at Farmington (50 minutes from the river) and Durango (1 hour and 15 minutes to the San Juan), and you can sometimes find competitive fares into these locations.

ACCESSIBILITY

You can easily reach the top four miles of quality water from SR 511. There are numerous parking areas, and anglers can easily move up and down the river. Most anglers wade the river, but be aware that a slippery, algae-covered bottom and cold water are substantial hazards. Several people have drowned in the river, so observe safe wading practices such as wearing a wading belt and felt-soled (or even studded) wading boots. A wading staff can provide extra security. Never wade in water beyond your ability. Signs at access points will caution you to get out of the river immediately if you hear the siren at the dam.

You can reach the north bank of the San Juan by going northwest on SR 173 at the town of Navajo Dam. Turn east on the dirt road to Cottonwood Campground. The road is a bit rough, and you want to avoid using it in wet weather. From the Simon Canyon Trailhead at the end of this road, a trail follows the north side of the river all the way to the dam. This is especially helpful in getting you away from other anglers when the river is too high to wade.

Once flows rise above 1,500 cfs, effective wade fishing becomes very difficult, and a drift boat becomes the best way to fish the river. If you don't have access to a drift boat, consider hiring one of the local guides during high-water periods. The stretch of river that is commonly floated is quite short (about three miles). Floaters put in at the Texas Hole and take out at the Gravel Pit boat ramp near the lower boundary of the quality water. Several paved fishing platforms also provide handicap access to the Texas Hole.

There is also a boat ramp just downstream from the town of Turley. This is a long float (about 11 miles downstream from the Gravel Pit access) with private lands on both sides of the river. To reach this hard-to-find access, go to the intersection of SR 511 and San Juan CR 4410 (at the Turley Cemetery), then head west 1.3 miles on SR 511 to the dirt road that goes north where the power lines cross the highway. Go north and stay on the main road that zigzags under the power lines. Watch for a low, faded brown sign that reads "public access path" and follow the arrow right, but not to the far right. The river is 1.1 miles from the highway if you stayed on the correct route. The bottom of the gravel ramp has been washed away and will be difficult to use until it is repaired. Check its condition before you launch.

CHECK RIVER FLOWS ON THE WEB
http://nm.water.usgs.gov/rt-cgi/gen_tbl_pg

WHEN TO GO

The San Juan provides good fishing opportunities all year long. If you have a flexible schedule, try to avoid weekends and holidays, when fishing pressure is greatest. By getting on the river early, or staying late, one can often find some welcome solitude.

It is a particularly good choice in the dead of winter, when snow and cold temperatures make most other trout water difficult and uncomfortable to fish. Daytime temperatures usually rise to the mid-40s, and snow rarely lasts long on the banks of the San Juan. Typical winter flows are around 500 cfs, and you can expect to find feeding fish, and other anglers, even on the coldest days.

High water comes in May and June most years and often reaches 4,500 cfs, nearly 10 times the normal winter flow. The reservoir normally "turns over" at this

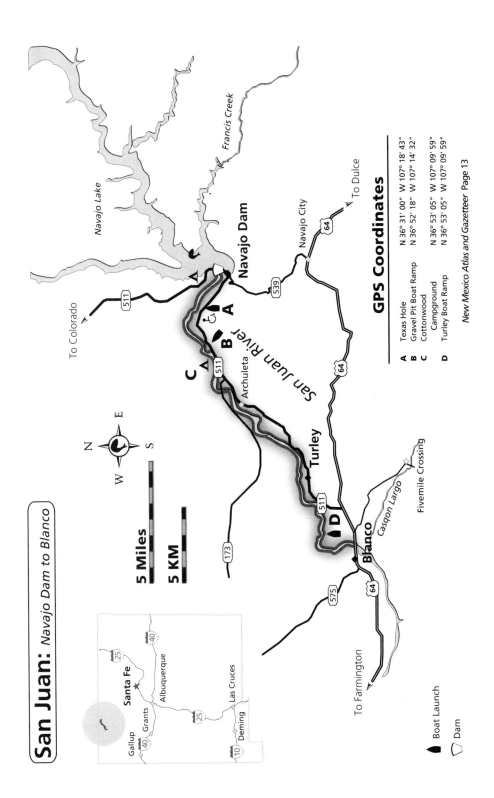

San Juan: *Navajo Dam to Blanco*

GPS Coordinates

A	Texas Hole	N 36° 31' 00" W 107° 18' 43"
B	Gravel Pit Boat Ramp	N 36° 52' 18" W 107° 14' 32"
C	Cottonwood Campground	N 36° 53' 05" W 107° 09' 59"
D	Turley Boat Ramp	N 36° 53' 05" W 107° 09' 59"

New Mexico Atlas and Gazetteer Page 13

Navajo Lake

Francis Creek

Navajo Dam

To Colorado

Navajo City

To Dulce

511

539

64

Archuleta

San Juan River

Turley

Blanco

Cañon Largo

Fivemile Crossing

173

511

511

64

575

64

To Farmington

▶ Boat Launch

◯ Dam

5 Miles

5 KM

N E S W

Santa Fe

Albuquerque

Grants

Gallup

Las Cruces

Deming

25

40

40

25

10

time, and more sediment comes in from feeder streams, so expect more turbid water. Floating the river and fishing some of the larger fly patterns is an effective way to deal with these conditions.

The best hatch activity of the year comes from July to September, as do the largest numbers of anglers. Be prepared for hot weather and be sure to carry water and wear wide-brimmed hats and long sleeves to protect you from the intense sun.

Everyone should experience the golden sunlight of a fall day on the San Juan. Both scenery and weather are at their best this time of year, and crowds begin to diminish a little, at least during midweek. Unlike their relatives in other waters, most San Juan rainbows spawn at this time of year. Expect clouded water for about a month when the lake turns over in November or December.

AREA ATTRACTIONS

Mesa Verde National Park is about 35 miles west of Durango, Colorado, or 65 miles north of Farmington, New Mexico. Mesa Verde was established in 1906 as the first national park dedicated to the preservation of the works and relics of pre-historic humans. It was also named as a world heritage site by the United Nations in 1978. Visitors can view a wide variety of artifacts and remarkably well-preserved structures, including spectacular cliff dwellings. Don't miss the opportunity to descend into a restored subterranean kiva. For more information, call Mesa Verde National Park at (970) 529-4465.

The strikingly preserved ruins of Mesa Verde National Park were named a World Heritage site by the United Nations in 1978.

RESOURCES

Cottonwood campground is next to the river and costs $10 per night or $14 with electrical hook-up. There are two handicap-accessible campsites and a dumping station. The campground at the Pine River area is just north of the dam and has full hook-ups for $18 per night. The other option for camping is at the Navajo Lake State Park, 25 miles east of the town of Bloomfield.

If you want to stay close to the river, the small town of Navajo Dam is your only option for accommodations.

Campgrounds

NAVAJO DAM
Navajo Lake State Park
1448 SR 511 #1
Navajo Dam, NM 87419
Phone number/s: (505) 632-2278

Lodging

NAVAJO DAM
Abe's Motel and Fly Shop
P.O. Box 6428
Navajo Dam, NM 87419
Phone number/s: (505) 632-2194
Web site: www.sanjuanriver.com

Rainbow Lodge
#51 County Road 4275
Navajo Dam, NM 87419
Phone number/s: (505) 632-5717,
toll-free (888) 328-1858
Fax: (505) 632-7618
Web site: www.sanjuanfishing.com
E-mail: cofishadv@fisi.net

Soaring Eagle
P.O. Box 6345
Navajo Dam, NM 87419
Phone number/s: (505) 632-3721
Fax: (505) 632-3721
Web site: www.soaringeagleoutfitters.com
E-mail: eaglefly@cyberport.com

Tackle Shops and Guide Services

DURANGO
Duranglers Flies and Supplies
923 Main Ave.
Durango, CO 81301
Phone number/s: (970) 385-408,
toll-free (888) FISH-DOG or 347-4346
Fax: (970) 385-1998
Web site: www.duranglers.com
E-mail: general@duranglers.com

Resolution Guide Services
P.O. Box 3361
Durango, CO 81302
Phone number/s: (970) 247-5639,
toll-free (888) 320-5639
E-mail: cguikema@hotmail.com

NAVAJO DAM
Abe's Motel and Fly Shop
SR 173, #1793
Navajo Dam, NM 87419
Phone number/s: (505) 632-2194
Web site: www.sanjuanriver.com

Rizuto's Guide Service
1796 SR 173
Navajo Dam, NM 87419
Phone number/s: (505) 632-3893,
toll-free (800) 525-1437
Web site: www.rizutos.com
E-mail: flyfishing@acs-online.net

Soaring Eagle
48 County Road 4370
Navajo Dam, NM 87419
Phone number/s: (505) 632-3721
Fax: 505-632-5621
Web site: www.soaringeagleoutfitters.com
E-mail: eaglefly@cyberport.com

UTAH

PHOTO: STEVE SCHMIDT

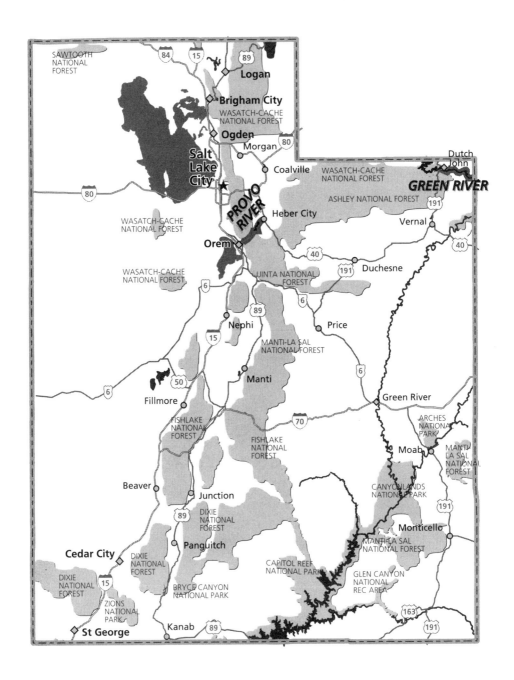

Utah

Utah is a land of great geographic diversity: striking red rock country in the south and snow-covered mountains in the north. It is the rivers of the north that have garnered most of the attention from fly fishers. Tall mountains with forests of pine and aspen make a beautiful backdrop for the great trout streams of Utah.

2000 GENERAL SEASON DATES AND BAG & POSSESSION LIMITS

Utah has a year-round general fishing season.

Species	2000 Daily Bag & Possession Limits
STATESIDE	
Trout, including salmon, grayling and hybrids	eight in the aggregate, except no more than two shall be lake trout/mackinaw
Whitefish	10

LICENSE FEES

A Wildlife Habitat Authorization is required on fishing licenses, other than a one-day license, for all anglers 14 and over. The fee is $6 for residents and nonresidents alike.

Fishing License	Age	Fee
RESIDENT		
Season	14 to 65	$20
Senior	65 and over	$9
Seven-day	14 and over	$11
Daily	14 and over	$6
NONRESIDENT		
Season	14 and over	$42
Seven-day	14 and over	$17
Daily	14 and over	$7

❐ A nonresident may purchase a one-day fishing stamp for $5 to extend a one-day or seven-day fishing license.

❐ A person, resident or nonresident, under 14 years of age may fish without a license and take half of the bag and possession limit or purchase a license and take the full bag and possession limit.

BOATING REGULATIONS

The Utah Division of Parks and Recreation regulates all boating activities. Boating regulations are published on its web site (*www.nr.state.ut.us/parks/boating*), or you can obtain a copy by calling (801) 538-7220.

Under Utah law, float tubes, kickboats and inflatable rafts are considered boats. Safety equipment required to be onboard a boat includes one properly fitted U.S. Coast Guard-approved Type I, II, III or V PFD for each person onboard. Children 12 years and under are required to wear a PFD.

RESOURCES

Utah Department of Fish & Game
Phone number/s: (801) 538-4700
Web site: www.nr.state.ut.us/dwr/dwr.htm

Recorded Fishing Information
Phone number/s: toll-free (877) 592-5169

Utah River Flows
Web site: http://svr1dutslc.wr.usgs.gov/rt-cgi/gen_tbl_pg?page=1
Web site: www.cuwcd.com/o&m/data.htm

Utah Division of Parks and Recreation
Phone number/s: (801) 538-7220
Web site: www.nr.state.ut.us/park/boating

Utah Travel Council
Phone number/s: (801) 538-1030
Web site: www.utah.com

Bureau of Land Management
Phone number/s: (801) 539-4001
Web site: www.ut.blm.gov

U.S. Forest Service
Phone number/s: (435) 789-1181 (Ashley)
Web site: www.fs.fed.us/recreation/states/ut.shtml

Green River below Flaming Gorge

It is easy to see why Major John Wesley Powell named this spectacular landscape Flaming Gorge. Witness the light reflecting off the glowing orange and fiery red vertical walls that tower above the clear river. You may come here to fish, but don't forget to spend a moment or two just taking in the rich natural beauty.

Butch Cassidy and Harry Longabaugh (alias The Sundance Kid) were cowboys in the Brown's Park area, along the banks of the Green River. During their outlaw days, they often returned to hide out in this isolated country, where they made it a point to get along with the locals. This "Wild Bunch" liked to think of themselves as frontier Robin Hoods and were known to have donated excess booty to John Jarvie, who ran the General Store. You can visit the store and several other original structures from the turn of the century at the Jarvie Ranch.

The Green of this frontier period was a warm, muddy, high desert river. The character of the river changed when Flaming Gorge Dam was finished in 1962. The river still didn't reach its potential as a trout fishery until 1978, when changes were made to control the temperature of the water leaving the dam. Special regulations have also helped preserve the fish population.

Much of the Green now has all the attributes of a spring creek — an abundance of large fish, clear water and prolific insect hatches. The Green is also a large, powerful river that lends itself to floating and fishing from a variety of watercraft. Well-maintained trails also give the wading angler good access to much prime water. The large numbers of fish give the fly fisher a unique opportunity to observe trout behavior in clear emerald water that flows through steep red rock canyons lined with ponderosa pines.

FISH SPECIES
Rainbow, cutthroat, and brown trout as well as hybrid cuttbows

HIGHLIGHT
Sight fishing for lots of big trout

TIP
Pause and look for fish before entering the river

SEASON
Open year-round

SPECIFIC REGULATIONS AND FEES

From the Colorado state line in Brown's Park upstream to Flaming Gorge Dam, including Gorge Creek, a tributary entering the Green River at Little Hole:

❏ Artificial flies and lures only.
❏ Closed to fishing from a boat with a motor between the Utah-Colorado state line and Flaming Gorge Dam.
❏ Licensed anglers, trout limit is three: two under 13 inches and one over 20 inches.
❏ Unlicensed anglers under 14 years of age, trout limit is two: two under 13 inches or one under 13 inches and one over 20 inches.

You will need a parking pass to use the access at the dam or Little Hole. The cost is $2 per day or $20 for the season; passes can be purchased at either parking area.

TACTICS

To float or not to float is the question on the Green. There is good access for anglers either walking or wading on the northeast bank of the river from the dam to just above Red Creek, and this approach simplifies logistics. However, floating greatly increases the amount of water that can be effectively fished.

Fly fishers will appreciate the incredibly long drag-free drifts that are possible from a boat traveling at the speed of the current. Floating anglers can access the southeast bank of the river, which receives less pressure, and can cover many more river miles in a day than their wading counterparts. If you decide to float, be sure your equipment and skills are up to the challenge, or consider booking a trip with one of the many licensed guides who row the river regularly. There are several good outfitters on the river to help everyone from beginner to expert get the most out of their time on the water.

The blue-winged olive is probably the most important hatch of the year. The hatch can span three months in the spring, and on a good afternoon, there are places where one can see hundreds of trout feeding on blue-winged olives. Use leaders of at least nine feet and tippet down to 5x or finer. Parachute Adams, comparaduns, and thorax patterns in sizes 16 to 20 are all effective. For difficult fish, a Quigley cripple can be the answer.

PHOTO: DENNIS BREER / TROUT CREEK FLIES

Scott Grange pulled this fish of a lifetime from the Green's clear, emerald waters.

Hatch Chart   AVAILABILITY

Food Items	J	F	M	A	M	J	J	A	S	O	N	D
Midges	X	X	X	X	X	X	X	X	X	X	X	X
Scuds	X	X	X	X	X	X	X	X	X	X	X	X
Blue-winged olives			X	X	X					X	X	X
Pale morning duns						X	X	X				
Tricos									X			
Craneflies	X	X	X	X	X	X	X	X	X	X	X	X
Caddisflies						X	X	X	X			
Terrestrials					X	X	X	X	X	X		

Insects	Suggested Fly Patterns
Midges	Griffith's gnats (#16-22), grizzly midges (#16-22), Adams (#16-22), mating midges (#16-20), midge pupae, gray, cream, brown, red and black (#20-26), midge emergers, black and peacock (#20-26), brassies (#16-20), tungsten bead-head midge pupae, brown and black (#12-16)
Scuds	olive, tan, pink and orange scuds (#14-18)
Blue-winged olives	parachute Adams (#16-20), thorax BWOs (#16-20), olive comparaduns (#16-20), CDC emergers, olive (#16-20), Quigley cripples, olive (#16-20), pheasant tails (#16-20), hare's ears (#16-20), bead-head pheasant tails (#16-20), bead-head hare's ears (#16-20), WD40s (#18-20), RS2s (#18-20)
Pale morning duns	thorax PMDs (#14-16), cream parachutes (#14-16), cream comparaduns (#16-20), Quigley cripples, cream (#16-20), rusty spinners (#14-16), CDC emergers, cream (#16-20), pheasant tails (#14-16), hare's ears (#14-16), bead-head pheasant tails (#14-16), bead-head hare's ears (#14-16)
Tricos	trico spinners (#18-22), thorax tricos (#18-22), parachute Adams (#18-22), pheasant tails (#18-20)
Craneflies	cranefly larvae, olive, sand and cream (#8-12)
Caddisflies	elk-hair caddis (#16-18), partridge caddis (#16-18), CDC elk-hair caddis (#16-18), sparkle caddis (#16-18), X-caddis (#16-18), peeking caddis (#14-16), chamois caddis (#14-16)
Terrestrials	Dave's hoppers (#8-12), Henry's Fork hoppers (#8-12), Chernobyl ants (#4-10), fur ants, black (#14-18), CDC ants (#14-18), black foam cicadas (#8-12), deer-hair beetles, black (#14-16), hi-vis foam beetles (#14-16)

In late May, experienced anglers begin listening with anticipation for a buzzing in the trees. This is usually the first sign of the cicada hatch. The large, clumsy terrestrial insects can cause big trout to take more risks when the hatch is on. Cicadas have cyclic populations, so insect numbers can vary widely from one year to the next. The most popular patterns are good floaters in sizes 6 to 10 with bodies of black foam and calf-tail wings.

Nymph fishing is very popular and effective on the Green. Tungsten bead-head nymphs have been very successful since they were introduced. One popular technique is to fish a "dry and dropper." This is most commonly a cicada or another large, good-floating dry fly with a bead-head nymph hanging 18 to 48 inches below. Tying tippet to the bend of the hook on the large dry fly won't compromise its hooking ability.

The largest fish in the river feed on other fish. If you would like to catch a real trophy, use streamer flies up to eight inches or longer. Fish them close to the banks. Fast-sinking shooting heads or sink tips help take your fly down to these big trout. Streamers that imitate small rainbow trout work well, especially shortly after stocking has taken place.

HOW TO GET THERE

Anglers flying in will most likely want to go to Salt Lake City. Rental cars are easy to obtain and it is a 3- to 3 1/2-hour drive to Dutch John from the airport. Skywest Airlines does have regular service to Vernal. However, Vernal is still one

PHOTO: STEVE SCHMIDT

Emmett Heath — Dean of the Green — rows the Class III rapids at Red Creek.

Expect to see large numbers of fish like this in the clear water.

hour from Flaming Gorge Dam, and additional transportation is necessary. One can fly a private charter to the Dutch John Airport as well. There are also two shuttle services available in the area (see Resources).

The direct route from Salt Lake City is to take I-80 East 110 miles to Exit 34 at Fort Bridger, Wyoming. Follow SR 414 through town and turn right at Lyman at the four-way stop. Pass through Mountain View and continue southeast. Wyoming SR 414 will become Utah SR 43 and continue to Manila, Utah. Turn south onto SR 44 in Manila and climb up into the Uinta Mountains, eventually turning east onto US 191. This will bring you to the Flaming Gorge Lodge and then over Flaming Gorge Dam to the town of Dutch John. An alternate route is to take I-80 East to US 40 and continue east to Vernal. From Vernal, head north on US 191 to the junction with SR 44.

ACCESSIBILITY

There are three main sections of the Green River between Flaming Gorge Dam and the Colorado border. The "A Section" consists of seven miles of water from the dam to the access site at Little Hole. The "B Section" refers to the eight miles of river from Little Hole to the boat ramp at Indian Crossing in Brown's Park. The "C Section" is approximately 17 miles of river from Indian Crossing to the Utah/Colorado state line.

The A Section has the highest density of fish, more consistently clear water, and the easiest access. Not surprisingly, it also has most of the fishing pressure, as well as the vast majority of recreational boaters. If you would rather not share the river with others, plan your trip for off-season (October to March), fish midweek, or plan to be on the water either earlier or later than the majority of anglers.

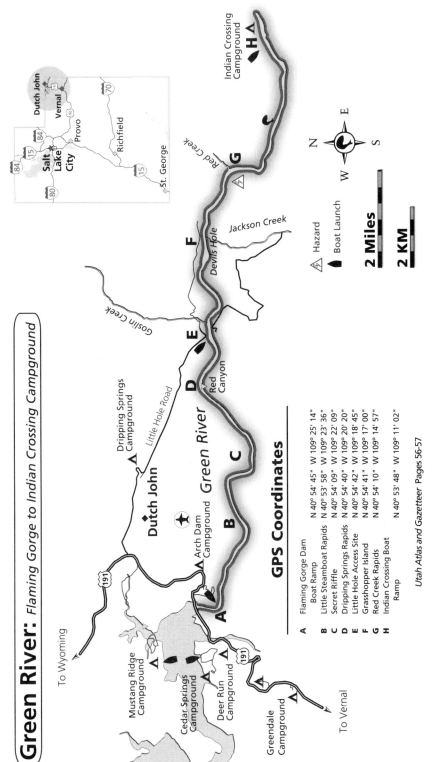

Green River: *Flaming Gorge to Indian Crossing Campground*

To Wyoming

Mustang Ridge Campground

Cedar Springs Campground

Deer Run Campground

Greendale Campground

To Vernal

Dripping Springs Campground

Little Hole Road

Dutch John

Arch Dam Campground

Goslin Creek

Green River

Red Canyon

Devils Hole

Jackson Creek

Red Creek

Indian Crossing Campground

Dutch John
Vernal

Salt Lake City
Provo
Richfield
St. George

GPS Coordinates

A	Flaming Gorge Dam Boat Ramp	N 40° 54' 45" W 109° 25' 14"
B	Little Steamboat Rapids	N 40° 53' 58" W 109° 23' 36"
C	Secret Riffle	N 40° 54' 09" W 109° 22' 09"
D	Dripping Springs Rapids	N 40° 54' 40" W 109° 20' 20"
E	Little Hole Access Site	N 40° 54' 42" W 109° 18' 45"
F	Grasshopper Island	N 40° 54' 41" W 109° 17' 00"
G	Red Creek Rapids	N 40° 54' 10" W 109° 14' 57"
H	Indian Crossing Boat Ramp	N 40° 53' 48" W 109° 11' 02"

Utah Atlas and Gazetteer Pages 56-57

⚠ Hazard

⬛ Boat Launch

N E S W

2 Miles

2 KM

Map 1of 2

Green River: *Indian River Campground to Colorado*

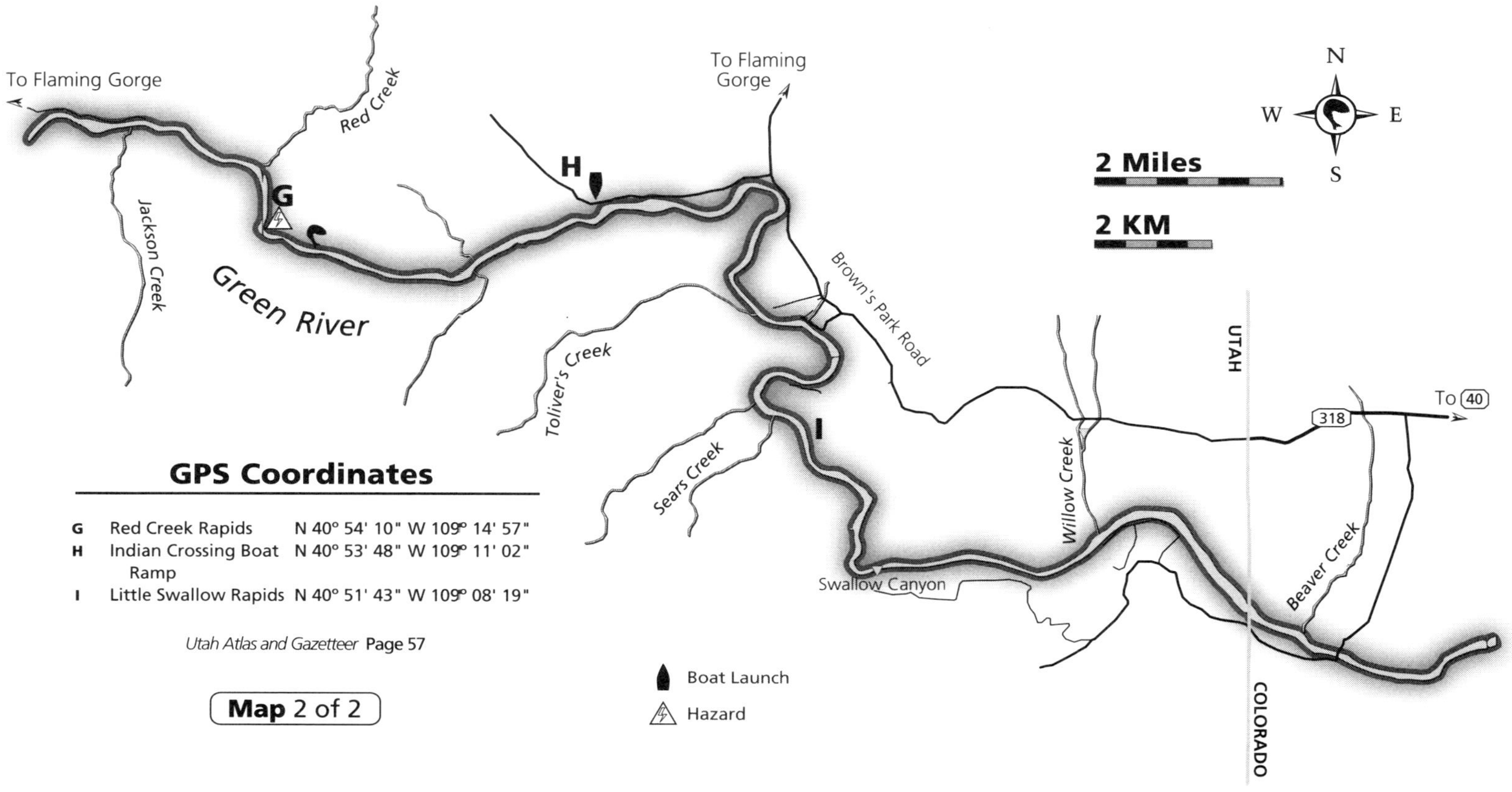

2 Miles

2 KM

N
E
W
S

To Flaming Gorge

To Flaming Gorge

Red Creek

Jackson Creek

Green River

G

H

To Flaming Gorge

Toliver's Creek

Sears Creek

Brown's Park Road

Swallow Canyon

Willow Creek

Beaver Creek

318

To 40

UTAH
COLORADO

Boat Launch
Hazard

GPS Coordinates

G Red Creek Rapids   N 40° 54' 10" W 109° 14' 57"

H Indian Crossing Boat N 40° 53' 48" W 109° 11' 02"
    Ramp

I Little Swallow Rapids N 40° 51' 43" W 109° 08' 19"

Utah Atlas and Gazetteer Page 57

Map 2 of 2

About ¼ mile east of Flaming Gorge Dam, a paved road leads to a parking area and boat ramp. A maintained foot trail goes from here to the next access at Little Hole, a distance of seven miles. The trail can be reached from the south end of the upper parking area or from the boat ramp. If you are launching a watercraft, prepare everything in the upper parking area, as there is a limited amount of room at the boat launch. Make sure you have necessary safety equipment, such as a spare oar or paddle, bail bucket or pump, and an approved Personal Flotation Device (PFD), Type III or better, for all passengers — plus a spare. There are several large Class II to III rapids on this section of the river. Make sure that your skills and watercraft are adequate.

There are still good numbers of fish on the B Section below Little Hole and considerably fewer anglers. The water will be clear for the first three miles, but after Red Creek it can be too muddy to fish, depending on run-off. Floating anglers can make a full day of these first three miles, but all the anglers in this section will be concentrated here if Red Creek is known to be running. To reach Little Hole and the beginning of the B Section, from US 191 turn east on Little Hole Road, 0.1 miles north of the turnoff to Dutch John. Six miles of paved road will take you to the access site. The foot trail from the dam continues down river another 2.7 miles to Trails End. There are three boat ramps here, but it is still a good idea to rig your watercraft as completely as possible before backing down to the water. Most rapids on this section are Class I, but Red Creek is Class III. If you are not prepared to negotiate a large, powerful rapid with many rocks and obstacles, or line your craft around it, you should avoid this section. Once you have safely passed Red Creek Rapids, you may remove your PFD. Note: While this section is only eight miles by river, the shuttle route is over 40 miles, much of it dirt that requires four-wheel-drive in wet weather and can become impassable in extreme weather. Also, any substantial flow in Red Creek can make the last four miles of this section unfishable.

Fishing the C Section in Brown's Park can vary a great deal with conditions. On a good day, you can catch many fish that are, on average, even larger than those in the upper portion of the river — and you may not see another angler. A bad day might mean few, if any, trout while fighting wind and dirty water. Brown's Park Road parallels this section, and there are several access points along it. From Dutch John, go north on US 191, then go right at the turnoff marked "Clay Basin" and "Brown's Park." It is about 26 miles to the river from here. There are several turns and forks; just stay on the main road. There is a newly paved section, but most of the road is dirt — and Clay Basin is aptly named. When wet, the road becomes very slick, and four-wheel drive is a must. From US 40 in Vernal, one can take a fairly rough route to Brown's Park over Diamond Mountain. Turn north onto US 191 (Vernal Avenue). Turn right at the sign for Diamond Mountain and Brown's Park (500 North). Stay left at the junction that appears in about three miles. Stay left at the "Y" another 5.8 miles ahead. It will be about 25 miles before you reach the left turn to Brown's Park. Stay on this road through Crouse Canyon and into Colorado before crossing the Green on the very narrow Swinging Bridge. Turn left at the junction to cross back into Utah. Note: This route is not suitable for large or heavy vehicles.

WHEN TO GO

The blue-winged olive hatch is the first really productive hatch of the year. It generally starts at the end of March. By April, the hatch becomes fairly consistent, with any overcast or rainy afternoon producing excellent dry-fly fishing from Secret Riffle to Washboard Rapid.

When the blue-wings start to fade in late May, the cicadas begin to show up and can be very important through June. These large terrestrial insects have a cyclic population, so they can vary a great deal from year to year.

The dog days of July and August can find the Green a bit slower; but afternoon hatches of caddis on the A Section, midmorning PMDs in Browns Park, and hopper and ant fishing down the entire river can all be rewarding.

Flows above 4,000 cfs can be difficult for wading anglers, and the bridge at Indian Crossing (the start of C Section) can be impassable to anglers floating the river. Fishing can be difficult for one to three days after a major change in flows. In recent years, an effort has been made to change flows gradually, as abrupt changes are detrimental to fishing. When flows are stable, fishing can be good at a wide range of levels.

> **CHECK RIVER FLOWS ON THE WEB**
> http://svr1dutslc.wr.usgs.gov/rt-cgi/gen_tbl_pg?page=1

RESOURCES

There are 15 river camps on the B Section between Little Hole and Indian Crossing. These campsites can be reserved at Little Hole on the day you launch.

The two BLM campgrounds in Brown's Park (Bridge Hollow and Indian Crossing), the five campsites across the river from Little Hole, and the 14 campsites on the river between Indian Crossing and the Colorado state line (C Section) are all available on a first-come, first-served basis.

For camping reservations in the Ashley National Forest, call toll-free at (877) 444-6777 or (800) 280-2267. You can also make reservations online at *http://maps.reserveusa.com/static/ut1.html*. Handicap-accessible sites are available at Dripping Springs and Firefighters.

Campgrounds

ASHLEY NATIONAL FOREST

For more information, contact the Ashley Ranger District at (435) 784-3445.

- ❐ Greendale Group
- ❐ Dripping Springs
- ❐ Cedar Springs
- ❐ Firefighters

Lodging

DUTCH JOHN

Flaming Gorge Lodge
155 Greendale, US 191
Dutch John, UT 84023
Phone number/s: (435) 889-3773
Fax: (435) 889-3788
Web site: www.fglodge.com
E-mail: lodge@fglodge.com

Red Canyon Lodge
790 Red Canyon Road
Dutch John, UT 84023
Phone number/s: (435) 889-3759
Fax: (435) 889-5106
Web site: www.redcanyonlodge.com

Spring Creek Ranch (B&B)
P.O. Box 284
Dutch John, Utah 84023
Phone number/s: (307) 350-3005
Fax: (307) 350-3047
Web site: www.quickbyte.com/springcreek

Tackle Shops and Guide Services

DUTCH JOHN

Green Rivers Outfitters
US 191, LIttle Hole Road
Dutch John, UT 84023
Phone number/s: (435) 885-3338
Fax: (435) 885-3370
Web site: www.utahgro.com
E-mail: greenriver@cisna.com
Permittee Ashley National Forest

Old Moe Guide Services
P.O. Box 308
Dutch John, UT 84023
Phone number/s: (435) 885-3342 (also fax)
Web site: www.quickbyte.com/oldmoe
E-mail: gwerning@union-tel.com
Permittee Ashley National Forest

Trout Creek Flies
108 2nd Ave.
Dutch John, UT 84023
Phone number/s: (435) 885-3355,
toll-free (800) 835-4551
Fax: (435) 885-3356
E-mail: info@fishgreenriver.com
Web site: www.fishgreenriver.com
Permittee Ashley National Forest

SALT LAKE CITY

Anglers Inn
2292 S. Highland Drive
Salt Lake City, UT 84106
Phone number/s: (801) 466-3921,
toll-free (888) 426-4466
Web site: www.anglersfly.com
Permittee Ashley National Forest

Spinner Fall Fly Shop
2645 E. Parley's Way
Salt Lake City, UT 84109
Phone number/s: (801) 466-5801,
toll-free (800) 959-3474
Fax: (801) 466-3029
Web site: www.spinnerfall.com
Permittee Ashley National Forest

Western Rivers Flyfisher
1071 E. 900 S.
SLC, UT 84105
Phone number/s: (801) 521-6424,
toll-free (800) 545-4312
Fax: (801) 521-6329
Web site: www.wrflyfisher.com
E-mail: info@wrflyfisher.com
Permittee Ashley National Forest

VERNAL

Big Foot Fly Shop
38 N. 400 W.
Vernal, UT 84078
Phone number/s: (435) 789-4960
(Fly-fishing equipment only)

Shuttle Services

DUTCH JOHN

Green River Outfitters
US 191, Little Hole Road
Dutch John, UT 84023
Phone number/s: (435) 885-3338
Web site: www.utahgro.com

Flaming Gorge Lodge
155 Greendale, US 191
Dutch John, UT 84023
Phone number/s: (435) 889-3773
Web site: www.fglodge.com
E-mail: lodge@fglodge.com

Area Attractions

John Jarvie Ranch
For more information, contact the Park Ranger at (435) 885-3307 or the BLM Vernal Office at (435) 781-4400.

Provo River

The river is named after Etienne Provost, a portly French-Canadian mountain man who discovered the Provo while trapping in the Uinta and Wasatch mountains in 1824 and 1825. American trappers also harvested fur here after Jedediah Smith's expedition in 1843. The first settlers arrived in the Heber Valley in the spring of 1859, and the pastoral riverscape has seen many changes over the generations.

Some of these changes have been quite beneficial to the fly fishers of today. Deer Creek Dam was completed in 1941, creating a tailwater fishery that has been an angling tradition for over half a century. Much of the river above Deer Creek Reservoir was channeled in the 1950s to control flooding — an impact that reduced the river's potential as a fishery. Work began on Jordanelle Dam in the 1980s. As the reservoir filled in 1997, the river between the reservoirs began to exhibit high-quality fishing.

The Provo between Jordanelle and Deer Creek is commonly called the Middle Provo. It runs through the pastures and chalet-style homes of Heber Valley beneath majestic Mount Timpanogos.

More of the Middle Provo will become productive as the Utah Reclamation Mitigation and Conservation Commission has begun a $30 million project that will restore this section of the river to a more natural condition, removing the dikes and creating meanders and islands that will add two miles of river and another 10 miles of side channel. This restoration could potentially double the number of trout per mile when it is completed in 2004.

The canyon water below Deer Creek Reservoir is commonly called the Lower Provo, a stretch of high-quality water that parallels the highway for six miles to the Olmstead Diversion Dam. Despite the recent highway construction that has reduced some of the intimate feel of the canyon, this is still a productive and beautiful part of the Provo.

Both sections of the river receive fairly heavy angling pressure, not surprisingly, due to its close proximity to the major cities of the Wasatch Front. Angler surveys in 1995 revealed over 220,000 angler days on the Provo — 30 percent more than Utah's famous section of the Green River. All this popularity means that visiting fly fishers will find easy access to the river, competent guides, and comfortable accommodations to complement some healthy trout.

FISH SPECIES
Rainbow, cutthroat and brown trout

HIGHLIGHT
Green drake hatch

TIP
Wear studded wading boots on the Middle Provo

SEASON
Open year-round

SPECIFIC REGULATIONS

Upstream from Olmstead Diversion Dam to Deer Creek Reservoir:
❏ Artificial flies and lures only.
❏ Brown trout limit is two under 15 inches.
❏ Closed to possession of cutthroat and rainbow trout. All rainbow and cutthroat trout and their hybrids must be immediately released.

From Charleston Bridge just above Deer Creek Reservoir upstream to the Jordanelle Dam, including the Valeo Diversion, the Wasatch Diversion and the streams that return flows from these diversions directly to the Provo River:
❏ Artificial flies and lures only.
❏ Brown trout limit is two under 15 inches.
❏ Closed to the possession of cutthroat and rainbow trout. All rainbow and cutthroat trout and their hybrids must be immediately released.

Hatch Chart   AVAILABILITY

Food Items	J	F	M	A	M	J	J	A	S	O	N	D
Sow bugs	X	X	X	X	X	X	X	X	X	X	X	X
Midges	X	X	X	X						X	X	X
Blue-winged olives			X	X	X				X	X	X	
Pale morning duns						X	X	X				
Green drakes							X					
Skwala stoneflies				X	X							
Golden stoneflies						X	X					
Caddisflies							X	X	X			
Terrestrials							X	X	X			

TACTICS

The Middle and the Lower Provo are quite different in character, insect populations and water type.

Trout on the Lower Provo can be taken using a variety of methods. Nymphing is very popular. Sow bugs, hare's ears, pheasant tails, and caddis nymphs tied to 4x or 5x leaders will usually connect with trout in the deeper runs. Strike indicators are useful. These fish see a lot of flies over the course of a season. Be sure that your nymphs are down on the bottom; pay careful attention to your drift. The Provo periodically surrenders some very large brown trout to dedicated nymph fishers.

If you want to fish dry flies, look for slower pools and eddies, and don't ignore the banks. You will often find rising fish under the brush at the river's edge. It takes good casts and realistic drifts to catch these fish. Fly fishers can look for good morning midge hatches beginning in February. Mating midge patterns and Griffith's gnats in sizes 18-20 fished on long, light leaders (12 feet long tapered down to 6x) can bring fish to the surface on frosty canyon mornings.

Insects	Suggested Fly Patterns
Sow bugs	Marabou sow bugs (#16-20), dubbed sow bugs (#16-20), Hump's cress bugs (#16-20)
Midges	mating midges, tan (#16-18), Griffith's gnats (#16-22), Adams (#16-22), soft hackles, peacock (#16-20), midge pupae, gray, cream, brown, red and black (#20-26), midge emergers, black and peacock (#20-26)
Blue-winged olives	parachute Adams (#16-20), thorax BWOs (#16-20), olive comparaduns (#16-20), sparkle duns, olive (#16-20), Quigley cripples, olive (#16-20), CDC emergers, olive (#16-20), Barr emergers (#16-20), pheasant tails (#16-20), hare's ears (#16-20), bead-head pheasant tails (#16-20), bead-head hare's ears (#16-20), WD40s (#18-20), RS2s (#18-20)
Pale morning duns	thorax PMDs (#14-16), cream parachutes (#14-16), cream comparaduns (#16-20), Quigley cripples, cream (#16-20), rusty spinners (#14-16), CDC emergers, cream (#16-20), Barr emergers (#16-18), pheasant tails (#14-16), hare's ears (#14-16), bead-head pheasant tails (#14-16), bead-head hare's ears (#14-16)
Green drakes	green drake Wulffs (#8-12), olive paradrakes (#10-12), olive comparaduns (#10-12), Quigley cripples, olive (#8-12), soft-hackle emergers, olive (#8-12), CDC emergers, olive (#10-14), hare's ears, olive (#10-14), zug bugs (#10-14)
Skwala stoneflies	olive stimulators (#6-10), stonefly nymphs, brown (#6-10), Chernobyl ants (#6-10), girdle bugs, black and brown (#6-10), yuk bugs, black, brown and olive (#6-10), woolly buggers, black, brown and olive (#6-10)
Golden stoneflies	yellow stimulators (#10-16), prince nymphs (#10-16), bead-head prince nymphs (#10-16), golden stonefly nymphs (#10-16), copper Johns (#10-16)
Caddisflies	elk-hair caddis (#16-18), partridge caddis (#16-18), CDC elk-hair caddis (#16-18), sparkle caddis (#16-18), X-caddis (#16-18), peeking caddis (#14-16), chamois caddis (#14-16)
Terrestrials	Dave's hoppers (#8-12), Henry's Fork hoppers (#8-12), Chernobyl ants (#6-10), foam cicadas (#8-12), fur ants, black (#14-18), CDC ants (#14-18), deer-hair beetles, black (#14-16), hi-vis foam beetles (#14-16)

Peter Rigstad proves that dedicated nymph fishers can catch some very large browns in the Provo.

In spring, expect blue-winged olives to hatch in the early afternoon. Pale morning duns will begin to appear midafternoon in the summer months. Flows in early summer are normally higher and faster as the Lower Provo delivers irrigation water to Utah Valley. Caddis are also common in summertime. Best activity is late evening until dark, or the first hour of the morning.

The lower mile of the Middle Provo just above Deer Creek gets quite a few spawning fish moving up in the fall and winter months. While this is expected of the browns, there is also a fall and winter spawning variety of rainbow trout.

Springtime brings blue-winged olives to the Middle, and nymph and dry-fly imitations will both produce fish. Fly fishers often overlook big brown stoneflies, or skwalas. Large dries can be effective, or cast weighted girdle bugs into pools and riffled water. Golden stoneflies appear in late June — a dry-and-dropper rig can be quite effective. A yellow stimulator with a prince nymph or cased caddis can be a good combination.

My favorite event of the year is the green drake hatch, which usually comes in early July. This hatch is often of short duration, but the big mayflies can trigger a feeding binge. Water is often still fairly high and trout are in excellent condition, so landing fish can be more challenging than hooking them. Try Quigley cripple patterns in faster water, or soft hackles in slower, shallower pools. Stay with 4x leaders during high water to give yourself a better chance to bring fish to net.

Caddis are the mainstay of late summer on the Middle Provo. Cased caddis nymphs work in the pools during midday, but best activity is early morning and late evening. Traditional dry flies will take fish, as will partridge and olive soft hackles, which can be fished on the swing for explosive takes. Just cast the fly into the rings left by a rising fish and prepare yourself.

Greg Pearson of Western Rivers Flyfisher also reports good fishing during summer months with unweighted streamers fished on the swing. Spruce flies or brown trout fry imitations cast into larger runs work best with this approach.

Brown trout in both sections of the Provo will spawn in October and November. Streamer fishing is often best in the early mornings before sunlight reaches the river. If you feel strikes to a streamer but are unable to hook up, try streamers with stinger hooks, or try articulated leeches with the hook placed close to the rear of the fly. Many anglers fish glo-bugs or other egg imitations during the spawn. While effective, it is also disruptive to fish more focused on reproduction than eating. You can limit your impact on spawning fish — and ultimately the health of the river — by avoiding spawning beds or simply staying away from the river altogether.

HOW TO GET THERE

Salt Lake City International is a stop for most major airlines. Anglers arriving by air will find a variety of rental vehicles — the preferred way to reach the river. If

Dry-fly fishing can be great on the slower pools of the Provo.

Provo River: *Jordanelle Reservoir to Deer Creek Reservoir*

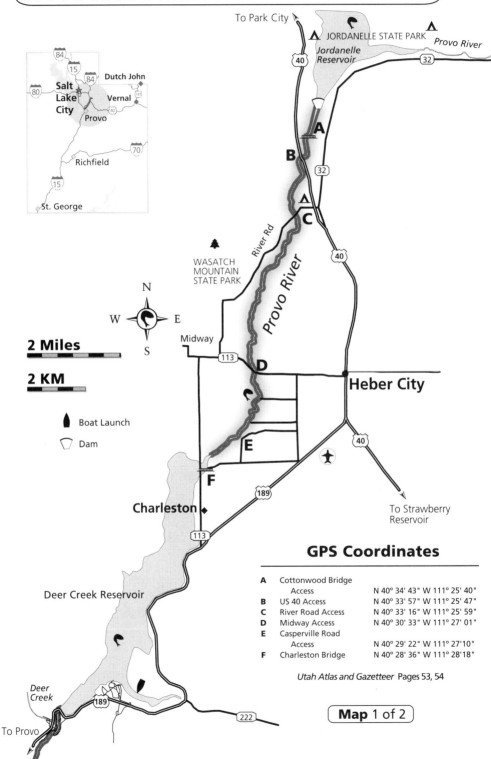

To Park City

JORDANELLE STATE PARK

Jordanelle Reservoir

Provo River

40

32

A

32

B

River Rd

40

C

WASATCH MOUNTAIN STATE PARK

N

W E

S

Provo River

Midway

113

D

Heber City

E

40

F

189

To Strawberry Reservoir

Charleston

113

Deer Creek Reservoir

Deer Creek

189

222

To Provo

2 Miles

2 KM

🔲 Boat Launch

⬠ Dam

Inset map:
84
15
84 Dutch John
80 Salt Lake City
Vernal
Provo
Richfield
70
15
St. George

GPS Coordinates

A	Cottonwood Bridge Access	N 40° 34' 43" W 111° 25' 40"
B	US 40 Access	N 40° 33' 57" W 111° 25' 47"
C	River Road Access	N 40° 33' 16" W 111° 25' 59"
D	Midway Access	N 40° 30' 33" W 111° 27' 01"
E	Casperville Road Access	N 40° 29' 22" W 111° 27'10"
F	Charleston Bridge	N 40° 28' 36" W 111° 28'18"

Utah Atlas and Gazetteer Pages 53, 54

Map 1 of 2

Provo River: *Deer Creek Reservoir to Olmstead Diversion*

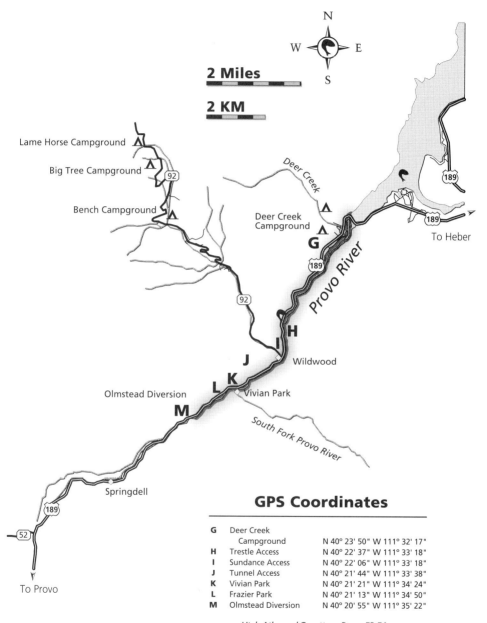

N
W E
S

2 Miles

2 KM

Lame Horse Campground

Big Tree Campground

92

Bench Campground

Deer Creek

189

Deer Creek Campground

G

189

To Heber

92

Provo River

H
I
J

Wildwood

K
L Vivian Park

Olmstead Diversion

M

South Fork Provo River

Springdell

189

52

To Provo

GPS Coordinates

G	Deer Creek Campground	N 40° 23' 50" W 111° 32' 17"
H	Trestle Access	N 40° 22' 37" W 111° 33' 18"
I	Sundance Access	N 40° 22' 06" W 111° 33' 18"
J	Tunnel Access	N 40° 21' 44" W 111° 33' 38"
K	Vivian Park	N 40° 21' 21" W 111° 34' 24"
L	Frazier Park	N 40° 21' 13" W 111° 34' 50"
M	Olmstead Diversion	N 40° 20' 55" W 111° 35' 22"

Utah Atlas and Gazetteer Pages 53-54

Map 2 of 2

Nice browns like this are only a short drive from Provo and Salt Lake City.

you prefer not to rent a vehicle, many hotels and resorts will provide shuttles from the airport. Some guide services can arrange to pick you up at your lodgings.

US 189 follows the Lower Provo River from Orem to Deer Creek Reservoir. From I-15, take the 800 North exit in Orem (Exit 275) and follow the signs for Sundance and Provo Canyon. It is only 14 miles from the Interstate to Deer Creek Reservoir and 23 miles to Charleston Bridge, where the Middle Provo reaches Deer Creek Reservoir.

To reach the Middle Provo from Salt Lake City, take I-80 East to US 40, then go east on US 40 until you pass Jordanelle Reservoir and cross the Provo River. A left turn onto SR 32 and another quick left takes you to Jordanelle Dam. If you turn right at SR 32 from US 40, you will parallel the river on your way to Midway. You can also take US 189 from Provo or Heber and turn off at Midway, reaching the Middle Provo at Charleston Bridge.

ACCESSIBILITY

The Provo is quite accessible both above and below Deer Creek. Access is a little more widely spaced on the Middle Provo. Most of this section has levees down both sides with a two-track road on top, so walking up and down the river is pleasant. Leave all gates as you found them; respect private property. The dikes will be removed during the reconstruction, but access will be improved with more parking, restrooms and trails. The streambed of the Middle is composed of slippery cobble rock, which can be difficult to walk on in low flows, not to mention high water.

Consider wearing studded wading boots and/or carry a wading staff.

The Lower Provo has many turnouts closely spaced along US 189, but be very careful when entering back onto the highway. Traffic is highway speed and often hard to see. This section generally wades easily, but can still be very intimidating when the water is high. The trestle access is particularly nice when the river is too high to cross, as the old bridge gives you access to the far bank.

CHECK RIVER FLOWS ON THE WEB
http://www.cuwcd.com/o&m/data.htm

WHEN TO GO

Morning midge fishing on the Lower Provo during February and March is usually best before the sun hits or during overcast conditions. Dress for cold weather.

Blue-wings show up in late March on the Lower Provo and early April on the Middle Provo. Weather can be beautiful at this time, and anglers can enjoy a few runs of spring skiing at Park City or Sundance before catching the blue-winged olive hatch in the early afternoon.

Late May or early June usually brings high water on the Middle Provo. Wading is dangerous at flows above 600 cfs. The inner tube and raft hatch on the Lower Provo gets started about Memorial Day. These recreational floaters seem to disturb anglers more than trout, so don't give up. You can often catch fish right after they pass by, especially in the deeper runs.

Around the first of July, flows decrease on the Middle — while they increase on the Lower Provo. Look for golden stoneflies on both sections, green drakes

PHOTO: STEVE SCHMIDT

You'll often find rising fish under the brush at the river's bank.

PHOTO: STEVE SCHMIDT

The Provo River is easy to wade as long as the water is not high.

hatching above Deer Creek Reservoir, and the pale morning duns going off below. Expect good caddis fishing all along the river in the late evening and early mornings.

Break out your streamers in September and October when the cottonwoods turn golden. Fishing can be inconsistent, but a beautiful autumn day on the river is its own reward.

AREA ATTRACTIONS

Try a ride on the Heber Valley Railroad that runs alongside the river in Provo Canyon. Step back into the past and board a vintage coach pulled by a steam-powered locomotive.

After a hard day of fishing, experience the ambiance of a classic country resort in Midway. Soak your bones in the thermal waters of the Homestead's unique underground crater.

RESOURCES

For anglers preferring to mix a bit of nightlife with fishing, Park City offers a ski town atmosphere and is an easy drive to both the Middle and Lower Provo. For lodging accommodations, go online to the Park City Chamber of Commerce's web site at *www.parkcityinfo.com* or call Park City Reservations at (800) 453-5789.

To camp in Utah's state parks, only telephone reservations are accepted. In the Salt Lake area, call (801) 322-3770 or toll-free at (800) 322-3770.

Campgrounds

PROVO
Deer Creek Park Campground
Provo Canyon US 189
Provo, UT 84604
Phone number/s: (801) 225-9783

STATE PARKS
Jordanelle State Park
Hailstone Recreation Site & Marina
SR 319 (Mayflower Exit on US 40)
Park City, UT 84060
Phone number/s: (435) 645-9540

Rock Cliff Recreation Site
SR 32 (between Kamas and Heber)
Kamas, UT 84036
Phone number/s: (435) 783-3030

Wasatch Mountain State Park
Midway, UT 84049
Phone number/s: (435) 654-3961

Lodging

SUNDANCE
Sundance Resort
North Fork Provo Canyon
RR 3 Box A-1
Sundance, UT 84604
Phone number/s: (435) 225- 4107,
toll-free (800) 892-1600
Fax: (435) 226-1937
Web site: www.sundance-utah.com
E-mail: sales@sundance-utah.com

MIDWAY
The Homestead Resort
700 N. Homestead Drive
Midway, UT 84049
Phone number/s: (435) 654-1102,
toll-free (800) 327-7220
Web site: www.homesteadresort.com
E-mail: info@homesteadresort.com

Inn On The Creek
375 Rainbow Lane
Midway, UT 84049
Phone number/s: (435) 654-0892,
toll-free (800) 654-0892
Web site: www.innoncreek.com

Johnson Mill Bed & Breakfast
100 N. Johnson Mill Road
Midway, UT 84049
Phone number/s: (435) 654-4333,
toll-free (888) 272-0030
Fax: (435) 657-1457
E-mail: oldmill@shadowlink.net

Tackle Shops and Guide Services

SALT LAKE CITY
Anglers Inn
2292 S. Highland Drive
Salt Lake City, UT 84106
Phone number/s: (801) 466-3921,
toll-free (888) 426-4466
Web site: www.anglersfly.com

Fish Tech
6153 Highland Dr.
Salt Lake City, UT 84121
Phone number/s: (801) 272-8808
Fax: (801) 272-6935

Four Seasons Fly Fishers
6591 S. 1460 E.
Murray, UT 84123
Phone number/s: (801) 288-1028,
toll-free (800) 498-5440
Web site: utahflyfish.com
E-mail: info@utahflyflish.com
(Guide service and lodging at Johnson Mill)

Spinner Fall Fly Shop
2645 E. Parley's Way
Salt Lake City, UT 84109
Phone number/s: (801) 466-5801,
toll-free (800) 959-3474
Fax: (801) 466-3029
Web site: www.spinnerfall.com

Western Rivers Flyfisher
1071 E. 900 S.
Salt Lake City, UT 84105
Phone number/s: (801) 521-6424,
toll-free (800) 545-4312
Fax: (801) 521-6329
Web site: www.wrflyfisher.com
E-mail: info@wrflyfisher.com

PARK CITY

Trout Bum 2
4343 N. SR 224, Suite 101
Park City, UT 84098
Phone number/s: (435) 658-1166,
toll-free (877) 878-2862
Web site: www.troutbum2.com
E-mail: troutbum2@uswest.net

Area Attractions

Heber Valley Railroad
450 S. 600 W.
Heber City, UT 84032
Phone number/s: (435) 654-5601
Fax: (435) 654-3709
Web site: www.hebervalleyrr.org

WYOMING

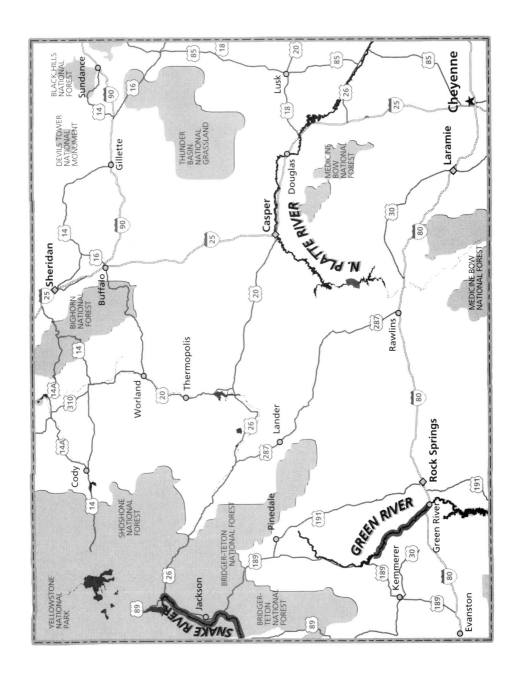

Wyoming

With more wildlife than people, Wyoming has been called "The Big Empty" by local comedians. For the fly fisher, the statistic of 4.91 people per square mile suggests the potential for solitude. In Wyoming, you may have only the wind and wildlife for companions rather than other anglers.

FISHING ACCESS LAWS

In Wyoming, the landowner controls access on the land, including riverbanks, islands and river bottoms. It is legal to float down a river in a boat or float tube, but floaters are not permitted to anchor or step on private land unless they are portaging to avoid a water hazard. The landowner's permission is required to enter or fish from private land.

2000 GENERAL SEASON DATES AND BAG & POSSESSION LIMITS

Fishing is permitted year-round, except where noted in special regulations.

Species	2000 Daily Bag & Possession Limits
STATEWIDE	
Trout, salmon and grayling in combination	six, only one over 20 inches
Brook trout, eight inches or less	10, in addition to daily limits (does not apply in the Green River drainage in Lincoln, Sublette and Sweetwater counties)
Whitefish	50

LICENSE FEES

Wyoming requires the purchase of a conservation stamp, valid for one year, with season licenses. Conservation stamps are not required for daily or 10-day youth licenses.

❏ Fishing licenses are required for resident and nonresident anglers 14 years or older. Exceptions are waters where fishing preserve permits or landowner fishing regulations apply.

❏ Resident youth under 14 do not need a license and their creel limit is the same as those requiring licenses.

❏ Nonresident youth under 14 do not need a license if accompanied by an adult possessing a valid Wyoming fishing license; however, the nonresident youth's creel limit shall be limited by the fishing license held by the accompanying adult.

❏ Lifetime licenses available only from the Cheyenne Headquarters Office.

Fishing License	Age	Fee
RESIDENT		
Lifetime	18 and over	$250
Season	18 and over	$15
Youth Season	14 to 18	$3
Daily	18 and over	$3
NONRESIDENT		
Season	18 and over	$65
Youth Season	14 to 18	$15
Youth 10-day	14 to 18	$10
Daily	18 and over	$6

BOATING REGULATIONS

The Wyoming Game and Fish Department regulates watercraft activities. Watercraft regulations are published on its web site (see Resources for the full address) or you can get a copy by calling (307) 777-4600.

In Wyoming, float tubes are not required to carry a PFD. However, once an inflatable or kickboat is rigged with oars, it is considered a "vessel" and a Coast Guard-approved PFD is required onboard as well as a sound-producing device, such as a whistle or horn.

RESOURCES

Wyoming Travel & Tourism
Phone number/s: toll-free (800) 225-5996
Web site: www.wyomingtourism.org

Wyoming Game and Fish Department
Phone number/s: (307) 777-4600,
toll-free within Wyoming (800) 842-1934
Web site: http://gf.state.wy.us

Wyoming Watercraft and Important Boating Information
Phone number/s: (307) 777-4600,
toll-free within Wyoming (800) 842-1934
Web site: http://gf.state.wy.us/HTML/regulations/regulations.htm#watercraft

Wyoming Outfitters & Guides Association
Phone number/s: (307) 527-7453

Wyoming State Parks and Historic Sites
Phone number/s: (307) 777-6323
Web site: http://commerce.state.wy.us/sphs/index1.htm

Grand Teton National Park
Phone number/s: (307) 739-3399,
for information packet (307) 739-3600
Web site: www.nps.gov/grte

Bureau of Land Management
Phone number/s: (307) 775-6256
Web site: www.wy.blm.gov

National Forest Service
Phone number/s: (307) 739-5500 (Bridger-Teton)
Web site: www.fs.fed.us/recreation/states/wy.shtml

Rewards await the angler who explores Wyoming's "Big Empty."

Green River below Fontenelle

T he Oregon Trail was the only practical route to the western U.S. in the mid-1800s, and South Pass (60 miles east of Fontenelle) was the key that opened the door for westward migration. More than 350,000 pioneers trudged their way across the 2,000-mile trail, and one in 10 died along the way. Treacherous river crossings claimed many lives, and the Green River was one of the worst, drowning 37 of these emigrants in 1850 alone. A strong American sentiment during this period was the belief in "Manifest Destiny" — a powerful urge to travel west and lay claim to a piece of land, despite the hardships and cruelties of the new frontier. This urge to "go west" stands out as the greatest mass migration in human history.

HIGHLIGHT
A high measure of solitude

TIP
Look for trout where you find rocks in the river

FISH SPECIES
Rainbow, cutthroat and brown trout (lake trout and kokanee salmon are present in the fall)

SEASON
Open year-round

The Green River has now been tamed by dams. Visitors can cross with impunity on modern bridges, but anglers traveling to this stretch of water still face some risks. The wind can roar though the dry sage with a force that makes fly fishing unpleasant or even impossible. Rowing a raft or drift boat downriver can become an exercise in frustration when it really starts to blow. When conditions are more agreeable, anglers can still have difficulty finding fish. The Green River in Wyoming has a lower density of trout (630 trout per mile in a 1999 survey) than many of the other great rivers of the West. They tend to concentrate in specific areas, leaving some stretches nearly devoid. So why bother with the Green in Wyoming? Because the river holds some truly exceptional fish — large, strong and well-proportioned. Rob Keith, a fisheries biologist with Wyoming Game and Fish, reports trout in the 7- to 8-pound class sampled in electro-shocking surveys, and he believes that larger fish are present. Angler numbers are very low and will likely stay that way, since the windy conditions and often difficult fishing will keep many from making a second visit. A trip here can yield your largest trout of the season or leave you disappointed and frustrated.

Mark Forslund, of Four Seasons Fly Fishers, sums up this section of the Green well: "Fly fishing the way it used to be — big trout on a lonely, windswept river."

This tailwater fishery was formed in the early 1960s after the completion of Fontenelle Reservoir. The first 4 ½ miles below the dam are open to bait fishing and harvest of up to six trout. As a result, this section receives heavy angling pressure and most of the fish are removed from the river before they reach their full size. However, once you go below the Sweetwater Road 8 (CCC) Bridge and head into the Seedskadee Wildlife Refuge, fewer anglers ply these waters and most captured trout are released. The upper mile of the river does become more interesting in the fall when it reopens after November 7. Fly fishers get a chance to cast to lake trout and kokanee, along with the other three species of trout that inhabit the Green.

SPECIFIC REGULATIONS AND FEES

Green River from Fontenelle Dam downstream approximately one mile to the U.S. Geological Survey gauge station (cable crossing) at the Weeping Rocks campground in Sweetwater County:

❏   Closed to fishing from October 7 to November 7.

Green River from Sweetwater Road 8 (CCC) Bridge, 4.5 miles below Fontenelle Dam, downstream to the Big Sandy River in Sweetwater County:

❏   The creel limit on trout shall be one per day or in possession. All trout less than 20 inches shall be released to the water immediately.
❏   Fishing is permitted with artificial flies or lures only.

TACTICS

This river is a bit unusual in that you will sometimes find trout holding in unexpected places, while other stretches of good-looking water may be empty. The best advice is to keep moving until you find a concentration of fish. Anglers new to

PHOTO: TOM FERRIS

Fishing guide Guy Turck with a 27 1/2-inch Green River rainbow taken on a large streamer.

Hatch Chart AVAILABILITY

Food Items	J	F	M	A	M	J	J	A	S	O	N	D
Midges	X	X	X	X	X	X	X	X	X	X	X	X
Annelid worms	X	X	X	X	X	X	X	X	X	X	X	X
Blue-winged olives				X	X					X	X	
Pale morning duns						X	X					
Tricos								X	X			
Yellow sallys							X					
Caddisflies				X	X	X	X	X	X			
Terrestrials							X	X	X			

the river can benefit by floating, covering more water in their search for good areas. Fly fishers who have spent a lot of time here often prefer to wade the runs they know to hold fish.

In general, when you find larger rocks and boulders in the river, you will find good numbers of trout. There are also several "sills" in the river, where habitat has been improved by placing rocks in a ridge or bar from bank to bank. Nymphing below these structures is often productive.

If you elect to float, the best approach is to fish large dry flies near the banks or on the eddy line just out from shore. Adding a smaller dry fly or a nymph behind the attractor will improve your chances of hooking up. Where you find one fish, there will usually be more. Streamers are also a good way to cover a lot of water

PHOTO: LARRY TULLIS

Mark Forslund of Four Seasons Fly Fishers with a stocky Green River trout.

Insects	Suggested Fly Patterns
Midges	Griffith's gnats (#16-22), Adams (#16-22), midge pupae, cream, brown and black (#18-22), brassies (#16-20)
Annelid worms	San Juan worms, orange and red (#10-14), red serendipities (#10-14)
Blue-winged olives	parachute Adams (#16-20), thorax BWOs (#16-20), olive comparaduns (#16-20), Quigley cripples, olive (#16-20), CDC emergers, olive (#16-20), pheasant tails (#16-20), hare's ears (#16-20), bead-head pheasant tails (#16-20), bead-head hare's ears (#16-20)
Pale morning duns	thorax PMDs (#14-16), cream parachutes (#14-16), cream comparaduns (#16-20), Quigley cripples, cream (#16-20), rusty spinners (#14-16), CDC emergers, cream (#16-20), pheasant tails (#14-16), hare's ears (#14-16), bead-head pheasant tails (#14-16), bead-head hare's ears (#14-16)
Tricos	trico poly spinners (#18-22), trico CDC spinners (#18-22), parachute Adams (#18-22), pheasant tails (#18-20)
Yellow sallys	yellow stimulators (#10-14), yellow seducers (#10-14), elk-hair caddis, yellow (#10-14), yellow humpies (#10-14), prince nymphs (#10-14)
Caddisflies	elk-hair caddis (#16-18), partridge caddis (#16-18), CDC elk-hair caddis (#16-18), sparkle caddis (#16-18), X-caddis (#16-18), peeking caddis (#14-18), chamois caddis (#14-18)
Terrestrials	Dave's hoppers (#8-12), Henry's Fork hoppers (#8-12), Turck's tarantulas (#8-12), Chernobyl ants (#6-10), black, yellow and olive humpies (#6-10), fur ants, black (#14-18), CDC ants (#14-18), deer-hair beetles, black (#14-16), hi-vis foam beetles (#14-16)
Streamers	Clouser minnows, dark shades (#4-8), woolly buggers, olive, black, brown and gold (#4-8), muddler minnows (#4-8), baby brown trout (#4-8), olive, copper, gold and black zonkers (#4-8)

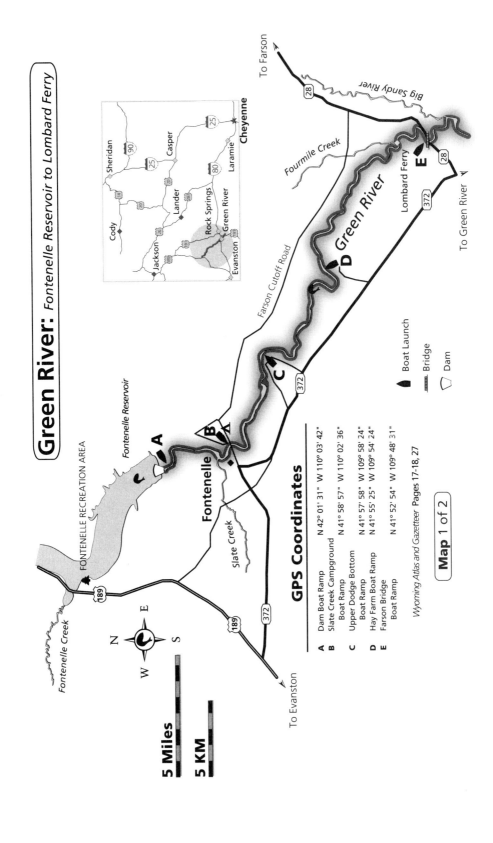

Green River: *Fontenelle Reservoir to Lombard Ferry*

GPS Coordinates

A Dam Boat Ramp   N 42° 01' 31" W 110° 03' 42"

B Slate Creek Campground
    Boat Ramp   N 41° 58' 57" W 110° 02' 36"

C Upper Dodge Bottom
    Boat Ramp   N 41° 57' 58" W 109° 58' 24"

D Hay Farm Boat Ramp   N 41° 55' 25" W 109° 54' 24"

E Farson Bridge
    Boat Ramp   N 41° 52' 54" W 109° 48' 31"

Wyoming Atlas and Gazetteer Pages 17-18, 27

Map 1 of 2

FONTENELLE RECREATION AREA

Fontenelle Reservoir

Fontenelle Creek

Fontenelle

Slate Creek

To Evanston

To Green River

Lombard Ferry

Green River

Farson Cutoff Road

Fourmile Creek

Big Sandy River

To Farson

5 Miles

5 KM

Boat Launch
Bridge
Dam

Sheridan
Cody
Jackson
Casper
Lander
Rock Springs
Green River
Evanston
Laramie
Cheyenne

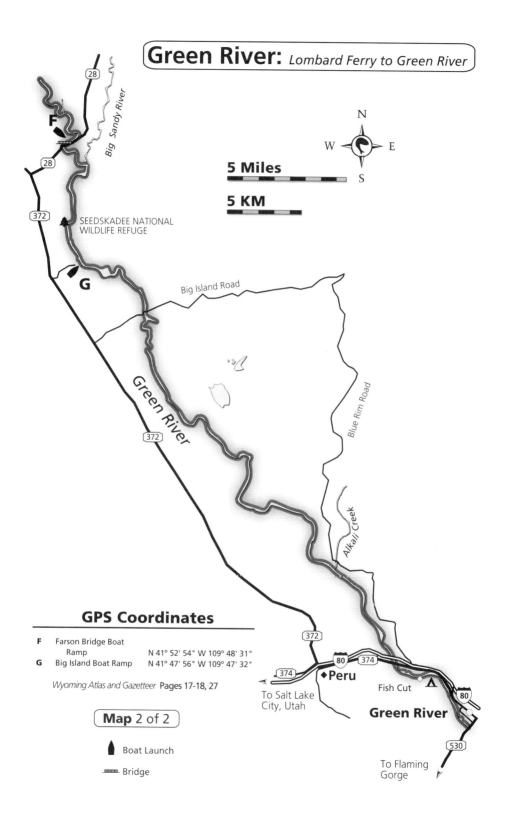

Green River: *Lombard Ferry to Green River*

28

F

28

372

SEEDSKADEE NATIONAL
WILDLIFE REFUGE

G

Big Island Road

Big Sandy River

Green River

372

Blue Rim Road

Alkali Creek

5 Miles

5 KM

N
W E
S

GPS Coordinates

F   Farson Bridge Boat
Ramp   N 41° 52' 54" W 109° 48' 31"
G   Big Island Boat Ramp   N 41° 47' 56" W 109° 47' 32"

Wyoming Atlas and Gazetteer **Pages 17-18, 27**

Map 2 of 2

🔻 Boat Launch

▥ Bridge

372

80

374

374

80

530

◆**Peru**

Fish Cut

Green River

To Salt Lake
City, Utah

To Flaming
Gorge

while drifting the river. This is especially effective if the water is high or in the late fall. The best streamers for the Green are heavily weighted, with lead eyes or the new tungsten cone-heads. High density sink-tips or shooting-head lines like the Teeny T200 work best. During late summer and early fall, there is so much weed breaking loose and drifting down the river that streamer fishing becomes unpractical.

Nymphing is usually the most productive method when you find concentrations of fish. The San Juan worm is probably the single most effective nymph pattern on the river, but don't be afraid to imitate other aquatic insects during hatch periods. In late fall, when kokanee salmon are dying off below the dam, an Alaskan-style flesh fly can be quite effective, especially for lake trout found right below the dam.

This stretch of the Green, like many western tailwaters, takes on the characteristics of a big spring creek. When trout are actively rising, they can be as difficult and picky as fish anywhere, especially during the trico or blue-winged olive hatches. Extend your leaders out to 12 feet and taper down to 6x if the wind will allow. Conflicting current seams caused by the heavy weed growth make getting a good drift quite a challenge. Experiment with your position and the shape of your cast, and keep mending until you get it right.

HOW TO GET THERE

Salt Lake City is about a three-hour drive from the Green River below Fontenelle Reservoir. There is also daily air service to Rock Springs (one hour to the river) from Denver on United Airlines.

Bill Shan battled afternoon winds to cast a Turck's tarantula in front of this big cutthroat.

To reach the Green River below Fontenelle Reservoir in Wyoming from Salt Lake City, go northeast 90 miles on I-80, then north 62 miles on US 189. Turn east on SR 372 for another eight miles to reach Fontenelle, Wyoming. From Rock Springs, take I-80 West about 22 miles to Exit 83, then turn northwest onto SR 372. It is 40 miles to the town of Fontenelle.

ACCESSIBILITY

This portion of the Green River flows mainly across public lands, and almost all of the water under special regulations is on the Seedskadee Wildlife Refuge. Not surprisingly, the best fishing is found between the Sweetwater Road 8 (CCC) Bridge and the mouth of the Big Sandy. The four miles below the dam are heavily fished with bait, so most larger trout are quickly harvested, and fish density declines as you go below US 28.

For most floaters, the river is quite easy to navigate, as long as winds are not too strong. There are fairly well-placed boat ramps. There are also a good number of access points for shorebound anglers, but bluffs along the banks will limit your ability to move up and down the river freely.

Seedskadee Wildlife Refuge does not allow camping within its boundaries, but Slate Creek campground is just above the refuge, and Weeping Rock and Tailrace campgrounds are just below the dam. Please stay on existing roads and abide by any road closures. You will see several "water gaps" along the river. These are generally rock-walled pools on the edge of the river that give cattle access to water. Try to avoid disturbing livestock using these areas.

CHECK RIVER FLOWS ON THE WEB
http://www.uc.usbr.gov/wrg/crsp/crsp_40_fn.txt

WHEN TO GO

Early season fishing can be slow, especially when spring winds kick up. Nymphing is the best bet in this early time, unless you find fish feeding on blue-winged olives.

Many veterans of this section of the Green wait until June before heading out to the river, when fish begin to look up for caddis. Large dry flies will also become effective in early summer. If the water is high (say above 2,500 cfs.), fish will concentrate along the deeper banks, so streamer fishing really picks up. By July and August, dry-fly fishing is best in the morning and evenings, and nymphing is the best way to hook better fish during midday.

Sometime in early September, much of the aquatic vegetation begins to die off and float down the river. Streamer fishing becomes very frustrating as you must constantly remove debris from your fly. The weeds clear out in a few weeks, and in early November, the first mile of river below the dam reopens. This presents fly fishers with some interesting opportunities as they will find kokanee salmon and lake trout in this section. The lake trout are generally right up in the outlet channel immediately below the dam (a boat provides the best access). Kokanee will be found spawning in the greatest numbers around the island ½ mile below the dam. In the refuge, you can expect good fishing in the late season with streamers and nymphs. Keep your eyes open for afternoon risers when the blue-winged olives hatch.

AREA ATTRACTIONS

If the wind blows you off the river, drive over to South Pass City for the day. It is about 75 miles from the Green River on US 28. This pioneer route through the Rockies was a gold rush town in the 1860s. The South Pass City State Historic Site includes a visitor's center and 25 buildings from the 1800s that are being restored. Visitors can try their luck at panning for gold or walk in the footsteps of the pioneers by taking a hike on the old Oregon Trail. For more information, go online at *http://commerce.state.wy.us/sphs/south1.htm.*

RESOURCES

The Fontenelle Store is just minutes from the river. The store rents drift boats, provides shuttles, and stocks some tackle and groceries. Lodging is available in LaBarge and Kemmerer. Both towns are a 30-minute drive from the river below the dam, with Kemmerer offering many more options for both meals and rooms. Green River and Rock Springs are about a one-hour drive and have a wide variety of restaurants, lodging and tackle shops for the visiting angler.

The Fontenelle Recreation complex has four campgrounds. All are first-come, first-served.

Tailrace, Weeping Rock and Slate Creek campgrounds all offer primitive camping along the river. Slate Creek is just above the Sweetwater Road 8 (CCC) Bridge, and is the most convenient site for floaters who want to fish the refuge.

If the campgrounds along the river are full, Fontenelle Creek campground at Fontenelle Reservoir has running water and restrooms. There is a $5 per night fee, so it does not usually fill up.

Lodging

GREEN RIVER

Oak Tree Inn
1170 W. Flaming Gorge Way
Green River, WY 82935
Phone number/s: (307) 875-3500

KEMMERER

Antler's Motel
419 Coral St.
Kemmerer, WY 83101
Phone number/s: (307) 877-4461

LABARGE

Wyoming Inn
129 W. Birchcreek (N. US 189)
LaBarge, WY 83123
Phone number/s: (307) 386-2654

Tackle Shops and Guide Services

GREEN RIVER

Highland Desert Flies
218 Uinta Drive
Green River, WY 82935
Phone number/s: (307) 875-2358

Wind River Sporting Goods
420 Uinta Drive
Green River, WY 82935
Phone number/s: (307) 875-4075

KEMMERER

Fontenelle Store
19 Fontenelle S. County Road 316
Kemmerer, WY 83101
Phone number/s: (307) 877-4844

Solitary Angler
P.O. Box 363
Kemmerer, WY 83101
Phone number/s: (307) 877-9459,
(505) 776-5585
Web site: www.losrios.com/losrios
E-mail: van@laplaza.org

SALT LAKE CITY

Four Seasons Fly Fishers
6591 S. 1460 E.
Murray, UT 84123
Phone number/s: (801) 288-1028,
toll-free (800) 498-5440
Web site: www.utahflyfish.com
E-mail: info@utahflyfish.com

North Platte River — Miracle Mile

At the turn of the last century, much of the western United States remained empty for want of reliable water for agriculture. To remedy this situation, Congress passed the Reclamation Act of 1902, ushering in the U.S. Reclamation Service, the predecessor to the Bureau of Reclamation. Among its first projects was Pathfinder Dam on the North Platte, which was completed in 1909. Seminoe Dam was built upstream and completed in 1939, and Kortes Dam was added in 1951 to act as an afterbay dam to Seminoe for power production. The purpose of building these large water projects was to "reclaim" arid lands for human use and to create homes for Americans on family farms. By happy coincidence, the short stretch of river that remained between Kortes Dam and the impounded waters of Pathfinder Reservoir also created an ideal environment for trout.

The tailwater below Kortes now has consistent water temperatures supporting a variety of aquatic foods that allow trout to grow in its rich waters year-round, and the river's resident fish are deep-bodied and thick. As if this weren't good enough, massive Pathfinder Reservoir is also home to a large population of trout that can exceed 10 pounds, and when that insistent urge to reproduce strikes them, they also find their way up into this "Miracle" section of the North Platte. When these migratory trout join the river's year-round residents, it creates the ideal situation, with lots of fish that average 16 inches and have the potential to exceed 10 pounds.

While this may sound like an angler's paradise, there is a price to be paid. The Miracle Mile is in southcentral Wyoming on the edge of the Great Plains, and winds are strong and persistent. Some fly fishers joke that you need only stand on the West Bank and let the wind carry out your line. The big spawning fish do not come into the river in the warm summer months, but during the cold and stormy periods of late fall and early spring, and it can take a resolute angler to put in the time necessary to land one of the North Platte's trophy trout.

SPECIAL REGULATIONS

North Platte River from Kortes Dam downstream to the confluence with Sage Creek (Miracle Mile) in Carbon County:

- ❏ The creel limit on trout shall be two per day or in possession. Only one trout shall exceed 20 inches.
- ❏ Closed to night fishing (8 p.m. to 6 a.m.) during the month of April.

TACTICS

Miracle Mile trout have a lot of food available to them under the surface. Pull some moss off the rocks up in the canyon and you will find it full of scuds. The river also has plenty of aquatic worms, mayfly nymphs and midge larvae, along with some caddis. Catch a trout here and it will be immediately apparent that they are well-fed, and they seldom need to risk their safety by feeding on top. Nymphs are the answer, and like many other tailwater fisheries, small patterns are most effective. At higher flows, trout are forced to the bottom or the edges of the river, so be sure you get down to the bottom with your nymphs and concentrate your efforts along the banks and eddy lines.

Streamer fishing is very productive on this stretch of the North Platte, and the big flies are visible at a greater distance when the river is murky. The yellow and brown Platte River Special is as effective as when it was first created, and you can also use other bright patterns like yellow zonkers or the yellow yummies (yellow woolly buggers with yellow rubber-legs) popular in western Montana. When the river is at lower flows, a heavily weighted fly fished with a floating line is easy to control. It can be worked effectively around the rocks up in the canyon water above the bridge, or you can keep the fly above the thick weeds that grow in the river down toward the lake. If the river is pumping along at higher flows, you may want to use a fairly dense (Type IV or V) sink-tip line to get down to the fish.

The upper end of the Miracle Mile is steeper, with rocky rapids that provide holding areas for trout.

Hatch Chart AVAILABILITY

Food Items	J	F	M	A	M	J	J	A	S	O	N	D
Midges	X	X	X	X	X	X	X	X	X	X	X	X
Scuds	X	X	X	X	X	X	X	X	X	X	X	X
Annelid worms	X	X	X	X	X	X	X	X	X	X	X	X
Blue-winged olives			X	X	X			X	X	X	X	
Pale morning duns							X	X	X			
Tricos								X	X			
Yellow sallys							X	X				
Caddisflies						X	X	X	X	X		
Terrestrials							X	X	X			

Insects	Suggested Fly Patterns
Midges	Griffith's gnats (#16-22), Adams (#16-22), palamino midges (#18-22), brassies (#16-20), serendipities (#16-22)
Scuds	olive, tan and amber scuds (#14-18), flashback scuds, olive, tan and amber (#14-18)
Annelid worms	San Juan Worms, red and wine (#12-16)
Blue-winged olives	parachute Adams (#16-20), olive comparaduns (#16-20), Quigley cripples, olive (#16-20), CDC emergers, olive (#16-20), pheasant tails (#16-20), hare's ears (#16-20), hare's ears, olive (#16-20), bead-head pheasant tails (#16-20), bead-head hare's ears (#16-20), RS2s (#16-20)
Pale morning duns	cream parachutes (#16-20), cream comparaduns (#16-20), Quigley cripples, cream (#16-20), rusty spinners (#14-16), pheasant tails (#16-20), flashback pheasant tails (#16-20), bead-head pheasant tails (#14-16), bead-head hare's ears (#14-16)
Tricos	trico spinners (#18-22), CDC tricos (#18-22), pheasant tails (#18-22), flashback pheasant tails (#16-22)
Yellow sallys	yellow stimulators (#14-18), yellow sallys (#14-18),red fox squirrel nymphs (#16-18), prince nymphs (#16-18)
Caddisflies	elk-hair caddis (#16-20), partridge caddis (#16-20), Hemingway caddis (#16-20), X-caddis, olive and brown (#16-18), sparkle pupae, olive and brown (#16-20), peeking caddis (#16-18)
Terrestrials	Dave's hoppers (#6-10), Henry's Fork hoppers (#6-10), fur ants, black (#16-20), flying ants, deer-hair beetles, black (#16-18), foam beetles, black (#16-18)

HOW TO GET THERE

Casper and Laramie are the two closest airports to the Miracle Mile of the North Platte with regular service. To reach the Miracle Mile from Casper, head southwest 29 miles on SR 220 (Cy Avenue), then go south 10 miles on CR 407 (Cottonwood Road). Turn west on Kortes Road (CR 291) for another 19 miles. Driving time is about 1 ½ hours.

If you are driving up from Laramie, it will take almost three hours. The simplest route is to go west about 90 miles on I-80. Take exit 219 at Sinclair, then go north on Seminoe Road and follow the signs to the Miracle Mile and Kortes Dam, reaching the river in about 37 miles. The stretch of Seminoe Road from the Reservoir to Kortes Dam is gravel surfaced with steep grades and tight turns as it traverses the Seminoe Mountains. It is not recommended for large RVs and may require snow tires and tire chains to drive it safely in winter months.

ACCESSIBILITY

Once you reach the river, access is very easy with public lands on both sides of the river. Moore Road (3108) follows the river's West Bank and Sage Creek, and Kortes Road gives anglers access to the east bank. There are 11 access areas with primitive camping and/or picnicking. These are fairly evenly spread up and down both sides of the river, except for the steep canyon just below Kortes Dam. Unlike many rivers, anglers are able to camp on the banks of the North Platte.

There are two concrete handicap-accessible fishing platforms with concrete access trails. But both platforms are quite small and not well-placed for mobility-challenged fly fishers.

PHOTO: JEFF BECK

The Miracle Mile's resident fish are deep-bodied and thick.

North Platte: *Kortes Dam to Sage Creek*

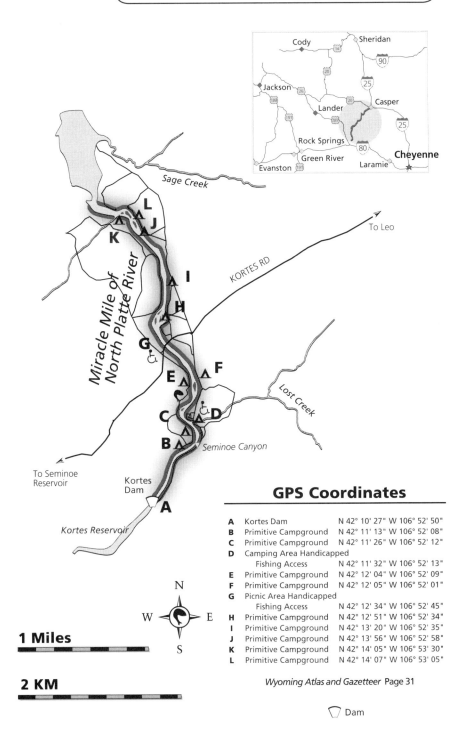

Sage Creek

To Leo

KORTES RD

Miracle Mile of
North Platte River

L
J
K
I
H
G
E F
C D
B
Seminoe Canyon

Lost Creek

To Seminoe
Reservoir

Kortes
Dam

A

Kortes Reservoir

GPS Coordinates

A	Kortes Dam	N 42° 10' 27" W 106° 52' 50"
B	Primitive Campground	N 42° 11' 13" W 106° 52' 08"
C	Primitive Campground	N 42° 11' 26" W 106° 52' 12"
D	Camping Area Handicapped Fishing Access	N 42° 11' 32" W 106° 52' 13"
E	Primitive Campground	N 42° 12' 04" W 106° 52' 09"
F	Primitive Campground	N 42° 12' 05" W 106° 52' 01"
G	Picnic Area Handicapped Fishing Access	N 42° 12' 34" W 106° 52' 45"
H	Primitive Campground	N 42° 12' 51" W 106° 52' 34"
I	Primitive Campground	N 42° 13' 20" W 106° 52' 35"
J	Primitive Campground	N 42° 13' 56" W 106° 52' 58"
K	Primitive Campground	N 42° 14' 05" W 106° 53' 30"
L	Primitive Campground	N 42° 14' 07" W 106° 53' 05"

Wyoming Atlas and Gazetteer Page 31

N
W E
S

1 Miles

2 KM

⬭ Dam

Water releases from Kortes Dam can vary from a mandated low of 500 cfs to a high of 3,000 cfs. Dam operators are required to ramp flows up and down so changes should not be extremely sudden, but they do vary quite a bit with power demands. There is no boat ramp available on this section of the North Platte due to frequent water surges from Seminoe Dam. When wading, always pay attention to water levels and don't get trapped by rising water.

The Miracle Mile actually consists of about 5 ½ miles of river, and the bridge over the river divides it neatly in half. Upstream the riverbed is steeper with some rocky rapids that provide holding areas for trout. As you go farther up into the canyon below Kortes Dam, the road hems in the river and it is a scramble down jumbled rocks to the river. Wading or just walking the banks here is difficult to dangerous, and some of the rock is well-polished and very slippery. Below the bridge, the river exhibits a more gentle gradient and spreads out around several islands as it make its way across the Sage Brush Flat down to Pathfinder Reservoir.

> **CHECK RIVER FLOWS ON THE WEB**
> http://www.gp.usbr.gov/htbin/hydromet_arcplt30?KORR&QD

WHEN TO GO

The Miracle Mile of the North Platte is a year-round fishery and can be productive during any month, but you may have trouble driving to the river after winter storms. During November and December, large brown trout move up into the river from Pathfinder Reservoir. Add these big migratory fish to the river's good population of resident trout and things can get interesting. Streamflows from Kortes Dam are normally low and clear at this time. Streamer fishing comes on strong, and the yellow and brown Platte River Special is one of the most popular patterns.

Rainbow and cutthroat trout get that spawning urge in the spring and begin to move up from Pathfinder in February. Spawning continues through April, and this late winter, early spring period is probably the best time of year to fish the Miracle Mile. Be sure to pack warm clothes and expect high winds.

The summer months can provide good fishing on this section of the North Platte, even though the lake-run trout are absent. The river's resident fish don't often feed on top, so concentrate on nymphing. Summer flows will typically be quite high, around 3,000 cfs, and water can often be quite murky.

RESOURCES

Rawlins and Casper are both a one-hour drive from the river and offer a wide variety of amenities. The Miracle Mile Ranch offers the only lodging on the river and has cabins and a store. There are many primitive campsites on both sides of the river.

Seminoe State Park is only about 12 miles from the Miracle Mile, but you will have to drive up over the mountain on the steep and twisting gravel road to reach the river. Limited services and facilities are available during the winter months. Tire chains and/or four-wheel-drive vehicles only are recommended during winter weather from Seminoe State Park north to the Miracle Mile. Overnight camping permits are $4 for residents and $9 for nonresidents.

Campgrounds

CASPER

Casper KOA Kampgrounds
2800 E. Yellowstone Highway
Casper, WY 82604
Phone number/s: (307) 237-5155

HANNA

Miracle Mile Ranch
Hanna, WY 82327
Phone number/s: (307) 325-6710

RAWLINS

Rawlins KOA Kampgrounds
205 E. SR 71
Rawlins, WY 82301
Phone number/s: (307) 328-2021

Western Hills Campground
2500 Wagon Circle St.
Rawlins, WY 82301
Phone number/s: (307) 324-2592

Lodging

CASPER

Best Western Inn
2325 E. Yellowstone Highway
Casper, WY 82604
Phone number/s: (307) 234-3541

Days Inn
301 E. "E" St.
Casper, WY 82609
Phone number/s: (307) 234-1159

RAWLINS

Best Western Inn
23rd & W. Spruce St.
Rawlins, WY 82301
Phone number/s: (307) 324-2737

HANNA

Miracle Mile Ranch
Hanna, WY 82327
Phone number/s: (307) 325-6710

RAWLINS

Days Inn
2222 E. Cedar St.
Rawlins, WY 82301
Phone number/s: (307) 324-6615

Tackle Shops and Guide Services

CASPER

Platte River Fly Shop
5033 Alcova SR 220
Casper WY, 82604
(307) 237-5997
E-mail: Platterat@aol.com

RAWLINS

Bi-Rite Sporting Goods
313 W. Cedar St.
Rawlins, WY 82301
Phone number/s: (307) 324-3401

SARATOGA

Great Rocky Mountain Outfitters
216 E. Walnut Ave.
Saratoga, WY 82331
Phone number/s: (307) 326-8750
Fax: (307) 326-5390
Web site: www.grmo.com
E-mail: GRMO@union-tel.com

Snake River

HIGHLIGHT
Grandeur of the
Tetons

TIP
Fishes best from a boat

FISH SPECIES
Snake River fine-
spotted cutthroat trout

SEASON
Open from April 1
to October 31

Few angling vistas compare with the lofty grandeur of the Teton Mountains as witnessed from the Snake River in Grand Teton National Park. The high point of Grand Teton scrapes the sky more than 7,000 feet above the river at its base, and each time the mountains reappear around a river bend they display a different perspective. Knife-edged ridges appear or fade away, proud spires break the horizon, and the afternoon shadows force their way across the cirques and high snow fields as the sun clears and slips behind these world-famous peaks.

While the Tetons may be the most visually impressive range in the Rocky Mountain chain, they are also the youngest. Movement along the Teton Fault only began somewhere between 5 and 9 million years ago. While the earth's crust west of the fault rose to form the four peaks, the east side dropped, creating the Jackson Hole Valley. While this uplifting gave the Tetons their height, glaciers as thick as 2,000 feet have sculpted them into their present shape, carving out U-shaped canyons and the large depressions that became lakes as the ice receded. While the last surge of ice melted 15,000 years ago, this craggy range still holds a dozen glaciers. Visitors to Grand Teton National Park can hike 10 miles up the south fork of Cascade Canyon to the Schoolroom Glacier, which exhibits all the classic glacial characteristics. Much of the rough and jagged appearance of the range's peaks has come about in more recent times. Frost wedging exerts prying forces, which splits rocks free from the mountain face, leaving the sharp ridges and pinnacles apparent today.

Jackson Hole has a long history of attracting tourists to enjoy the valley's hunting, fishing and bracing mountain air. Local residents began guiding outsiders in the late 1800s, and dude ranches began to spring up around the turn of the century. The wild and scenic nature of this high valley and impressive mountain range were recognized for the national treasures that they are in 1929, when Congress established Grand Teton National Park to preserve the land and its indigenous wildlife.

One of the most striking native creatures is the Snake River fine-spotted cutthroat trout. Though genetically very similar to the Yellowstone cutthroat, it is visually quite different, as it is heavily peppered with a multitude of tiny black spots. These trout are as beautiful as their home at the foot of the Tetons, with the golden hues along their backs fading into silver flanks, highlighted by rosy cheeks and brilliant fiery orange throat slashes. Although they don't often reach trophy size, their willingness to eat large dry flies has won them a place in the hearts of many fly fishers.

Note: This is the same river that is referred to as the South Fork of the Snake when it emerges from Palisades Reservoir in Idaho.

SPECIFIC REGULATIONS AND FEES

Within Grand Teton National Park:
❒ There is a $20 per car entrance fee, good for both Yellowstone and Grand Teton National Parks.
❒ A boat permit is required. For nonmotorized craft, the charge is $5 for seven days or $10 for an annual permit. No motors are permitted on the river.
❒ All boats must have a properly fitted U.S. Coast Guard-approved PFD for each person, and PFDs must be worn at all times when on the Snake River.
❒ Unlike Yellowstone, fishing in the Grand Teton National Park requires a Wyoming fishing license.

The Snake River bottom from Menor's Ferry at Moose north to the Buffalo Fork confluence:
❒ Closed to human access from December 15 to April 1.

Snake River proper from Yellowstone National Park downstream to Palisades Reservoir in Teton County:
❒ Closed to fishing from November 1 through March 31.
❒ Closed to whitefish fishing from March 1 through March 31.

Snake River proper for a distance of 150 feet below the downstream face of Jackson Lake Dam, Grand Teton National Park in Teton County:
❒ Closed to fishing throughout the calendar year.

Snake River proper from 150 feet below Jackson Lake downstream to the gauging station 1,000 feet below Jackson Lake Dam in Teton county:
❒ The creel limit on trout shall be three per day or in possession.
❒ Only one trout shall exceed 20 inches.
❒ The use or possession of fish, part thereof or fish eggs for bait is prohibited.

Snake River proper from 1,000 feet below Jackson Lake Dam (at gauging station) downstream to the SR 22 Bridge (Wilson Bridge) in Teton county:
❒ The creel limit on trout shall be three per day or in possession.
❒ Only one trout shall exceed 18 inches.
❒ All trout between 12 and 18 inches (inclusive) shall be released to the water immediately. Fishing is permitted with artificial flies and lures only.

Snake River proper from the SR 22 Bridge (Wilson Bridge) downstream to West Table boat ramp in Teton county:
❒ The creel limit on trout shall be three per day or in possession.
❒ Only one trout shall exceed 12 inches.

Snake River from West Table boat ramp in Teton County to Sheep Gulch boat ramp in Lincoln County:
❒ Use of internal combustion motors is prohibited.

Don't try this at home: Trained professionals cool off after an afternoon of hot fishing on the Snake.

Hatch Chart   AVAILABILITY

Food Items	J	F	M	A	M	J	J	A	S	O	N	D
Midges	X	X	X	X	X	X	X	X	X	X	X	X
Blue-winged olives			X	X					X	X	X	
Pale morning duns						X	X	X				
Gray drakes						X	X					
Mahogany duns								X	X			
Yellow sallys						X	X	X				
Salmonflies						X	X					
Golden stoneflies							X	X				
Caddisflies						X	X	X	X	X		
Terrestrials							X	X	X			

TACTICS

The resident fine-spot cuts often orient themselves to deeper pools and current seams. Undercut banks and brush piles will hold good fish in the upper sections of the river. In the canyons downstream, expect to find fish just above fast water or rapids and right against vertical rock walls. Most of the Snake is still unconstrained by dikes, so new side channels are created every year. These smaller channels can hold good numbers of fish, and you may find active feeders.

Fly selection on the Snake River can be a fairly simple proposition compared to other rivers. Hatches are usually sparse, and the trout seldom get selective to a single insect, so feeding fish are often willing to sample a variety of different flies. For much of the river's short season, anglers can offer up large dry flies with the assurance that they will not be ignored. Turck's tarantulas, double humpies, Chernobyl ants and other large attractor-type flies are standard fare along with hoppers, trudes and royal Wulffs.

"Wiggle that thing," says Morrison Simms, a Jackson Hole native and guide for Jack Dennis Fishing. Her years of experience on the river have shown that the resident trout often respond to some movement from a big dry fly, especially leggy patterns like Turck's tarantulas and grasshoppers.

If fish are really keyed into movement, then you may want to try streamers. Just because these Snake River trout will eat dry flies doesn't mean they will pass up a big meal served subsurface. Sinking or sink-tip lines can help take your fly down to the fish, which will often be found along deep eddy lines. Try muddlers, woolly buggers, zonkers and yuk bugs.

If you are more comfortable nymphing, then look for even-depth tail-outs with moderate current, or float your flies down along undercut banks and the sides of rocks. Basic patterns like hare's ears and prince nymphs should produce fish.

Insects	Suggested Fly Patterns
Midges	Griffith's gnats (#16-20), grizzly midges (#16-20), Adams (#16-20) brassies (#16-20), serendipities (#18-22)
Blue-winged olives	parachute Adams (#16-18), thorax BWOs (#16-18), Quigley cripples, olive (#16-20), pheasant tails (#14-18), hare's ears (#14-18)
Pale morning duns	cream comparaduns (#16-18), cream parachutes (#16-18), sparkle duns, cream (#16-18), CDC loopwing emergers, cream (#16-18), Quigley cripples, cream (#16-18), rusty spinners (#16-20), pheasant tails (#16-18), hare's ears (#16-18)
Gray drakes	gray Wulffs (#10-12), parachute Adams (#10-16), muskrat nymphs (#12-14), pheasant tails (#12-14), bead-head pheasant tails (#12-14)
Mahogany duns	Harrop's hair-wing duns, brown (#14-16), sparkle duns, brown (#14-16), pheasant tails (#14-16), bead-head pheasant tails (#14-16)
Yellow sallys	yellow stimulators (#10-14), Flint's stones (#10-14), elk-hair caddis, yellow (#10-14), yellow humpies (#10-14), prince nymphs (#10-14)
Salmonflies	sofa pillows (#6-10), Mac Salmons (#6-10), orange stimulators (#6-10), bullethead salmonflies (#6-10), rubber-legs, black (#6-10), Bitch Creek nymphs (#6-10), Brook's stone nymphs (#6-10)
Golden stoneflies	yellow stimulators (#8-12), prince nymphs (#8-10), bead-head prince nymphs (#8-10), golden stonefly nymphs (#6-10), Bitch Creek nymphs (#6-10), copper Johns (#10-14)
Caddisflies	elk-hair caddis (#12-16), Goddard caddis (#12-16), CDC elk-hair caddis (#12-16), X-caddis (#12-16), peeking caddis (#12-16), chamois caddis (#12-16)
Terrestrials	Turck's tarantulas (#6-8), double humpies (#6-8), Dave's hoppers (#8-12), Henry's Fork hoppers (#8-12), Chernobyl ants (#6-10)

Guide's day off: Morrison Simms gets a chance to cast a fly herself.

HOW TO GET THERE

The Jackson Hole Airport is about seven miles north of town next to the river. Aircraft approach on a course parallel to the mountains, and passengers are treated to a view of the Tetons from a remarkable perspective. There is regular air service into Jackson, but you may find considerably cheaper fares by flying into Idaho Falls, a two-hour drive to Jackson, or Salt Lake City, which is about a five-hour drive to Jackson. If you prefer to let someone else do the driving, call the Jackson Hole Express shuttle (800-652-9510), which has two daily departures from Salt Lake City.

Idaho Falls is about 100 miles east of Jackson. US 26 East will take you directly to Jackson. To reach Jackson from Salt Lake City, take I-15 North about 200 miles to Exit 118 in Idaho Falls. Follow US 26 for about 70 miles through Swan Valley to the town of Alpine. From Alpine, US 26 follows the Snake River northeast for another 35 miles to Jackson.

ACCESSIBILITY

The Snake is a large, brawling mountain river with powerful currents and some large rapids. Spring floods often rearrange the river's braided channels, and large trees are washed into the river, creating sweepers and log jams that present a real hazard to floaters, especially in the faster sections. Whether wading or floating the Snake, always treat it with respect; know your limitations and stay within them.

Below Jackson Dam, there is a launch area, but no ramp, and floaters must lift their craft over the parking barriers and slide them down to the water. It is two

miles down to the next access at Cattleman's Bridge, which does have an unimproved ramp where boats can be launched from trailers. Another three miles will
bring floaters to Pacific Creek Landing. This upper five miles of river is considered
the beginner water on the Snake River in Grand Teton National Park and can be
floated in rafts, drift boats or canoes. You will need to negotiate Cattleman's Bridge
(portage required above 5,000 cfs) if you float the length of this stretch, and there
is some very slow water above Pacific Creek. There are several small springs that
enter the river in this stretch of stillwater, and you can find fish concentrated in the
cooler areas they create.

   The float from Pacific Creek to Deadman's Bar is about 11 miles and requires
an intermediate level of river-running skills to negotiate safely. The main hazards
are sweepers and log jams. Floaters need to keep a careful lookout for downstream
hazards and choose channels carefully. This section does give floaters excellent
views of the Tetons with a different perspective around every bend.

   From Deadman's Bar to Moose Landing, the river covers about 10 miles.
Schwabachers Landing is between these two access points, about five miles below
Deadman's Bar, but it is situated on a side channel that is only accessible during
higher flows. Be sure to check it in advance if you intend to use it as a take-out.
From Moose to Wilson Bridge is another 12 miles. The Snake River from
Deadman's Bar to Wilson Bridge is faster than the water upstream, with more
braided channels. Floaters need advanced river-running skills and competence with

PHOTO: LEONARD KLEIMAN

**Guy Turck with ace client Darren Kleiman and a 22-inch Snake River fine-
spotted cutthroat trout that fell prey to a grasshopper near Jackson Hole.**

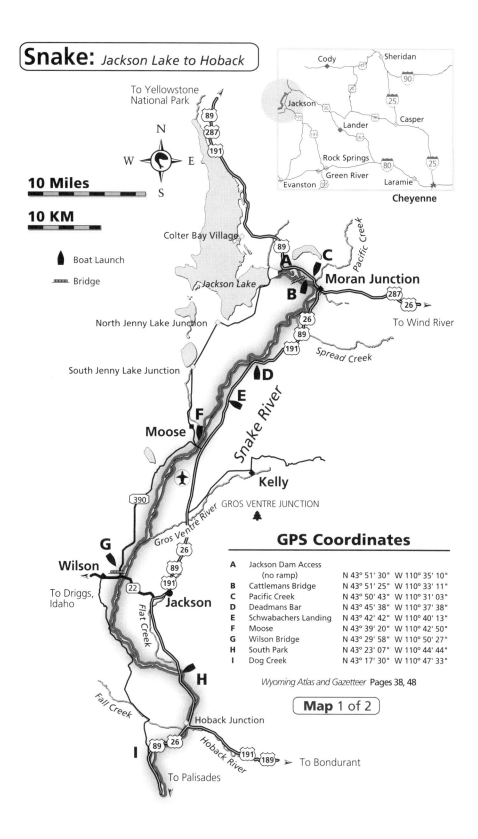

Snake: *Jackson Lake to Hoback*

Cody
Sheridan
Jackson
Lander
Casper
Rock Springs
Green River
Evanston
Laramie
Cheyenne

To Yellowstone National Park

N
W · E
S

10 Miles

10 KM

▲ Boat Launch

⎯ Bridge

Colter Bay Village

Jackson Lake

Pacific Creek

Moran Junction

To Wind River

North Jenny Lake Junction

Spread Creek

South Jenny Lake Junction

Snake River

Moose

Kelly

GROS VENTRE JUNCTION

Gros Ventre River

Wilson

To Driggs, Idaho

Flat Creek

Jackson

GPS Coordinates

A	Jackson Dam Access (no ramp)	N 43° 51' 30" W 110° 35' 10"
B	Cattlemans Bridge	N 43° 51' 25" W 110° 33' 11"
C	Pacific Creek	N 43° 50' 43" W 110° 31' 03"
D	Deadmans Bar	N 43° 45' 38" W 110° 37' 38"
E	Schwabachers Landing	N 43° 42' 42" W 110° 40' 13"
F	Moose	N 43° 39' 20" W 110° 42' 50"
G	Wilson Bridge	N 43° 29' 58" W 110° 50' 27"
H	South Park	N 43° 23' 07" W 110° 44' 44"
I	Dog Creek	N 43° 17' 30" W 110° 47' 33"

Wyoming Atlas and Gazetteer Pages 38, 48

Map 1 of 2

Fall Creek

Hoback Junction

Hoback River

To Bondurant

To Palisades

Snake: *Hoback to Palisades Reservoir*

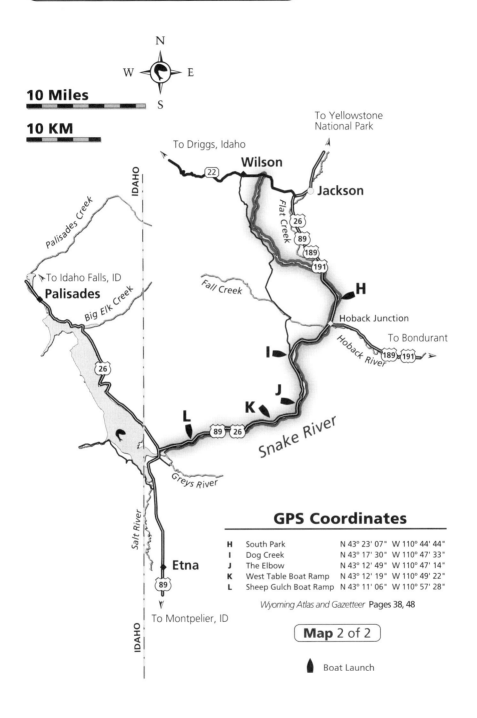

N
W   E
S

10 Miles

10 KM

To Yellowstone National Park

To Driggs, Idaho

Wilson 22

Jackson

IDAHO

Flat Creek

26
89
189
191

Palisades Creek

H

To Idaho Falls, ID

Fall Creek

Palisades

Big Elk Creek

Hoback Junction

To Bondurant

Hoback River 189 191

26

I

J

K

L 89 26

Snake River

Greys River

Salt River

GPS Coordinates

H	South Park	N 43° 23' 07"	W 110° 44' 44"
I	Dog Creek	N 43° 17' 30"	W 110° 47' 33"
J	The Elbow	N 43° 12' 49"	W 110° 47' 14"
K	West Table Boat Ramp	N 43° 12' 19"	W 110° 49' 22"
L	Sheep Gulch Boat Ramp	N 43° 11' 06"	W 110° 57' 28"

Wyoming Atlas and Gazetteer **Pages 38, 48**

Etna

89

IDAHO

To Montpelier, ID

Map 2 of 2

Boat Launch

Incredible views of the Tetons await anglers around every bend of the Snake in Teton National Park.

their chosen craft before they attempt this section. Even major channels may be blocked, so it is advisable to float this section with someone who knows it well before attempting it on your own. You will exit Teton National Park about five miles downstream from Moose, and great views of the Teton Range continue until you exit the park waters.

Below Wilson Bridge and before West Table, there are three launch sites: South Park at the US 89 bridge just south of Jackson; Dog Creek (also known as Prichard); and the Elbow. There is currently no launch at Astoria, but one should reopen in the future once road construction is completed. While this water is still quite powerful, competent floaters should not find it overly difficult.

Unless you are well-prepared for large Class III rapids with holes, breaking waves and dangerous rocks and ledges, you will want to get out at West Table. From this launch site down to Sheep Gulch is the Alpine Canyon of the Snake, which draws whitewater fans throughout the spring and summer. The canyon holds good numbers of trout, and there is minimal fishing pressure since most visitors focus their attention on the rapids. Fishing is best at the lowest flows, and you will have to keep an eye out for other river traffic. Unless you have good equipment and excellent river-running skills, consider hiring one of the talented local guides to row you through the canyon.

Although wading only provides limited access to the river, some good areas for shorebound anglers are at Cattleman's Bridge (it is collapsed and you won't be able to cross it) and Schwabacher's Landing, which is situated on a side channel. If you have a four-wheel-drive vehicle and don't mind a rough ride, River Road runs along the river for many miles inside the park, providing river access in several places.

WHEN TO GO

The season on the Snake opens April 1, and run-off at this altitude is often delayed to mid-May, giving anglers a good window for some early season trout fishing. Be prepared for unpredictable weather and variable fishing if you plan a trip here in the spring.

For most Snake River fly fishers, the season begins when the high waters of spring begin to recede in mid-July. Fishing with big dry flies gets better and better as waters levels drop. August brings good fishing that normally improves into September as the cottonwoods lining the river turn golden. Snow can arrive in the month of October at this altitude, so watch the weather and pack warm clothes if you set your sights on a late-season trip on the Snake.

CHECK RIVER FLOWS ON THE WEB
http://wyoming.usgs.gov./rt-cgi/gen_tbl_pg

RESOURCES

Jackson is a booming, flamboyant tourist town. If you are looking for shopping or nightlife, it is the place to stay. For a more "low-key" experience, Teton Village offers a variety of accommodations and restaurants in a quiet mountain setting.

Jackson Hole lodging ranges from budget to five-star hotels, with a choice of condos, B&Bs and dude ranches added to the mixture. For more information, contact Jackson Hole Central Reservations at (800) 443-6931 or go online to *www.jacksonhole.com/lodging/hotels.html.*

Campgrounds

JACKSON

Lone Eagle Campground Resort
Star Route, Box 45C
Jackson, WY 83001
Phone number/s: (307) 733-1090,
toll-free (800) 321-3800

Snake River Park KOA Kampgrounds
9705 S. US 89
Jackson, WY 83001
Phone number/s: (307) 733-7078,
toll-free (800) 562-1878
Fax: (307) 733-0412

Virginian RV Park
750 W. Broadway
Jackson, WY 83001-1052
Phone number/s: (307) 733-7189,
toll-free (800) 321-6982

Wagon Wheel Campground
525 N. Cache
Jackson, WY 83001
Phone number/s: (307) 733-4588

MORAN

Colter Bay RV Park/Tent Village
P.O. Box 240
Moran, WY 83013
Phone number/s: (800) 628-9988

Grand Teton Park RV Resort and Cabins
P.O. Box 92
Moran, WY 83013
Phone number/s: (307) 543-2483,
toll-free (800) 563-6469

Lodging

JACKSON

Anglers Inn
265 N. Millward
Jackson, WY 83001-1247
Phone number/s: (307) 733-3682
E-mail: anglersinn@wyoming.com

Hitching Post Lodge
460 E. Broadway, Box 4397
Jackson, WY 83001
Phone number/s: (307) 733-2606,
toll-free (800) 821-8351
Fax: (307) 733-8221
E-mail: HitchingPost@wyoming.com

Rusty Parrot Lodge
175 N. Jackson St.
Jackson, WY 83001
Phone number/s: (307) 733-2000

TETON VILLAGE

Hostel
3325 McCollister Drive
Teton Village, WY 83025
Phone number/s: (307) 733-3415

Jackson Hole Ski Area and Resort
7658 Teewinot
Teton Village, WY 83025
Phone number/s: (307) 733-2292

Tackle Shops and Outfitters

JACKSON

High Country Flies
185 N. Center St.
Jackson, WY 83001
Phone number/s: (307) 733-7210
Web site: www.highcountryflies.com

Jack Dennis Fishing
50 E. Broadway
Jackson, WY 83001
Phone number/s: (307) 733-3270,
toll-free (800) 570-3270
Fax: (307) 733-4540

Orvis
485 W. Broadway St.
Jackson, WY 83001
Phone number/s: (307) 733-5407

TETON VILLAGE

Westbank Anglers
3670 N. Moose-Wilson Road
Teton Village, WY 83025
Phone number/s: (307) 733-6483

Raft Rentals

HOBACK JUNCTION

Rent-A-Raft/Jackson Hole Outdoor Center
Lewis Landing
10925 S. US 89
Hoback Junction, WY
Phone number/s: (307) 733-2728

Shuttle Services

JACKSON

Holly Frank
Phone number/s: (307) 690-9390

John Clark
River Shuttles
Phone number/s: (307) 690-5646

YELLOWSTONE NATIONAL PARK

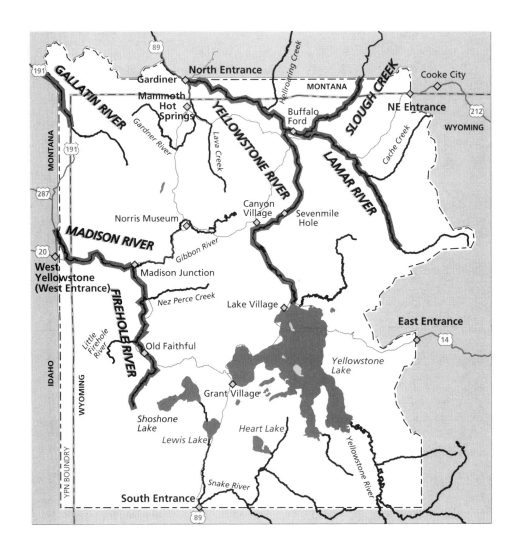

Yellowstone National Park

 t 2.2 million acres, the country's first national park has plenty of room for fly fishers who journey here in pursuit of trout. Being entirely public lands, visitors have free access to all areas of the park, except where restricted for safety or environmental protection. This vast mountainous preserve has remained relatively unaffected by man, and anglers can find fish populations flourishing in pristine rivers.

GENERAL SEASON AND DAILY BAG &POSSESSION LIMITS

The general fishing season in the park begins on the Saturday of Memorial Day weekend through the first Sunday in November and is open each day from 5 a.m. to 10 p.m. No fishing is allowed from any road bridge or boat dock.

Species	2000 Daily Bag & Possession Limits
PARKWIDE REGULATIONS	
Cutthroat trout	catch-and-release only
Grayling	catch-and-release only
Mountain whitefish	two fish, any size
Rainbow trout	two fish, any size
Brown trout	two fish, any size
Brook trout	five fish, any size
Lake trout	two fish, any size

LICENSE FEES

A permit is required to fish in Yellowstone. Anglers 12 to 15 years of age are required to obtain a nonfee permit. Children 11 years of age or younger may fish without a permit when supervised by an adult. The adult is responsible for the child's actions. Fishing permits are available at all ranger stations, visitor centers and Hamilton General Stores. No state fishing license is required in Yellowstone National Park.

Fishing License	Age	Fee
PARK VISITORS		
Season	16 and over	$20
Ten-day	16 and over	$10
Youth permit	12 to 15	free

GENERAL TACKLE RESTRICTIONS

❐ Flies may have only one hook with a single point. Up to two flies may be used on a single leader.
❐ Leaded fishing tackle such as leaded split-shot sinkers, weighted jigs (lead molded to a hook) and soft lead-weighted ribbon for nymph fishing are not allowed (see below).

NONTOXIC FISHING

Yellowstone National Park has implemented a nontoxic fishing program. Nationwide, over 3 million waterfowl die from lead poisoning through ingestion. Because lead from fishing tackle concentrates in aquatic environments, tackle such as leaded split-shot sinkers, weighted jigs and soft-weighted ribbon for fly fishing are prohibited. Only nontoxic alternatives to lead are allowed.

BOATING REGULATIONS

A boat permit is required for all types of vessels. No boats, canoes, kayaks, rafts or float tubes are allowed on park rivers and streams, with the exception of the waterway between Lewis and Shoshone Lake where only hand-propelled craft are permitted.

CAMPGROUNDS

Yellowstone National Park has 12 campgrounds. Camping is only permitted in designated campgrounds and limit of stay is 14 days between June 15 and September 15, and 30 days during the rest of the year.

Five of Yellowstone's campgrounds are operated by AmFac Parks & Resorts and accept reservations. Bridge Bay, Canyon, Grant Village and Madison campgrounds offer rest rooms, fire grates, and tables accessible to campers with disabilities. The RV park has accessible flush toilets, but there are no tables or fire grates because of its proximity to bear habitat. For camping reservations, call (307) 344-7311.

❐ Bridge Bay — open from mid-May to mid-September ($15)
❐ Canyon — open from early June to early September ($15)
❐ Grant Village — open from mid-June to early October ($15)
❐ Madison campground — open from early May to late October ($15)
❐ Fishing Bridge RV Park — open from mid-May to mid-September ($27)

Seven of Yellowstone's campgrounds are operated by the National Park Service and are on a first-come, first-served basis. During the peak season (early July to late August), these campgrounds are usually full by late morning. Indian Creek, Lewis Lake, Pebble Creek, Slough Creek and Tower Fall have accessible vault toilets. Lewis Lake and Slough Creek campgrounds have an accessible campsite.

❏   Mammoth — open year-round ($12)
❏   Norris — open from mid-May to late September ($12)
❏   Indian Creek — open from early June to mid-September ($10)
❏   Lewis Lake — open from early June to late October ($10)
❏   Pebble Creek — open from early June to the end of September ($10)
❏   Tower Fall — open from mid-May to the end of September ($10)

BACKCOUNTRY CAMPING

Yellowstone has a designated backcountry campsite system, and a permit is required for all overnight stays. Permits may be obtained only in person and no more than 48 hours in advance of your trip. Permits are free and available from most ranger stations and visitor centers.

For a nonrefundable $15 fee, backcountry campsites may be reserved in advance, but only by mail or in person. Reservations are booked on a first-come, first-served basis. Forms for making advance reservations are available by writing to: Backcountry Office, P.O. Box 168, Yellowstone National Park, WY 82190, by calling (307) 344-2160, or by downloading them from the Online Backcountry Trip Planner at *ww.nps.gov/yell/publications/pdfs/backcountry/index.htm*.

PARK ENTRANCES

❏   North Entrance — US 89 from I-90 at Livingston, Montana
❏   Northeast Entrance — US 212 from I-90 at Billings, Montana, or SR 296 from Cody, Wyoming
❏   West Entrance — US 191 from Bozeman, Montana, or US 20 from Idaho Falls, Idaho
❏   East Entrance — US 16 from Cody, Wyoming
❏   South Entrance — US 89 from Jackson, Wyoming

ENTRANCE FEES

The entrance fee is $20 for a private, noncommercial vehicle; $15 for each snowmobile or motorcycle; or $10 for each visitor entering by foot, bike, ski, etc. This fee provides the visitor with a seven-day entrance permit for both Yellowstone and Grand Teton national parks. Commercial tours are subject to a separate fee schedule. Golden Age, Eagle and Access passports are honored and provide free admission to the park.

ACCESSIBILITY

The park's major sites can be viewed by automobile. Some trails and facilities are wheelchair accessible. For online information about accessibility, go to *www.nps.gov/yell/planvisit/access/index.htm*.

RESOURCES

Banking Services

Automated teller machines are located at Old Faithful Inn, Lake Yellowstone Hotel, Mammoth Hot Springs Hotel, Old Faithful Snow Lodge, Grant Village and Snow Lodge.

Tackle Shops and Outfitters

You can purchase fishing permits at any of the Hamilton Stores found throughout the park. These stores have some fly tackle and flies. Fly selection is limited, and the flies are generally of poor quality. Your best option is to stock up outside the park. For a complete listing of outfitters in the area, go online to *www.nps.gov/yell/planvisit/todo/fishing/ibp_fish.htm.*

Yellowstone National Park
P.O. Box 168
Yellowstone National Park, WY 82190-0168
Phone number/s: (307) 344-7381
Web site: www.nps.gov/yell/index.htm

AmFac Parks and Resorts
P.O. Box 165
Yellowstone National Park, WY 82190
Phone number/s: (307) 344-7311
Fax: (307) 344-7456
Web site: www.ynp-lodges.com

Yellowstone National Park Lodges (operated by AmFac)
AmFac Parks and Resorts
P.O. Box 165
Yellowstone National Park, WY 82190
Phone number/s: (307) 344-7311
Fax: (307) 344-7456
Web site: http://amfac.worldres.com

Yellowstone National Park (unofficial)
Web site: http://travelyellowstone.com

Yellowstone National Park Traveler Resources
Web site: www.areaparks.com/yellowstone

The best bet for handicap-accesssible fly fishing in Yellowstone is by Mount Washburn on the Madison River.

Firehole River

HIGHLIGHT
Incomparable scenery
and abundant wildlife

TIP
Try swimming caddis
patterns

FISH SPECIES
Brown and rainbow
trout with brookies in
the higher reaches

SEASON
Saturday of Memorial
Day weekend through
the first Sunday in
November

Few experiences in fly fishing can surpass a day spent on the banks of the legendary Firehole. Some of fly fishing's best anglers have plied these waters for generations, and annual pilgrimages to the Firehole continue today. This unique and beautiful, clear stream runs through verdant meadows, pine forest and surrealistic geyser basins. Steam rises in plumes from the many hot springs and fumaroles, and when the wind shifts you may smell the tang of sulfur in the air. Wild bison roam the flats while elk let forth with their mournful bugle in the evening. End your day at the incredible log Old Faithful Inn, and it may not matter whether you hooked that big rainbow or not.

The Old Faithful Inn is a famous Yellowstone landmark, built just after the turn of the century, and is the largest log structure in the world. Constructed of native stone and contorted lodgepole pine, the Inn's asymmetry is intended to mimic the chaos of nature that surrounds it. The expansive hotel lobby is 65 feet high with a massive stone fireplace. Even more impressive than its architecture is the Inn's location, just 200 yards from Old Faithful itself and only a couple of miles from the Firehole's best fishing

The average fish are only 10 to 12 inches, but larger individuals reach 16 to 18 inches and, on rare occasion, exceed 20. These trout see many flies pass over their heads on the surface of the clear water, while the footsteps of careless anglers resonate through the undercut banks. As you might guess, fishing can be difficult here, especially if you have your heart set on capturing one of the Firehole's bigger trout.

SPECIFIC REGULATIONS

The Firehole River (not including the tributaries):
❏ Restricted to fly fishing only (artificial flies only may be used to attract and catch fish regardless of the type of rod or line).

The Firehole River and its tributaries:
❏ Anglers may keep two brown trout under 13 inches.
❏ Catch-and-release only for rainbow.

The Firehole River from the road bridge ½ mile upstream of Old Faithful to the road bridge at Biscuit Basin (2 ½ miles downstream of Old Faithful):
❏ Closed to fishing.

Few experiences rival an early morning of fly fishing the legendary Firehole.

See the section on Yellowstone National Park on page 345 for entrance fees and parkwide regulations.

TACTICS

Most of the hatches on the Firehole are comprised of small insects, and you will usually be casting flies size 16 and smaller on relatively slick water. Longer leaders of 12 feet tapered to 5x will work for most dry-fly fishing conditions. Approach the water quietly; most of the better fish will be right along the banks. Once you find a larger fish, adjust your position or your cast to get the best drift possible.

If you find yourself having difficulty catching rising fish with traditional dry flies during caddis hatches, try flies that imitate a swimming caddis. These patterns fish well with drag or even when fished on a downstream swing and can help compensate for poor drifts. You will find these flies very useful wherever you travel, not just on the Firehole. Adult caddisflies are good swimmers, and swimming or diving imitations can be especially effective when adults swarm the river in the evening.

The water warms very early in the season on the Firehole, and midday fishing is often fruitless. The best fishing is usually found in the early mornings or the last hour of the evening. As the Firehole's trout are subject to a great deal of thermal stress, it is a good idea to carry a thermometer and check temperatures before fishing. When the water rises above 68 degrees, hooking and playing trout adds to the cumulative stress they are already experiencing and mortality increases. Consider limiting your fishing to the early morning hours or visit one of the other rivers in the park.

Nymphing on the Firehole can be effective, and as there are no whitefish above the falls, anglers are spared the frustration of discovering that the trout they thought they just hooked is no trout at all. Bead-head nymphs can be quite effective, or you can use nonlead shot to get your bugs down to the fish.

The Firehole below the falls is distinctly different from the rest of the river. This is strong, fast water that holds golden stones and even some salmonflies. In June, forget the tiny flies that work up above and tie on a big sofa pillow or stimulator with a bead-head dropper. From late October until fishing closes in the park (the first Sunday of November), you have the chance to catch large spawning fish up from Hebgen Lake. Break out your sink-tip lines and weighted streamers if you want to hook up with these large migratory fish. Remember that lead-weighted flies are not allowed in the park. Streamers tied with tungsten cone-head or tungsten underbodies will reach fish more effectively in the deeper runs.

HOW TO GET THERE

The West Entrance of Yellowstone National Park is only 30 miles from Old Faithful and only 12 miles from the confluence of the Firehole and Gibbon rivers. There is regular air service into West Yellowstone from June 1 to September 30. If you are flying in to fish the Firehole in the early or late season, try Jackson Hole. It

PHOTO: MARK WILLIAMS

The slick waters of the Firehole require long leaders and a careful presentation.

Hatch Chart

AVAILABILITY

Food Items	J	F	M	A	M	J	J	A	S	O	N	D
Midges					X	X	X	X	X	X	X	
Blue-winged olives					X	X			X	X		
Pale morning duns					X	X						
Flavs						X						
Yellow sallys						X	X					
Salmonflies						X						
Caddisflies						X	X	X	X	X		
Terrestrials							X	X	X	X		

Insects	Suggested Fly Patterns
Midges	Griffith's gnats (#16-22), grizzly midges (#16-22), midge pupae, black, cream and red (#20-26), bead-head midges, black, red and brown (#16-18), midge emergers, black and peacock (#20-26)
Blue-winged olives	parachute Adams (#18-24), thorax BWOs (#18-24), olive comparaduns (#18-24), sparkle duns, olive (#18-24), Quigley cripples, olive (#18-24), CDC emergers, olive (#18-24), pheasant tails (#16-20), hare's ears (#16-20), bead-head pheasant tails (#16-20), bead-head hare's ears (#16-20)
Pale morning duns	thorax PMDs (#16-20), cream parachutes (#16-20), cream comparaduns (#16-20), Quigley cripples, cream (#16-20), rusty spinners (#16-20), CDC emergers, cream (#16-20), pheasant tails (#14-16), bead-head pheasant tails (#14-16)
Flavs	green drake Wulffs (#14-16), olive parachutes (#14-16), olive comparaduns (#14-16), Quigley cripples, olive (#14-16), CDC emergers, olive (#14-16), hare's ears, olive (#14-16)
Yellow sallys	yellow stimulators (#14-18), yellow sallys (#14-18), red fox squirrel nymphs (#16-18)
Salmonflies	sofa pillows (#6-10), Mac Salmons (#6-10), orange stimulators (#6-10), rubber-legs, black (#6-10), Bitch Creek nymphs (#6-10), Brook's stone nymphs
Caddisflies	elk-hair caddis (#16-18), partridge caddis (#16-18), CDC elk-hair caddis (#16-18), sparkle caddis (#16-18), parachute caddis (#16-18), bead-head diving caddis (#16-18)
Terrestrials	Dave's hoppers (#10-12), Dave's crickets (#10-12), fur ants, black (#16-20), CDC ants, black (#16-18), flying ants (#16-20), deer-hair beetles, black (#14-18), hi-vis foam beetles (#14-18)

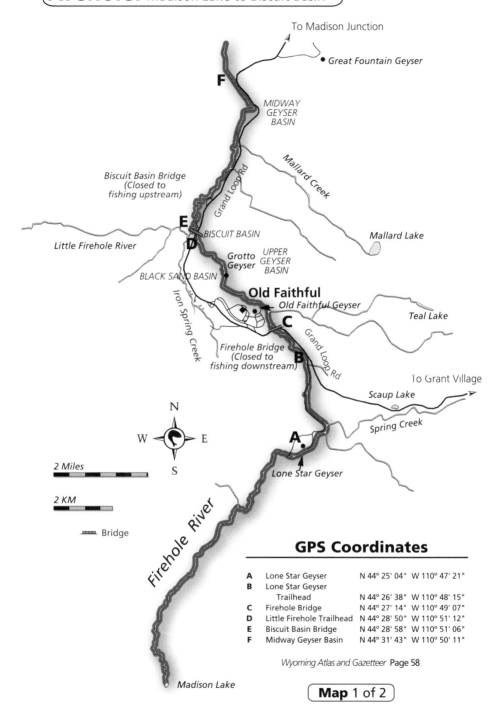

Firehole: *Madison Lake to Biscuit Basin*

To Madison Junction

• Great Fountain Geyser

F

MIDWAY GEYSER BASIN

Mallard Creek

Grand Loop Rd

Biscuit Basin Bridge
(Closed to fishing upstream)

Mallard Lake

E
BISCUIT BASIN
D

Little Firehole River

Grotto Geyser

UPPER GEYSER BASIN

BLACK SAND BASIN

Old Faithful

Old Faithful Geyser

Teal Lake

Iron Spring Creek

C

Firehole Bridge
(Closed to fishing downstream)

B

Grand Loop Rd

To Grant Village

Scaup Lake

N
W E
S

A

Lone Star Geyser

Spring Creek

2 Miles

2 KM

Bridge

Firehole River

GPS Coordinates

A	Lone Star Geyser	N 44° 25' 04" W 110° 47' 21"
B	Lone Star Geyser Trailhead	N 44° 26' 38" W 110° 48' 15"
C	Firehole Bridge	N 44° 27' 14" W 110° 49' 07"
D	Little Firehole Trailhead	N 44° 28' 50" W 110° 51' 12"
E	Biscuit Basin Bridge	N 44° 28' 58" W 110° 51' 06"
F	Midway Geyser Basin	N 44° 31' 43" W 110° 50' 11"

Wyoming Atlas and Gazetteer Page 58

Madison Lake

Map 1 of 2

Firehole: Biscuit Basin to Madison Junction

To Mammoth Hot Springs

To West Yellowstone

Harlequin Lake

Madison Junction

West Entrance Rd

Grand Loop Rd

Gibbon River

Madison River

K

Λ

J

Firehole River

GPS Coordinates

E	Biscuit Basin Bridge	N 44° 28' 58" W 110° 51' 06"
F	Midway Geyser Basin	N 44° 31' 43" W 110° 50' 11"
G	Goose Lake	N 44° 32' 32" W 110° 50' 32"
H	Goose Lake Trailhead	N 44° 34' 02" W 110° 50' 07"
I	Trailhead to Upper Nez	
	Perce Creek	N 44° 34' 11" W 110° 48' 56"
J	Firehole Falls	N 44° 37' 51" W 110° 51' 46"
K	Madison Junction	
	Picnic Area	N 44° 38' 34" W 110° 51' 35"

Wyoming Atlas and Gazetteer **Page 58**

Nez Perce Creek

CULEX BASIN

I

Grand Loop Rd

Sentinel Creek

H

LOWER GEYSER BASIN

Fountain Paint Pot

Λ

G

Λ

Goose Lake

Firehole Lake

White Dome Geyser

Great Fountain Geyser

Fairy Creek

Fountain Flat Dr

Lower Basin Lake

White Creek

F

Midway Bluff

Map 2 of 2

N
W   E
S

2 Miles

2 KM

Spray Geyser
Imperial Geyser

Grand Prismatic Spring

MIDWAY GEYSER BASIN

Mallard Creek

╍╍╍ Bridge

Biscuit Basin Bridge
(Closed to fishing upstream)

E

BISCUIT BASIN

Little Firehole River

Mallard Lake

Grotto Geyser

To Old Faithful

The Firehole cuts a steep canyon at the falls.

is about 100 miles away, but you will drive past the majestic Tetons on your way to Yellowstone's South Entrance.

From West Yellowstone, enter the park on West Entrance Road and drive east about 14 miles to Madison Junction, then turn south on Grand Loop Road, which will parallel the river from the Madison until it leaves the road at the Lone Star Geyser trailhead.

If you drive up from Jackson Hole, take US 89 (also US 26 or US 191) north for almost 60 miles to Yellowstone's South Entrance. Continue north for 22 miles on South Entrance Road, then turn west for 19 miles on Grand Loop Road to reach the Firehole downstream from Old Faithful.

ACCESSIBILITY

Some of the best of the classic Firehole water will be found between Biscuit Basin and the Muleshoe Bend. The river is closed to fishing above the bridge at Biscuit Basin for about 3 ½ miles, and it can get quite warm below Midway Geyser Basin. There are several turnouts along this stretch of Grand Loop Road. The Firehole is never very far away from the pavement, so getting to the water doesn't present much of a problem. Wading is not particularly difficult either, but some of the river bottom is composed of old hot spring deposit and there are some sharp drop-offs and holes, so use caution. The water is clear enough that you can misjudge the depth.

There is trail access away from the road on two sections of the Firehole. One goes up to Lone Star Geyser and follows the river for about four miles above Keppler Cascade. Both the river and the fish — mostly brook trout — run a bit smaller up here, but you will find few other anglers, and this section is not plagued by the excessively high summer temperatures that affect the river below Old Faithful. The Firehole enters a steep canyon about six miles from the trailhead, and you will find no fish above. Another trail begins on the Fountain Flats Road, which you can hike or bike the 2 ½ miles to reach the Firehole by Goose Lake. Fishing in this stretch of the river suffers from all the warm geothermal inflow, but you can still find good conditions in the cooler months.

When the Firehole gets too warm in the summer months, many of its trout move to cooler waters up the tributary streams. Nez Perce Creek will hold fish above the warmwater inflow in Culex Basin. It is only a little

An angler fishes an evening caddis hatch at Mule Shoe Bend on the Firehole.

over one mile to the creek if you park at the trailhead at Mary Mountain, but this area doesn't open until June 16. The Little Firehole will also hold fish and can be reached from its trailhead just above Biscuit Basin. The lower mile of the stream is a cool water haven to Firehole trout, but hooking and landing them in this small water is challenging.

The canyon below Firehole Falls is steep and rocky with pools and pocket water. Use care wading and consider carrying a wading staff. Firehole Canyon Drive follows the river to the falls and is narrow with very little room for parking. Instead, leave your vehicle at the Madison Junction picnic area for a short, easy stroll to the confluence. You will need to either wade across the Gibbon or walk to the bridge just upstream.

WHEN TO GO

If water levels are not too high, the Firehole will fish well when it opens on the Saturday of Memorial Day weekend; it can be a good bet for the park's season opener. Lucky anglers may catch the limited salmonfly hatch below the falls in early June. Good fishing continues until the middle or end of June, perhaps even into July in cool, wet years.

With all the geothermal water flowing into the Firehole, it fishes poorly through much of the summer, generally from the first of July to mid-September. During the heat of the summer, try fishing above the Firehole Bridge or even above Keppler Cascade. The Little Firehole and Nez Perce Creek can also be good options during the heat of the summer.

When the weather cools in late September, you may share the steaming geysers with none but the elk and bison or occasional coyote. The fish will be keyed in on small blue-winged olives or caddis. October can bring some incredible days to the Firehole, with hungry but difficult fish presenting a challenge under fall skies.

RESOURCES

For a complete listing of resources in Yellowstone National Park, please refer to page 345.

Campgrounds

YELLOWSTONE NATIONAL PARK

For camping reservations at Yellowstone National Park, contact:

AmFac Parks and Resorts
P.O. Box 165
Yellowstone National Park, WY 82190
Phone number/s: (307) 344-7311
Fax: (307) 344-7456
Web site: www.ynp-lodges.com

❑   Grant Village
❑   Madison

National Park Service
first-come, first-served basis

❑   Lewis Lake

Lodging

YELLOWSTONE NATIONAL PARK

For lodging reservations, contact:

AmFac Parks and Resorts
P.O. Box 165
Yellowstone National Park, WY 82190
Phone number/s: (307) 344-7311
Fax: (307) 344-7456
Web site: http://amfac.worldres.com

❑   Grant Village
❑   Lake Lodge Cabins
❑   Lake Yellowstone Hotel & Cabins
❑   Old Faithful Lodge and Cabins
❑   Old Faithful Snow Lodge

WEST YELLOWSTONE

Comfort Inn
638 Madison Ave.
West Yellowstone, MT 59758
Phone number/s: (406) 646-4212,
toll-free (888) 264-2466
Web site: w-yellowstone.com/comfortinn

Pine Shadows Motel
530 Gibbon Ave.
West Yellowstone, MT 59758
Phone number/s: (406) 646-7541,
toll-free (800) 624-5291
Web site: www.wyellowstone.com/clients/
pineshadows/

Yellowstone Inn and Cabins
601 US 20
West Yellowstone, MT 59758
Phone number/s: (406) 646-7633,
toll-free (800) 858-9224
Web site: www.wyellowstone.com/
yellowstoneinn/
E-mail: kate@aicom.net

Tackle Shops and Outfitters

WEST YELLOWSTONE

Blue Ribbon Flies
315 Canyon St.
West Yellowstone, MT 59758
Phone number/s: (406) 646-7642

Bud Lilly's Trout Shop
39 Madison Ave.
West Yellowstone, MT 59758
Phone number/s: (406) 646-7630,
toll-free (800) 854-9559
Web site: www.budlillys.com

Jacklin's Fly Shop
105 Yellowstone Ave.
West Yellowstone, MT 59758
Phone number/s: (406) 646-7336
Fax: (406) 646-9729
Web site: www.wyellowstone.com/
jacklinsflyshop
E-mail: bjacklin@jacklinsflyshop.com

Madison River Outfitters
117 Canyon St.
West Yellowstone, MT 59758
Phone number/s: (406) 646-9644,
toll-free (800) 646-9644
Web site: www.flyfishingyellowstone.com

Gallatin River

FISH SPECIES
Rainbow, cutthroat, cuttbows, and brown trout

TIP
This cold river fishes best during the heat of the day

HIGHLIGHT
Grasshopper fishing in August

SEASON
Saturday of Memorial Day weekend through the first Sunday in November

The Gallatin River section in Montana was the setting for the fishing scenes in *A River Runs Through It*, but you won't have to worry about swimming through rapids to land your big fish. The waters in Yellowstone National Park are much more tame than the whitewater found below.

Named for Albert Gallatin, the Secretary of the Treasury who helped plan and finance Lewis and Clark's Voyage of Discovery, the river begins at the outflow of Gallatin Lake at 8,600 feet. From this point, it descends 1,200 feet over the next 13 miles to US 191 at the Bighorn trailhead. From the trailhead downstream to the Yellowstone National Park boundary, there are 12 miles of beautiful meadow water easily accessible from the road.

The Gallatin in Yellowstone National Park is simple, unpretentious water. It is normally kind to rookie fly fishers, and basic dry flies will usually do the trick. The waters of the Gallatin flow clear and cold most of the summer — much colder than nearby neighbors like the Madison and the Firehole. This quality makes the Gallatin a good choice during late July and August, when other streams suffer from summer doldrums. You can sleep in or linger over coffee, as this river fishes best when the sun is well up in the sky. Another benefit is that cold water stays well oxygenated, so when you hook one of this river's stocky rainbow trout, expect it to get airborne time and time again. This wadeable, small river produces fish that run about 13 to 14 inches with some up to 18. Yet stories of 20-inch browns still circulate wherever the Gallatin's faithful anglers congregate.

Even in mid-July, the water remains cold and waders are a good idea.

Hatch Chart

Food Items	J	F	M	A	M	J	J	A	S	O	N	D
Midges			X	X	X	X	X	X	X	X	X	
Blue-winged olives			X	X	X	X	X	X	X	X	X	
Pale morning duns							X	X				
Green drakes							X					
Flavs							X	X				
Golden stoneflies						X	X					
Salmonflies						X	X					
Caddisflies						X	X	X	X	X		
Terrestrials							X	X	X			
Attractors							X	X	X			

AVAILABILITY

SPECIAL REGULATIONS

This stretch of the Gallatin River falls under general park regulations. See page 345 for Yellowstone National Park fees and regulations.

TACTICS

The Gallatin is a simple stream under most conditions. If you find one of its larger aquatic insect species hatching when you arrive, just tie on a reasonable imitation and begin fishing your way upstream. In the absence of any significant

Cast grasshopppers tight against deep undercut banks for the river's biggest browns.

Insects	Suggested Fly Patterns
Midges	Griffith's gnats (#16-20), grizzly midges (#16-20), Adams (#16-20), brassies (#16-20), serendipities (#18-20)
Blue-winged olives	parachute Adams (#16-20), thorax BWOs (#16-20), Quigley cripples, olive (#16-20), pheasant tails (#14-18), hare's ears (#14-18)
Pale morning duns	comparaduns, cream (#14-18), thorax duns, cream (#14-18), cream parachutes (#14-18), sparkle duns, cream (#14-18), Quigley cripples, cream (#14-18), rusty spinners (#16-20), pheasant tails (#14-18), hare's ears (#14-18)
Green drakes	green drake Wulffs (#10-12), olive paradrakes (#10-12), olive comparaduns (#10-12), Quigley cripples, olive (#10-12), soft-hackle emergers, olive (#8-12), hare's ears, olive (#10-14), zug bugs (#10-14)
Flavs	green drake Wulffs (#14-16), olive parachutes (#14-16), olive comparaduns (#14-16), Quigley cripples, olive (#14-16), soft hackles, partridge and green (#14-16), CDC emergers, olive (#14-16), hare's ears, olive (#14-16)
Golden stoneflies	yellow stimulators (#8-12), prince nymphs (#8-12), bead-head prince nymphs (#8-12), golden stonefly nymphs (#6-10), Bitch Creek nymphs (#6-10)
Salmonflies	sofa pillows (#6-10), Mac Salmons (#6-10), orange stimulators (#6-10), rubber-legs, black (#6-10), Bitch Creek nymphs (#6-10) Brook's stone nymphs (#6-10)
Caddisflies	elk-hair caddis, tan and black (#14-18), CDC elk-hair caddis (#14-18), parachute caddis, olive, tan and brown (#14-18), partridge caddis (#14-18), soft-hackle caddis pupae (#14-18)
Terrestrials	Dave's hoppers (#8-12), parachute hoppers (#8-12), Dave's crickets (#10-12), fur ants, black (#16-20), CDC ants, black (#16-18), deer-hair beetles, black (#14-18), hi-vis foam beetles (#14-18)
Attractors	royal Wulffs (#12-16), gray Wulffs (#12-16), Rio Grande trudes (#12-16), peacock trudes (#12-16), Chernobyl ants (# 6-10)

hatch, select your favorite attractor. If fishing is a little slow with the big dry flies, try adding a small bead-head dropper.

The dry/dropper combination is most effective in the riffled water that is home to the Gallatin's scrappy rainbows. If you are looking for one of the river's large brown trout, cast your fly up against deep, undercut banks. Grasshoppers and other terrestrials are the best choice for fishing tight to the riverbank.

Fishing streamers can also be effective in this smaller water. Try stripping woolly buggers and zonkers. Sink-tip lines can be effective, but well-weighted flies work best by sinking quickly right at the river's edge. Remember that you are still in Yellowstone National Park and lead is not allowed.

HOW TO GET THERE

There is regular air service into Bozeman year-round and into West Yellowstone from June 1 to September. Most anglers who visit this water will make the Gallatin a side trip while based in West Yellowstone.

Give a wide berth to the moose who roam the river.

To reach the Gallatin from West Yellowstone, head north on US 191 along Grayling Creek. You will pass Divide Lake just before you reach the river near the Bighorn trailhead, about 21 miles north of West Yellowstone.

From Bozeman, drive 60 miles south on US 191 to reach the Gallatin at the national park boundary.

ACCESSIBILITY

The Gallatin meets US 191 near the Bighorn trailhead. If you are looking for a backcountry experience, head up the Bighorn Pass Trail to the upper stretches of the river. You can hike a loop over Fawn Pass and connect with the Fan Creek Trail. From the Bighorn trailhead downstream, the Gallatin follows US 191 all the way to the park boundary. There are several turnouts and parking areas at major trailheads, making it simple for anglers to gain access to the river.

If you want to get a little farther away from the road, hike downstream from Fawn Pass trailhead (near mile marker 22), or fish the river between mile marker 26 and 27 (includes the confluence with Specimen Creek).

The river is moderately swift and powerful when the water is high. The bottom is composed of cobble rock and gravel, making wading difficult in places. This river is cold enough to justify waders through much of the summer.

The thick willows along the bank can impede an angler's progress, as well as hide the valley's stoic moose. Be careful of North America's largest ungulate — they may seem peaceful and immobile, but they can charge quickly if anglers encroach too close or spook them out of their resting spot. One would be wise to be careful of all wildlife in this wild area — take your time, make some noise and always maintain a safe distance.

CHECK RIVER FLOWS ON THE WEB
http://montana.usgs.gov./rt-cgi/gen_tbl_pg

Gallatin: *Gallatin Lake to YNP Boundary*

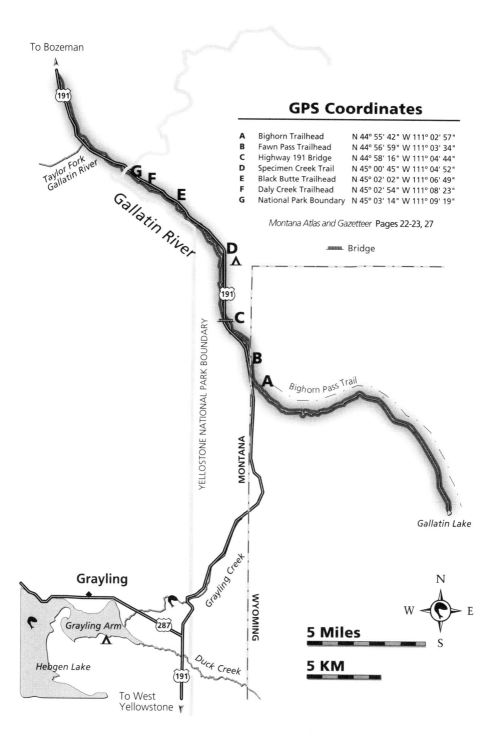

To Bozeman

191

Taylor Fork
Gallatin River

Gallatin River

G F

E

D

191

C

B

A

Bighorn Pass Trail

Gallatin Lake

YELLOWSTONE NATIONAL PARK BOUNDARY

MONTANA

WYOMING

Grayling

Grayling Creek

287

Grayling Arm

Hebgen Lake

Duck Creek

191

To West
Yellowstone

GPS Coordinates

A	Bighorn Trailhead	N 44° 55' 42" W 111° 02' 57"
B	Fawn Pass Trailhead	N 44° 56' 59" W 111° 03' 34"
C	Highway 191 Bridge	N 44° 58' 16" W 111° 04' 44"
D	Specimen Creek Trail	N 45° 00' 45" W 111° 04' 52"
E	Black Butte Trailhead	N 45° 02' 02" W 111° 06' 49"
F	Daly Creek Trailhead	N 45° 02' 54" W 111° 08' 23"
G	National Park Boundary	N 45° 03' 14" W 111° 09' 19"

Montana Atlas and Gazetteer **Pages 22-23, 27**

Bridge

N
W E
S

5 Miles

5 KM

WHEN TO GO

Although the Gallatin opens on Memorial Day weekend, it does not normally fish well until spring run-off recedes. This may occur in late June of low water years, but July is a safer bet for planning a trip. July fishing can include salmonflies and green drakes, making for some memorable days when things go your way.

As the dog days of summer stretch into August, hopper fishing really picks up and provides some of the best fishing most years. Indian summer days of September are beautiful in this high country, and terrestrial fishing usually holds up through the end of the month. If you visit the Gallatin in October, dress warm and look for aggressive brown trout willing to chase streamers.

RESOURCES

West Yellowstone is an ideal base to fish the Gallatin. Lodging, restaurants and shops are plentiful. If you prefer to stay in the park, refer to page 345 for Yellowstone National Park resources.

Campgrounds

GALLATIN NATIONAL FOREST

For more information, contact the Hebgen Lake Ranger District at (406) 823-6961.

❏   Bakers Hole

Lodging

BIG SKY

Big Sky Ski & Summer Resort
One Lone Mountain Trail
Big Sky, MT 59716
Phone number/s: (406) 995-5000

Comfort Inn Of Big Sky
47214 Gallatin Road
Big Sky, MT 59716
Phone number/s: (406) 995-2333

GALLATIN GATEWAY

Corral Bar Café & Motel
42895 Gallatin Road
Gallatin Gateway, MT 58730
Phone number/s: (406) 995-4249

WEST YELLOWSTONE

Pine Shadows Motel
530 Gibbon Ave.
West Yellowstone, MT 59758
Phone number/s: (406) 646-7541

Tackle Shops and Guide Services

BIG SKY

East Slope Anglers
US 191
Big Sky, MT 59716
Phone number/s: (406) 995-4369

BOZEMAN

River's Edge
2012 N. 7th Ave.
Bozeman, MT 59715
Phone number/s: (406) 586-5373

WEST YELLOWSTONE

Bud Lilly's Trout Shop
39 Madison Ave.
West Yellowstone, MT 59758
Phone: (406) 646-7801,
toll-free (800) 854-9559
Web site: www.budlillys.com

Madison River Outfitters
117 Canyon St.
West Yellowstone, MT 59758
Phone number/s: (406) 646-9644,
toll-free (800) 646-9644
Web site: www.flyfishingyellowstone.com

Lamar River

The restoration of free-ranging wolves has come to represent true wildness in America. The Lamar Valley has been at the center of their controversial return from exile. During the 1930s, the last gray wolves were killed in Yellowstone Park. As wolves disappeared from the landscape, the delicate balance of predator-prey relationships was greatly altered. With the wolves gone, elk populations in Yellowstone began to go up and down in boom and bust cycles, with catastrophic winter mortality rates every five or 10 years. In the 1980s, wolf restoration became the hot topic, pitting ranchers against environmentalists. Wolves, it was now recognized, help to keep a prey population fit. As the poet Whitman wrote, "What whittle the antelope so swift but the wolf's tooth."

In 1995, a complex and controversial federal wolf recovery program was instituted in Yellowstone National Park. The program would restore nature's dominion yet provide human-made amendments to protect the livestock industry vital to the regional economy. A total of 31 wolves were released in 1995 and 1996, and they quickly established themselves as breeding packs. Successful reproduction has allowed the park's wolf population to increase to more than 115 by the year 2000. With 11 wolf packs roaming the Lamar River region, anglers casting flies in the early morning hours or late evenings have the rare opportunity to hear the haunting howl of the wolf or even glimpse a pack coming down from the hills to hunt.

Just as the wild and unaltered character of the Lamar Valley makes it an ideal home for native species like wolves and buffalo, the same holds true for the indigenous Yellowstone cutthroat. Today, fly fishers will find trout that have adapted to this specific environment over centuries and continue to thrive in the Lamar's waters. These colorful fish average around 14 inches, but you can expect a few to reach sizes of 18 inches or more. Cutthroat are considered less wary than the other species of trout and more tolerant of a novice angler's clumsy presentations. This quality, combined with the wide-open meadows and easy access, make the Lamar a good choice for new fly fishers to "wet their feet."

SPECIFIC REGULATIONS

The Lamar River upstream from Calfee Creek and all tributaries upstream from and including Calfee Creek:

❏   Anglers may keep two cutthroat trout, any size.

Hatch Chart

Food Items	AVAILABILITY											
	J	F	M	A	M	J	J	A	S	O	N	D
Midges			✗	✗	✗	✗	✗	✗	✗	✗	✗	
Blue-winged olives								✗	✗	✗		
Pale morning duns							✗	✗	✗			
Gray drakes							✗	✗	✗	✗		
Green drakes							✗	✗				
Callibaetis							✗					
Salmonflies							✗					
Golden stoneflies							✗	✗				
Caddisflies							✗	✗	✗			
Terrestrials							✗	✗	✗	✗		

TACTICS

The salmonflies and golden stoneflies hatch sporadically in early July. The fish may not key into these bugs very well, but it does get them looking up, and they will continue to feed on dry flies the rest of the season. Weeks after the big bugs are gone, large attractor-type dry flies such as stimulators, trudes and royal Wulffs will work. If you find that trout are coming up to examine your offering, then turning away, try adding a smaller dry fly or nymph as a dropper.

With its expansive meadows and grassy, undercut banks, the Lamar could be considered the quintessential terrestrial trout stream. The banks of the Lamar are

The canyon stretch of the Lamar offers good angling opportunities.

Insects	Suggested Fly Patterns
Midges	Griffith's gnats (#16-20), Adams (#16-20), black gnats (#14-20), brassies (#16-20), bead-head midge pupae (#16-20)
Blue-winged olives	parachute Adams (#16-20), thorax BWOs (#16-20), olive comparaduns (#16-20), Quigley cripples, olive (#16-20), pheasant tails (#16-20), hare's ears (#16-20), bead-head pheasant tails (#16-20), bead-head hare's ears (#16-20)
Pale morning duns	thorax PMDs (#14-16), cream parachutes (#14-16), cream comparaduns (#16-20), rusty spinners (#14-16), pheasant tails (#14-16), hare's ears (#14-16), bead-head pheasant tails (#14-16), bead-head hare's ears (#14-16)
Gray drakes	gray Wulffs (#12-16), parachute Adams (#12-16), gray comparaduns (#12-16), pheasant tails (#12-14), bead-head pheasant tails (#12-14)
Green drakes	green drake Wulffs (#8-12), olive parachutes (#10-12), Quigley cripples, olive (#8-12), soft-hackle emergers, olive (#8-12), hare's ears, olive (#10-14), zug bugs (#10-14)
Callibaetis	parachute Adams (#14-16), callibaetis thorax duns (#14-16), hare's ears (#14-16)
Salmonflies	sofa pillows (#6-10), orange stimulators (#6-10), rubber-legs, black (#6-10), Bitch Creek nymphs (#6-10), Brook's stone nymphs (#6-10)
Golden stoneflies	yellow stimulators (#8-12), bead-head prince nymphs (#8-10), golden stonefly nymphs (#6-10), copper Johns (#10-14)
Caddisflies	elk-hair caddis (#16-18), CDC elk-hair caddis (#16-18), soft-hackle caddis pupae (#16-18), peeking caddis (#14-16)
Terrestrials	Dave's hoppers (#8-12), Henry's Fork hopper (#8-12), fur ants, black (#14-18), CDC ants (#14-18), deer-hair beetles, black (#12-16), hi-vis foam beetles (#12-16)

well-supplied with grasshoppers, ants and beetles. Frequent afternoon winds knock these shore-dwellers onto the water, and trout quickly learn to appreciate this bounty. Through August and September your favorite hopper patterns should produce plenty of action. Cast them next to grassy banks with good flow and water depth and get them as close to the bank as possible. A common technique is to cast your fly right onto the bank, then pull just enough to drop it on the water's edge. Leaders of 7 ½ to 9 feet and 3x or 4x tippets will help you turn the big hoppers. The leader's shortness will help with accuracy, especially if the wind is up, and the heavy tippets will keep your fly attached on those inevitable occasions when you get hung up on the bank.

Green drakes and gray drakes can provide some of the season's best fishing on this water. Both of these hatches usually come later to the Lamar than other area waters, but it is always a good idea to carry some imitations of these large mayflies, even if they are just size 10-14 Adams. The green drakes normally hatch through the day. Gray drakes can be sporadic during the day, but the greatest numbers can often appear at sunset. If you see a few around, it can be worth your while to stay late on the river.

For some unforgettable evening entertainment in the park, forget the campfire program and fish the Lamar's caddis hatch into darkness — when the winds are calm and other anglers have given up for the day. The hatch may come and go in spurts throughout the evening, so anglers who wait out the slow periods may have the river to themselves when the fish really start to work. Fished astutely, this reliable

Evening entertainment on the Lamar River.

evening hatch can reward the angler with some beautiful cutthroat. The greatest activity can come just as it gets too dark to see your flies on the water. If you continue to fish a dry fly at this point, simply set the hook anytime you detect a splash in the vicinity of your fly. If you keep your casts and drifts short, you will maintain a good sense of your fly's location. Another effective approach is to switch to a soft hackle or other swimming caddis imitation when darkness descends. These can be cast downstream and across, then allowed to swing on a taut line. You won't need to see your fly, since any takes will be telegraphed up your line and trout will often hook themselves. Your last memory of the evening may well be the biggest fish of the day. Be sure to bring a flashlight to find your way safely back to the car.

HOW TO GET THERE

Anglers flying into the region will find Cody, Wyoming, or West Yellowstone, Montana to be the closest airports with regular service. West Yellowstone airport only has regular service from June 1 to September 30. You might consider Billings as well, if you would like to enter Yellowstone by driving the full length of the scenic Beartooth Highway.

From Cody, go northwest 17 miles on SR 120 to SR 296 (Chief Joseph Highway), which you will follow northwest for another 45 miles. This highway joins US 212 (Beartooth Highway) 14 miles east of Cooke City. Head west 20 miles to the Northeast Entrance of Yellowstone National Park. The Lamar will be another 14 miles west.

From West Yellowstone, enter the park on West Entrance Road and drive east about 14 miles to Madison Junction, then turn north on Grand Loop Road. Follow this scenic park road north, then east, for 52 miles to Tower Junction. Turn east on Northeast Entrance Road, which follows the Lamar.

If you come from Billings, take I-90 southwest about 15 miles to Exit 434, where you can get onto US 212 (Beartooth Highway). You will reach the park boundary in 113 miles, but expect steep mountain roads. This highway generally opens in time for the Memorial Day weekend, but you can check in advance at *http://www.nps.gov/yell/planvisit/orientation/travel/roadopen.htm* or call Yellowstone National Park Visitor Services at (307) 344-2115.

ACCESSIBILITY

Yellowstone's Northeast Entrance Road follows the lower 14 miles of the Lamar, and the river is never more than a mile away. There are several turnouts along the road and in many areas, a short walk of less than ½ mile will put you on the river and away from other anglers. The Lamar is steep and bouldery from its confluence with the Yellowstone up to the point where it is joined by Slough Creek. Anglers can reach the confluence of the Lamar and Yellowstone by parking on the east side of the Northeast Entrance Road bridge over the Yellowstone and following the trail downstream for about ½ mile.

Lamar Canyon begins at the Lamar Bridge and extends upstream about 2 ½ miles where it opens up into a broad valley shared by free-ranging bison, grizzly bears and wolves. Anglers will find about seven miles of the Lamar's classic meadow water here, and most of it is only a short stroll from the road. Be sure to give wildlife a wide berth. Remember that the park is their home and we, humans, are the visitors.

Above Soda Butte Creek, the Lamar leaves the road and access is by trail. There are two trailheads ¼ mile apart: the Lamar River and the Lamar River Stock trailheads. The two trails meet and provide access to the upper Lamar. There is a footbridge crossing Soda Butte Creek at the Lamar River trailhead, but you will have to wade Soda Butte if you use the stock trailhead. It's about a 2-mile hike to the Lamar River trail ford, and fording conditions are posted at the trailhead. Two miles farther up the trail is Cache Creek, one of the better tributaries that hold small cutthroat. There are four backcountry campsites at Cache Creek along the Lamar. Be sure to reserve a campsite in advance if you plan to turn this day trip into an overnight stay. From Cache Creek to the headwaters, the Lamar is steep and what fish the waters hold are smaller than those you will find downstream. If you want to experience the backcountry without the hike, Beartooth Plateau Outfitters of Cooke City offers day and overnight horseback fishing trips.

Note: There is a temporary closure of the north side of the highway between the Lamar River Stock Trailhead and the Lamar River Trailhead to reduce human impact on wolves coming down to water. Stopping or standing along this ¼-mile stretch of the Northeast Entrance Road is prohibited, but you can join the dedicated wolf watchers who spend hours glued to their spotting scopes at either of the two Lamar River trailheads.

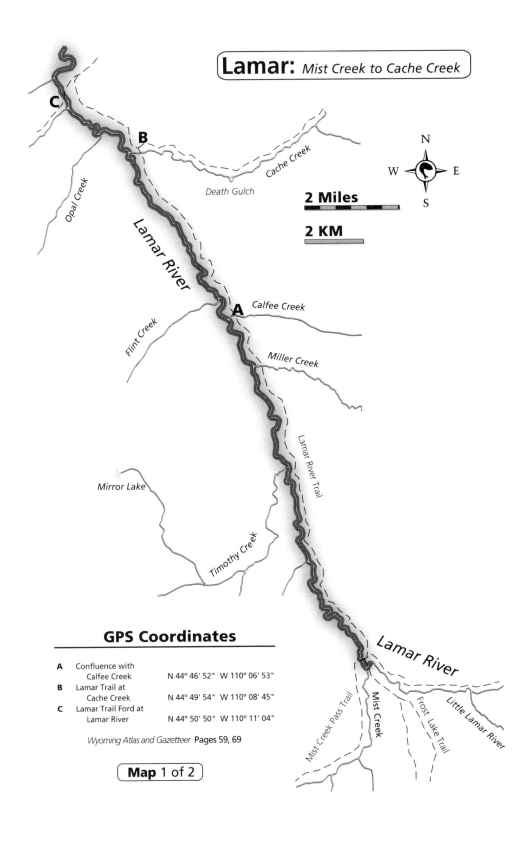

Lamar: *Mist Creek to Cache Creek*

N
W E
S

2 Miles

2 KM

C

B

Cache Creek

Death Gulch

Opal Creek

Lamar River

A Calfee Creek

Flint Creek

Miller Creek

Lamar River Trail

Mirror Lake

Timothy Creek

GPS Coordinates

A Confluence with
   Calfee Creek   N 44° 46' 52" W 110° 06' 53"
B Lamar Trail at
   Cache Creek   N 44° 49' 54" W 110° 08' 45"
C Lamar Trail Ford at
   Lamar River   N 44° 50' 50" W 110° 11' 04"

Wyoming Atlas and Gazetteer **Pages 59, 69**

Map 1 of 2

Lamar River

Mist Creek Pass Trail

Mist Creek

Frost Lake Trail

Little Lamar River

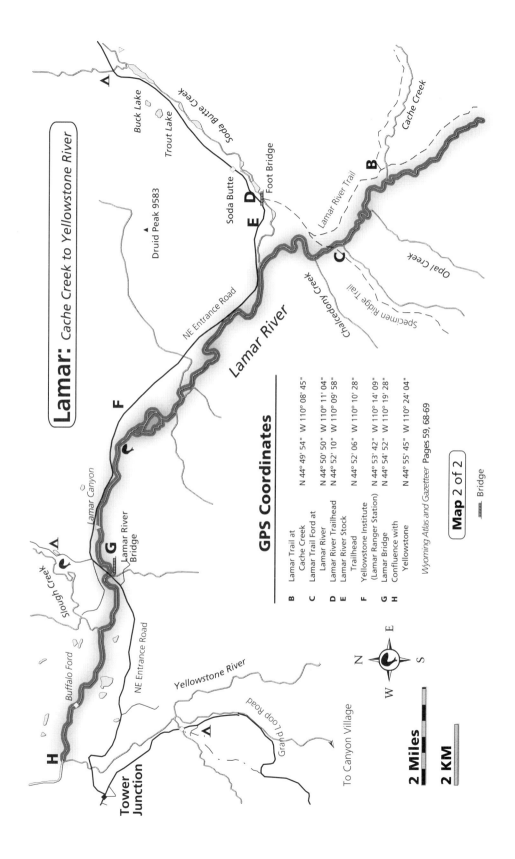

Lamar: *Cache Creek to Yellowstone River*

Buck Lake

Trout Lake

Soda Butte Creek

Druid Peak 9583

Soda Butte

Foot Bridge

NE Entrance Road

Lamar River Trail

Cache Creek

Opal Creek

Specimen Ridge Trail

Chalcedony Creek

Lamar River

Lamar Canyon

Slough Creek

Lamar River Bridge

Buffalo Ford

NE Entrance Road

Yellowstone River

Grand Loop Road

To Canyon Village

Tower Junction

GPS Coordinates

B	Lamar Trail at Cache Creek	N 44° 49' 54" W 110° 08' 45"
C	Lamar Trail Ford at Lamar River	N 44° 50' 50" W 110° 11' 04"
D	Lamar River Trailhead	N 44° 52' 10" W 110° 09' 58"
E	Lamar River Stock Trailhead	N 44° 52' 06" W 110° 10' 28"
F	Yellowstone Institute (Lamar Ranger Station)	N 44° 53' 42" W 110° 14' 09"
G	Lamar Bridge	N 44° 54' 52" W 110° 19' 28"
H	Confluence with Yellowstone	N 44° 55' 45" W 110° 24' 04"

Wyoming Atlas and Gazetteer Pages 59, 68-69

N W E S

2 Miles

2 KM

Map 2 of 2

Bridge

WHEN TO GO

The Lamar River's short fishing season begins late, since run-off from the rugged Absaroka Range can extend well into summer. When the sun's rays begin to melt the high altitude snow, the Lamar becomes a mass of mud and silt, which is eroded from the old glacial beds and soft banks of the river's upper reaches and carried downstream through May and June. By mid-July, anglers can usually wade the Lamar, but even minor rains can cloud the river and make it unfishable for days. If dirty water foils your plans to fish the Lamar, remember that Slough Creek and the Yellowstone River are close by and less subject to clouding.

This river really comes into its own in August and September when land-born insects are at their peak and water is normally low and clear. October can bring on some great gray drake fishing, especially during inclement weather (see note on gray drakes on page 387). Experiencing an Indian summer day in the Lamar Valley is like stepping back in time with wild buffalo grazing the

Coyotes, and the more elusive wolves, frequent the Lamar Valley.

open grasslands in the golden sunlight of autumn. Take a moment to lay your rod aside, sit down in the tall grass and turn your back to the road. You will see spread before you a scene from the American West as witnessed by the early explorers of this wild landscape.

AREA ATTRACTIONS

While it may be difficult to divert your attention from the glories of Yellowstone National Park, the Beartooth Highway (US 212) is called "America's most spectacular drive" for good reason. Providing a summer link between Cooke City and Red Lodge, Montana, it ascends to nearly 11,000 feet through stunning alpine scenery full of wildflowers and high lakes on its route across the majestic Beartooth Plateau. While it is only 65 miles between the two towns, plan on several hours for the drive. The road rises over 6,000 feet and includes an incredible series of switchbacks as it climbs up out of Rock Creek Canyon.

RESOURCES

Staying in the park or nearby Cooke City are the best choices when fishing the Lamar and nearby Slough Creek and Yellowstone River. The plain but cozy cabins at Roosevelt Lodge, located at Tower Junction, offer the closest lodging. The Roosevelt Lodge offers meals throughout the day, and there is a gas station at the junction. There is camping at Slough Creek campground, but it is often full, while Pebble Creek is just seven miles northeast of the Lamar and usually has some open campsites. Silver Gate and Cooke City offer more options for lodging and restaurants, and these towns are just down the road from Yellowstone's Northeast Entrance, which is only 15 miles from the river.

Campgrounds

YELLOWSTONE NATIONAL PARK

National Park Service
first-come, first served basis

❑ Pebble Creek
❑ Slough Creek
❑ Tower Fall

Lodging

COOKE CITY

Elk Horn Lodge
Hwy 212
Cooke City, MT 59020
Phone number/s: (406) 838-2332

High Country Motel
Hwy 212
Cooke City, MT 59020
Phone number/s: (406) 838-2272

YELLOWSTONE NATIONAL PARK

For lodging reservations, contact:

AmFac Parks and Resorts
P.O. Box 165
Yellowstone National Park, WY 82190
Phone number/s: (307) 344-7311
Fax: (307) 344-7456
Web site: www.ynp-lodges.com
Online reservations:
www.travelyellowstone.com/hotels

❑ Roosevelt Lodge Cabins

Fly Shops and Outfitters

COOKE CITY

Beartooth Plateau Outfitters
320 Main St.
Cooke City, MT 59020
Phone number/s: (406) 838-2328,
toll-free (800) 253-8545

Greater Yellowstone Flyfishers
206 W. Main St.
Cooke City, MT 59020
Phone number/s: (406) 838-2468 (summer),
(406) 586-2489 (year-round)

Madison: *Madison Junction to YNP Boundary*

GPS Coordinates

A	Madison Junction Picnic Area	N 44° 38' 34" W 110° 51' 35"
B	Mount Haynes Overlook	N 44° 38' 41" W 110° 55' 27"
C	Nine Mile Hole	N 44° 38' 51" W 110° 55' 55"
D	Seven Mile Bridge	N 44° 39' 49" W 110° 57' 53"
E	Riverside Drive	N 44° 39' 18" W 110° 59' 33"
F	Two Ribbons Trail	N 44° 39' 09" W 111° 01' 48"
G	Barnes Pool Number One Access	N 44° 39' 58" W 111° 04' 04"
H	Barnes Pool Number Two Access	N 44° 40' 12" W 111° 04' 15"
I	Cardiac Hill Trail At Highway 191	N 44° 41' 32" W 111° 06' 04"
J	Cardiac Hill Trail at Beaver Meadows	N 44° 41' 25" W 111° 05' 31"
K	Park Boundary	N 44° 42' 12" W 111° 05' 47"
L	Baker's Hole Campground	N 44° 42' 13" W 111° 06' 01"

Montana Atlas and Gazetteer Pages 22-23

2 Miles

2 KM

N W E S

Bridge

Madison River

HIGHLIGHT
Trophy-sized browns
in the autumn

TIP
Hike to Beaver Meadows
for solitude

FISH SPECIES
Brown and rainbow trout,
with a few brookies and
grayling

SEASON
Saturday of Memorial Day
weekend through the first
Sunday in November

The summer of 1988 was one of drought and fire in the Rocky Mountains, and Yellowstone, in particular, experienced the full force of nature's regenerative cycle. Extremely dry conditions, careless humans, lightning and relentless winds created one of the worst fire seasons in living memory. Before the fires were finally extinguished in late fall, they would burn nearly 800,000 of the 2.2 million acres in Yellowstone National Park. More than 25,000 firefighters, including the U.S. Army and Marines, would stand on the fire lines and defend the park against the ravenous flames, yet the implacable forces of nature would beat them back into retreat time and time again.

There were 13 named fires in the Yellowstone region that summer — and the North Fork fire was one of the largest. It started just outside the boundary of the park, and quickly grew into a wind-driven monster that roared through tinder-dry lodgepole stands along the Madison River. It defied the efforts of firefighters to contain it and would eventually threaten both West Yellowstone and Old Faithful. Ten years after that scorching season, a drive along the Madison draws your eyes toward the thin, bare trunks of charred trees outlined against the horizon. Yet in the circle of life, the end of one thing often marks the beginning of another. Down closer to the ground, young lodgepole pines have begun to grow up, a result of seeds being released by the fire's heat.

While the fires brought about a marked change in the landscape along the banks of the Madison, it had little effect on the river or its trout. It still holds good numbers of resident rainbow and brown trout that average around 12 inches, with some larger fish reaching 18 inches or more. The trophy fish that the Madison is renowned for make their home in Hebgen Lake. They move up into the park waters of the Madison when the frost paints the leaves with the rich colors of fall and the first snows settle on the Yellowstone Plateau. These lake fish can be very large, running from 16 to 20 inches, but some will exceed 2 feet. Their bright spawning colors seem to mimic the fall foliage, and many a winter fish story has described battles won or lost against these powerful migratory fish.

SPECIFIC REGULATIONS AND FEES

The Madison River (not including the tributaries):
❐   Restricted to fly fishing only (artificial flies only may be used to attract and catch fish regardless of the type of rod or line).

Hatch Chart AVAILABILITY

Food Items	J	F	M	A	M	J	J	A	S	O	N	D
Midges					X	X	X	X	X	X	X	
Blue-winged olives					X	X			X	X	X	
Pale morning duns						X	X	X				
Green drakes						X	X					
Tricos								X	X			
Little yellow sallys						X	X					
Salmonflies						X	X					
Caddisflies						X	X	X	X	X		
Terrestrials							X	X	X	X		
Streamers										X	X	

❑ Anglers may keep two brown trout under 13 inches.
❑ Catch-and-release only for rainbow and grayling.

TACTICS

In the steep and rocky sections of the river, like the Barns Pools, there are good populations of salmonflies and other small stoneflies. Sofa pillows and large attractor dry flies work well on top, and streamers and large rubber-leg nymphs are effective underneath. Smaller nymphs will take fish, but you may catch several whitefish for every trout. A large dry fly with a bead-head dropper is a good way to cover the water in search of fish when there are no active risers. Short, stiff leaders will turn over the big flies in the wind and place them accurately against the banks. Try 7 ½-foot 3x leaders while the tippet to the nymph can be stepped down to 4x.

Trico and pale morning dun hatches will take place on slower stretches of the river; adjust your tactics to these conditions. Use leaders of nine to 12 feet tapered down to 5x or 6x. When fish are keyed on the small mayflies, your best presentations will be downstream or slightly down and across.

The evening caddis hatches can occur up and down the length of the river in both slow and riffled water. Fish smaller, more realistic patterns in the slow sections, like parachute caddis or CDC elk-hair caddis. Traditional elk-hair caddis and Goddards caddis will float better in the faster water. Soft-hackle caddis pupae will take fish on the swing, and this technique simplifies drifts while increasing the percentage of fish hooked.

When the big fish start to move up from the lake, it is time to dig out your warm clothes and head for the Madison above Hebgen Lake. Blaine Heaps of Bud Lilly's Trout Shop has been guiding out of West Yellowstone for nearly 20 years and has several suggestions for anglers who want to chase these big lake fish. Most fly fishers will do well nymphing with big rubber-legs tied to a nine-foot 3x leader, or add size 6 to 8 prince nymphs on a 4x dropper. Look for fish at the bottoms of riffles as they come into pools or the edges of the deep undercut banks. Good casters may want to try stripping big weighted streamers on a 10-foot sink-tip line.

Insects	Suggested Fly Patterns
Midges	Griffith's gnats (#16-22), grizzly midges (#16-22), midge pupae, black, cream and red (#20-26), bead-head midges, black, red and brown (#16-18), midge emergers, black and peacock (#20-26)
Blue-winged olives	parachute Adams (#16-20), thorax BWOs (#16-20), olive comparaduns (#16-20), sparkle duns, olive (#16-20), Quigley cripples, olive (#16-20), CDC emergers, olive (#16-20), pheasant tails (#16-20), hare's ears (#16-20), bead-head pheasant tails (#16-20), bead-head hare's ears (#16-20)
Pale morning duns	thorax PMDs (#14-18), cream parachutes (#14-18), cream comparaduns (#14-18), Quigley cripples, cream (#14-18), rusty spinners (#14-18), CDC emergers, cream (#14-18), pheasant tails (#14-18), bead-head pheasant tails (#14-18)
Green drakes	green drake Wulffs (#10-12), olive paradrakes (#10-12), olive comparaduns (#10-12), Quigley cripples, olive (#10-12), soft-hackle emergers, olive (#10-12), CDC emergers, olive (#10-14), hare's ears, olive (#10-14), zug bugs (#10-14)
Tricos	trico spinners (#18-22), CDC tricos (#18-22), parachute Adams (#18-22)
Little yellow sallys	yellow stimulators (#14-18), yellow sallys (#14-18), red fox squirrel nymphs (#16-18)
Salmonflies	sofa pillows (#6-10), Mac Salmons (#6-10), orange stimulators (#6-10), rubber-legs, black (#6-10), bitch creek nymphs (#6-10), Brook's stone nymphs (#6-10)
Caddisflies	elk-hair caddis (#16-18), partridge caddis (#16-18), CDC elk-hair caddis (#16-18), sparkle caddis (#16-18), parachute caddis (#16-18), soft-hackle caddis pupae (#16-18)
Terrestrials	Dave's hoppers (#10-12), Dave's crickets (#10-12), fur ants, black (#16-20), CDC ants, black (#16-18), flying ants (#16-20), deer-hair beetles, black (#14-18), hi-vis foam beetles (#14-18)
Streamers	olive, copper and gold zonkers (#4-8), spruce flies, light and dark (#4-8), articulated leeches, black, olive and purple (#4-8), woolly buggers, black and olive (#4-8), woolhead sculpins, black and olive (#4-8)

PHOTO: MARK WILLIAMS

The Madison River plays host to a spawning run of large fish from Hebgen Lake in the fall, giving anglers a shot at true trophy fish.

Streamer leaders of six-foot 2x will straighten out on the cast and let you "put the wood to 'em" when you hook up. Try big (#4-8) zonkers, spruce flies and woolly buggers. If you have a spey rod that doesn't get enough use, bring it to the Madison in the fall. Fish soft-hackle prince nymphs or similar flies (#6-8) on a traditional swing, with nine- to 10-foot leaders tapered down to 3x — and be prepared for some vicious strikes. Blaine recommends either parking at Bakers Hole and fishing upstream, coming out to a car at the Cardiac Hill Access or starting at Cardiac and fishing up to Barns Pools.

HOW TO GET THERE

If you come to fish the Madison in Yellowstone National Park, West Yellowstone provides the best base of operations, particularly in the last few weeks of the season when many of the park's facilities shut down for the winter. For anglers flying in from out of the region, there is regular air service into West Yellowstone from June 1 to September 30. Idaho Falls and Bozeman are a two-hour plus drive from West Yellowstone and have year-round air service.

To reach the Madison from West Yellowstone, enter the park on West Entrance Road. Drive east and the Madison will soon come into view. From Idaho Falls, find your way to US 20 and drive northeast about 110 miles to the West Entrance at West Yellowstone. If you are driving from Bozeman, point your vehicle south on US 191. You will reach West Yellowstone in a little over 80 miles.

ACCESSIBILITY

Yellowstone National Park's West Entrance Road follows the Madison for the first 13 miles of its course. Anglers can stroll to the confluence from the Madison Junction picnic area, or there are many turnouts that will take you right to the river's edge. The river turns north about one mile from the park entrance, and an unmarked dirt road will take anglers to the renowned Cable Car Run and Barns Pools. This road is the first road going north after you enter the park, about ½ mile east of the West Entrance. It is about one mile to the upper access and 1½ miles to the lower.

The Mount Haynes Overlook has a handicap-accessible wooden walkway and fishing platform that is well-placed on fairly good water, giving people with limited mobility a good chance to catch a Madison River trout. There are also two handicap-accessible campsites at Bakers Hole Campground, and a good gravel trail to a small wooden fishing platform.

If you would like to get away from the traffic on the main road, Riverside Drive will give you an extra measure of quiet. The Gneiss Creek Trail on the north side of the Seven Mile Bridge will give you access to almost a mile of the far bank of the river.

If it is true solitude you are looking for, then hike down the river from the Barns Pools access or come up from Bakers Hole. Be aware that Bakers Hole campground is just outside Yellowstone National Park, and you will need a Montana license to fish west of the park boundary. As the river twists and turns through here,

PHOTO: MARK WILLIAMS

The Madison's early morning mist can wash an angler's cares away.

While the Madison's resident fish average about 12 inches, some do get considerably larger.

crossing the boundary several times, it is wise to carry both licenses if you intend fishing this area. The Cardiac Hill Trail is not much of a trail, but it is only ½ mile to the river midway between Bakers Hole and Barns Pools. Park by the boulders and follow the old two-track over the edge of the hill to the park boundary. The trail is faint and hard to follow from here to the river, so it may be easier to use it to walk down to the Madison and fish your way up to the Barns Pools.

Wading the Madison is not particularly challenging; however, it is a large, powerful river that can take even the most experienced angler for a swim. Some stretches have abrupt drops and boulders that can be obscured by weed beds, and there are fallen trees that can trip the unwary. The stretch between Seven Mile Bridge and Nine Mile Hole has a soft and treacherous bottom and is best avoided. A portion of the river upstream from the bridge is normally closed for trumpeter swan nesting in spring and early summer.

WHEN TO GO

The Madison in the park may fish well on Yellowstone's opening day (the Saturday of Memorial Day Weekend), but bad weather and high water can make things difficult. The best fishing at this time is usually underneath — bring your streamers and big rubber-legged nymphs. The fish will begin to look up when the salmonflies hatch in late June or early July, and once they have gotten a taste for the big bugs, they will remember them for several weeks.

Good fishing continues into the summer until the water warms up, which can begin in July during low water years. During the hot days of summer, you may want to shift your attention to other waters or confine your efforts to early mornings or the late-evening caddis hatch. Water can begin to cool in August, just in time for the great trico hatch that can last through September.

In October, the air has a bite to it and the colors have begun to turn. Big browns begin to move up out of Hebgen Lake, and sizeable rainbows follow to feed on their eggs. This is the fly fisher's best chance of the year to catch a trophy fish in the Madison. The memory of a giant brown trout will help ease the pain of a long, cold winter.

CHECK RIVER FLOWS ON THE WEB
http://wyoming.usgs.gov./rt-cgi/gen_tbl_pg

RESOURCES

If you prefer to stay outside of the park, then West Yellowstone is your best bet. This low-key tourist town has a wide choice of accommodations, campgrounds, restaurants and shopping. For a complete listing of West Yellowstone lodging and attractions, visit its web site at *www.westyellowstone.com*.

Charred memories of the 1988 Yellowstone fires linger a dozen years later.

Campgrounds

GALLATIN NATIONAL FOREST

For more information, contact the Hebgen Lake Ranger District at (406) 823-6961.

❑ Bakers Hole Campground

YELLOWSTONE NATIONAL PARK

For camping reservations at Yellowstone National Park, contact:

AmFac Parks and Resorts
P.O. Box 165
Yellowstone National Park, WY 82190
Phone number/s: (307) 344-7311
Web site: www.ynp-lodges.com
Online reservations:
www.travelyellowstone.com/camping

❑ Grant Village
❑ Madison

National Park Service
first-come, first-served basis

❑ Lewis Lake

Lodging

YELLOWSTONE NATIONAL PARK

For lodging reservations, contact:

AmFac Parks and Resorts
P.O. Box 165
Yellowstone National Park, WY 82190
Phone number/s: (307) 344-7311
Fax: (307) 344-7456
Web site: www.ynp-lodges.com
Online reservations:
www.travelyellowstone.com/hotels

❑ Grant Village
❑ Lake Lodge Cabins
❑ Lake Yellowstone Hotel & Cabins
❑ Old Faithful Lodge and Cabins
❑ Old Faithful Snow Lodge

WEST YELLOWSTONE

Comfort Inn
638 Madison Ave.
West Yellowstone, MT 59758
Phone number/s: (406) 646-4212,
toll-free (888) 264-2466
Web site: w-yellowstone.com/comfortinn

Pine Shadows Motel
530 Gibbon Ave.
West Yellowstone, MT 59758
Phone number/s: (406) 646-7541,
toll-free (800) 624-5291
Web site: www.wyellowstone.com/clients/
pineshadows/

Yellowstone Inn and Cabins
601 US 20
West Yellowstone, MT 59758
Phone number/s: (406) 646-7633,
toll-free (800) 858-9224
Web site: www.wyellowstone.com/
yellowstoneinn
E-mail: kate@aicom.net

Tackle Shops and Outfitters

WEST YELLOWSTONE

Blue Ribbon Flies
315 Canyon St.
West Yellowstone, MT 59758
Phone number/s: (406) 646-7642

Bud Lilly's Trout Shop
39 Madison Ave.
West Yellowstone, MT 59758
Phone number/s: (406) 646-7630,
toll-free (800) 854-9559
Web site: www.budlillys.com

Jacklin's Fly Shop
105 Yellowstone Ave.
West Yellowstone, MT 59758
Phone number/s: (406) 646-7336
Fax: (406) 646-9729
Web site: www.wyellowstone.com/
jacklinsflyshop
E-mail: bjacklin@jacklinsflyshop.com

Madison River Outfitters
117 Canyon St.
West Yellowstone, MT 59758
Phone number/s: (406) 646-9644,
toll-free (800) 646-9644
Web site: www.flyfishingyellowstone.com

Slough Creek

There is probably no water in Yellowstone National Park that has laid claim to the hearts and minds of fly fishers as has Slough Creek. It is one of the park's most fertile streams and produces excellent hatches as well as strong and heavy cutthroat trout. The clear, smooth waters of its upper meadows allow anglers to watch their intended quarry as they attempt to deceive and seduce the creek's beautifully colored fish. Just as "familiarity breeds contempt," so does the remoteness of Slough Creek's meadows preserve the mystique of these distant waters. Few souls have a regular opportunity to cast a fly on the Slough, and most of us must be content with an annual pilgrimage at best. Even the most jaded fly casters can't help but fantasize about the day ahead and what fish it may hold as they trudge their way up the steep slope that separates the meadows from the ordinary world.

HIGHLIGHT
Backcountry fishing in alpine meadows

TIP
Sight fish and stalk the bigger trout

FISH SPECIES
Almost entirely cutthroat, with a few rainbows below the campground

SEASON
Saturday of Memorial Day weekend through the first Sunday in November

Slough Creek and its big cutthroat trout seem designed to delight anglers. Large enough to harbor a few giants, the creek is small enough to invite intimacy and is easily wadeable at all but the highest flows. The long walk to the upper meadows minimizes overcrowding and discourages those who are impatient and unwilling to earn their fish. Open meadows let anglers concentrate on the trout rising in front of them instead of where to place their backcast, and encourage frequent bouts of introspection while lying in the long grass watching the clouds of summer sail overhead.

What fly fisher doesn't enjoy casting dry flies to large, feeding fish? That is exactly what the Slough offers through most of its season. If you prefer challenging conditions and educated fish, just stay on the lower meadow water below the campground. If your slow-water technique is still developing, then lace up your hiking boots and head for one of the upper meadows, where even fairly new fly casters can expect to hook a big trout or two under most conditions.

As if Slough Creek's great fishing isn't enough for some anglers, the alpine meadow setting between the ridges and rugged peaks of the Absaroka Range should be. This wild country has always been protected from the negative effects of civilization. Spend a night or two camped along the creek's bank, and you may catch a glimpse of a wild grizzly bear wandering through the meadow or hear the howl of wolves as the sun slides behind the peaks that encircle this fly-fisher's paradise.

Hatch Chart AVAILABILITY

Food Items	J	F	M	A	M	J	J	A	S	O	N	D
Midges					X	X	X	X	X	X	X	
Blue-winged olives					X	X		X	X	X		
Pale morning duns						X	X	X				
Gray drakes							X	X				
Green drakes							X	X				
Yellow sallys							X	X				
Salmonflies						X	X					
Caddisflies							X	X	X	X		
Terrestrials							X	X	X	X		

SPECIFIC REGULATIONS

Slough Creek falls under general park-wide regulations (see page 345). As most of the trout in Slough Creek are cutthroats, it is effectively a catch-and-release fishery.

TACTICS

The lower meadow will test your presentation skills. You will need soft, accurate casts and a drag-free drift to take these wary fish. Use longer leaders of 12 feet. Match your tippet size to the flies you are casting; you may need 4x to turn over big grasshoppers, or go down to 6x if the fish are selecting pale morning duns. When the gray drakes are on, you may see them in limited numbers throughout the afternoon, but the real excitement will usually come in the last light of day. Schedule your fishing time so that you can take advantage of this late-evening bounty. Be persistent — it can get quite dark before these big mayflies show up in numbers — and bring a light for the walk out.

The upper meadows of Slough Creek fish very differently than the water below. Although increased angler pressure has had some effect on the indiscriminate cutthroat of this remote water, they normally exhibit a reasonable degree of tolerance for the less-than-perfect technique. This is fairly easy spring creek fishing, but slow, clear water and an abundance of food still allow fish to pass on a fly that drags or doesn't mimic the insect they are feeding on. Long, light leaders will help you fool trout when casting smaller flies. If you are fishing hoppers or other large flies, moderate-length leaders will allow extra control in the frequent afternoon winds.

Take the time to observe the stream ecosystem and see if you can identify and match any active hatches. The nice thing about Slough Creek, especially in late summer and into September, is that many of the fish are always willing to eat terrestrials. Ants are extremely effective by late July, as are hoppers and beetles. If you're unsuccessful matching the hatch, then just turn to imitations of land-born insects.

Insects	Suggested Fly Patterns
Midges	Griffith's gnats (#16-22), grizzly midges (#16-22), Adams (#16-22), midge pupae, cream, red and black (#18-22), brassies (#16-20), serendipities (#18-22), midge emergers, black and peacock (#18-22)
Blue-winged olives	CDC comparaduns, olive (#16-22), parachute Adams (#16-22), thorax BWOs (#16-22), no-hackle duns, olive (#18-22), CDC loopwing emergers, olive (#18-22), Quigley cripples, olive (#16-20), pheasant tails (#16-20), hare's ears (#16-20), WD40s (#16-20), RS2s (#16-20)
Pale morning duns	CDC comparaduns, cream (#16-20), thorax duns, cream (#16-20), cream parachutes (#16-20), sparkle duns, cream (#16-20), no-hackle duns, cream (#16-20), CDC loopwing emergers, cream (#16-20), Quigley cripples, cream (#16-18), floating nymphs, cream (#16-20), rusty spinners (#16-20), cream spinners (#16-20), pheasant tails (#16-18), hare's ears (#16-18)
Gray drakes	gray Wulffs (#10-12), parachute Adams (#10-12), gray comparaduns (#10-12), muskrat nymphs (#12-14), pheasant tails (#12-14), bead-head pheasant tails (#12-14)
Green drakes	green drake Wulffs (#8-12), olive paradrakes (#10-12), olive comparaduns (#10-12), Quigley cripples, olive (#8-12), soft-hackle emergers, olive (#8-12), CDC emergers, olive (#10-14), hare's ears, olive (#10-14), zug bugs (#10-14)
Yellow sallys	yellow stimulators (#14-18), yellow sallys (#14-18), red fox squirrel nymphs (#14-18), prince nymphs (#14-18)
Salmonflies	sofa pillows (#6-10), Mac Salmons (#6-10), orange stimulators (#6-10), rubber-legs, black (#6-10), Bitch Creek nymphs (#6-10), Brook's stone nymphs (#6-10)
Caddisflies	elk-hair caddis, tan and black (#16-20), CDC elk-hair caddis (#16-20), CDC caddis, black (#16-20), parachute caddis, olive, tan and brown (#16-20), partridge caddis (#16-20), soft-hackle caddis pupae, caddis sparkle pupae, olive, tan and brown (#16-20)
Terrestrials	Dave's hoppers (#10-12), Dave's crickets (#10-12), fur ants, black (#16- 20), CDC ants, black (#16-18), deer-hair beetles, black (# 14-18), hi-vis foam beetles (# 14-18)

If you walk into Slough Creek and find yourself having one of those phenomenal days when most fish seem willing to eat your fly, please remember that catch-and release fishing still causes some mortality. Instead of going for large numbers of fish caught, consider casting only to fish above a certain size. This approach will limit the impact you have on the fishery, while challenging your skills and improving your chances of landing one of the creek's larger fish.

HOW TO GET THERE

West Yellowstone is the closest airport to Slough Creek (regular air service from June 1 to September 30), and is about 1 hour and 45 minutes away. Cody is the next closest at 2 ½ hours and Billings is 3 ½. If you drive

Lower Slough Creek's deep undercut banks are home to some large and educated cutthroat trout. Use soft, accurate casts and drag-free drifts to take these wary fish.

over from Billings, you can experience the Beartooth Highway, considered one of the most scenic drives in America.

From Cody, Wyoming, go northwest 17 miles on SR 120 to SR 296 (Chief Joseph Highway), which you will follow northwest for another 45 miles. This will join US 212 (Beartooth Highway) 14 miles east of Cooke City. Head west 20 miles to the Northeast Entrance of Yellowstone National Park. Slough Creek will be another 20 miles west.

From West Yellowstone, enter the park on West Entrance Road and drive east about 14 miles to Madison Junction, then turn north on Grand Loop Road. Follow this scenic park road north, then east, for 52 miles to Tower Junction. Turn east on Northeast Entrance Road for about six miles to reach the turnoff to Slough Creek.

If you come from Billings, take I-90 southwest about 15 miles to Exit 434, where you can get onto US 212 (Beartooth Highway). You will reach the park boundary in 113 miles, but expect steep mountain roads. Slough Creek is 20 miles west of the northeast park entrance. This highway generally opens in time for the Memorial Day weekend, but you can check in advance at *www.nps.gov/yell/planvisit/* or call Yellowstone National Park Visitor Services at (307) 344-2115.

The second meadow at Slough Creek is a fly-fishing Shangri-la that brings many anglers back for an annual pilgrimage.

A NOTE ON GRAY DRAKES

There are two species of mayflies in the West that are commonly referred to as "gray drakes," yet they have very different habits even though found in similar waters.

The most common is *Siphlonurus occidentalis*, a two-tailed slender mayfly that prefers slower waters such as quiet pools and backwaters. The nymphs of this species are strong swimmers and will migrate to shore prior to emergence. The emergent form crawls out on streamside vegetation before its transformation to the dun stage — hence, these duns are not readily available to trout. The spinner stage is of greater importance to fly fishers and their quarry, especially around dusk, when mating and egg-laying normally occur. While the dun of this species is gray, the spinner is brown, with a distinctive horseshoe marking on the ventral surface of the abdomen.

The other species of "gray drake" is classified as *Timpanoga hecuba*. It is a rather stout mayfly with three tails, which are short in the dun stage. The nymphs of this species occur on silty rocks and wood debris in limited current. As they are poor swimmers, the duns emerge in midstream. *T. hecuba* can emerge anywhere from July through October, but get the most attention from anglers in autumn when inclement weather can keep them on the water for a long time, creating a very good hatch. These large mayflies are most important on the Lamar River and Slough Creek of Yellowstone Park. John Juracek and Craig Mathews refer to this species in *Fishing Yellowstone Hatches* as a type of green drake.

ACCESSIBILITY

The lower stretch of Slough Creek is the easiest to reach. There are about three miles of meadow water downstream from Slough Creek campground with several turnouts that are either on the creek or a short walk from it. The last ½ mile of Slough Creek drops into a steep canyon as it rushes to its confluence with the Lamar River. This lower meadow of the Slough fishes like a classic spring creek. Relatively high numbers of anglers mean that you will need to resort to more subtle fly-fishing tricks for success.

For most anglers, the real attraction is the upper meadows. But there is a price to be paid. You will start to climb right from the trailhead and gain 400 feet in the first mile — a tough way to warm up in the morning. After the first mile, the trail is much easier. It is actually a wagon trail that is used by the Silver Tip Lodge (on Slough Creek just north of the park boundary) and is very easy walking. It is wide enough for two anglers to walk side by side and tell stories about the fish they caught (or didn't) on the way out. The first meadow is about two miles in and has about two miles of fishable water. The second meadow is a five-mile hike with over three miles of delightful meadow water. The third meadow is eight miles in and beyond the range of most day hikers; it has five or more miles of unpressured water.

If you really want to maximize your fishing time, then spend a night or two at one of the backcountry campsites on Slough Creek. The first one (2S1) is near the downstream end of the second meadow; the second (2S2) is another ½ mile up the trail; and the third (2S3) is near the middle of the second meadow. The remaining four campsites (2S4, 2S6 and the stock party sites 2S7 and 2S8) are clustered between the second and third meadows.

The upper meadows of Slough Creek are in prime grizzly bear habitat. Be sure you don't surprise one of these large animals. Hike with others and make noise while you move along the trail. Bear bells will alert grizzlies to your presence. Many people rely on pepper spray as a bear deterrent. Practice using the spray in advance, as it is difficult to learn a new skill when a 500-pound carnivore is charging you. If you are camping on the creek, be sure to familiarize yourself with Yellowstone National Park's regulations on keeping a clean and "bear-safe" camp.

If backpacking is not your style, call the folks at Beartooth Plateau or Slough Creek Outfitters, who can provide horsepack trips into the Slough for one or more days.

WHEN TO GO

Slough Creek should fish well as soon as run-off subsides, usually in early or mid-July. Terrestrial fishing runs from late July into September, providing some of the best fishing of the Slough's short season. Expect to find other anglers on the creek during this period.

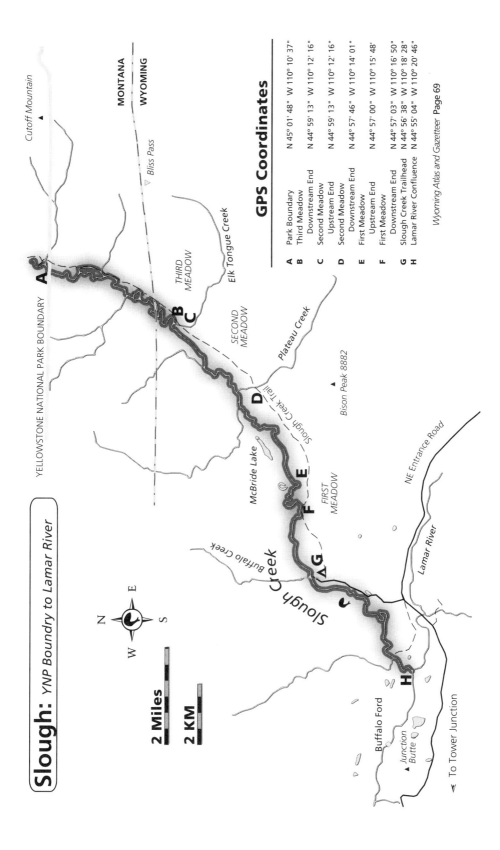

Slough: *YNP Boundry to Lamar River*

2 Miles

2 KM

N / E / S / W

Cutoff Mountain

MONTANA

WYOMING

Bliss Pass

YELLOWSTONE NATIONAL PARK BOUNDARY

THIRD MEADOW

SECOND MEADOW

Elk Tongue Creek

Plateau Creek

Bison Peak 8882

Slough Creek Trail

McBride Lake

FIRST MEADOW

Buffalo Creek

Slough Creek

NE Entrance Road

Lamar River

Buffalo Ford

Junction Butte

To Tower Junction

GPS Coordinates

A	Park Boundary	N 45° 01' 48"	W 110° 10' 37"
B	Third Meadow	N 44° 59' 13"	W 110° 12' 16"
	Downstream End		
C	Second Meadow	N 44° 59' 13"	W 110° 12' 16"
	Upstream End		
D	Second Meadow	N 44° 57' 46"	W 110° 14' 01"
	Downstream End		
E	First Meadow	N 44° 57' 00"	W 110° 15' 48'
	Upstream End		
F	First Meadow	N 44° 57' 03"	W 110° 16' 50"
	Downstream End		
G	Slough Creek Trailhead	N 44° 56' 38"	W 110° 18' 28"
H	Lamar River Confluence	N 44° 55' 04"	W 110° 20' 46"

Wyoming Atlas and Gazetteer Page 69

Wild cutthroat from Slough Creek's second meadow.

By late September, Slough Creek becomes a quiet and often solitary place to chase late-season cutthroats. Just be willing to take a chance on weather. Some of the best gray drake fishing of the season can come in October. Cool, wet weather makes it difficult for the big mayflies to dry their wings after they emerge, and they remain available to the trout for a much longer period, making it seem like a much heavier hatch.

RESOURCES

With only 29 campsites, the Slough Creek campground fills up fast in the summer. There are seven backcountry campsites in the meadows and advanced reservations and a permit are required. Permits, which are free and available from most ranger stations and visitor centers, may be obtained only in person and no more than 48 hours in advance of your trip. The closest ranger station to Slough Creek is at Tower Junction.

For a nonrefundable $15 fee, backcountry campsites may be reserved in advance, but only by mail or in person. Reservations are booked on a first-come, first-served basis. Forms for making advance reservations are available by writing to: Backcountry Office, P.O. Box 168, Yellowstone National Park, WY 82190, by calling (307) 344-2160, or by downloading them from the Online Backcountry Trip Planner at *www.nps.gov/yell/publications/pdfs/backcountry/index.htm*.

If you're based in West Yellowstone, it's a two-hour drive to Slough Creek. This is workable if you only plan to fish a day on the Slough, but you are better off staying in the Tower Junction area or Cooke City if plan to spend more time on this great water.

Campgrounds

YELLOWSTONE NATIONAL PARK

National Park Service Campgrounds
first-come, first-served basis

- ❏ Pebble Creek
- ❏ Slough Creek
- ❏ Tower Fall

GALLATIN NATIONAL FOREST

*For more information, call the Gardiner
Ranger District at (406) 848-7375.*

- ❏ Colter
- ❏ Soda Butte

Lodging

COOKE CITY, MT

Elk Horn Lodge
Hwy 212
Cooke City, MT 59020
Phone number/s: (406) 838-2332

High Country Motel
Hwy 212
Cooke City, MT 59020
Phone number/s: (406) 838-2272

YELLOWSTONE NATIONAL PARK

For lodging reservations, contact:

AmFac Parks and Resorts
P.O. Box 165
Yellowstone National Park, WY 82190
Phone number/s: (307) 344-7311
Fax: (307) 344-7456
Web site: www.ynp-lodges.com
Online reservations:
www.travelyellowstone.com/hotels

- ❏ Roosevelt Lodge Cabins

Tackle Shops and Outfitters

COOKE CITY

Beartooth Plateau Outfitters, Inc
PO Box 1127
Cooke City, MT 59020-1127
Phone number/s:
(406) 838-2328 (June to September)
(406) 445-2293 (October to May)
toll-free (800) 253-8545
Web site: www.beartoothoutfitters.com

Greater Yellowstone Flyfishers
211 W. Main St.
Cooke City, MT 59020
Phone number/s: (406) 838-2468 (summer),
(406) 586-2489 (year-round)

LIVINGSTON

Slough Creek Outfitters
136 Deep Creek Road
Livingston, MT 59047
Phone number/s: (406) 222-6642
Web site: www.sloughcreek.com

Yellowstone River

HIGHLIGHT
Stonefly hatch in early July

TIP
Hike into Black Canyon for great fishing without the crowds

FISH SPECIES
Yellowstone cutthroat, brown, rainbow, cuttbows and brook trout

SEASON
Varies depending on the stretch of river

T he Yellowstone is the park's most famous trout river and deservedly so. Its drainage encompasses 60 percent of the national park, is perhaps the best-preserved large river system in the country, and includes one of the world's largest alpine lakes. It emerges from Yellowstone Lake as a wide, idyllic spring creek that flows smoothly and calmly (except for LeHardy Rapids) through the grassy meadows and stands of lodgepole pine down to Chittenden Bridge. At the head of the Grand Canyon of the Yellowstone, the river begins a furious descent from the plateau as it cuts its way though the golden-hued rock that gives the river its name. Upper Yellowstone Falls is an awesome display of nature's force as it drops 109 feet into the deep canyon, yet it is dwarfed by the Lower Yellowstone Falls just downstream — nearly three times its height at 308 feet. As you stand at the brink of the Lower Falls, you can feel a deep, steady rumble through your feet as thousands of gallons of water per second pound the bedrock at the base of the falls.

The river hosts an incredible migration of large Yellowstone cutthroat trout from Yellowstone Lake that move into the river to spawn. Historic Fishing Bridge was placed just below the river's mouth so that anglers could comfortably and easily harvest these large fish. Hundreds of trout were taken daily until it became apparent that the runs were diminishing. The regulations of today are much stricter and have helped to restore this marvel of nature to its former glory. Anglers can no longer keep trout from the upper river, and fishing is only allowed on about eight of the 16 miles of river between the lake and the start of the Grand Canyon at Chittenden Bridge. The strict catch-and-release policy and protected sanctuary sections ensure that our generation and those to follow can experience this incredible fishery.

The dominant trout in the river is the Yellowstone cutthroat, which average 15 to 18 inches in the upper section of the river when the migratory lake fish are present. There are some trout crossing the 20-inch mark. This section of the river is entirely cutthroat, but you will begin to see a few rainbow by the time the river reaches the mouth of the Lamar. The average size is a bit smaller on the lower river below the falls, running from about 12 to 15 inches with some fish stretching to 18 inches or more. Brook trout can occasionally be caught in side streams, and there are brown trout below Knowles Falls.

Whichever stretch of the Yellowstone you choose to fish, it can be a moving and powerful experience that gives anglers a glimpse of what our wild fisheries must have been like before they were heavily affected by humans.

SPECIFIC REGULATIONS

The Yellowstone River and its tribu-
taries between Chittenden Bridge
(near Canyon) and Yellowstone
Lake:

❑ Fishing season opens July
   15.
❑ This area is catch-and-release
   only.

Fishing Bridge, including an area
one mile downstream (toward
Canyon) and ¼ mile upstream
(toward Yellowstone Lake) of the
bridge:

❑ Permanently closed to
   fishing.

The Yellowstone River and its tribu-
tary streams through Hayden Valley
— from the confluence of Alum
Creek upstream (toward Yellowstone
Lake) to Sulphur Caldron:

❑ Permanently closed to
   fishing.

The Yellowstone River for 100
yards upstream and downstream
of LeHardy Rapids:

**The Lower Falls of the Grand Canyon of the
Yellowstone.**

❑ Permanently closed to fishing.

The entire west channel of the Yellowstone River near the road at Buffalo Ford:

❑ Permanently closed to fishing.

The Yellowstone River from Chittenden downstream through the Grand Canyon of the
Yellowstone to a point directly below Silver Cord Cascade:

❑ Closed to fishing.

Agate and Cottonwood Creeks and portions of the Yellowstone 100 yards of these creeks:

❑ Open to fishing on July 15.

TACTICS

Fishing the Yellowstone in early July normally means just one thing:
salmonflies in one of the canyons. Water will still be high and fast, if it is fishable
at all. Trout will be forced to feed along the edges of the river — in pockets and
eddies where the current is slow enough to allow them to hold. Don't waste your

Hatch Chart — AVAILABILITY

Food Items	J	F	M	A	M	J	J	A	S	O	N	D
Midges					X	X	X	X	X	X	X	
Blue-winged olives						X	X	X	X	X		
Pale morning duns							X	X	X			
Gray drakes							X	X	X			
Green drakes							X	X				
Flavs							X	X				
Tricos								X	X	X		
Callibaetis								X				
Golden stoneflies							X	X	X	X		
Salmonflies							X					
Caddisflies						X	X	X	X			
Terrestrials								X	X	X		

Insects	Suggested Fly Patterns
Midges	Griffith's gnats (#16-22), Adams (#16-22), black gnats (#14-20), midge pupae, cream, brown and black (#14-22), brassies (#16-20), bead-head midge pupae (#16-20)
Blue-winged olives	parachute Adams (#16-20), thorax BWOs (#16-20), olive comparaduns (#16-20), Quigley cripples, olive (#16-20), CDC emergers, olive (#16-20), pheasant tails (#16-20), hare's ears (#16-20), bead-head pheasant tails (#16-20), bead- head hare's ears (#16-20)
Pale morning duns	thorax PMDs (#14-16), cream parachutes (#14-16), cream comparaduns (#16-20), Quigley cripples, cream (#16-20), rusty spinners (#14-16), CDC emergers, cream (#16-20), pheasant tails (#14-16), hare's ears (#14-16), bead-head pheasant tails (#14-16), bead-head hare's ears (#14-16)
Gray drakes	gray Wulffs (#12-16), parachute Adams (#12-16), gray comparaduns (#12-16), spinners, black and gray (#10-12), muskrat nymphs (#12-14), pheasant tails (#12-14), bead-head pheasant tails (#12-14)
Green drakes	green drake Wulffs (#8-12), olive paradrakes (#10-12), olive comparaduns (#10-12), Quigley cripples, olive (#8-12), soft-hackle emergers, olive (#8-12), CDC emergers, olive (#10-14), hare's ears, olive (#10-14), zug bugs (#10-14)

Insects	Suggested Fly Patterns
Flavs	green drake Wulffs (#14-16), olive parachutes (#14-16), olive comparaduns (#14-16), Quigley cripples, olive (#14-16), soft-hackle emergers, olive (#14-16), CDC emergers, olive (#14-16), hare's ears, olive (#14-16)
Tricos	trico poly spinners (#18-22), trico CDC spinners (#18-22), parachute Adams (#18-22), pheasant tails (#18-20)
Callibaetis	parachute Adams (#14-16), callibaetis thorax duns (#14-16), Quigley cripples, light gray (#14-16), CDC comparaduns, light gray (#14-16), hare's ears (#14-16)
Golden stoneflies	sofa pillows (#6-10), Mac Salmons (#6-10), orange stimulators (#6-10), bullethead salmonflies (#6-10), rubber-legs, black (#6-10), Bitch Creek nymphs (#6-10), Brook's stone nymphs (#6-10)
Salmonflies	yellow stimulators (#8-12), prince nymphs (#8-10), bead-head prince nymphs (#8-10), golden stonefly nymphs (#6-10), Bitch Creek nymphs (#6-10), copper Johns (#10-14)
Caddisflies	elk-hair caddis (#16-18), partridge caddis (#16-18), CDC elk-hair caddis (#16-18), sparkle caddis (#16-18), X-caddis (#16-18), peeking caddis (#14-16), bead-head peeking caddis (#14-16)
Terrestrials	Dave's hoppers (#8-12), Henry's Fork hoppers (#8-12), fur ants, black (#14-18), CDC ants (#14-18), deer-hair beetles, black (#14-16), hi-vis foam beetles (#14-16)

time casting to the middle of the river. If you are ahead of the main hatch, the fish may not be oriented to feeding on the surface yet, and rubber-legs or other stonefly nymphs will likely be your best choice. If the hatch has begun in earnest, you will find the shed skins from the large nymphs and adults in the brush along the banks in the mornings, or salmonflies flying over the river once the sun warms their large bodies. Tie your favorite salmonfly imitation onto a short, stiff leader and carefully work your way up or down the riverbank. The highest concentrations of trout often seem to be near the mouths of feeder streams that flow into the Yellowstone.

Once the water subsides in the canyon stretches of the Yellowstone, anglers should revert to standard nine-foot leaders of 4x or 5x. Summer hatches include golden stoneflies and caddis. As late summer moves into fall, blue-winged olives become more important to surface feeders. The water near Tower Falls provides some good fishing with these small mayfly imitations until the end of the season.

The Yellowstone above the falls provides a very different fishing experience than that in the Grand Canyon or Black Canyon. This world-famous stretch of fly-fishing water is heavily fished as soon as it opens on July 15, and the average fish is caught and released several times during the relatively short season. Though they have a reputation for being easier to seduce than the other trout species, they can become quite selective to a particular hatch, and anglers who pay attention to the smaller details will catch more fish. Long, light leaders are often not necessary, but will improve your success. Big yellow stimulators (#8) work well in the early season, particularly in the faster water above and below LeHardy Rapids. Sight fishing is usually much more productive on this river than fishing blind. Bring your polarized glasses and walk slowly while you look for fish. You will often find them stacked along the banks. In the first few weeks of the season, downstream presentations are not necessary, but the cutthroat that remain in the river can become much more difficult to catch as the weeks go by.

The difficulty increases when you find multiple overlapping hatches, which is fairly common on this productive water. Late July and August often bring the full gamut of moving-water hatches, as well as stillwater species like callibaetis below Fishing Bridge.

If you find yourself stumped by the Yellowstone's complicated hatches, just pull out your streamer box and select a black woolly bugger or strip leech. You can easily reach the fish with a floating line as long as you add shot (nontoxic only, no lead). Casting streamers will allow you to cover a large area with your fly, and you will likely find some willing fish. You can use this method throughout the season. Fish numbers decline greatly by late fall, but then so do the number of anglers.

This Black Canyon cutthroat couldn't resist a big dry salmonfly. This stretch of the river was empty in early July while other park waters were crowded.

HOW TO GET THERE

If you are flying in to fish the Yellowstone River in the park, West Yellowstone is the most convenient airport — regular service from June 1 to September 30 — and is a one-hour-plus drive from much of the fishing on this great river. If you plan to fish the lower portion of the river through Black Canyon, then Bozeman airport is only two hours from Gardiner and the North Entrance, where access to the Yellowstone River in the park begins. If you want to fish the water around Buffalo Ford, then the airport at Cody is a two-hour drive.

From West Yellowstone, enter the park and take West Entrance Road to Madison Junction, then turn north on Grand Loop Road. After about

Black Canyon of the Yellowstone River.

13 miles, turn east on Norris Canyon Road, which will bring you again to Grand Loop Road. Turn south if you intend to fish above the falls. Turn north if the lower portion of the Grand Canyon or Black Canyon is your planned destination.

If you fly into Bozeman, drive east 26 miles on I-90 to Livingston, then turn south for another 53 miles on US 89 to reach Gardiner. The Yellowstone is near the North Entrance of the park.

If driving into the park from Cody, go west about 50 miles to the East Entrance. Go west 26 miles on East Entrance Road to reach the Yellowstone River at Fishing Bridge.

ACCESSIBILITY

The Yellowstone between the lake and the falls is a gentle river that is easy to wade. Grand Loop Road gives easy access to much of this stretch. There are several closed areas along this stretch, so be sure you understand the regulations and know where you are. Expect other anglers on this famous water. Once the river enters the Grand Canyon of the Yellowstone, it becomes steep, fast and very difficult to wade at all. You will need to hike to get to the river, but once there you will be able to fish for the Yellowstone's big cutthroats in solitude. That's the beauty of the Yellowstone: Walking for a mile can put you off into the wild, while hordes of tourists crowd the park's roads.

The Yellowstone is permanently closed to fishing for the first 1 ¼ miles below the lake, including Fishing Bridge. There is about 2 ½ miles of water open to fishing (after July 15), which runs from one mile below Fishing Bridge to 100 yards above LeHardy Rapids. Access is by way of the Howard Eaton Trail, hiking south one mile from Fishing Bridge, or from turnouts along Grand Loop Road. This section is mostly smooth, slow water. It holds larger fish that have come down from Yellowstone Lake to spawn. They will be present from the season opener until perhaps as late as mid-August, when the majority will have returned to the deep waters of the lake.

The Yellowstone is open to fishing again from 100 yards below LeHardy rapids to Sulphur Caldron, which includes another three miles of river and the famous Buffalo Ford. Access is again from Grand Loop Road or the Howard Eaton Trail, which is north of the ford and about five miles from the Fishing Bridge access. Once water levels have dropped (usually into August), anglers as well as buffalo can cross the river here if caution is exercised. The river bottom at the ford is composed of gravel and will hold post-spawn fish in good numbers at the season opener. These big cutthroat will begin to move back to the lake a few weeks into the season, so if you don't find many fish, move upstream above LeHardy. Remember, the entire west channel of the Yellowstone River near the road at Buffalo Ford is permanently closed to fishing.

The river in beautiful Hayden Valley is also closed to fishing until it goes below Alum Creek. There is another 2 ½ miles of the Yellowstone open to fishing after July 15, and it gets less pressure than the river upstream. As this section is farther from the lake, it hosts lower numbers of Yellowstone Lake's spawning trout, which tend to leave here even earlier. Access is again from Grand Loop Road or the Howard Eaton Trail, starting at the trailhead in the picnic area just east of Chittenden Bridge. The river is closed to fishing below the bridge.

Below the Great Falls of the Yellowstone, the first possible access is at Sevenmile Hole. Anglers can hike right down into the Grand Canyon of the Yellowstone. It is five miles one way, and you will drop over 1,000 feet in the last 1 ½ miles. If you have strong knees, this is not such a big deal, until you realize that you have to come back out the same way you came in. There are three backcountry campsites on the river in Sevenmile Hole, so that you can spend a night or two before attempting the hike out. Be sure to reserve your campsite in advance.

The next hike-in point is at Agate Creek off the Specimen Ridge Trail — an even more brutal hike than Sevenmile Hole. It is a bit more than seven miles to hike in. You climb 1,400 feet over the first four miles, then in the last 1 ¾ miles drop 1,200 feet to the river. You will want to stay at the single backcountry campsite on the river, as climbing back out the same day probably won't be an attractive option.

Tower Falls provides the first access below Yellowstone Falls that is really suitable for a day trip. The trail to the falls leads almost to the river and is a relatively easy ¼ mile. The riverbank is fairly gentle here and continues so for a few miles upstream.

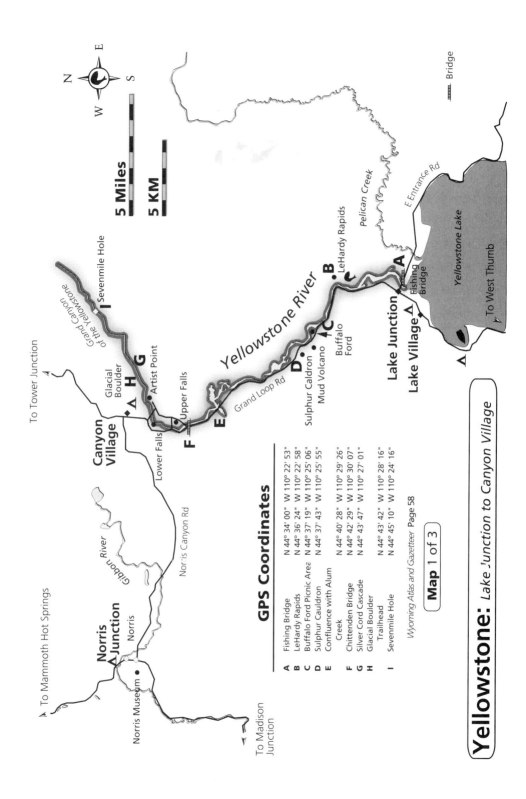

To Tower Junction

To Mammoth Hot Springs

Norris Junction
Norris
Norris Museum

To Madison Junction

Canyon Village

Grand Canyon of the Yellowstone
Sevenmile Hole
Glacial Boulder
Artist Point
Lower Falls
Upper Falls

Gibbon River

Norris Canyon Rd

Grand Loop Rd

Yellowstone River

Sulphur Caldron
Mud Volcano
Buffalo Ford

LeHardy Rapids
Pelican Creek

Lake Junction
Fishing Bridge
Lake Village

E Entrance Rd

Yellowstone Lake

To West Thumb

N W E S

5 Miles

5 KM

Bridge

GPS Coordinates

A	Fishing Bridge	N 44° 34' 00" W 110° 22' 53"
B	LeHardy Rapids	N 44° 36' 24" W 110° 22' 58"
C	Buffalo Ford Picnic Area	N 44° 37' 19" W 110° 25' 06"
D	Sulphur Cauldron	N 44° 37' 43" W 110° 25' 55"
E	Confluence with Alum Creek	N 44° 40' 28" W 110° 29' 26"
F	Chittenden Bridge	N 44° 42' 29" W 110° 30' 07"
G	Silver Cord Cascade	N 44° 43' 47" W 110° 27' 01"
H	Glacial Boulder Trailhead	N 44° 43' 42" W 110° 28' 16"
I	Sevenmile Hole	N 44° 45' 10" W 110° 24' 16"

Wyoming Atlas and Gazetteer Page 58

Map 1 of 3

Yellowstone: *Lake Junction to Canyon Village*

Yellowstone: *Canyon Village to Tower Junction*

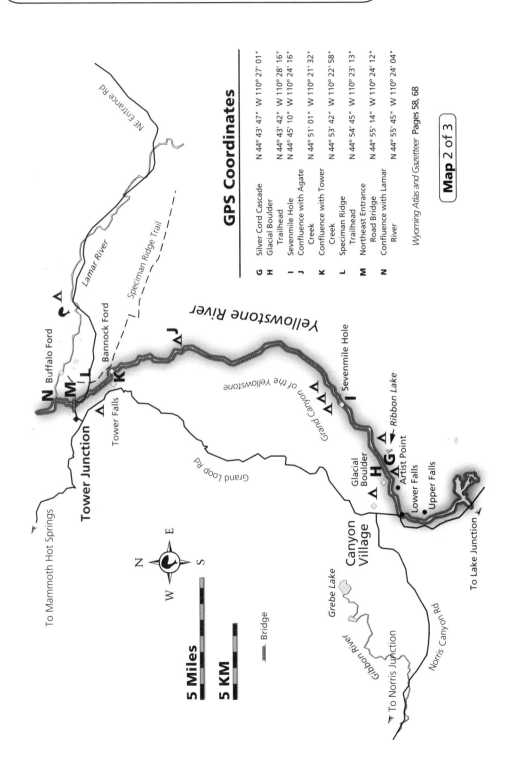

GPS Coordinates

G   Silver Cord Cascade   N 44° 43' 47"   W 110° 27' 01"
H   Glacial Boulder
      Trailhead   N 44° 43' 42"   W 110° 28' 16"
I   Sevenmile Hole   N 44° 45' 10"   W 110° 24' 16"
J   Confluence with Agate
      Creek   N 44° 51' 01"   W 110° 21' 32"
K   Confluence with Tower
      Creek   N 44° 53' 42"   W 110° 22' 58"
L   Specimen Ridge
      Trailhead   N 44° 54' 45"   W 110° 23' 13"
M   Northeast Entrance
      Road Bridge   N 44° 55' 14"   W 110° 24' 12"
N   Confluence with Lamar
      River   N 44° 55' 45"   W 110° 24' 04"

Wyoming Atlas and Gazetteer Pages 58, 68

Map 2 of 3

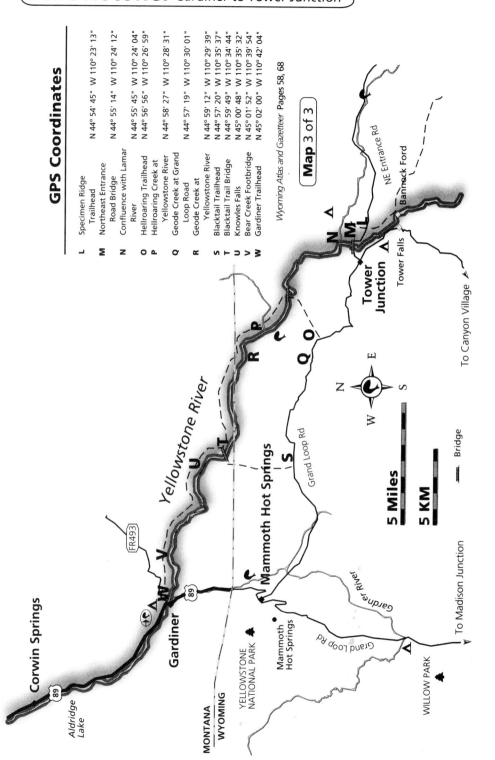

The Yellowstone and its big, hungry cutthroat are only one mile from the main road at the Hellroaring trailhead.

You can get on the river at the Northeast Entrance Road Bridge over the Yellowstone and head upstream or downstream. On the northeast side of the bridge, there is a parking area and a trail that goes down to the Yellowstone's confluence with the Lamar. Riverbanks are very steep through here, making access a challenge.

The Hellroaring trailhead, four miles northwest of Tower Junction, provides access to Black Canyon, with a hike of only one mile, although it is a fairly steep drop of about 600 feet to the river. The trail hits the river at a suspension bridge over an inaccessible gorge, but both banks are walkable just upstream. On the north side of the bridge, take the trail that swings east for almost ½ mile, when you will see the river below you at the bottom of a steep but passable bank. On the south side you can take the Garnet Hill trail for a hundred feet or so until you see a fork to the right that will take you down to where Elk Creek meets the river. If you elect to stay on the Garnet Hill Trail, it is about 3 ½ miles from this junction back out to Northeast Entrance Road, less than ½ mile east of Tower Junction. You will be able to drop down to the river and fish in several areas, until the trail finally leaves the river to cross a long sagebrush flat on the way back to the road.

There is a reasonable off-trail route into Black Canyon for the adventurous. Simply park at the sign for Geode Creek on Grand Loop Road (about six miles west of Tower Junction) and follow the tiny creek down to the Yellowstone. A very helpful young clerk at Madison River Outfitters in West Yellowstone directed me to this route during the peak of the salmonfly hatch in 1988, and it still stands as one of the most incredible fly-fishing experiences I have ever known. It is a little over two miles down to the river, but you will lose nearly 1,400 feet of elevation, which you will have to earn back on the way out. Cliffs above and below Geode Creek will restrict your passage, so this is not a place for large groups.

The Blacktail Trail is a good option for an all-day or overnight trip. The trail starts seven miles east of Mammoth and is just over four miles down to the river. The first three miles climb up and down over rolling hills, and the last mile drops sharply to the river. There is good fishing upstream from the bridge on both sides of the banks, which are reasonably accessible. If you cross the river and hike downstream two miles along the trail, you will reach Knowles Falls, which forms an upstream barrier to brown trout.

The Gardiner trailhead is in an odd spot, but it puts you on the river in about ¼ mile. You can just fish upstream until you've had enough, then stroll back down to the trailhead, making this one of the least strenuous options to fish in Black Canyon. To reach the trailhead from the Yellowstone River Bridge on US 89, go north one block and turn onto Fourth Street and immediately take the right fork, which is Jardine Road. Turn right onto White Lane and the trailhead sign will be on your right just before the LDS Church. There is limited parking here, so get someone to drop you off if possible. This trailhead and the first ½ mile of riverbank is outside the park, and the river crosses outside the boundary again around Bear Creek. It is a good idea to have both Yellowstone National Park and Montana fishing licenses if you are going to fish this section.

These big shucks on streamside rocks are an indicator that the salmonfly hatch has begun.

A word of warning: While fishing in either the Grand Canyon or Black Canyon of the Yellowstone, remember that they are both "works in progress," and the river is constantly digging its way deeper into the earth. The edge of the river is steep, and rocks are often loose and prone to shift as well as being polished smooth by the rushing water. The river is incredibly powerful, especially in the early season, and a slip into deep water could have dire consequences. Fish with others if possible, leave an itinerary with someone, and always exercise caution and good judgment in the backcountry.

WHEN TO GO

Below Chittenden Bridge the Yellowstone opens with the rest of the park, but there is usually not much point in fishing it until run-off subsides. This may happen at the end of June in low water years, but the river is not normally fishable until mid-July. The big event of the year on this lower part of the river is the salmonfly hatch, if it comes when the river has dropped to fishable levels. Check with local fly shops to find out where the hatch is on the river. It will start down near Livingston and move up the river. Being ahead or behind the hatch can produce good fishing, but there is nothing quite like timing it so that you are present when the big bugs are emerging en masse. This lower part of the river will continue to fish well through the summer, even though the attention of most anglers will be focused on the upper water. Fish big dry flies or match hatches as you find them. If you are camping on the river, eat an early dinner. Late evening can produce some of the day's best fishing; expect good numbers of caddis at dark.

The open portions of the upper river from Fishing Bridge to Chittenden will be a mob scene when they open on July 15 — and for good reason. Large numbers of native Yellowstone cutthroat trout come downstream from Yellowstone Lake to spawn in this part of the river. By the time the river opens, most fish will have completed their mission and will be feeding to regain their strength. Fish average about 16 inches, but there are good numbers in the 18-inch range, and some will stretch to 20. Fish are easy to spot and catch in the early season, but trout numbers dwindle quickly as these migratory lake fish return to their home. This fact, combined with the river's complex hatches, can make for increasingly difficult fishing as the season progresses. The upside of late-season fishing here is that angler numbers decline, and hopper fishing can be quite good in August.

If you are planning a trip and are trying to decide if you should include the Yellowstone in your itinerary, keep in mind that low water years produce the best fishing on the Yellowstone, while other park waters like the Madison or Firehole benefit from high water.

> **CHECK RIVER FLOWS ON THE WEB**
> http://wyoming.usgs.gov./rt-cgi/gen_tbl_pg

RESOURCES

Gardiner is the gateway town to the north entrance to Yellowstone National Park and is a good alternative to staying in the park, but it is a long drive if you are interested in the Yellowstone above the falls. Canyon Village and Tower Junction are located toward the middle of the park section of this famous river, while Mammoth and Lake Village are at either end.

A complete listing of Yellowstone National Park resources can be found on page 345.

Campgrounds

GALLATIN NATIONAL FOREST

For more information, call the Gardiner Ranger District at (406) 848-7375.

❑   Tom Miner

GARDINER

Rock Mountain Campground
14 Jardine Road
Gardiner, MT 59030
Phone number/s: (406) 848-7251

Yellowstone RV Park & Campground
117 US 89 South
Gardiner, MT 59030
Phone number/s: (406) 848-7496

YELLOWSTONE NATIONAL PARK

For camping reservations at Yellowstone National Park, contact:

AmFac Parks and Resorts
P.O. Box 165
Yellowstone National Park, WY 82190
Phone number/s: (307) 344-7311
Fax: (307) 344-7456
Web site: www.ynp-lodges.com
Online reservations:
www.travelyellowstone.com/camping

❑   Bridge Bay
❑   Canyon
❑   Fishing Bridge RV Park

National Park Service Campground
first-come, first-served basis

❑   Tower Fall
❑   Mammoth

Lodging

GARDINER

Best Western by Mammoth Hot Springs
US 89
Gardiner, MT 59030
Phone number/s: (406) 848-7311,
toll-free (800) 828-9080
Fax: (406) 848-7120
Web site: www.bestwestern.com

Super 8 Motel of Gardiner –
Yellowstone Super 8
US 89 South
Gardiner, MT 59030
Phone number/s: (406) 848-7401,
toll-free (800) 800-8000
Fax: (406) 848-9410
Web site: http://yellowstonesuper8.
simplenet.com
E-mail: super8@gomontana.com

Yellowstone River Motel
14 Park St.
Gardiner, MT 59030
Phone number/s: (406) 848-7303 ,
toll-free (888) 797-4837
Fax: (406) 848-7304

YELLOWSTONE NATIONAL PARK

For lodging reservations, contact:

AmFac Parks and Resorts
P.O. Box 165
Yellowstone National Park, WY 82190
Phone number/s: (307) 344-7311
Fax: (307) 344-7456
Web site: www.ynp-lodges.com
Online reservations:
www.travelyellowstone.com/hotels

❑   Canyon Lodge and Cabins
❑   Mammoth Hot Springs
     Hotel & Cabins
❑   Roosevelt Lodge Cabins

Tackle Shops and Outfitters

GARDINER

Parks' Fly Shop
202 2nd St. South
Gardiner, MT 59030
Phone number/s: (406) 848-7314

Coldwater Game Fish

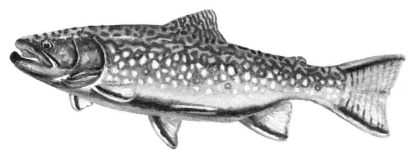

Brook Trout. Exhibiting a wide range of colors, they may be olive to blue-gray on the back to white on the belly. Red spots, usually with bluish halos around them, are present on the sides. Characteristic light wavy marks on the back are a distinguishing feature. An obvious white and then black stripe along the fore edge of each of the lower fins aids in separating brook trout from most other trout. Caudal fin is square or lightly forked.

Brown Trout. It is a very hardy trout that competes well with other fishes and endures marginal water qualities better than most trout. It generally has golden-brown hues with yellow under parts. The males during spawning are often brilliantly splashed with crimson spots circled with blue halos. Its upper body is usually profusely dappled with large, irregular dark-chocolate spots. It is quite carnivorous and sports a stronger, sharper set of teeth than most trout. Brown trout often grow to considerable sizes in excess of 10 pounds.

Cutthroat Trout. Cutthroats are best distinguished by their crimson slash along the lower jaw. They lack the iridescent pink stripe of the rainbow trout. The *Bonneville cutthroat* has sparsely scattered, very distinctly round spots over the upper body. They are clothed in subdued colors of silver-gray to charcoal upper body with subtle hues of pink on flanks during spawning. Cutthroats, particularly the Bear Lake strain, often lack the bright crimson jaw slash that at times may be yellow.

The *Colorado River cutthroat* trout evolved in the Colorado/Green river drainages and is noted for its brilliant coloration. The males, in spawning condition, have bright crimson stripes along their sides and their stomachs are often crimson. Spotting is usually concentrated posteriorly.

The *Snake River cutthroat* trout, pictured above, is also known as "fine spot." It varies from the other subspecies by having smaller, more numerous spots.

The *Yellowstone cutthroat* is lightly spotted, with distinctly round spots concentrated toward the tail area. Today, the native strains are becoming more extensively used in the sport fisheries programs and are being reintroduced to many of their former habitats.

Grayling. Silvery to light purple colors on the sides and bluish-white on the belly are the distinctive colors of grayling. They are relatively slender and are most easily distinguished by their long, high, bright purple, sail-like dorsal fin.

Kokanee Salmon. Kokanee are bright silvery fish with no definitive spotting pattern. Kokanee have a dark blue back with silvery sides. As the spawning season approaches, both male and female kokanee turn a deep red (shades from gold to orange to red) and the lower jaw of the male develops a characteristic hook common to the Pacific salmon. A deeply forked tail also distinguishes them from rainbow, cutthroat and brown trout.

Lake Trout. These fish have a background color of gray-brown overlaid with light spots that vary in intensity with age and environment. The background color covers the back, sides and fins and serves to highlight the lighter gray spots. Trout in large lakes are sometimes so silvery that the spots are difficult to see. Spotting is usually more intense on small fish. The caudal fin is deeply forked. The mouth is large and terminal with strong teeth on both jaws.

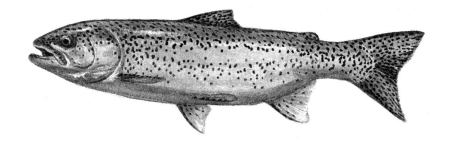

Rainbow Trout. Colors vary greatly, with patterns depending on habitat, size and maturity. Stream residents and migrant spawners are darker and have more intense colors than lake residents or nonspawners. Lake residents tend to be silvery. A mature rainbow is dark green to bluish on the back with silvery sides. The reddish horizontal band typifies the species. The belly may be white to silvery. Irregular black spots are usually present on the head, back and sides.

Fish and Game by State

Arizona Game & Fish Department
2221 W. Greenway Road
Phoenix, AZ 85023-4399
Phone: (602) 942-3000
Web site: www.gf.state.az.us

Colorado Division of Wildlife
6060 Broadway
Denver, CO 80216
Phone: (303) 297-1192
Web site: www.dnr.state.co.us/wildlife

Idaho Department of Fish and Game
P.O. Box 25
Boise, ID 83707-0025
Phone number/s: (203) 334-3700
Web site: www.state.id.us/fishgame
E-mail: idfginfo@idfg.state.id.us

Montana Fish, Wildlife & Parks
1420 East Sixth Ave.
Helena, MT 59620
Phone number/s: (406) 444-2535
Web site: www.fwp.state.mt.us

**New Mexico Department
of Game and Fish**
Villagra Building
408 Galisteo St.
Santa Fe, NM 87504-5112
Phone number/s: (505) 827-7905,
toll-free (800) 862-9310
Web site: www.gmfsh.state.nm.us

Utah Division of Wildlife Resources
1594 W. North Temple
Salt Lake City, UT 84114-6301
Phone number/s: (801) 538-4700
Web site: www.nr.state.ut.us/dwr/dwr.htm

Wyoming Game and Fish Department
Information Section
5400 Bishop Blvd.
Cheyenne, WY 82006-0001
Phone number/s: (307) 777-4600
toll-free (800) 842-1934
Web site: http://gf.state.wy.us

Other Blue Ribbon Rivers

COLORADO

General Season: Open year-round.

Animas River, Southwestern Colorado

Fish Species: Brown, cutthroat and rainbow trout.
Special Regulations: Yes, see current proclamation. Gold Medal water.
Local Contact: Duranglers Flies and Supplies, Durango, (888) FISH-DOG.

Blue River, Central Colorado

Fish Species: Brook, brown, cutthroat and rainbow trout; kokanee.
Special Regulations: Yes, see current proclamation. Gold Medal water.
Local Contact: Cutthroat Anglers, Silverthorne, (888) 876-8818.

Dolores River, Southwestern Colorado

Fish Species: Brown, rainbow and cutthroat trout.
Special Regulations: Yes, see current proclamation.
Local Contact: Duranglers Flies and Supplies, Durango, (888) FISH-DOG.

South Platte River below Spinney Reservoir, Central Colorado

Fish Species: Brown and rainbow trout.
Special Regulations: Yes, see current proclamation. Gold Medal water.
Local Contact: The Blue Quill Angler, Evergreen, (800) 435-5353.

Taylor River, Central Colorado

Fish Species: Brown and rainbow trout; kokanee.
Special Regulations: Yes, see current proclamation.
Local Contact: High Mountain Drifter, Gunnison, (970) 641-4243.

Yampa River, Northwestern Colorado

Fish Species: Brook, brown, cutthroat and rainbow trout.
Special Regulations: Yes, see current proclamation.
Local Contact: Steamboat Fishing Co., Steamboat Springs, (970) 879-6552.

IDAHO

General Season: Open the Saturday before Memorial Day through November 30.

Middle Fork of the Salmon River, Central Idaho

Fish Species: Cutthroat and rainbow trout.
Special Regulations: Yes, see current proclamation.
Local Contact: Schaefers Guide Service, Vida, Oregon, (541) 896-3789.

MONTANA

General Season: Open the third Saturday in May through November 30.

Clark Fork River, Western Montana

Fish Species: Brown, cutthroat and rainbow trout.
Special Regulations: See proclamation; some stretches open year-round.
Local Contact: Grizzly Hackle International Fishing, Missoula, (800) 297-8996.

Gallatin River, Southwestern Montana

Fish Species: Brown, cutthroat, cuttbow and rainbow trout.
Special Regulations: Yes, open year-round.
Local Contact: East Slope Anglers, Big Sky, (406) 995-4369.

Stillwater River, South Central Montana

Fish Species: Brook, cutthroat and rainbow trout.
Special Regulations: See current proclamation; some stretches open year-round.
Local Contact: Bighorn Fly & Tackle Shop, Billings, (406) 656-8257.

NEW MEXICO

General Season: Open year-round.

Chama River, North Central New Mexico

Fish Species: Brown and rainbow trout; kokanee.
Special Regulations: Stretches designated as special trout waters.
Local Contact: Los Rios Anglers, Taos, (505) 758-2798.

UTAH

General Season: Open year-round.

Logan River, Northern Utah

Fish Species: Brook, brown, cutthroat and rainbow trout.
Special Regulations: Yes, see current proclamation; also water closures.
Local Contact: Western Rivers Flyfisher, Salt Lake City, (800) 545-4312.

WYOMING

General Season: Open year-round.

Greys River, Western Wyoming

Fish Species: Snake River fine-spotted cutthroat.
Special Regulations: Yes, see current proclamation. No guide services permitted.
Local Contact: Jack Dennis Fishing, Jackson, (800) 570-3270.

For more information on these destinations, go online to *www.AmazingOutdoors.com*.

Federation of Fly Fishers

By LC "Bob" Burnham

The Federation of Fly Fishers, founded in Eugene, Oregon, in 1965, was formed to give fly fishing a unified voice, to promote fly fishing as a method of angling and to protect and expand fly-fishing opportunities. It is the only organized advocate for fly fishers on the national and regional level, and is now international in scope. By charter and inclination, the FFF is organized from the bottom up; each member club in North America and the world is a unique and self-directed group.

The FFF works to maintain the fly-fishing opportunities available today: cold-water, warmwater and saltwater, all fish in all waters. The FFF works to improve the fly-fishing opportunities for tomorrow — actively working to restore and conserve clean waters and healthy ecosystems for all sport species. The FFF believes that we need to protect all species and all fisheries habitat, and has encouraged catch-and-release of wild fish since 1965.

The FFF provides a forum for the exchange of fly-fishing knowledge, skills and techniques. The FFF published the first fly-fishing magazine in the world, *The Flyfisher*, today the journal of FFF activities, published four times per year. The FFF web page — *www.fedflyfishers.org* — is an award-winning source of information about the Federation of Fly Fishers activities and programs.

The FFF teaches the fly fishers of tomorrow the skills needed to be successful, and its energetic youth program introduces young people, as well as beginning fly fishers, to the allure of the sport.

Women Fly Fishers are an FFF original, having active women's involvement for over 28 years and an established national program aimed at educating women about fly fishing.

The FFF's International Fly Fishing Center in Livingston, Montana, is a unique facility, housing both an outstanding museum of fly fishing and the education center for the FFF. The museum includes exhibits of the history of fly fishing, with displays of equipment, outstanding art and flies tied by masters from around the world. The Lewis A. Bell Memorial Fly Fishing Library is available to visitors, writers and researchers. The IFFC provides school programs, including casting lessons, an equipment-loan program, and a surface-water testing kit and teachers' guide for high-school level students.

The fly-casting certification program was begun in 1992 for the purpose of enhancing the overall level of instruction in fly casting to beginning and experienced fly casters. The program includes instructor knowledge, casting proficiency and teaching ability.

For more information, contact: The Federation of Fly Fishers, P.O. Box 1595, Bozeman, MT 59771, (406) 585-7592, web site: www.fedflyfishers.org

LC "Bob" Burnham *is a lifetime member of the Federation of Fly Fishers.*

Index

AmazingOutdoors.com Resources

AmazingOutdoors.com AmazingOutdoors.com is the premier outdoors-related web site for recreation and information in the Intermountain West. The site features multimedia presentations, maps, magazine content from the past 13 years of *Utah Outdoors* magazine (formerly *Utah Fishing and Outdoors*), and news and feature stories dedicated to all forms of outdoor recreation. This content-intensive site includes the complete contents of many guidebooks from Falcon Publishing, those from AmazingOutdoors.com and its subsidiaries, and updated weather and fishing reports, including our weekly FishBytes e-mail. The site also offers an online retail shop where users can purchase thousands of items. Phone number/s: (801) 858-3450 or toll-free (800) 366-8824.

***Utah Outdoors* magazine** A monthly magazine describing the Intermountain West's best fishing, hiking, backpacking, mountain biking and exploring adventures. In-depth coverage of fishing on quality waters from the Yellowstone area through southern Idaho, all of Utah, and south to Wahweep and Lees Ferry in Arizona. Also covers family adventures and destinations. Mailed to subscribers; sold over the counter at stores throughout the region. *Utah Outdoors* magazine (*www.UtahOutdoors.com*) is a subsidiary of Amazing Outdoors.com. Phone number/s: (801) 858 3450 or toll-free (800) 366-8824.

Utah Boating Guide A comprehensive guide to all boatable waters in Utah. Provides maps and photos for all waters, along with descriptions of the waters, facilities, unique features and suggested activities. Also includes sections on boating skills, safety and regulations. Available at boat dealerships, bookstores and sporting goods stores. Phone number/s: (801) 858-3450 or toll-free (800) 366-8824.

Utah Camping Guide A comprehensive guide to public and private campgrounds in Utah and significant over-the-border destinations, including Grand Canyon and Yellowstone national parks, grouped by region. Provides directions to the campgrounds and describes facilities. Also provides basic information on planning campouts and on camping skills. Available at bookstores and sporting goods stores. Phone number/s: (801) 858-3450 or toll-free (800) 366-8824.

Utah Fishing Guide The most comprehensive guide ever published on fishing in Utah. Regulations and fishing tips for over 700 waters. GPS coordinates, maps, techniques and description of facilities. Extensive sections cover the Uinta and Boulder Mountain areas. Available at bookstores and sporting goods stores. Phone number/s: (801) 858-3450 or toll-free (800) 366-8824.

30 Days to Better Flycasting This guidebook teaches specific techniques that can help beginners or experienced fishers cast farther and more accurately. Available at bookstores and sporting goods stores. Phone number/s: (801) 858-3450 or toll-free (800) 366-8824.

Provo River Map and Fishing Guide shows access points, names, holes and describes effective fishing techniques. Available at bookstores and sporting goods stores. Phone number/s: (801) 858-3450 or toll-free (800) 366-8824.

FishBytes A weekly e-mail newsletter published by AmazingOutdoors.com. FishBytes is mailed every Wednesday evening and is designed to help anglers plan weekend fishing adventures. It contains the latest information possible on the best places to fish in the Intermountain Region, including information on hatches and fly patterns. This is a free service. To subscribe, follow the links on our web site: *www.AmazingOutdoors.com*. Phone number/s: (801) 858-3450 or toll-free (800) 366-8824.

Utah Trout Map A 3-D relief map of Utah showing and identifying trout waters. Color codes show the water's quality rating, making it easy to locate the best fishing in the state. This is a beautiful work suitable for framing and display as an art piece. It is also available as a fold-up map — throw it into the glove compartment and use it for field reference. Published by UtahOutdoors.com. Available at bookstores and sporting goods stores. Phone number/s: (801) 858-3450 or toll-free (800) 366-8824.

PHOTO: JEFF BECK

About the Author

Steve Cook holds a Bachelor's degree in Fisheries and Wildlife Management from Lake Superior State University in northern Michigan. He is an avid outdoorsman who has lived in and explored Utah for the past 15 years as a fly-fishing guide and instructor. When not in Utah, he works as a GPS surveyor in the remote areas of Alaska.

UTAH OUTDOORS
M A G A Z I N E

For the price of a night at the movies for two, you'll learn about the best places in Utah and surrounding areas to boat, fish, hike, camp, mountain bike and explore — every month, all year long. It's our job to know about the hot new destinations, the old favorites and the overlooked places — and to tell you all about them, with stories, maps and photos. We'll keep you informed, up-to-date and ahead of the crowds.

To start your subscription, just fill out the information on this card and mail it in. We'll bill you later.

For questions or credit card service call (800) 366-UTAH.

Name _____ Phone _____

Address _____

City _____ State _____ Zip _____

E-mail address _____

12 issues for $19.95*
*plus tax

Also...

If you're an outdoor enthusiast, you'll likely be interested in our other publications:

☐ **Utah Fishing Guide,** by Steve Cook, $24.95*
   Maps, GPS coordinates, accessibility, regulations and more — 591 pages, softbound

☐ **Utah Boating Guide,** by Chad Booth, $24.95*
   Waterways, facilities, camping, tips, maps, GPS coordinates and more   400 pages, softbound

☐ **Utah Camping Guide,** by Gaylen Webb, $19.95*
   Directions, descriptions, fees & reservations, tips and more — 240 pages, soft-bound

☐ **Utah Trout map,** $5.95*
   Ranks waters according to quality of fishing — 24"x32", two-sided, suitable for framing

☐ **Provo River map,** $5.95*
   Fishing the Provo River drainage and related waters — 24"x32", 2-sided

*Plus tax and shipping

Send no money now. Just return this card with your selections marked and we will bill you.
For faster service call: 1 (800) 366-UTAH or visit us on the web at www.AmazingOutdoors.com.

Name _____ Phone _____

Address _____

City _____ State _____ Zip _____

E-mail address _____

Amazing Outdoors.com

UtahOutdoors

P.O. Box 711126
Salt Lake City, UT 84171-1126

Amazing
Outdoors.com

P.O. Box 711126
Salt Lake City, UT 84171-1126